# THE COMMERCIAL EXCELLENCE PLAYBOOK

A Reflective Journey to Self-Diagnose Your Commercial Functions

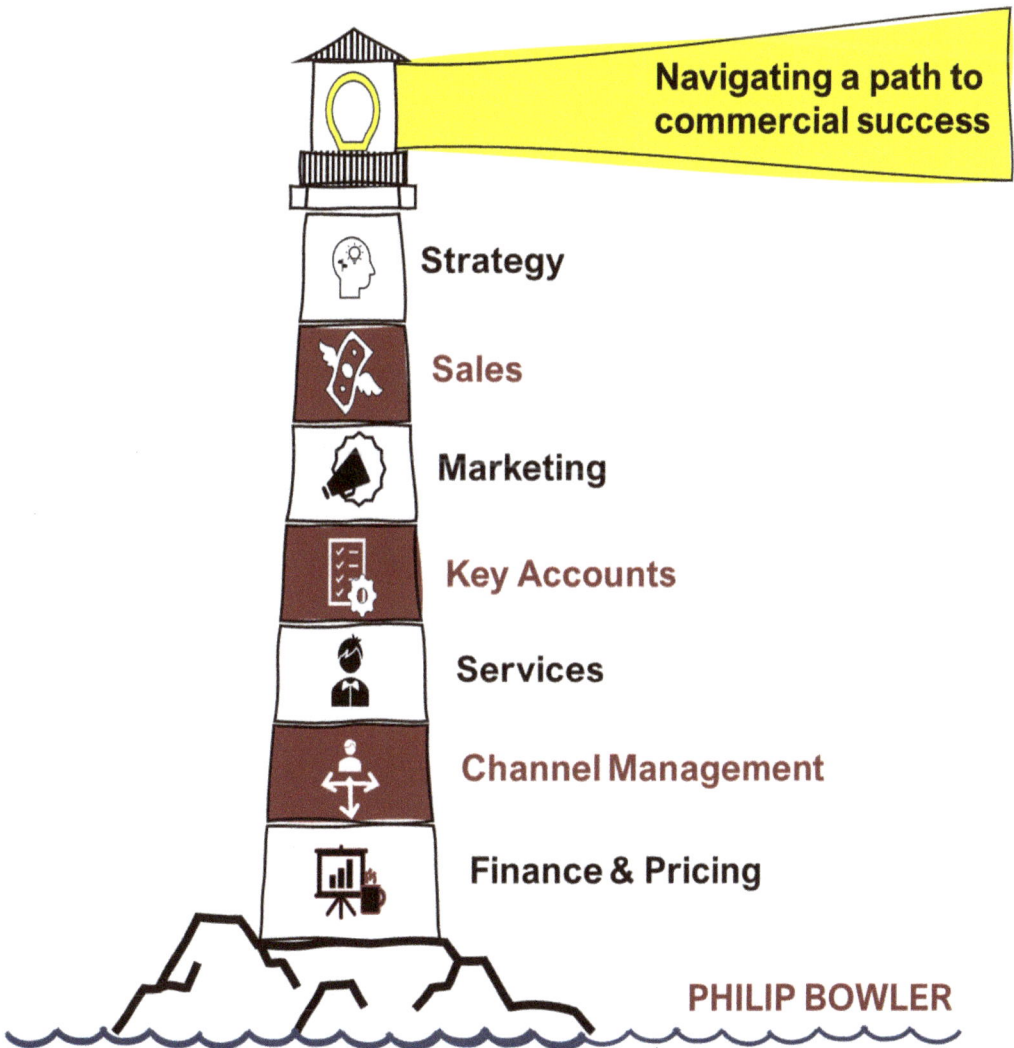

Navigating a path to commercial success

Strategy

Sales

Marketing

Key Accounts

Services

Channel Management

Finance & Pricing

PHILIP BOWLER

**Publisher's Note:**
Every effort has been made to ensure that the information contained in this book is accurate at the time of going to press, and the publisher and author cannot accept responsibility for any errors or omissions, however caused. No responsibility for loss or damage occasioned to the editor, the publisher or the author to accept any person acting or refraining from action.

# PREFACE

Over my eight years implementing commercial excellence principles across Asia Pacific, I often wanted a diagnostic tool that could give me the layout of a business and what to tackle first. Rolling out a corrective program is great, but how to know which one to roll out? This was always the domain of the big four consulting companies who were at the time charging the company I was with over $6 Million USD for the privilege. It struck me that for the average small to medium enterprise (SME) this could be extremely helpful, yet way, way, outside their affordability. So, I decided to write this book.

The other premise for this book is based upon the following: Everyone wants to know what to do, but no one likes to be told. So, I set about writing as a reflection piece. Thinking thorough 3 lenses for each area should enable you, the reader, to draw your own conclusions on the topics. In my career, I have been fortunate enough that every CEO / CFO / GM / Country Manager I've worked with has been smart and capable of understanding what should be done.

The pursuit of commercial excellence can often feel like navigating in the dark. Throughout this book we, we'll use the visual metaphor of a classical lighthouse.

A big thank you to Betty Petrillo, Stephen Hipkiss and Dr Terance Hart for helping me put this through its paces.

- Strategy
- Sales
- Marketing
- Key Accounts
- Services
- Channel Management
- Finance & Pricing

At the apex of the lighthouse is 'Strategy.' Guiding our endeavours, this is the overarching vision, defines the direction and objectives of the entire commercial operation. As we move down the lighthouse, we'll investigate the other areas that commercial excellence topics touch, like building blocks and foundations for our strategy to light the way.

If we think for a minute on a lighthouse, it's designed to illuminate danger, allowing safe passage. In this book we'll look through three lenses to understand the topic fully and for each chapter we'll consider different wavelengths that make up that topic. Just like the light from a lighthouse needs to be lensed to make the light bright and straight, and the bright white light is made up of all the different wavelengths of the visible spectrum.

This visual model will serve as our constant reference point, ensuring a cohesive and easily understandable exploration of this vital business discipline. You may want to skip ahead to chapters that you are facing challenges with right now. That is okay, this book will still work just as well front to back as it will deep dive only into specific chapters.

Tackling the whole book at once would potentially take you about a month, unless you already know the answers, but I suspect that in most cases you may need to go into the organisation and find out exactly how it's operating. If this is the case, the book can be handled one section a month and 1-2 chapters a week.

**Some chapters and maybe complete sections may not be relevant to your organisation as it is today**. That's to be expected, just skip them and choose the sections or chapters that may help you as your organisation is today.

If you follow through the scoring system and reflect on each section, you'll end up at the completion of the book with a full maturity assessment of the commercial areas of your business.

# TABLE OF CONTENTS

# QUICK START GUIDE

This section is designed to get you up and running with the book quickly. This is not your average read and forget book. To get the most out of the book you're going to need to understand how to view a topic or area, how to score yourself for that area and how to plot those scores. Don't stress! It's really quite simple.

We'll be looking at three main parts. First is the lenses. Each topic is written in three lenses. The lenses are AS IS today, What would be Ideal, and the Importance for your business.

In the second part, we'll cover a scoring system of 1-10 for each topic for the three lenses, combining those for a chapter score.

And finally, we'll plot those topic and chapter scores onto a plot at the end of each section, and a final one at the end of the book to put it altogether. There are a couple of scoring and plots at the end of the book so if you would prefer just photocopy them and use them as you go through.

## THE 3 LENSES

As mentioned earlier our lighthouse metaphor needs a bright light to illuminate our path. To do this and look at a topic completely we're going to look through three lenses to detail each aspect of commercial excellence.

This is to provide you with a guide for self-assessment. We'll pose a series of pointed questions or statements designed to prompt deep reflection on your organisation's current practices. Each question should be considered through three critical lenses:
the "AS IS," the "Ideal," and the "Importance / Relevance / Weighting"

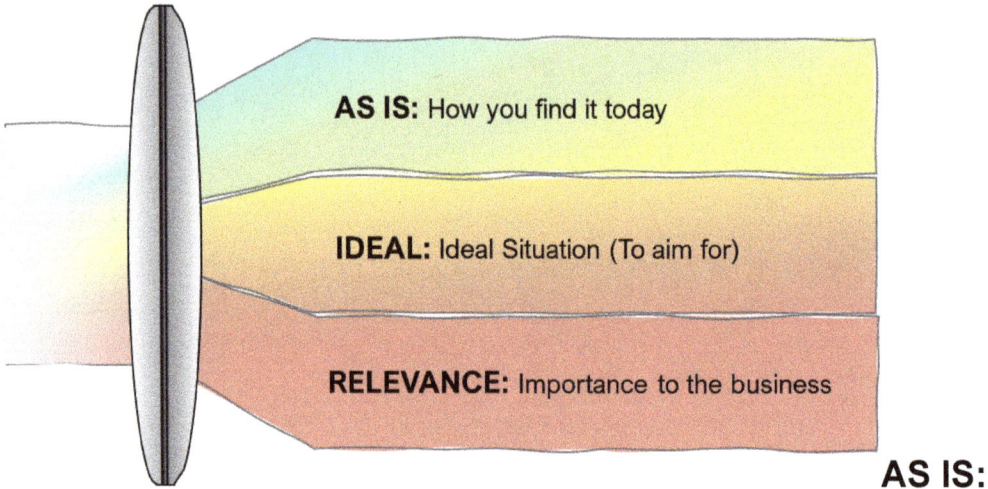

**AS IS:** How you find it today

**IDEAL:** Ideal Situation (To aim for)

**RELEVANCE:** Importance to the business

## AS IS:

The "AS IS" lens prompts you to honestly evaluate your current state—where you stand today.

## IDEAL:

The "Ideal" lens encourages you to define your ambitions—where you realistically aspire to be, given your resources and priorities. Recognizing that achieving a perfect "10 out of 10" in every area isn't always feasible or necessary, this lens focuses on identifying the most impactful areas for improvement.

## RELEVANCE:

Finally, the **"Importance / Relevance / Weighting for your organisation"** As that is a bit too wordy, let's just call it importance. But as you work through this lens, **please consider all three**: How important the aspect is to the business, how relevant the area is for the business, and what weighting you would put on addressing any issues you discover in that area.

This lens asks you to consider the importance of each question within the context of your specific market. What might be highly relevant for a medical device manufacturer, such as after-sales service and support, might be less critical for a pharmaceutical company. Stakeholder management, such as a Key Opinion Leader (KOL) or Influencer (I'll use the terms interchangeably), may be very important for a government organisation but completely irrelevant for a mechanic's business.

By examining each question through these three perspectives, you'll gain a nuanced understanding of your strategic alignment, market positioning, and competitive advantage. This structured approach will provide a solid understanding of the business and help you navigate your where to next and how to get there.

# SCORING:

Score how you are today

Score how you would like to be tomorrow

Identify the Gap from Tomorrow Vs Today

How Important to your business is it

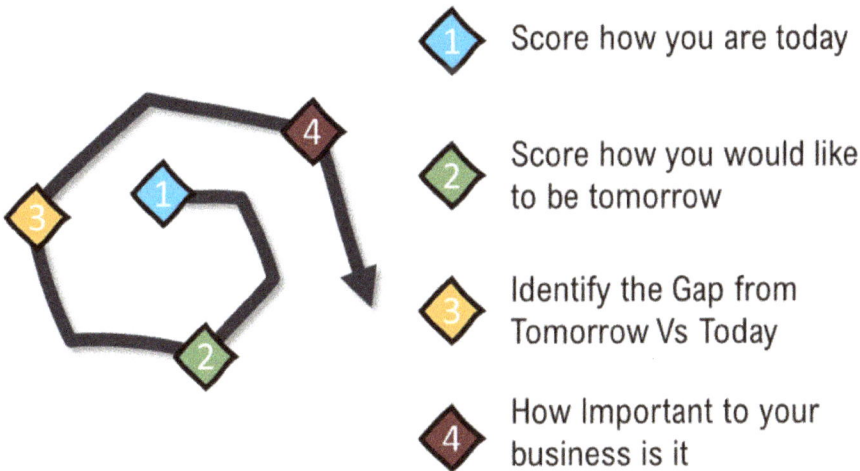

For each of the sections in this book there will be a box plot where you can score your organisation from 1–10 for the section. Don't be a fence-sitter – it's either favourable or it's not yet, so try not to choose 5. As you read the reflection questions, you may notice specific language, for example: "A documented process for..." If you have a process and it's not documented then it's more likely a scoring of 6 or 7 whereas a flowchart may be a 7-8, and an integrated document's record could represent a 9 or a 10. However, you score it won't matter as long as you score it the same way throughout the book so you can compare chapters and sections. I'd also recommend jotting a note in the spare pages so that when you re-visit this in the future you can easily see if you've made progress.

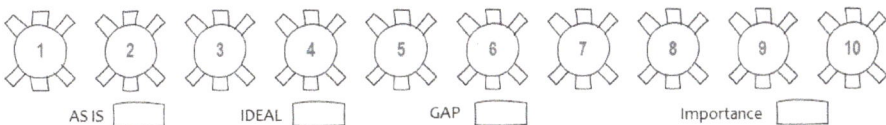

| 1 | 2 | 3 | 4 | 5 | 6 | 7 | 8 | 9 | 10 |

AS IS [      ]        IDEAL [      ]        GAP [      ]                Importance [      ]

In each number you will see three aspects: The circle, a vertical line, and a cross.

1: AS IS = 3, Ideal = 7, ∴ Gap = 4, and Importance / Relevance = 9
2: AS IS = 4, Ideal = 6, ∴ Gap = 2, and Importance / Relevance = 2
3: AS IS = 8, Ideal = 6, ∴ Gap = -2, and Importance / Relevance = 7

**Figure 1:** Scoring Examples

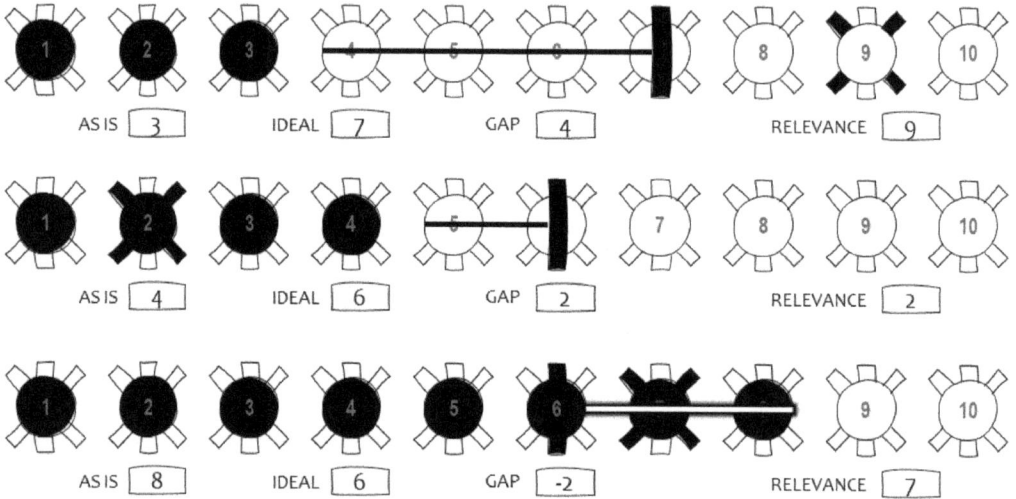

The circle is for marking where your organisation is today and the gap. Hold with me here, I'll get to how in a minute. The horizontal line is for your Ideal State Score and the cross is for you to record the weighting in importance for your organisation. Now going back to the gap. If you score your organisation a 3 out of 10 for "AS IS" and your Ideal (horizontal line) is a 7 out of 10, then if you're using a black pen, shade the 3 in fully and put a line through 4, 5, and 6 to the vertical line at 7 for Ideal.

**Figure 2:** Scoring Cell

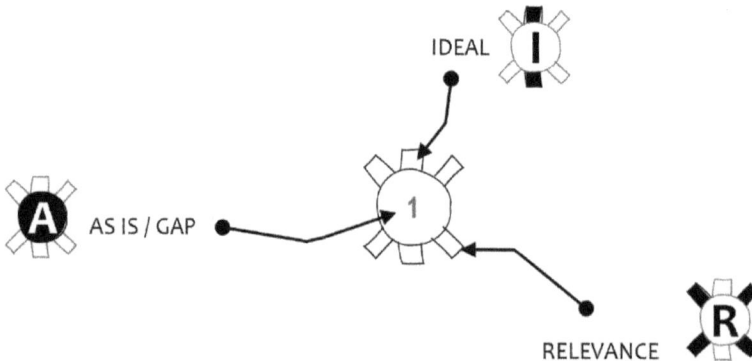

If you are not a visual person, then just put the numbers in the boxes. I am a visual learner so having the plots to work with as I go along is great for me.

Just keep the numbers somewhere you will need them to help diagnose each section. The other variable that I have when running this with clients is – what timeframe are we scoring over? The timeframe is up to you and depending upon how dynamic your business is you will need to come up with an appropriate one. My suggestion is that you score it within a reasonable amount of time. But not so long that your organisation could not react now!

At the end of the book, you will likely want to do something about your results. So, the timeframe needs to be long enough to get a good Ideal State but short enough that the important things for today are ranked as important. If you are unsure pick 18-24 months as a starting point.

Okay great so you have all these scores, now what do you do with them?
At the end of each section, you'll find a Plotting template, and at the end of the book we have a final copy for you to plot each of the section results. By doing this you'll get the ability to have a high-level overview of the company, each section will have aspects that are more sophisticated and some that you'll want to pay attention to. So if your biggest gap Between your As is and Ideal is Finance and Pricing, you'll know exactly what aspects in that big bucket you may want to work on first.

Okay, so let's now review what the plot looks like and how to use it.

# THE PLOT:

On the plot you will notice 2 axis $y$ being the GAP and $x$ being the Importance / Relevance to your organisation.

**Figure 3:**

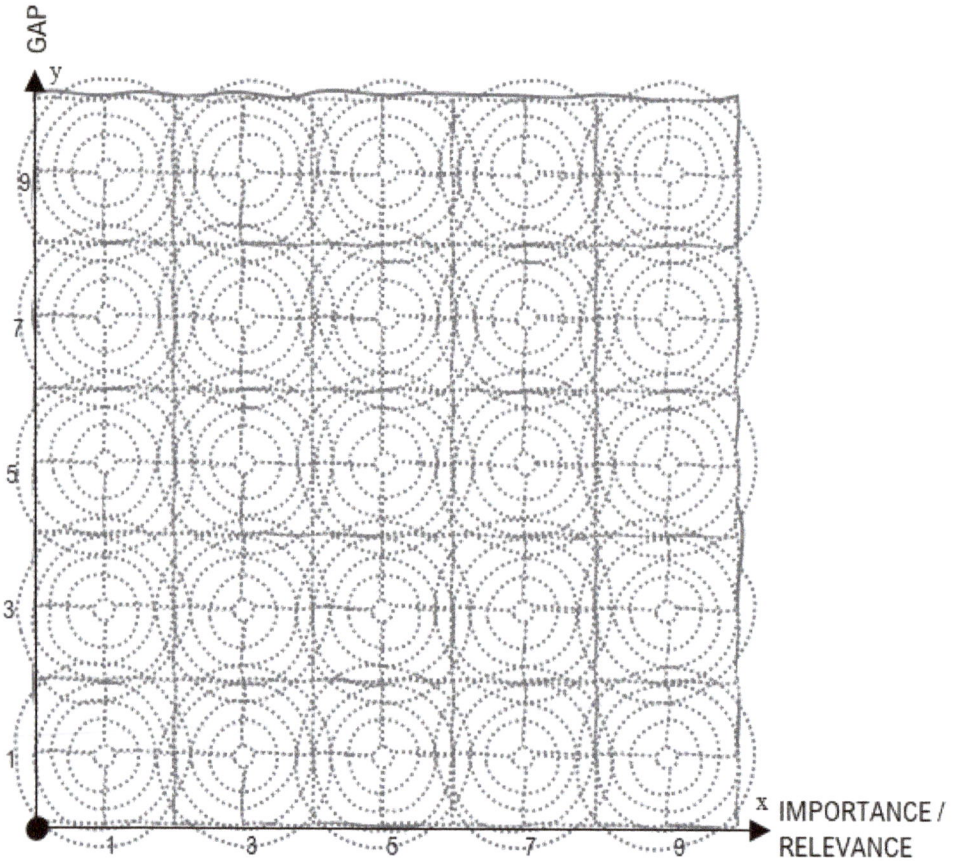

**Note:** The size of the Circle is in Reverse. The Lower the AS IS Score the Larger the Circle should be.

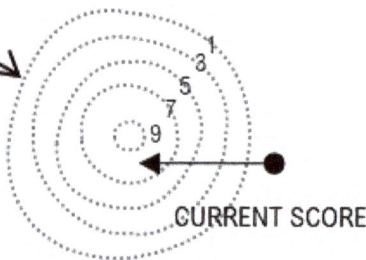

At the intersections you will notice expanding circles. These are to record your **AS IS** state. Notice the numbers for scoring the expanding circles are in reverse order. As your score gets larger, the size of the circle gets smaller. Therefore, a AS IS of 1 is the largest circle, and a AS IS score of 9 is the smallest circle.

Because it's in reverse, it easily shows where you have a lower maturity or system that has less sophistication.

For example, let's assume we have the below for Section 1: Strategic Direction, our scores are detailed in the following table:

| Chapter | AS IS | Ideal | Gap | Relevance |
|---|---|---|---|---|
| Strategy Development | 3 | 7 | 4 | 9 |
| Opportunity Selection | 7 | 8 | 1 | 6 |
| Success Drivers | 3 | 5 | 2 | 7 |
| Commercial Operating Model | 6 | 8 | 2 | 4 |

If we plotted the Section 1 on our graph it would look like this:

**Figure 4:** Example Section 1 Plot

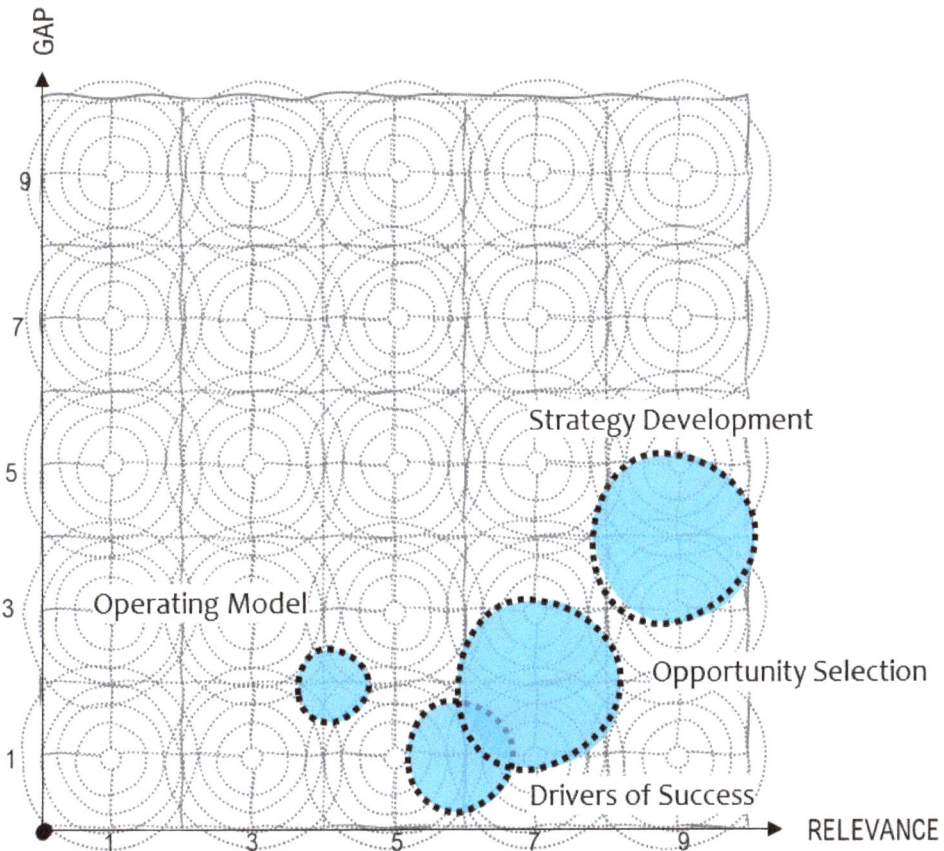

In Figure 4 we can see that the 4 aspects of strategy are plotted out as 4 circles of differing sizes.
So what does that mean? Let's consider how to read a plot.

## Reading the Plot Graphs

In the figure 5 below the plot graph is separated into areas for importance. And shows 2 example aspects. One being a priority for the organisation and 1 being a potential source of over resourcing.

**Figure 5:** How to interoperate a plot

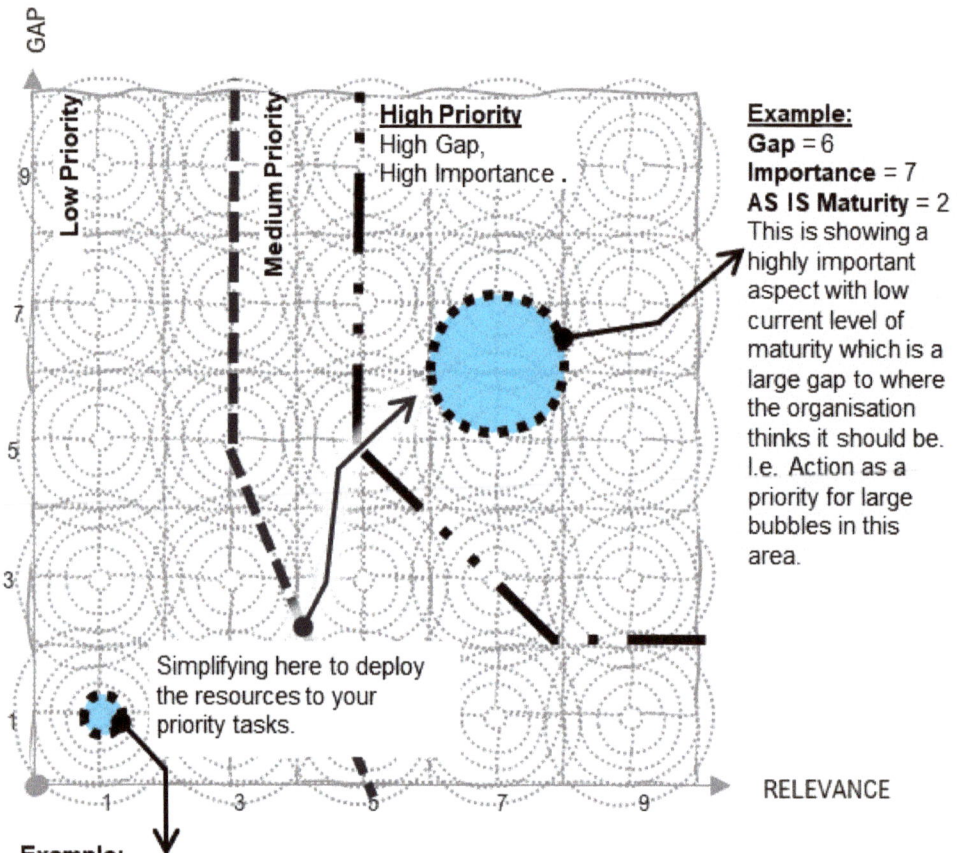

**High Priority**
High Gap,
High Importance .

**Example:**
**Gap** = 6
**Importance** = 7
**AS IS Maturity** = 2
This is showing a highly important aspect with low current level of maturity which is a large gap to where the organisation thinks it should be. I.e. Action as a priority for large bubbles in this area.

Simplifying here to deploy the resources to your priority tasks.

**Example:**
Gap = 1
Importance = 1
AS IS Maturity = 9
This is showing an aspect that is well under control and perhaps overly sophisticated for the organisations needs. You may want to see if you can Trim or simplify here.

As you move through the book a picture will emerge of where you are doing well and where to potentially focus your efforts. Looking for the larger sections that are closer to the top and closer to the right side.

* **Pro Tip:** I've used this book many times over and over to guide me through when I finish a project or start a new project. It's a great diagnostic tool for how your business is performing over time.

Remember, you won't be able to implement everything at once, so this book will help with prioritisation. Of course, you must also consider the required resources for implementation (throughout this book, "resources" includes time) and your current skills and expertise.

# POTENTIAL USE CASES FOR THIS BOOK:

- **THE NEW CEO:** The newly appointed CEO who wants to rapidly understand the status of the business.
- **NED UNDERSTANDING:** Board of Directors has several Non-Executive Directors that want / need to understand aspects of the business.
- **STRATEGIC PLANNING:** Just before a Strategic Planning Session to understand where the business is now.
- **CONSULTING:** As a consultant for the before and after picture to see the impact of their work. (Especially when before and after revenue growth has impact limitations).
- **COMMERCIAL EXCELLENCE PRACTICE:** As a commercial excellence practitioner as a reference guide.
- **MERGER & ACQUISITION READYNESS:** As a shared language for evaluating commercial strengths, weaknesses, and integration opportunities. A pre-merger due diligence tool that helps both parties see the same light.
- **SUCCESSION PLANNING:** as a checklist for outgoing and incoming leaders, ensuring continuity of commercial wisdom and focus.
- **BUSINESS TURNAROUND INITIATIVES:** As a compass, helping leaders prioritize which commercial functions to stabilize first
- **ANNUAL BOARD REVIEWS:** Annually to benchmark progress, recalibrate priorities, and ensure alignment across leadership

# LIGHTHOUSE METAPHOR:

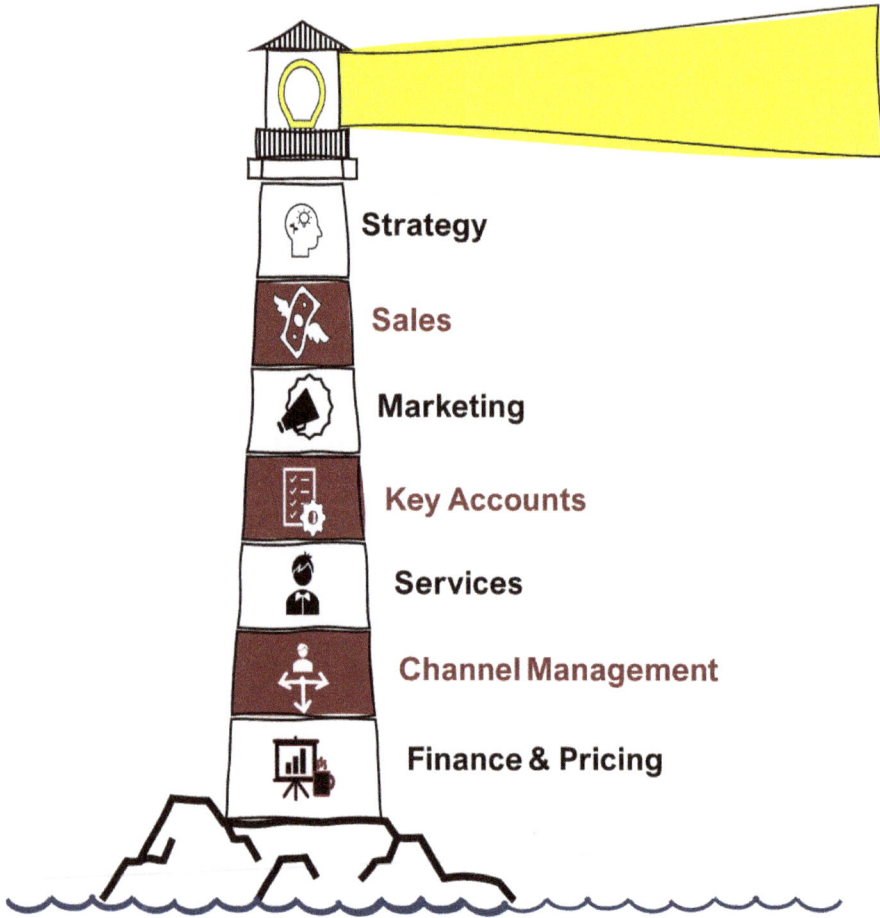

**Strategy**

**Sales**

**Marketing**

**Key Accounts**

**Services**

**Channel Management**

**Finance & Pricing**

To help guide us through the book, the light house graphic will guide us as to where we are. Commercial excellence is about two things:

**1.** Understanding where you are as an organisation at a point in time and

**2.** What you want to do about it. The commercial areas we're looking at are

**SALES & MARKETING**. I pull out a special section for
Key Accounts as I believe, even if you don't have a key account process, understanding the core aspects is helpful in your 1-5 largest accounts (I'll hazard a guess they represent 30-50% of your total potential in a given marketplace.)

The Commercial Excellence Playbook

Services is a way of capturing more value and or more loyalty from your existing customer base and customer care to ensure onboarding of new customers or prospects builds loyalty from before day 1.

I'm also from a technical and value based selling industry. Therefore, I'd suggest taking what you wish from the sections and leaving what's not relevant behind.

Channel Management or Distribution Management is an extension of the Go To Market (GTM or G2M) model and is often the first way a company moves into a new geography with existing products. Managing distribution is a different game than managing customers directly. Working with and through a partner organisation has its own specifics that are interesting, to say the least. Especially if you want to rapid, profitable growth.

Finance & Pricing: There are certain elements that for a commercial excellence program that finance needs to help prepare that are critical for being able to understand and take appropriate actions. I will also include here tender management as it's important from the industry that I have worked in, but it may well be irrelevant in yours. (Again, just skip the section if necessary). I don't know how many times in my career I've heard a sales rep say "We lost because of price". I call bull**** on that! So, we'll delve into pricing.

You'll notice that nearly all these aspects relate to a CRM system. Salesforce.com, for example, has modules for Sales, Marketing, Key Accounts, Services and Pricing. Yet CRM systems don't yet have an integrated approach. I'll watch this space for when they start to integrate all what must be custom add-ins from the big players into a standard offering for the rest of us.

# BEFORE YOU BEGIN:

The purpose of this book is for you, the reader, to self-evaluate your own business. The sections have been written not as a must, or you should do this. They are written to create reflection and interest on your part. It's therefore critically important that you have an honest self-assessment.

However, you read or score yourself doesn't matter as long as you score the same way through the entirety of the book, you'll get the benefit. There are no right or wrong answers here. You don't have to be 10 out of 10 at anything. If you are, you're probably over-invested in that area.

Enjoy the book – and I hope it helps you gain some valuable insights into your own business.

# SECTION 1: STRATEGY

## The Guiding Light at the Apex

*Strategy, strategic directions, assessing strategic alignment, market positioning, and competitive advantage*

**Strategy**

**Sales**

**Marketing**

**Key Accounts**

**Services**

**Channel Management**

**Finance & Pricing**

Are you steering your ship through foggy waters, or do you have a clear view of your destination? In today's rapidly evolving business landscape, having a well-defined strategic direction isn't just an advantage—it's a necessity. This chapter challenges you to make a critical examination of the alignment between your company's vision and its day-to-day operations. Are you truly positioned to outmanoeuvre your competitors, or are you simply treading water? Let's dive into the heart of strategic alignment, market positioning, and competitive advantage to ensure your business isn't just surviving but thriving in the face of change.

**Figure 6:** Strategy Stairway (5 stairs of Strategy Execution)

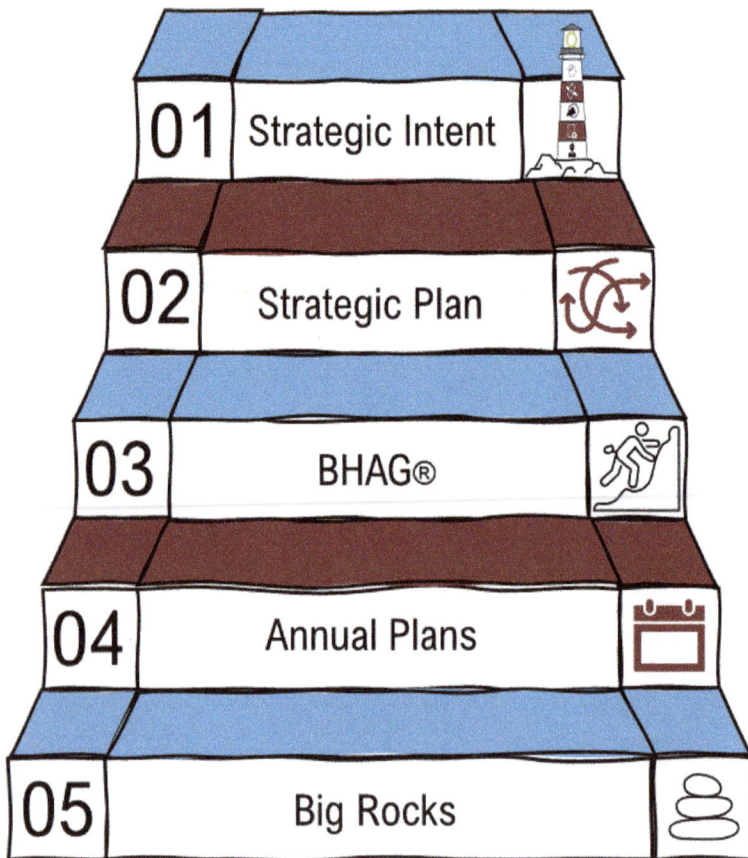

At the highest level lies the 'Strategic Intent'—the long-term vision set by the board of directors, providing overarching guidance to the executive team. This intent is then translated into a more concrete 'Strategic Plan,' a detailed roadmap by the executive team and presented back to the board for approval or rework. It should outline how they intend to achieve the strategic intent. This

The Commercial Excellence Playbook

plan informs the annual budget and business plans, defining the one-year objectives and priorities.

Often, these annual plans are anchored by BHAG's ® (Collins, 2004)—Big Hairy Audacious Goals—ambitious, long-term objectives that inspire and galvanise the organisation. To make these BHAGs more manageable and actionable, they are further broken down into 'Big Rocks'—key priorities or projects that must be completed within a specific timeframe to contribute to the larger BHAG ® . By examining how these different levels of strategic direction align and interact, we can gain a clear understanding of whether your organisation is effectively translating its long-term vision into concrete actions and measurable results.

In my experience, I have seen 1 of 2 things happen at most of the companies that I have had the pleasure to be involved with.

**1.** The board is made up of founders who can't let go and want to be involved in steps 1 though to 3. Whilst challenge testing and ensuring a robust process and stretch targets is one thing but they're not at the maturity level to step back or not willing to let go.
Or

**2.** Alternatively, the second is global multinationals where the Strategic intent and strategic (Strat) plan is not shared with the regional or country level executives. The control is set at a regional level, leaving the Matrix organisation to manage their parts without necessary checking or cross checking with the other. I've seen this lead to local CEOs pushing for their pet projects or acquisition targets that make 100% sense at a country level but are not aligned with the long-term goals of the company. A Statement of Strategic Intent in this case would help the region and countries make better decisions and focus on areas aligned to the vision rather than wasted effort able it with good intent.

Over this section, we will look at strategy over four key spectrums (Figure7). Each spectrum is broken into chapters to explore.

**Figure 7:** 4 Wavelengths of Strategy Section

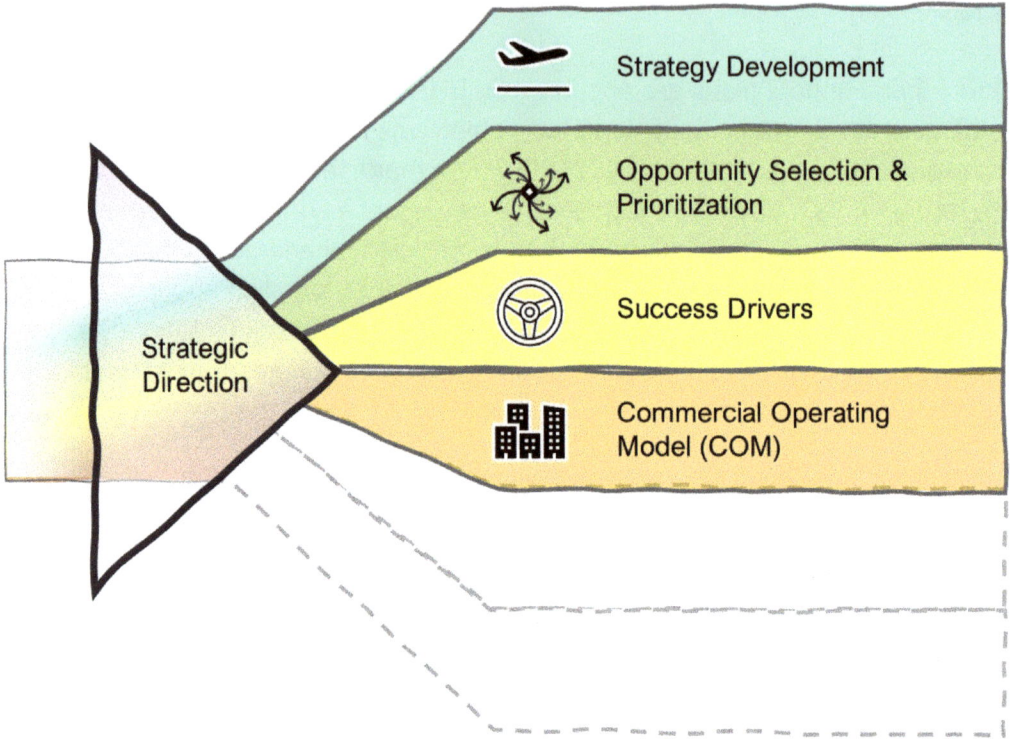

Strategy Development

Opportunity Selection & Prioritization

Success Drivers

Commercial Operating Model (COM)

Strategic Direction

# CHAPTER 1:
# Strategy Development

Score this chapter here

① 1  ② 2  ③ 3  ④ 4  ⑤ 5  ⑥ 6  ⑦ 7  ⑧ 8  ⑨ 9  ⑩ 10

AS IS ⬚   IDEAL ⬚   GAP ⬚   RELEVANCE ⬚

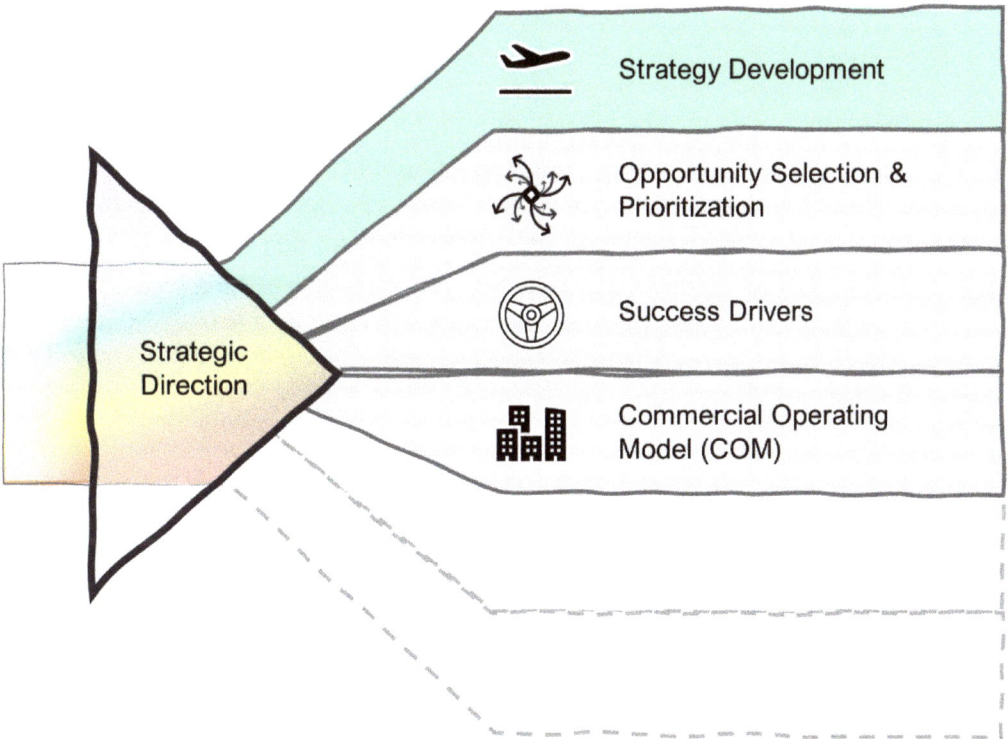

Strategic Direction

✈ Strategy Development

Opportunity Selection & Prioritization

Success Drivers

Commercial Operating Model (COM)

The first part of developing a strategy is to gather the needs and trends of both the customer base and where the market is going – what are the mega trends? How does the company gather the needs and priorities from its customers to develop its strategy?

The company is often not yet mature enough to have a process to do this, but naturally does through a founder or business development manager. Who has the information in their head/s? To diagnose this part, consider the customer needs below. Note your answers and look through the lenses at the area and you will soon understand where you are.

## CUSTOMER NEEDS:

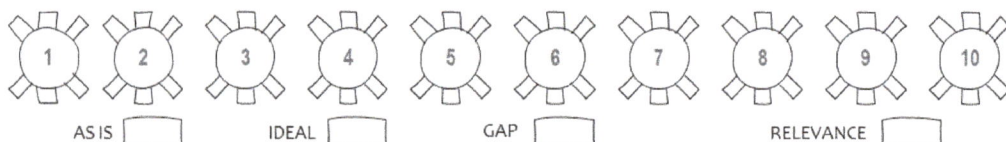

AS IS [          ]        IDEAL [          ]        GAP [          ]                RELEVANCE [          ]

The needs of the customer are crucial for understanding what do develop and what will sell. As the organisation matures (e.g. gets closer to a 10/10) on our scoring system, the Informal Ad hoc information gathering will move to more formal and planned. Not to say that the informal and Ad hoc avenues won't stay, but less weight will be placed upon them as the organisation gets bigger. The Informal Ad hoc may be extremely important for the future of a small enterprise with less than 100 employees but not even considered for global multinationals.

To make up your assessment of this area, think about where your organisation is currently gathering its customer insights from. Below (Figure 8) is a graphic with a few ways organisations typically gather these. Showing a Formal Vs Informal axis and Planned Vs Ad Hoc axis to classify methods for needs collection.

**Figure 8:** Customer Need Discovery

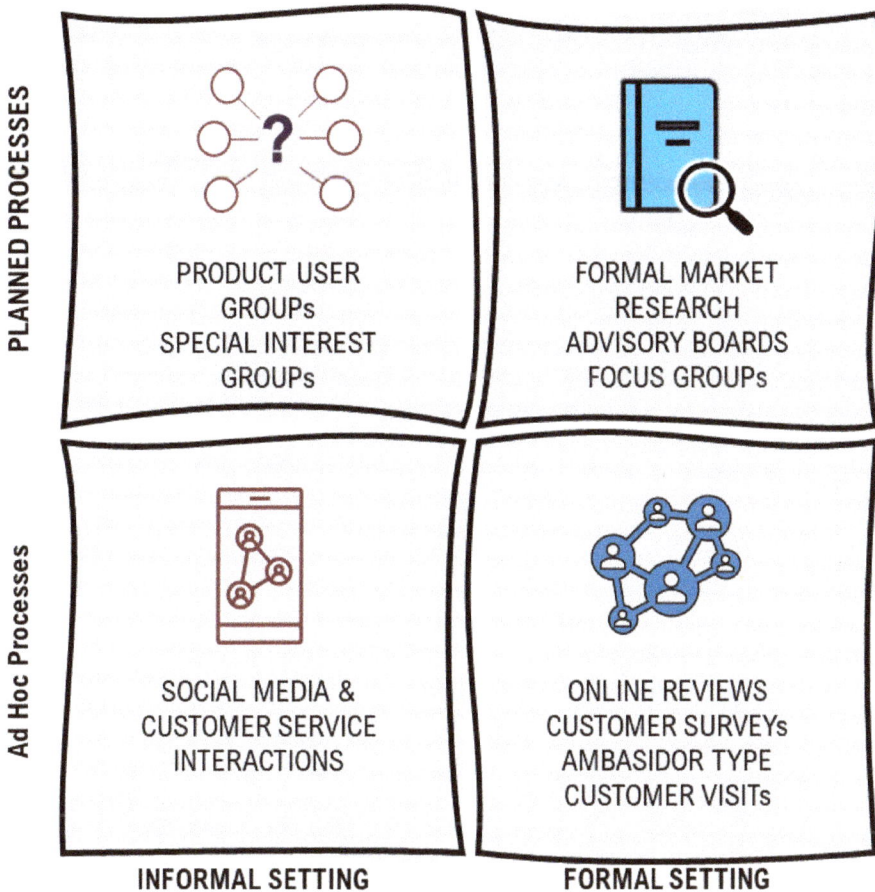

| | INFORMAL SETTING | FORMAL SETTING |
|---|---|---|
| **PLANNED PROCESSES** | PRODUCT USER GROUPs SPECIAL INTEREST GROUPs | FORMAL MARKET RESEARCH ADVISORY BOARDS FOCUS GROUPs |
| **Ad Hoc Processes** | SOCIAL MEDIA & CUSTOMER SERVICE INTERACTIONS | ONLINE REVIEWS CUSTOMER SURVEYs AMBASIDOR TYPE CUSTOMER VISITs |

# AS IS:

How does your organisation currently gather customer needs? Is it through formal market research, informal feedback, sales interactions, customer service logs, online reviews, or a combination of methods? How often is this done—only during strategic planning, ad hoc, or continuously? Where is this information stored—in CRM systems, spreadsheets, or simply in individual employees' minds? How do you currently filter out noise or conflicting feedback?

## IDEAL:

_How_ should your organisation gather customer needs? Ideally, this would involve a continuous, systematic process incorporating multiple data sources and feedback channels. This might include regular customer surveys, focus groups, social media monitoring, and analysis of customer behaviour data. Ideally, this information would be centralised in a robust system accessible to relevant teams, with logical processes for filtering and prioritising feedback based on its relevance and strategic importance.

## RELEVANCE:

How relevant are different methods of gathering customer needs to your specific market and business model? For example, in a B2B context with long sales cycles, direct interaction with key accounts might be paramount, while in a high-volume B2C market, social media monitoring and online reviews might be more critical. The relevance here prompts you to focus on the methods and frequency of data collection that are most impactful for your specific context.

## MARKET POSITION:

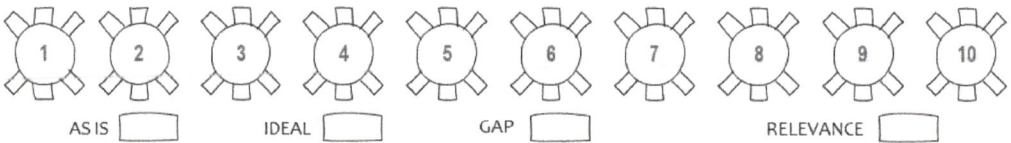

| AS IS | | IDEAL | | GAP | | | RELEVANCE | |

Market Position is where you sit in the marketplace. Are you number one – or one of many?

## AS IS:

How does your organisation currently assess its market position? Do you conduct formal market analysis, rely on industry reports, track competitor activities, analyse sales data, or use a combination of these methods? How often is this analysis performed? How is this information documented and shared within the organisation? How is this information used to inform strategic decisions? In the following matrix, where do your products / services fall?

# IDEAL:

Ideally, market position analysis should be an ongoing process, involving a combination of quantitative and qualitative research. This might include market sizing, competitive analysis, trend forecasting, customer segmentation, and SWOT analysis. An understanding of Blue Vs Red Ocean (Mauborgne, 2005) and the lifecycles of the product and service ranges as compared to those market conditions. Ideally, you will know for sure your position in the market. Ideally, you'll have some ability to understand the potential next steps for the market, and how the initial adaptors are (or would be) thinking about those steps.

This information should be systematically collected, stored in a central repository, and regularly reviewed by relevant teams. This analysis should directly inform strategic decisions, such as target market selection, product development, marketing campaigns, and pricing strategies. Where do you fit into this framework? (Figure 9)

**Figure 9:** Blue Ocean Normative Proposition

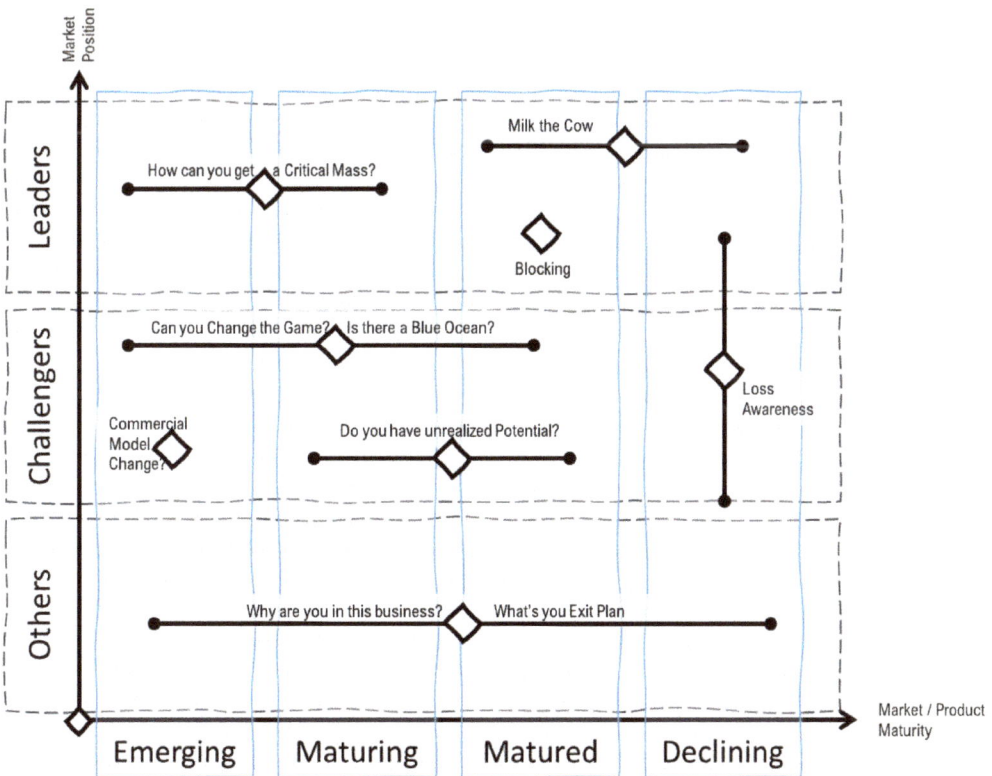

## RELEVANCE:

How relevant are different market analysis methods to your specific industry and competitive landscape? For example, in a rapidly developing tech market, real-time competitor tracking and trend analysis might be crucial, (if you can get up-to-date data) while in a more stable industry, historical market data and customer segmentation might be more important. The relevance lens encourages you to prioritise the data and analysis methods that are most impactful for your specific context.

## DIFFERENTIATION STRATEGY:

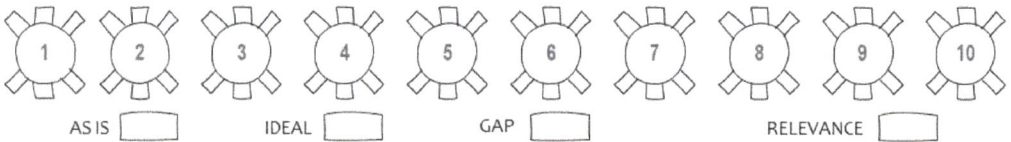

AS IS [    ]       IDEAL [    ]       GAP [    ]       RELEVANCE [    ]

Does your organisation have a well-defined and well-communicated unique value proposition. How is this reviewed and communicated to the organisation? What makes the organisation unique?

## AS IS:

Does your organisation currently have a clearly defined value proposition? Is it documented and communicated effectively both internally and externally? How was it developed—through formal market research, intuition, or a combination of both? How long has it been since it's been reviewed? Is it out of date? When preparing a Strat Plan, Business Plan, BHAG ® (Collins, 2004) or Big Rock (Harnish, 2014) is it discussed and incorporated into the thinking? How is the value proposition currently used in strategy formulation—is it a central guiding principle, or is it treated as a separate marketing exercise? What are the mission and vision statements? As business leadership expert and author Simon Sinek says, "Start with why." (SINEK, 2009). Is this communicated and lived at every level of the organisation does it drive your thinking?

## IDEAL:

Ideally, your organisation should have an interesting and clearly articulated Unique Value Proposition (UVP) that resonates with your target market and differentiates you from competitors. This UVP should be developed through rigorous market research and customer analysis, and it should be regularly reviewed and updated to ensure its continued importance. Ideally, the UVP should be a cornerstone of your strategic planning process, informing decisions related to product development, marketing, sales, and customer service.

## RELEVANCE:

The importance of a clearly defined and communicated UVP varies depending on how 'red' (highly competitive) your ocean is. In highly competitive markets, a strong UVP is essential for differentiation and customer acquisition. In less competitive markets, while still important, the emphasis might be on operational efficiency or other factors. The relevance lens prompts you to consider how critical a strong UVP is to your specific industry and competitive environment.

# COMPETITORS' UNIQUE VALUE PROPOSITION:

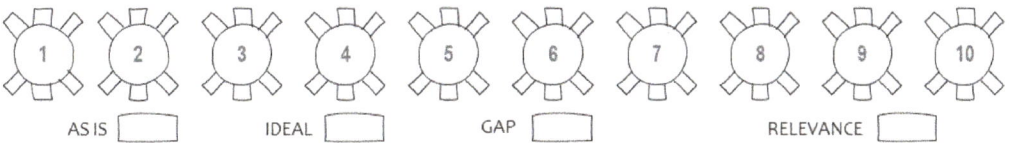

AS IS [    ]    IDEAL [    ]    GAP [    ]    RELEVANCE [    ]

Understanding your competitive landscape is crucial to understand if your UVP is truly differentiated.

## AS IS:

How does your organisation currently assess competitor value propositions? Do you analyse their marketing materials, websites, customer reviews, pricing strategies, or conduct competitive intelligence research? How systematically is this information gathered and analysed? Do you use this information to differentiate yourselves so you don't compete on the same axes? From the information, can we gather what part of the ANSOFF Matrix (Ansoff, 1957) they are going for? Do you know their Source of Volume (Dapena-Baron C. N., 2015), Their Price, Place and Promotion philosophy. How is it currently used in your strategy formulation? Is it used to inform differentiation strategies, pricing decisions, or marketing campaigns?

## IDEAL:

Ideally, your organisation should have a robust process for continuously monitoring and analysing competitor value propositions. This would involve gathering data from multiple sources, including competitor websites, marketing materials, customer reviews, industry reports, and potentially even direct customer feedback. This information should be systematically analysed to identify key differentiators, competitive advantages, and potential vulnerabilities. Ideally, this competitive analysis should directly inform your own strategy formulation, helping you to refine your UVP, identify opportunities for differentiation, and develop effective competitive strategies.

## RELEVANCE:

The depth and intensity of competitor analysis will vary depending on the competitive intensity of your market. In highly competitive markets with many similar offerings, a deep understanding of competitor UVPs is essential for survival and success.

# THE BUSINESS ENVIRONMENT:

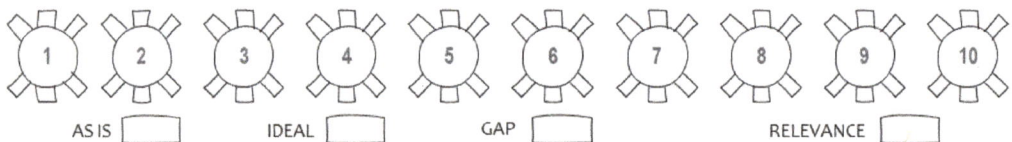

| AS IS | | IDEAL | | GAP | | | RELEVANCE | |

The need to adapt to external changes. There have been several re-counting stories of Kodak and the move from film to digital. We need to ensure we stay up to speed with mega trends and are clear on the direction we're heading. I expect many organisations will move towards AI integration models in their operations within the next five years. From a commercial excellence perspective, BCG and Bain and Co are the first of the big commercial excellence consulting companies who have already moved into Enterprise AI with Open AI (openai.com/business/).

## AS IS:

How does your organisation currently monitor and assess the business environment? Do you use formal methods like PESTLE (Aguilar, 1967) analysis (Political, Economic, Social, Technological, Legal, Environmental), Porter's Five Forces (Porter, 1979), or scenario planning? Do you rely on industry reports, news sources, or internal expertise? How frequently is this assessment conducted, and how is the information disseminated and used in strategy formulation? Is it a reactive or proactive process? Does your business utilise fully trade conferences and thought leaders? Does the business monitor its customers' customers? That's right – their customers! What are their wants, needs, desires? What is their online presence saying? Is your organisation leading or lagging in digital transformation and AI? Or is your business building an enterprise AI?

## IDEAL:

Ideally, your organisation should have a structured and ongoing process for monitoring the business environment. This would involve using a combination of frameworks and data sources to identify emerging trends, potential threats, and new opportunities. This process should be integrated into the strategic planning cycle, ensuring that commercial strategies are developed with a clear understanding of the external context. Ideally, this process would be proactive, allowing the organisation to anticipate changes and adapt its strategy accordingly.

## RELEVANCE:

The importance of a robust environmental assessment process varies depending on the dynamism and volatility of the industry. In rapidly changing industries, continuous monitoring and adaptation are essential for survival. In more stable industries, periodic reviews might be sufficient.

# NEW AND NOVEL:

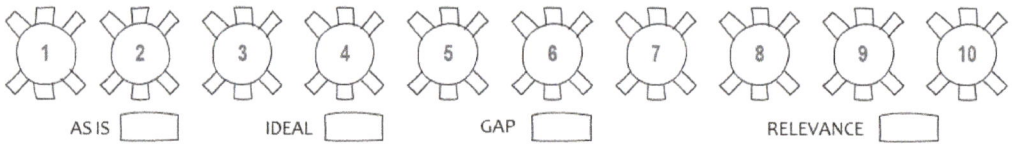

| | | | | | | | | | |
|---|---|---|---|---|---|---|---|---|---|
| 1 | 2 | 3 | 4 | 5 | 6 | 7 | 8 | 9 | 10 |

AS IS [   ]   IDEAL [   ]   GAP [   ]   RELEVANCE [   ]

What is the importance is new and novel products / services or business models for our strategy? Is the market moving into a different business model? Microsoft Office was late to software as a service model, yet Google Docs is still free (Well for now anyway, I would not be surprised if their current move into Google Workspaces isn't designed to re-capture value here). But I digress...

Have you considered using a different model? Maybe, an electronic sales force that sells purely by video conferencing or webinars. Do you have inside sales and lead generation engines? What digital or social marketing is done? Do you utilise KOLs as influencers and have them share your content? What about other platforms and marketplaces? Do you utilise AI tools to help the business? Explore the role of innovation and adaptation in your commercial strategy and require assessment through our three lenses, considering various modern sales and marketing approaches.

## AS IS:

How does your organisation currently prioritize innovation in products, services, or business models? Is there a formal process for generating and evaluating new ideas? How quickly does your organisation typically adopt new technologies or business models? How are emerging trends like electronic sales forces, video conferencing for sales, inside sales, digital marketing, social media marketing, influencer marketing, and online platforms/marketplaces currently being utilized? Is there a clear understanding of whether the market is shifting towards a different dominant business model?
What part of the ANSOFF Matrix (Ansoff, 1957) is the organisation focusing on? Is this aligned with what they are doing on the ground.

## IDEAL:

Ideally, your organisation should have a proactive approach to innovation, continuously exploring and evaluating new opportunities. This would involve actively monitoring market trends, customer needs, and technological advancements. There should be a structured process for evaluating the

26      

potential of new products, services, and business models, including assessing their alignment with the overall strategy and their potential return on investment. Ideally, the organisation would be agile and adaptable, capable of quickly adopting and integrating relevant new approaches like electronic sales forces, video conferencing, and various digital marketing strategies.

## RELEVANCE:

The importance of innovation and adaptation varies significantly depending on the industry and market dynamics. In rapidly evolving industries, continuous innovation is essential for survival. In more stable industries, a more incremental approach might be appropriate.

What is the R&D spend in our industry? For medical devices and medical diagnostics, the average is 10% (medium (8%) mode (7%) of their turnover on research and development).

The table below shows the R&D spending as a percentage of turnover (revenue) for their respective filings for 2023.

**Figure 10:** % of revenue spend on R&D for 2023 tax filings

| COMPANY | % T/O FOR R&D | COMPANY | % T/O FOR R&D |
|---|---|---|---|
| Roche | 22% | Illumina | 30.1% |
| bioMerieux | 12.5% | Bruker | 9.9% |
| Mindray | 9.8% | Qiagen | 9.8% |
| BioRad | 9.3% | Siemens | 8.6% |
| Sysmex | 6.8% | Danaher | 6.3% |
| GE Health Care | 6.2% | Abbott | 6% |
| Becton Dickenson | 5.9% | Thermo Fisher | 0.1% |

## LOW-COST COMPETITION:

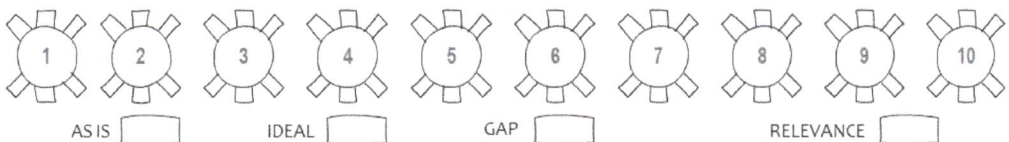

```
  1    2    3    4    5    6    7    8    9    10
AS IS [    ]   IDEAL [    ]   GAP [    ]        RELEVANCE [    ]
```

Over the years new entrants either coming in as a high cost or luxury end or at the low-cost end. Making it especially important to keep an eye on this end of your market. The long game is they will gain market share and as they gain acceptance, they will move up the value chain. Looking at the Australian car market, Kia and Hyundai were the cheap entrants in the 90s and 2000s and they are now as expensive and thought of as the same quality as the rest of the mid-tier market with new Chinese entrants such as Cherri, BYD and GWM now doing the same. Thinking about what the impact is in the short term and longer term as a risk to be considered in Strat planning processes. Low cost does not mean low profit. Mindray, a Chinese medical diagnostic equipment company, is a low-cost player in many Asian markets, yet it has one of the highest EDITs in the industry. The Strategy here is to enter the market as low cost and as you gain market share, increase pricing. In medical diagnostics / equipment, Mindray the Chinese equipment manufacturer here is a recent example. Interestingly, low cost does not equate to low margins. Mindray, whilst being low cost, actually has one of the highest net profit to turnover ratios of the sector. In their 2023 financial statements, they have a 33% EBIT on turnover.

## AS IS:

Does your organisation currently track low-cost competitors? How do you define "low-cost" in your market (e.g., lower prices, different business model, different target market)? How do you gather information about their strategies, pricing, marketing, and target customers? Is this information formally documented and analysed? How is this information currently used in your strategy formulation—does it influence pricing decisions, product development, or marketing efforts?

## IDEAL:

Ideally, your organisation should have a systematic process for identifying and monitoring low-cost competitors. This would involve defining specific criteria for identifying these competitors and regularly gathering data on their offerings, pricing, target markets, and strategies. This information should be analysed to understand their competitive advantages and potential threats to your business. Ideally, this analysis would directly inform your strategy, helping you to determine how to compete effectively against these low-cost players—whether through differentiation, cost reduction, or other strategies.

## RELEVANCE:

The importance of monitoring low-cost competitors depends on the market structure and competitive dynamics. In markets with high price sensitivity or where low-cost business models are prevalent, understanding these competitors is crucial. In markets where differentiation or other factors are more important, the focus on low-cost competitors might be less intense. If you're the large entity in the market, it's likely this is an area often overlooked. If your strategy is to cut pricing quickly to secure your market position this area is highly relevant.

# OBJECTIVE SETTING:

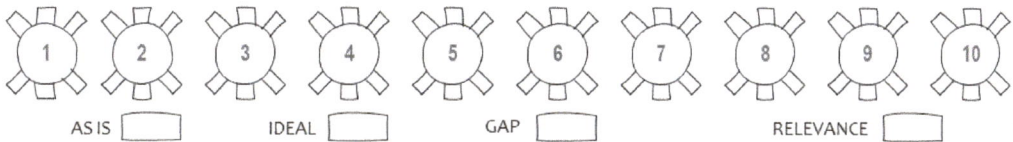

AS IS [    ]    IDEAL [    ]    GAP [    ]    RELEVANCE [    ]

How to translate our strategy into specific objectives (long term being strategic intent, medium term being our strategy, and short term being budgeting and quarterly objectives. This question addresses the crucial link between high-level vision and on-the-ground execution.

## AS IS:

How does your organisation currently translate its strategic intent into concrete objectives? Is there a formal process for setting long-term, medium-term, and short-term goals? How are these goals communicated and cascaded down through the organisation? How are budgets and quarterly objectives ('Big Rocks') aligned with the overall strategy? Are there clear metrics and KPIs used to track progress? How effectively does the organisation currently bridge the gap between strategic? thinking and tactical execution?

## IDEAL:

Ideally, there should be a clear and well-defined process for translating strategic intent into actionable objectives at all levels. This would involve a structured approach to setting long-term strategic goals, translating them into medium-term strategic plans, and then breaking these plans down into short-term, measurable objectives and quarterly 'Big Rocks.' (Harnish, 2014). This process should ensure alignment between all levels of the organisation and should include clear communication, defined responsibilities, and robust performance tracking mechanisms.

# RELEVANCE:

The level of formality and rigour required for this translation process will depend on the size and complexity of the organisation. In smaller organisations, a more informal approach might be sufficient, while larger organisations require more structured processes and systems.

What objectives can we set for?

# CHAPTER 2:

# Opportunity Selection & Prioritisation

Score this chapter here:

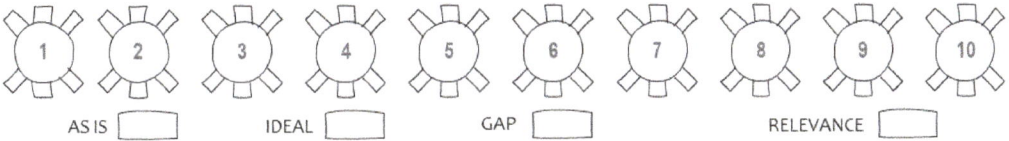

AS IS [     ]     IDEAL [     ]     GAP [     ]     RELEVANCE [     ]

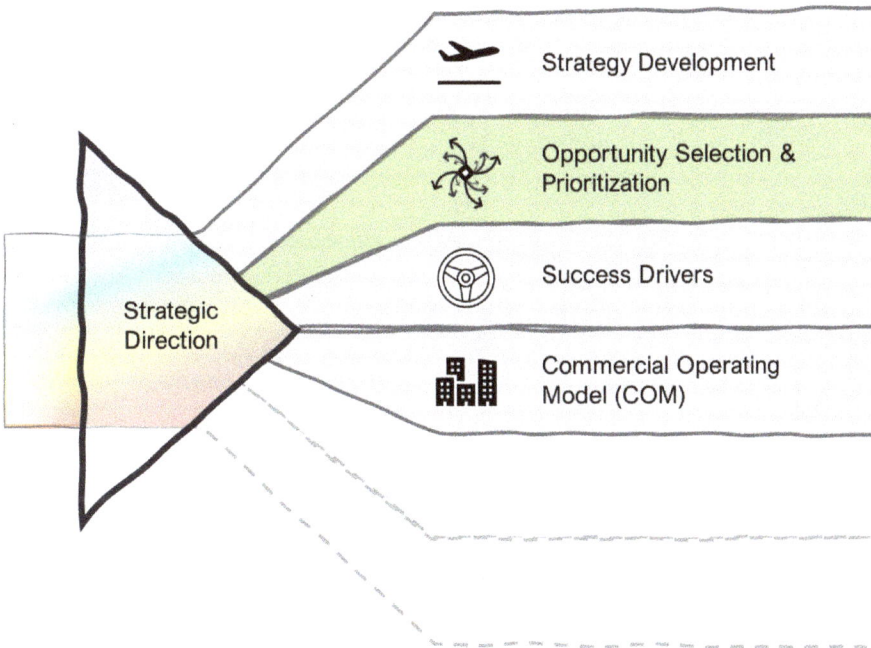

Strategy Development

Opportunity Selection & Prioritization

Success Drivers

Commercial Operating Model (COM)

Strategic Direction

This chapter is focused on how the organisation knows what to focus on. How it chooses product A vs product B and sell it to customer A or customer B.

# MARKETING SYSTEMS / STRATEGY INTEGRATION:

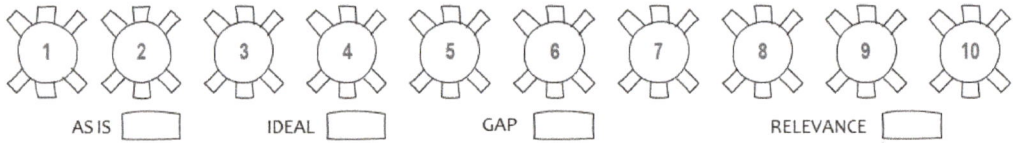

AS IS [    ]    IDEAL [    ]    GAP [    ]    RELEVANCE [    ]

Do we have a system where our sales and marketing know the strategic products / services for the company? There is a need to align sales and marketing to the overall strategic direction of the company.

Let's examine it through our three lenses:

## AS IS:

How does your organisation currently ensure that sales and marketing are aware of the strategic products/services? Is there a formal communication process, such as regular meetings, training sessions, or shared documentation? How effectively is this information cascaded down to **ALL LEVELS** of the sales and marketing teams? How is this knowledge used in day-to-day activities, such as sales pitches, marketing campaigns, and customer interactions? Are there any metrics or KPIs in place to measure the effectiveness of this alignment?

## IDEAL:

Ideally, there should be a seamless and continuous flow of information between strategy, sales, and marketing. This would involve not only communicating which products/services are strategic but also explaining _why_ they are strategic, their target markets, and their key value propositions. This could be achieved through regular cross-functional meetings, shared platforms for information sharing, and ongoing training programs. Ideally, sales and marketing would be actively involved in the strategic planning process, providing valuable market insights and feedback. There may be a financial component to this aspect. This would ensure that their activities are fully aligned with the company's overall strategic objectives.

## RELEVANCE:

The importance of this alignment depends on the complexity of the product/service portfolio and the go-to-market strategy. In organisations with a diverse range of offerings or complex sales processes, ensuring that sales and marketing are focused on the right products/services is crucial. In smaller organisations with simpler offerings, this alignment might be easier to achieve, but it's still important to maintain clear communication and shared understanding. The relevance lens prompts you to consider how critical this alignment is to your specific business context and market dynamics.

# INCENTIVE / STRATEGY ALIGNMENT:

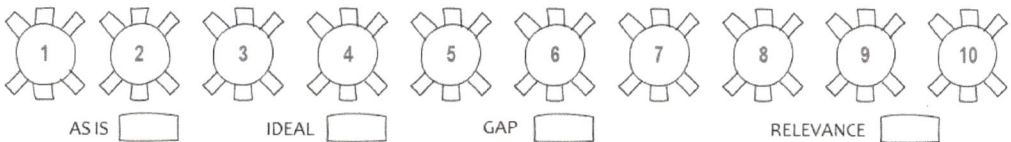

It's crucial to get appropriate execution in the right direction. Ensuring that the incentives of sales and marketing are aligned with the strategy of the company. This ensures that the entire commercial organisation is aligned on behaviours and outcomes and those are aligned with the strategy of the company.

Let's analyse it through our three lenses:

## AS IS:

How are sales and marketing teams currently motivated? What metrics are used to determine bonuses, commissions, or other rewards? Do these metrics directly reflect the strategic priorities of the company? For example, are sales teams motivated solely on revenue, or are other factors like customer acquisition cost, customer retention, or sales of strategic products also considered? Are marketing teams motivated on lead generation alone, or are factors like lead quality, brand awareness, or contribution to sales pipeline also taken into account? How often are incentive programs reviewed and adjusted to ensure continued alignment with the evolving strategy?

## IDEAL:

Ideally, sales and marketing incentives should be directly and transparently aligned with the company's strategic objectives. This means that the metrics used to determine rewards should reward behaviours that directly contribute to the achievement of strategic goals. For example, if the strategy is to increase market share in a new segment, sales incentives might prioritize new customer acquisition in that segment. If the strategy is to increase profitability, incentives might focus on selling high-margin products or reducing customer churn. Ideally, incentive programs should be regularly reviewed and adjusted to reflect changes in the strategy and market conditions.

## RELEVANCE:

The importance of aligning sales and marketing incentives with strategy depends on the complexity of the sales and marketing functions and the degree of strategic focus required. In organisations with complex sales processes or diverse product portfolios, ensuring alignment is crucial to avoid conflicting priorities and wasted effort. In smaller organisations with simpler sales and marketing functions, alignment might be easier to achieve, but it's still important to have clear and consistent incentives that drive the desired behaviours. The relevance lens prompts you to consider how critical this alignment is to your specific business context and the effectiveness of your strategy execution.

## CUSTOMER TARGETING:

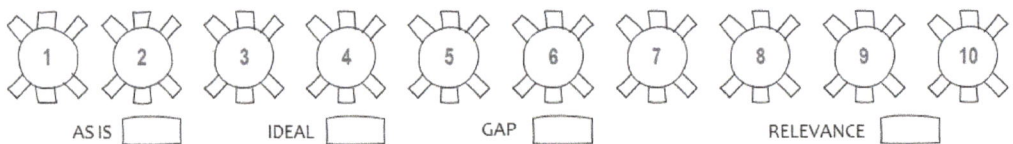

AS IS [ ]    IDEAL [ ]    GAP [ ]    RELEVANCE [ ]

Customer targeting systems are the process and procedure that guides the sales organisation who and what type of customer the organisation wants and needs. These systems ideally look at both the existing revenues of today but also the potential revenues of tomorrow for a customer or prospect. This differs from market segmentation – it's a customer-by-customer breakdown, which represents a true customer centric approach. In any given market segment, you will have many potential customers. Targeting is about who comes first.

Let's analyse it through our three lenses:

# AS IS:

How does your organisation currently define and segment its target customers? Does your customer system primarily focus on existing revenue streams, or does it also incorporate assessments of future potential? How do you identify and prioritize high-potential customers or customer segments? What data and metrics are used to assess future potential (e.g., market size, growth rate, customer lifetime value, potential for cross-selling/upselling)? How is this information used to inform sales and marketing strategies, resource allocation, and customer relationship management?

# IDEAL:

Ideally, your customer system should provide a holistic view of each customer, encompassing both their current value and their future potential. This would involve using a combination of quantitative and qualitative data to assess customer lifetime value, growth potential, and strategic fit. This information should be readily accessible to sales and marketing teams and should be used to prioritize customer interactions, tailor marketing campaigns, and develop customized sales strategies. Ideally, the system would also incorporate predictive analytics to identify emerging customer needs and anticipate future opportunities.

# RELEVANCE:

The importance of incorporating future potential into your customer system depends on the growth strategy of the organisation and the dynamics of the market. In rapidly growing markets or for organisations pursuing aggressive growth strategies, prioritizing high-potential customers is crucial. In more mature or stable markets, the focus might be more on maximizing value from existing customers. The relevance lens prompts you to consider how important it is for your organisation to balance the focus on existing revenue with the pursuit of future growth opportunities through a robust customer system.

# INCORPORATION OF RISK APPETITE:

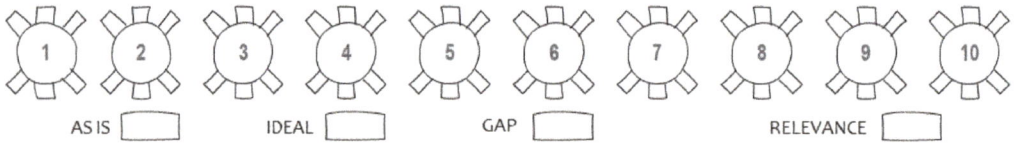

AS IS [    ]          IDEAL [    ]          GAP [    ]                    RELEVANCE [    ]

How is the acceptable level of risk assessed within the organisation? Is this incorporated into the strategy systems of the company. Aligning on the acceptable risk and therefore the unacceptable levels of risk can guide the organisation and limit or eliminate wasted efforts.
When we find opportunities for business (new product and/or new models) we have a system to assess the risk appetite set by the board.

Let's analyse it through our three lenses:

## AS IS:

How does your organisation currently assess the risk associated with new business opportunities? Is there a formal process for evaluating risk, and how is it linked to the board's established risk appetite? Has the board articulated the amount of risk it's willing for the employees to take? Are there specific criteria or metrics used to assess risk (e.g., financial risk, market risk, operational risk, reputational risk)? How is the board's risk appetite communicated and understood throughout the organisation? How are opportunities prioritized based on their risk profile and potential return? Is there a clear process for escalating high-risk opportunities to the board for review and approval?

## IDEAL:

Ideally, your organisation should have a well-defined and consistently applied risk assessment framework that is directly aligned with the board's risk appetite. This framework should provide clear guidelines and criteria for evaluating different types of risk associated with new opportunities. There should be a transparent process for escalating high-risk opportunities for the board for review and approval, ensuring that all major decisions are made within the defined risk parameters. Ideally, this process would not only identify potential risks but also outline mitigation strategies to minimize their impact.

## RELEVANCE:

The importance of a robust risk assessment process and clear alignment with the board's risk appetite depends on the organisation's industry, size, and growth strategy. In highly regulated industries or for organisations pursuing aggressive growth strategies, a more formal and rigorous risk assessment process is essential. In smaller organisations or those operating in more stable environments, a less formal approach might be sufficient, but it's still crucial to have a clear understanding of the board's risk tolerance and to ensure that new opportunities are evaluated accordingly. Many organisations do not relate risk to strategy. Personally, I believe this is a big oversight as they are intertwined.

> **Risk and strategy are two sides of the same coin. You cannot truly achieve one without considering the other.**

## ALIGNING OPPORTUNITIES WITH STRATEGY:

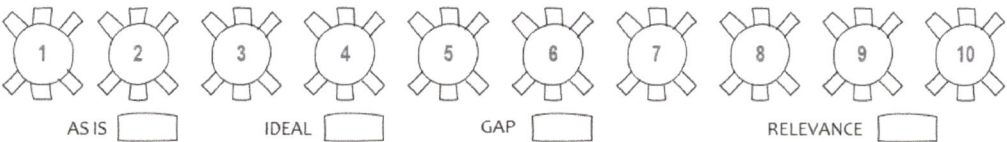

When finding opportunities, there should be a method for prioritising those opportunities that are aligned with the overarching strategy of the organisation. Let's analyse this through our three lenses:

## AS IS:

How does your organisation currently assess the strategic fit of new business opportunities? Is there a formal process for evaluating how new products or business models align with the overall company strategy? Are specific criteria or metrics used to assess strategic fit (e.g., alignment with target markets, core competencies, brand values, long-term goals)? How is this assessment documented and communicated? How does the organisation ensure that new opportunities don't divert resources or attention away from core strategic priorities?

## IDEAL:

Ideally, there should be a clear and consistently applied process for evaluating the strategic fit of all new business opportunities. This process should involve clearly defined criteria that are directly linked to the overarching company strategy. This ensures that resources are allocated to opportunities that have the greatest potential to contribute to the long-term success of the organisation. Ideally, this process would also involve assessing the potential impact of the new opportunity on existing business units and ensuring that there are no significant conflicts or cannibalization effects.

## RELEVANCE:

The importance of a robust strategic fit assessment process depends on the diversity of the organisation's business portfolio and the complexity of its strategic objectives. In organisations with a focused strategy and a narrow product/service portfolio, the assessment might be extremely simple. However, in diversified organisations with multiple business units and complex strategic goals, a more rigorous and structured approach is essential to ensure that new opportunities are truly aligned with the overall direction of the company. The relevance lens prompts you to consider how critical this alignment is to your specific business context and the effective execution of your overall strategy.

## OPPORTUNITY ESCALATION:

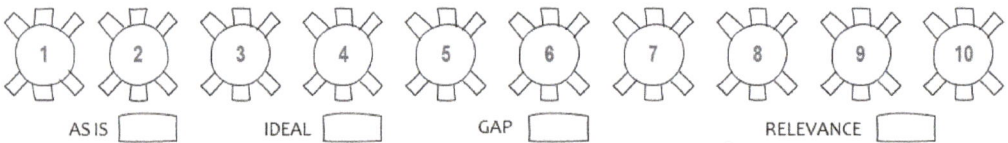

AS IS [    ]     IDEAL [    ]     GAP [    ]     RELEVANCE [    ]

It's important to analyse the way an organisation funnels business development, acquisition or merger targets, and commercial opportunities higher up the organisation. This is so that the right level of senior figure in the organisation can properly evaluate them. For instance, if it falls outside of the general sales opportunity pipeline for existing products but an opportunity exists for co-development, how does it get escalated up to the appropriate person within the organisation, so it's not lost?

Remember we're looking at the long-term strategy of the company here, not the day to day running. We're only talking about those opportunities that have the potential to change the strategy of the company. So, let's analyse it through our three lenses:

## AS IS:

How does your organisation currently communicate new **MARKET** opportunities to the board / decision makers? Is there a formal process for identifying, evaluating, and presenting these opportunities? What criteria are used to determine which opportunities are escalated? What format is used for these? (e.g., formal reports, presentations, informal discussions)? How often are these opportunities discussed? Is there a clear understanding of the board / decision makers' role in reviewing and approving new opportunities?

## IDEAL:

Ideally, there should be a well-defined and transparent process for funnelling new market opportunities to the board or those with the delegated authority. This process should include clear criteria for escalating opportunities based on factors such as potential impact, risk, and strategic fit. There should be a standardized format for presenting these opportunities to the board, ensuring that they receive all the necessary information to make informed decisions. This process should also include a mechanism for tracking the status of submitted opportunities and communicating the board's decisions back to the relevant teams.

## RELEVANCE:

The formality and complexity of this funnelling process will depend on the size and structure of the organisation, as well as the board's level of involvement in strategic decision-making. In smaller organisations, a more informal communication process might be sufficient. However, in larger organisations with more complex governance structures, a formal and well-documented process is essential to ensure that the board is aware of and can effectively oversee the evaluation of new market opportunities. The relevance lens prompts you to consider the appropriate level of formality and structure for your organisation to ensure effective communication and strategic oversight of new market opportunities.

# CHAPTER 3:

# Success Drivers

Score this chapter here

1  2  3  4  5  6  7  8  9  10

AS IS [    ]      IDEAL [    ]      GAP [    ]      RELEVANCE [    ]

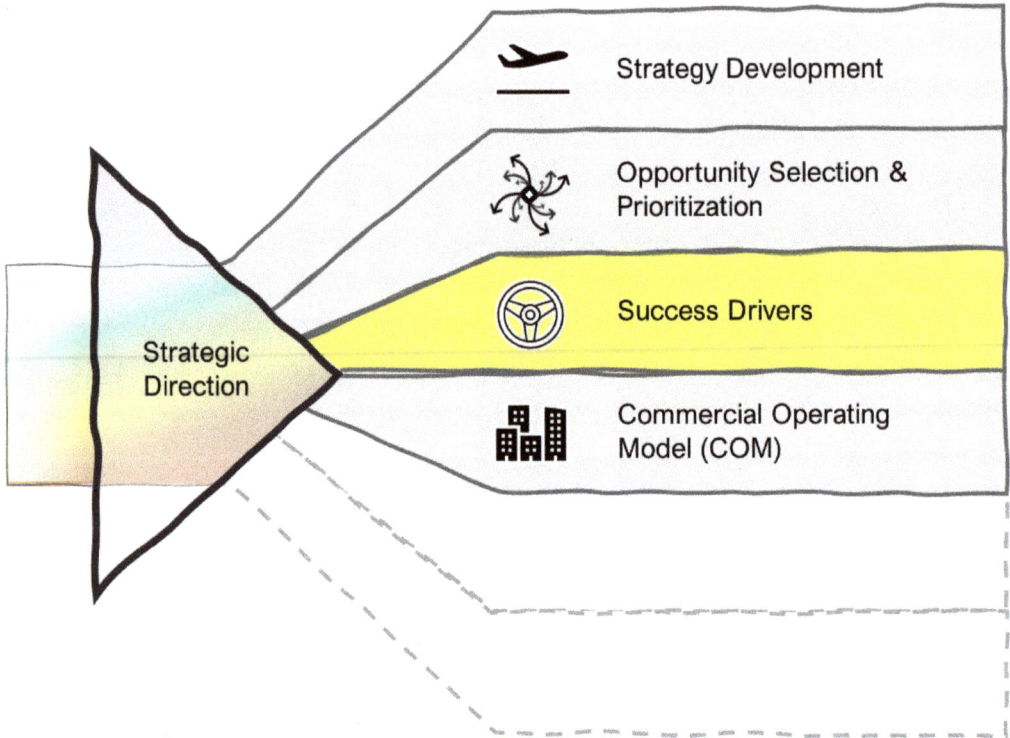

Strategy Development

Opportunity Selection & Prioritization

Success Drivers

Commercial Operating Model (COM)

Strategic Direction

This chapter focuses on the unique selling points that drive the success of the organisation.

## COMPETITION UNIQUE SELLING POINTS (USP):

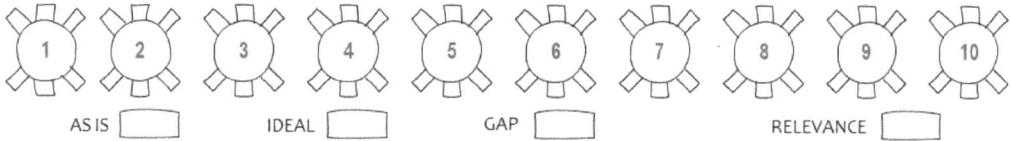

AS IS [    ]    IDEAL [    ]    GAP [    ]    RELEVANCE [    ]

Through the understanding of the competition's strategy and the tactics they are using to gain business, an organisation can understand how to position themselves and formulate their own drivers of success in the marketplace. Let's analyse it through our three lenses:

## AS IS:

How does your organisation currently gather information about competitors' strategies and tactics? Do you conduct formal competitive analysis, monitor their marketing materials and websites, analyse their pricing and sales data, attend industry events, or gather information from customers and suppliers? How systematically is this information collected, analysed, and disseminated within the organisation? How is this competitive intelligence used to inform your own strategies and tactics? Are there specific tools or technologies used for competitive monitoring?

## IDEAL:

Ideally, your organisation should have a robust and ongoing process for gathering and analysing competitive intelligence. This would involve using a variety of methods to gather data from multiple sources, including both publicly available information and primary research. This information should be systematically analysed to identify key competitor strategies, tactics, strengths, and weaknesses. This analysis should be regularly shared with relevant teams, including sales, marketing, product development, and strategy. Ideally, this process would be proactive, allowing the organisation to anticipate competitor moves and develop effective counter-strategies.

## RELEVANCE:

The importance of understanding competitor strategies and tactics depends on the competitive intensity of the market. In highly competitive markets, a deep understanding of competitor activities is essential for survival and success. In less competitive markets, while still important, the focus might be less intense. The relevance lens prompts you to consider how critical it is for your organisation to have a strong understanding of its competitive landscape and to use this knowledge to inform its own strategies and tactics.

## YOUR OWN USP:

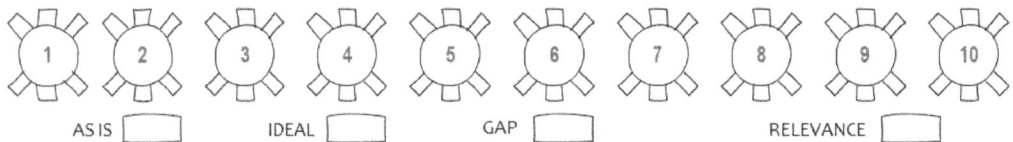

Through the understanding of the strategy of the company and the local tactics, we're able to understand and formulate our own unique selling point that is linked with our unique value proposition and use it to differentiate and compete in a blue ocean (less competition).

## AS IS:

How does the organisation currently gather the information about the market to formulate strategies? Is there a formal process to monitor and monitor the customers' wants and needs? How is that used to generate a unique value proposition and then crafted into unique selling points that are disseminated to the sales force?

## IDEAL:

The robust process for capturing the information in the field and feeding it back into the organisations marketing, this is then used as a counterpoint to other market information that forms a unique value proposition that's challenged tested and confirmed by customer advisory board or user groups etc to ensure it's accurate.

The Commercial Excellence Playbook

# RELEVANCE:

The importance of understanding our own sales tactics and strategies is highly dependent upon the size of the organisation and the number of product ranges and sales staff there are in the organisation.

What the competitions strategy is, and the tactics they are using to gain business. Through knowing this, an organisation can understand how to position themselves and formulate their own drivers of success in the marketplace.

# CHAPTER 4:

# Commercial Operating Model

Score this chapter here:

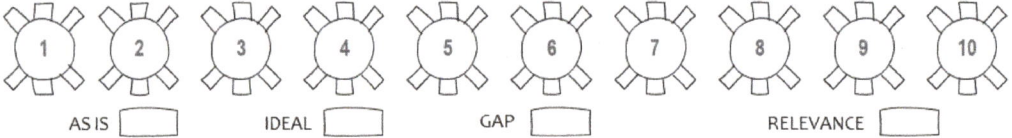

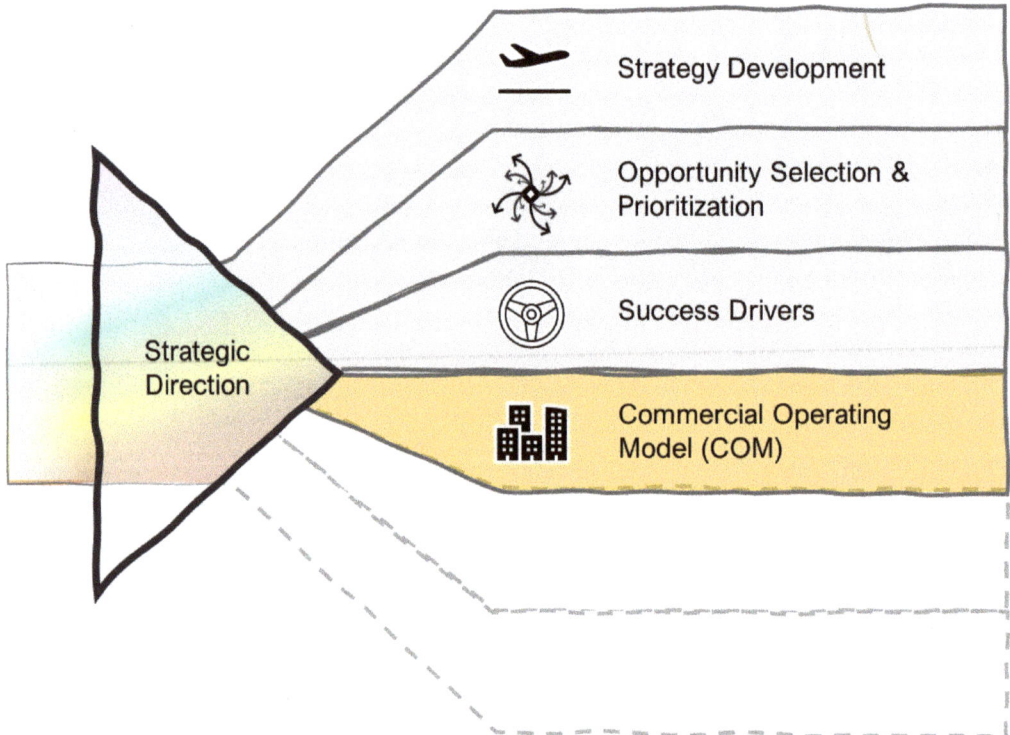

1  2  3  4  5  6  7  8  9  10

AS IS [    ]   IDEAL [    ]   GAP [    ]   RELEVANCE [    ]

Strategy Development

Opportunity Selection & Prioritization

Success Drivers

Commercial Operating Model (COM)

Strategic Direction

This chapter looks at the wavelength of how the organisation gets its products / services into customers' hands. The selection of a model can be very different depending on the strategy of the business.

As a guide to run through this chapter, here are the parts of a commercial operating model for a diagnostic, medical device or pharma company. This may look different for products or product groups or divisions or customer segments.

**Figure 11:** COM Canvas

Commercial Operating Model Canvas

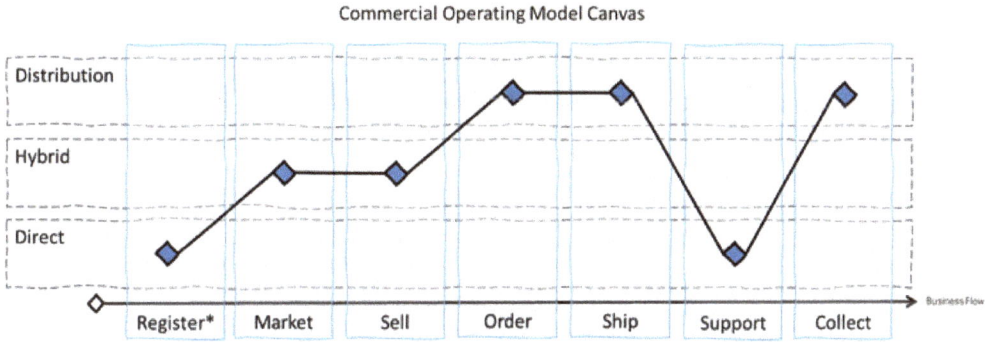

| | Register* | Market | Sell | Order | Ship | Support | Collect |

* Registration is required prior to marketing the products for Med Device, Diagnostics, Pharma etc.

In the model above, we can see that the business will hold registration of the product and the support functions internally whilst using a distributor for orders shipping and collections, and potentially both the distributor and the business doing sales and marketing activities.

**Figure 12:** A Pure Distribution Model:

Commercial Operating Model Canvas

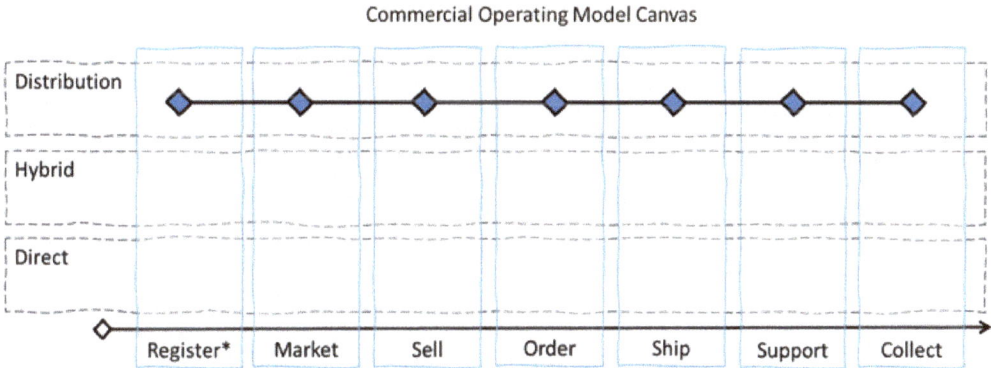

| | Register* | Market | Sell | Order | Ship | Support | Collect |

Whereas a pure Direct Model shown below (Figure 13):

**Figure 13:** A Pure Direct Model

## Commercial Operating Model Canvas

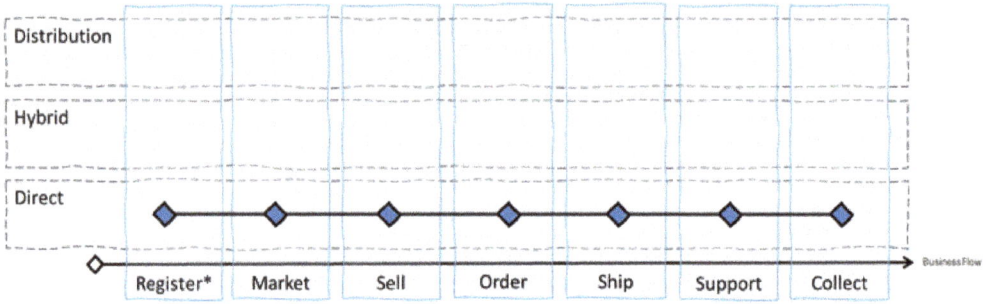

I use this canvas to quickly explain how we are going to market in a particular territory. The graph with explanatory notes below, and potentially a RACI process for each hybrid section is particularly helpful. This document is also very helpful when discussing with potential distributors or channel partners.

## Example RACI:

Figure 14 Below shows a RACI for an organisation with business development, key accounts, sales marketing and sales admin (ordering).

**Figure 14:** RACI for Hypothetical Principle Distributor Canvas

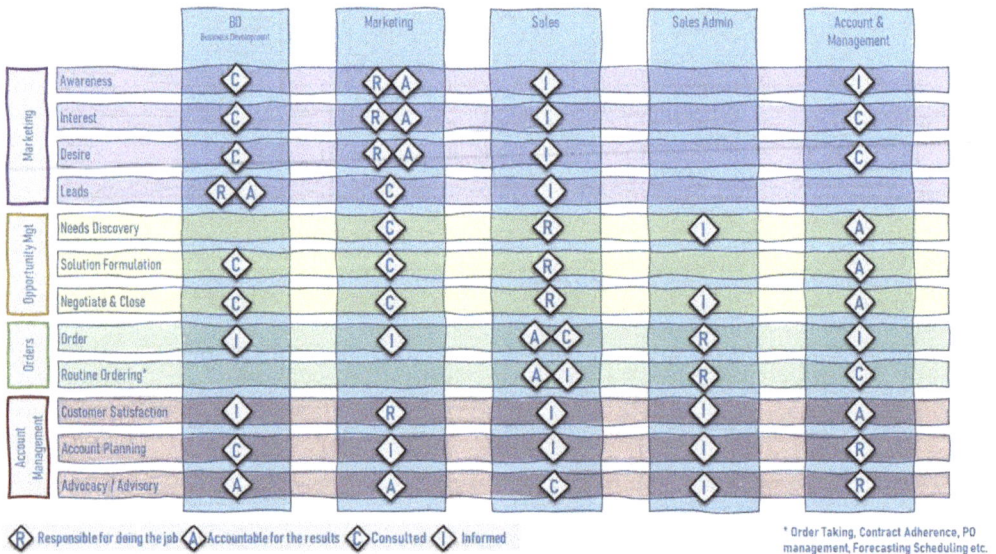

Each diamond would have explanatory notes attached.

# POTENTIAL AND THE COMMERCIAL OPERATING MODEL:

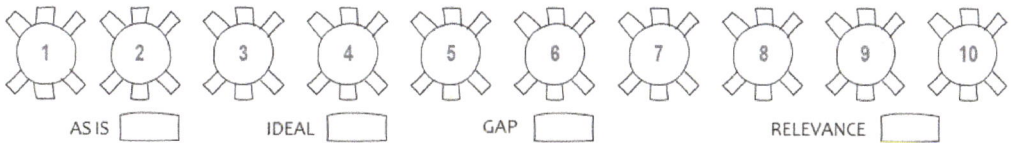

AS IS ☐  IDEAL ☐  GAP ☐  RELEVANCE ☐

Is the commercial operating model (COM) only focused on today? Consideration should be given to not only today's revenue but also the potential of future customers, with both existing products and a way to incorporate and re-evaluate when new products or services come on line. Again, let's analyse this through our three lenses:

## AS IS:

How does your current COM address both existing and potential customers? Does it incorporate different customer segments and their respective needs? Are there distinct processes and strategies for managing existing customer relationships versus acquiring new customers? Is this reflected in your COM Canvas? Does the COM outline how resources are allocated across different customer segments? Does the COM consider the customer journey and experience for both existing and potential customers?

## IDEAL:

Ideally, your COM Canvas should represent how the business will operate in a given territory. It will include both the existing customer base but also the potential of the territory and the potential of future growth in the marketplace. This may mean that there are several canvases to explain differing customer mixes, strategy and the potential or what if scenarios. The COM will incorporate what resources are needed to adequately cover the territory and what the business has available to it now and how it will deploy the resources it has.

## RELEVANCE:

The importance of incorporating both existing and potential customers into the COM depends on the organisation's growth strategy and the dynamics of the market. In rapidly growing markets, a strong focus on acquiring new customers is essential. In more mature markets, maximizing value from existing customers might be the primary focus. However, regardless of the market context, a well-designed COM should consider both existing and potential customers to ensure sustainable growth and long-term success.

# MARKET DYNAMICS AND THE COMMERCIAL OPERATING MODEL:

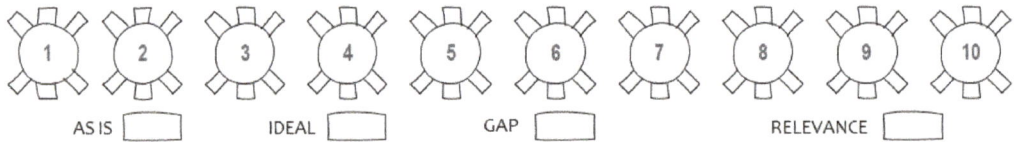

When assessing the COM, the current market situation must be considered. For example, if there are changes in the registration or regulations in an environment, the way we service that environment may change.

This emphasizes the dynamic nature of the commercial operating model and its responsiveness to market conditions. Let's analyse it through our three lenses:

## AS IS:

How does your organisation's COM currently incorporate market analysis? Are the market intelligence functions clear for the model? If your model is indirect or a hybrid who has the responsibility for monitoring the changes? How are they communicated and incorporated into the model? Is there a formal process for regularly reviewing the COM in light of changing market conditions? What data and information are used to assess the market (e.g., market size, growth rate, competitive landscape, customer trends)? How frequently is this market assessment conducted, and how are the findings used to adjust the COM? Are there specific triggers that prompt a review of the COM because of market changes?

## IDEAL:

Ideally, whether you're deciding how to first enter a new country or reviewing existing territories, a market assessment should be an integral and ongoing part of the COM. This means that the COM should not be a static document but a dynamic framework that is regularly reviewed and updated to reflect changes in

The Commercial Excellence Playbook

the market. For each of the pillars, review what the market conditions or changes are – and how that will affect the proposed or existing model. This would involve establishing logical processes for monitoring market trends, gathering competitive intelligence, and analysing customer behaviour. This information is used to identify opportunities and threats, and to adjust the COM accordingly. Ideally, the COM would be designed to be agile and adaptable, allowing the organisation to quickly respond to changing market conditions.

## RELEVANCE:

The importance of incorporating market assessment into the COM depends on the dynamism and volatility of the market. In transforming markets, continuous monitoring and adaptation are essential. In more stable markets, periodic reviews might be sufficient. However, regardless of the market context, it's crucial that the COM is not treated as a static document but is regularly assessed and adjusted to ensure its continued relevance and effectiveness. The relevance lens prompts you to consider how critical it is for your COM to be responsive to the specific market dynamics in which your organisation operates.

# PRODUCT / SERVICE PRIORITISATION AND THE COM:

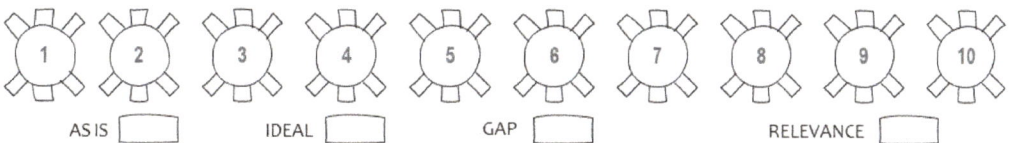

AS IS [    ]     IDEAL [    ]     GAP [    ]     RELEVANCE [    ]

Where a product or service is strategic and aligned or prioritised by our strategy, there needs to be a way to ensure that the COM is assessed to see if it's the best way to achieve the strategy of the organisation. Let's analyse it through our three lenses:

## AS IS:

How does your organisation's COM currently incorporate the strategy of priority products/services? Are the sales, marketing, and service processes within the COM specifically tailored to support the strategic objectives of these products/services? Are they incorporated into the COM Canvas? Do you have "reserve" customers within a territory? How does the COM address different stages of the product/service lifecycle (e.g., introduction, growth, maturity, decline)?

## IDEAL:

Ideally, the COM should consider how to best support the strategy of priority products/services. This means that all aspects of the COM, including sales processes, marketing campaigns, customer service protocols, and resource allocation, should be aligned, and where there are hybrid models there should be a RACI or appropriate documents the ensure there is no confusion.

## RELEVANCE:

The importance of aligning the COM with product/service strategy depends on the diversity of the product/service portfolio and the complexity of the market. In organisations that are fully direct or fully in-direct, the alignment should be simple. However, in models that are hybrid and with a diverse range of offerings, it's crucial to have a COM that can effectively support the unique strategies of each priority product/service. The relevance lens prompts you to consider how critical this alignment is to your specific business context and the successful execution of your product/service strategies.

## CONSTRAINT CONSIDERATIONS:

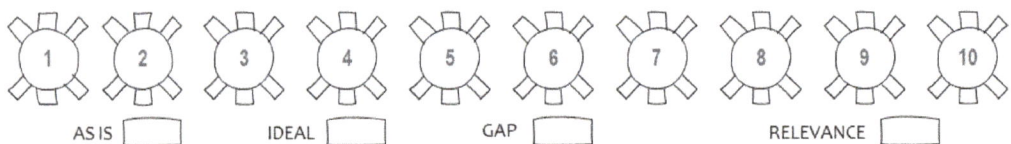

| AS IS | IDEAL | GAP | RELEVANCE |

Constraints need to be practically and feasibly incorporated into the commercial operating model. For example, when expanding into a new geography in Indonesia, the setting up of distribution may be step one, followed by a representative office for technical sales because of financial or cash flow constraints. In my position in Thailand, the Ministry of Health had a reputation of taking between 100 to more than 300 days to pay its accounts, especially with smaller organisations. They got paid, but it was not fast. This led me to working through distribution partners in a hybrid model to ensure my business did not have cash flow problems.

As the distributor was also supplying many other hospital supplies, slow or non-payment to them would cause the hospital sufficient problems to pay on time. Ever try to run a hospital without medicines? You're going to pay on time! I use this an example for thinking outside of the box around constraints because they may not be that obvious initially. Let's analyse this through our three lenses:

## AS IS:

How does your organisation's COM currently consider resource availability and costs? Does it include a clear assessment of the resources required to execute the various components of the COM (e.g., personnel, technology, budget, cash)? Is the customer easily accessible or geographically disperse? Is the market price or value-driven? Are the staff members sufficiently knowledgeable, do they have the right skills, and are they motivated for the territory? Do you have sufficient budget to go direct? What speed to you need to go at?

## IDEAL:

Ideally, the COM should incorporate the limitations of the business and the market in terms of cash, budget, staff (knowledge, skills and motivation) resource availability in the marketplace. It will consider the speed to go to market – and the resources required to support that speed. It will clearly define what needs to be done, but also how it will be resourced and at what cost.

## RELEVANCE:

The importance of explicitly considering resource availability, costs, and other market constraints depends on the organisation's size, resources, and growth strategy. In resource-constrained organisations or those pursuing aggressive growth strategies, careful resource planning and management are essential for determining how you will go to the market. In larger, more established organisations, resource availability might be less of a constraint, but competition for them may still exist. The relevance lens prompts you to consider how critical the constraints are for selecting the appropriate COM.

# TERRITORY FORMULATION:

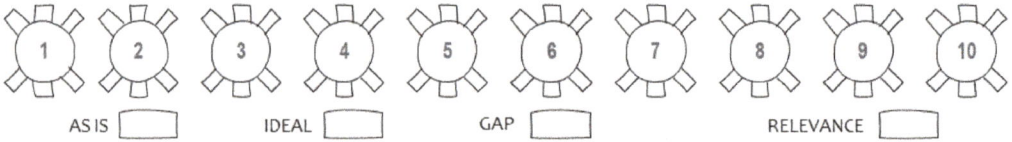

| | | | | |
|---|---|---|---|---|
| AS IS | IDEAL | GAP | | RELEVANCE |

Territories are more important than what they're first given credit for. Imagine you're a new sales rep and you've been allocated a territory of great loyal customers. Sounds perfect, right? But what if your compensation is linked to growth and you have an 80% profit share from your existing customers and minimal new customer potential. Meanwhile, your colleague smashes their targets because they have a territory with low or no penetration. You're probably not going to work as hard and will likely end up looking for a new job pretty soon...

This underlines why the set-up, type of customer, and future growth potential should all be considerations in your commercial model for territory management. Let's analyse this through our three lenses:

## AS IS:

How does your organisation currently define and manage sales territories? Are territories defined geographically, by customer type, or by other criteria? How does the COM incorporate an understanding of different customer types and their specific needs? Does the territory consider the future growth potential of different territories and customer segments? Are there specific metrics or KPIs used to track performance within different territories and customer segments?

## IDEAL:

Ideally, there will be a clear framework for defining and managing sales territories based on a thorough understanding of customer types and their future growth potential. This would involve segmenting customers based on relevant criteria (e.g., industry, size, needs, growth potential) and aligning sales territories accordingly. The territories would be set up to be of equal potential and opportunity richness.

## RELEVANCE:

The importance of explicitly considering sales territories, customer types, and future growth in the COM depends on the organisation's size, geographic reach, and market dynamics. In organisations with a large geographic footprint or diverse customer base, a well-defined territory management system is more critical. Whilst in smaller organisations with a more concentrated customer base, a less formal approach might be sufficient. However, regardless of the organisation's size, it's important that the territory set up is considered when assessing the appropriate COM.

# REGULATIONS:

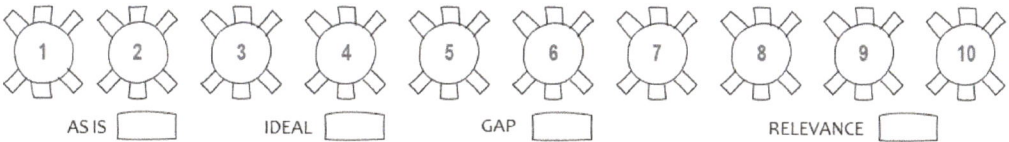

AS IS [ ]   IDEAL [ ]   GAP [ ]   RELEVANCE [ ]

Is your industry regulated? If so, how does this shape your commercial operating model? There is a crucial need for the commercial operating model to consider legal and regulatory constraints. Let's analyse it through our three lenses:

## AS IS:

How does your organisation's COM currently account for the regulatory environment? Are there processes in place to identify and monitor relevant regulations and legal requirements? Are these regulations considered during the design and implementation of the COM? Are there dedicated resources or expertise available to ensure compliance? How are changes in regulations communicated and incorporated into the COM? Are there any specific compliance metrics or audit processes in place?

## IDEAL:

Ideally, the COM should be designed with a thorough understanding of the relevant regulatory environment. This would involve conducting a comprehensive regulatory analysis during the formulation of the COM.

## RELEVANCE:

The importance of assessing the regulatory environment within the COM depends heavily on the industry and the specific regulations that apply. In highly regulated industries (e.g., medical diagnostics, medical devices and pharmaceuticals), a deep understanding of the regulatory landscape is essential. In less regulated industries, the focus might be less intense, but it's still crucial to ensure compliance with basic legal requirements. The relevance lens prompts you to consider how critical it is for your COM to address the specific regulatory environment in which your organisation operates.

## RANKING THE ASPECTS IMPORTANCE:

We've covered a number of topics in this section. Over the next two years how would you view their importance? If you listed each of the topics, which would rank highest and which would be lowest? This assessment can be used to help you determine the overall importance to your organisation – and allow you to make a single judgement on the section we will move into next.

# Section 1 Conclusion:

This chapter has laid the essential groundwork for our journey toward commercial excellence by focusing on <u>strategic direction</u>. We've explored a series of crucial questions, each designed to illuminate the 'AS IS,' 'Ideal,' and 'Relevance' of various strategic elements within your organisation. From defining strategic intent and translating it into actionable objectives and 'Big Rocks,' to understanding customer needs, market positioning, competitive landscapes, and the ever-evolving business environment, we've examined the critical factors that shape commercial success. We've also considered how these elements influence the design and adaptation of your commercial operating model, ensuring it aligns with strategic priorities, resource availability, regulatory requirements, and the specific dynamics of your market.

Recall the visual metaphor of the commercial temple. This chapter has focused on the very top of the structure—the 'strategy' that forms the roof and overarching direction for all other functions. We've delved into what constitutes a robust strategy, how it's translated into action, and how it considers the external

The Commercial Excellence Playbook

world. We've seen how critical it is to understand the interplay between the strategic intent set by the board, the strategic plan developed by the executive team, and the practical execution through budgets, objectives, and the COM.

Without a solid strategic foundation, the pillars of our temple cannot stand strong. With this crucial strategic context established, we now turn our attention to the first supporting pillar of our commercial temple: **Sales**. We will delve into the specific strategies, processes, and best practices that drive revenue generation and contribute to overall commercial success. We will examine how sales teams can effectively execute the strategic direction set in this chapter and contribute to achieving the organisation's overall objectives. Just as a temple relies on strong pillars to support its roof, so too does a commercially excellent organisation rely on a robust sales function to execute its strategy. We'll now explore how to build that strength.

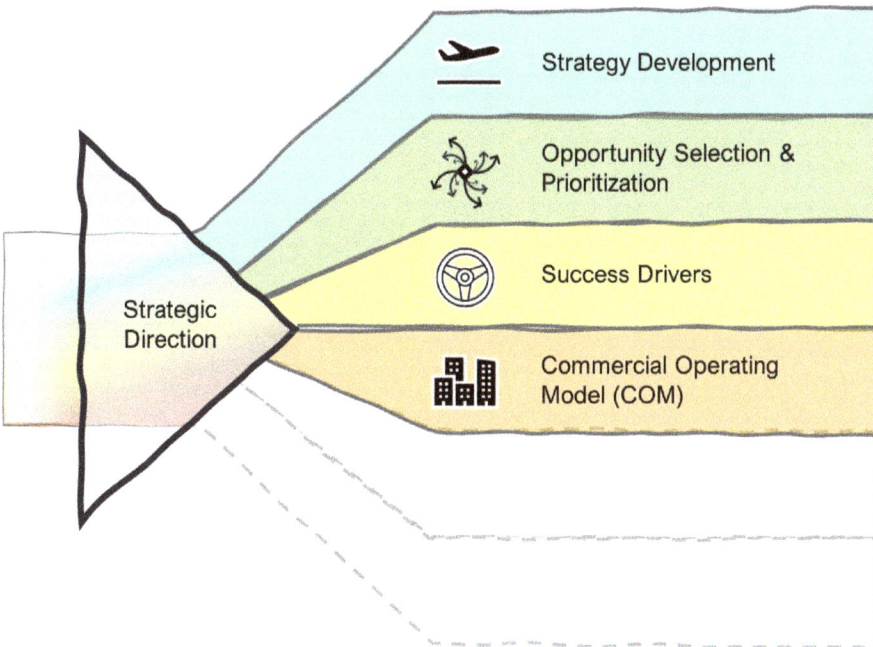

**Transfer the ratings at the beginning of each chapter here:**

| Chapter | AS IS | Ideal | Gap | Relevance |
|---|---|---|---|---|
| Strategy Development | | | | |
| Opportunity Selection | | | | |

| Success Drivers | | | | |
|---|---|---|---|---|
| Commercial Operating Model | | | | |

Is there one area that is better or worse than the others?

Plot the chapters into the Strategy Box Plot.

# STRATEGY BOX PLOT:

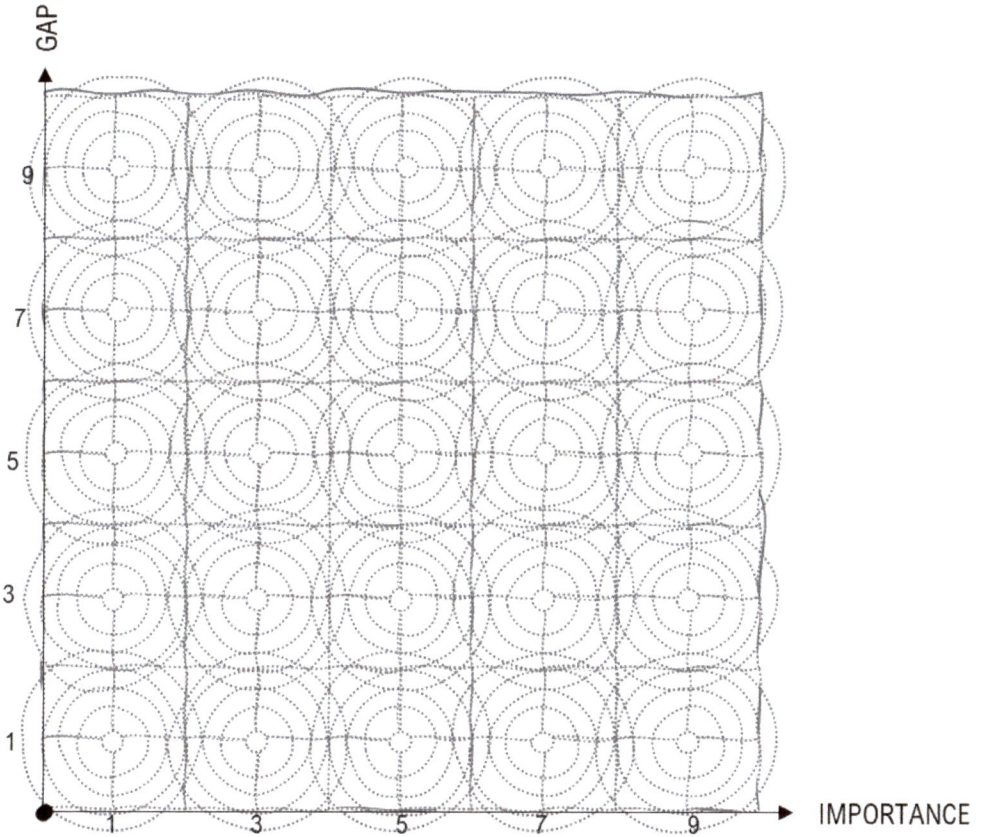

# OVERALL STATUS OF STRATEGY ALIGNMENT:

AS IS [    ]    IDEAL [    ]    GAP [    ]    RELEVANCE [    ]

Looking at the box plot what is your assessment of your company's strategy?

# SECTION 2:
# SALES

Sales – The Revenue Generation Engine of the Business

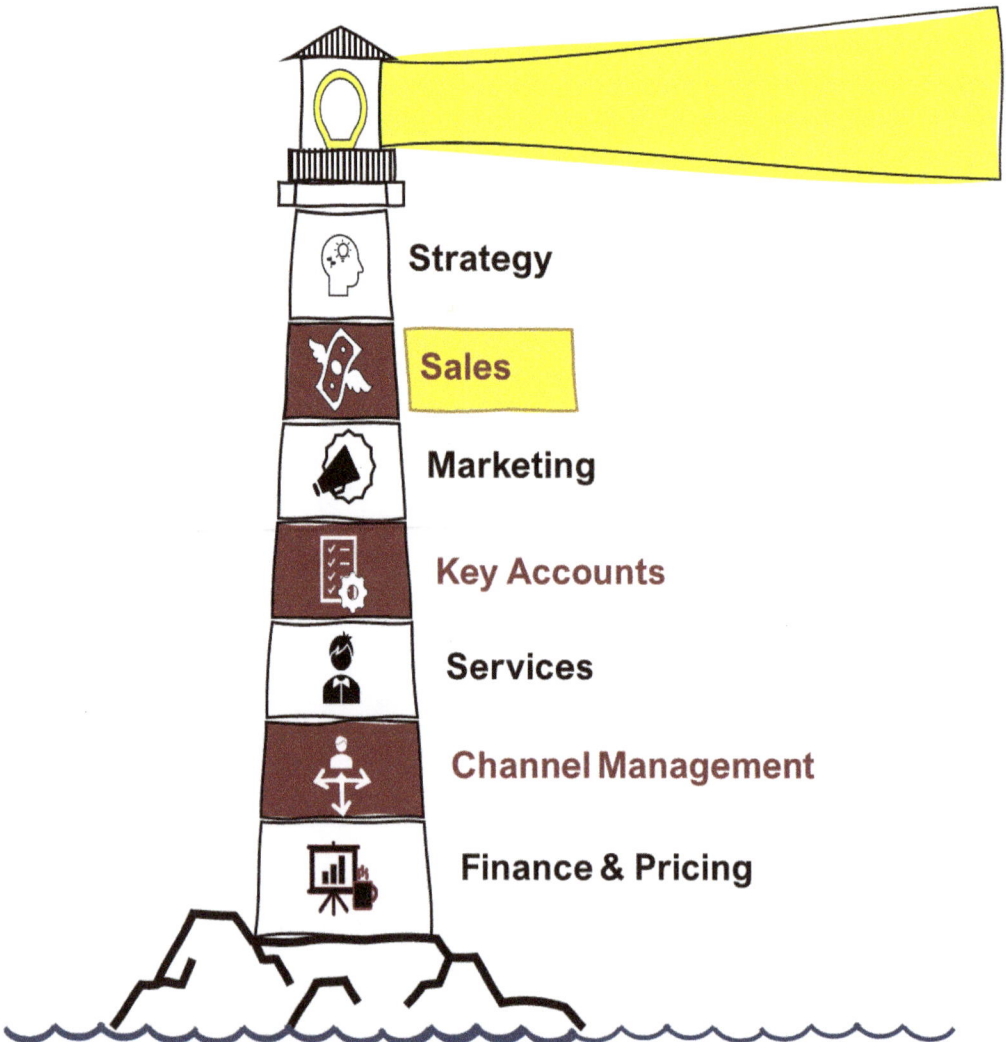

Strategy

Sales

Marketing

Key Accounts

Services

Channel Management

Finance & Pricing

Is your sales team a well-oiled machine, or are they struggling to keep pace with market demands? In today's hyper-competitive business environment, a robust sales strategy isn't just about closing deals—it's about creating value at every

The Commercial Excellence Playbook

customer touchpoint. This chapter challenges you to critically examine your sales processes, team capabilities, and performance metrics. Are you truly leveraging your sales force as a strategic asset, or are you leaving money on the table? Let's dive into the heart of sales excellence, exploring how to align your sales efforts with your overall business strategy and drive sustainable growth in an ever-evolving marketplace.

In this section, we will look at the way the organisation conducts sales. To do this, we will look closely at the six parts of the sales spectrum.

**Figure 15:** The Six Wavelengths for Sales Performance

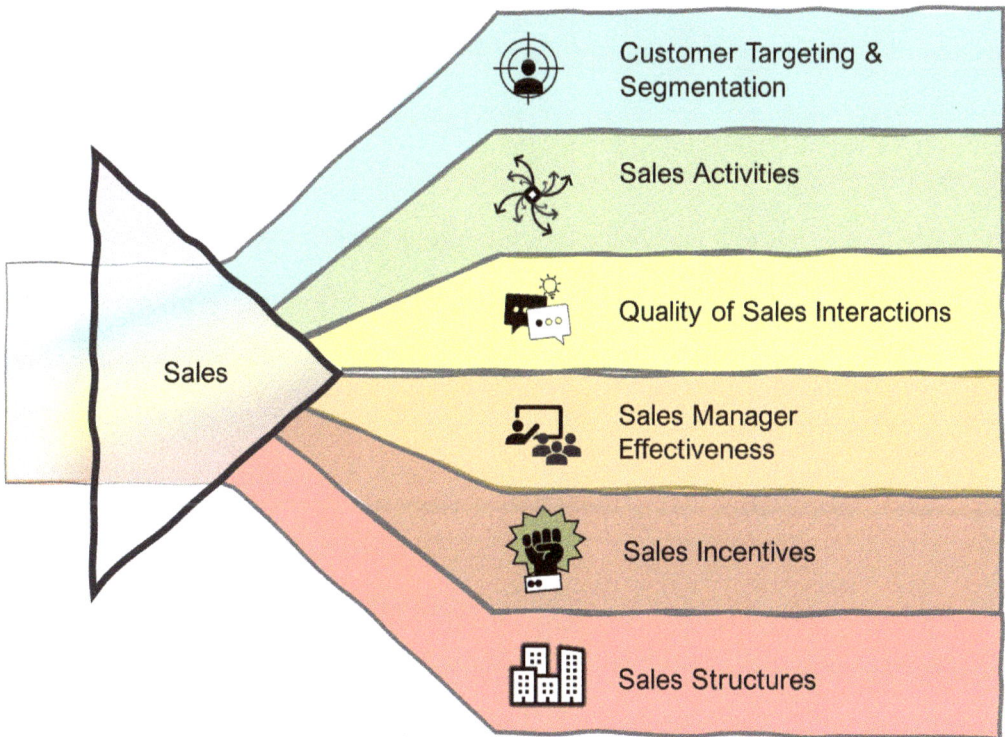

# CHAPTER 5:

# Customer Targeting & Segmentation

- Customer Targeting & Segmentation
- Sales Activities
- Quality of Sales Interactions
- Sales Manager Effectiveness
- Sales Incentives
- Sales Structures

Sales

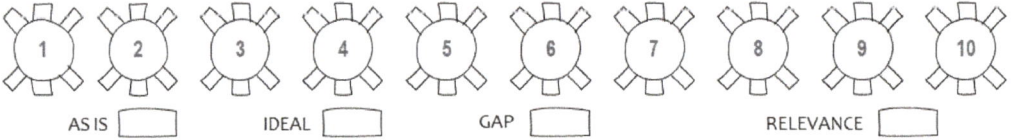

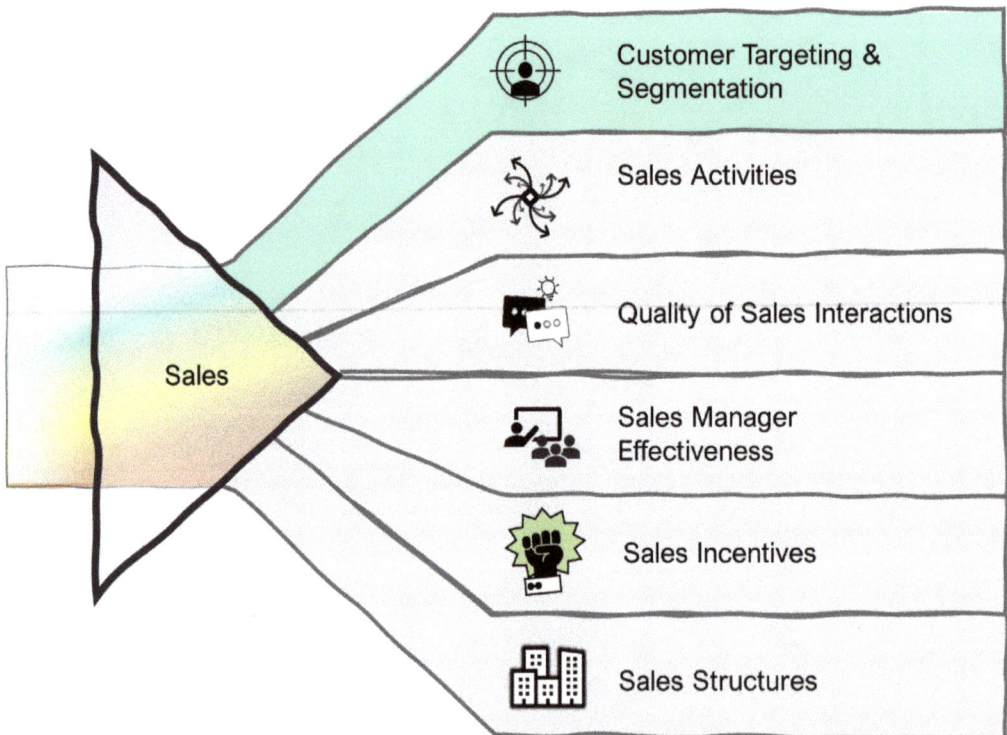

In this section we will explore how your organisation chooses which prospects and customers to grow with and how it communicates this to the organisation.

# CUSTOMER TARGETING STRATEGY:

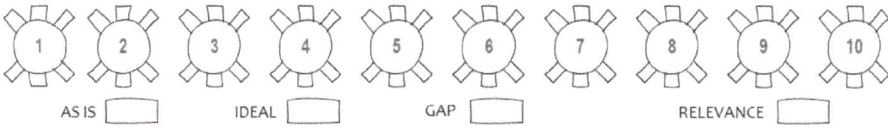

AS IS [        ]     IDEAL [        ]     GAP [        ]     RELEVANCE [        ]

Let's look at having a clear strategy and purpose when targeting customers. Using customer criteria to leverage the right customer will help to grow both revenue and profitability. What types of customers are relevant for your business? Do you currently have segmentation criteria or could you implement this type of process? Can you segment on potential and existing revenues? Have you ever looked at what customers are more likely to buy certain product ranges, and what are the priorities of your product portfolio?

Even a low medium and high ABCD rating (Figure 16) here can help align the organisation. Which is the most and least or non-visited segments? This is in analysing sales performance maturity, similar to how we analysed strategic direction in previous exchanges.

**Figure 16:** Customer Targeting Classification

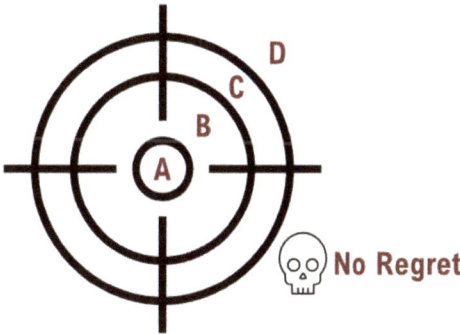

Here's the breakdown:

## AS IS:

How does your organisation currently segment and target customers? What criteria are used (e.g., demographics, industry, size, purchasing behaviour, needs)? Is this segmentation documented and clearly communicated to the sales team? How are priorities assigned to different customer segments (high, low, non-visited)? Is there a formal process for reviewing and updating the segmentation and targeting strategy? How is the product portfolio aligned with these segments? How effectively does this segmentation drive sales efforts and resource allocation? Are there tools or technologies used to support this process (e.g., CRM, marketing automation)?

## IDEAL:

Ideally, your organisation should have a well-defined and data-driven segmentation and targeting strategy. This would involve using relevant customer-specific criteria to create distinct segments with unique needs and characteristics. The prioritization of these segments should be based on factors such as revenue potential, profitability, strategic fit, and growth potential. The product portfolio should be clearly aligned with these segments, ensuring that the right products are offered to the right customers. The segmentation and targeting strategy should be regularly reviewed and updated to reflect changes in the market and customer base. This process should be supported by appropriate tools and technologies. A simple targeting system of A – D class customers and a No Regret segment can be useful.

## RELEVANCE:

The importance of a sophisticated segmentation and targeting strategy depends on the diversity of your customer base and the complexity of your market. In markets with highly diverse customer needs, a robust segmentation strategy is crucial for effective sales and marketing. In markets with a more homogenous customer base, a simpler approach might be sufficient. The relevance lens prompts you to consider how critical it is for your organisation to have a clear and effective segmentation and targeting strategy given your specific market dynamics and business objectives. This prioritization ensures efficient resource allocation and maximizes the impact of sales efforts.

## TARGETING ALIGNMENT:

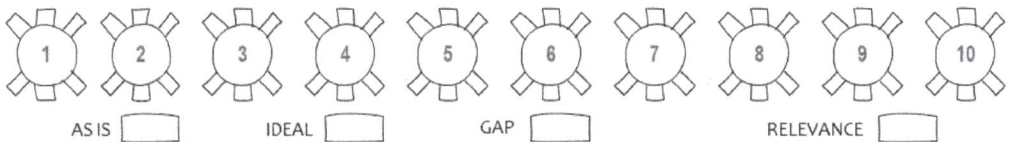

| 1 | 2 | 3 | 4 | 5 | 6 | 7 | 8 | 9 | 10 |

AS IS [    ]      IDEAL [    ]      GAP [    ]      RELEVANCE [    ]

How well do your Sales, Key Account Management, Distributor Management, Marketing, Pricing and Remote Selling Teams (i.e. Inside Sales / Tele-sales), align with your strategy on targeting customers? This is both in terms of alignment between the departments, but also in being aligned with the overall strategy.

## AS IS:

How well aligned is your current segmentation and targeting strategy across different functions? Are Sales, Key Account Management, Distributor Management, Marketing, Pricing, and Remote Selling Teams all using the same customer segmentation and targeting definitions? Are these definitions clearly communicated and understood across all teams? Are there any inconsistencies or conflicts in how different teams approach customer segmentation and targeting? How are these inconsistencies addressed? Are there any metrics or KPIs used to measure the effectiveness of cross-functional alignment & what are they telling you?

## IDEAL:

Ideally, there should be complete alignment in segmentation and targeting across all relevant functions. This ensures that all teams are working towards the same goals and that customer interactions are consistent and coordinated. Clear, consistent definitions should be established and communicated to all teams. Regular cross-functional meetings and training sessions should be conducted to ensure shared understanding and address any inconsistencies. Yearly kick-off meetings are a great avenue for this. There should be mechanisms in place to track the effectiveness of this cross-functional alignment and identify areas for improvement.

## RELEVANCE:

The importance of this alignment depends on the complexity of your sales and marketing operations and the degree of interaction needed between different teams. In organisations with complex sales processes or multiple channels, ensuring alignment is crucial to avoid confusion, duplication of effort, and inconsistent customer experiences. In smaller organisations with simpler structures, achieving alignment might be less challenging. The relevance lens prompts you to consider how critical this cross-functional alignment is to the effectiveness of your overall sales and marketing efforts and the customer experience.

# SEGMENTATION BUY IN:

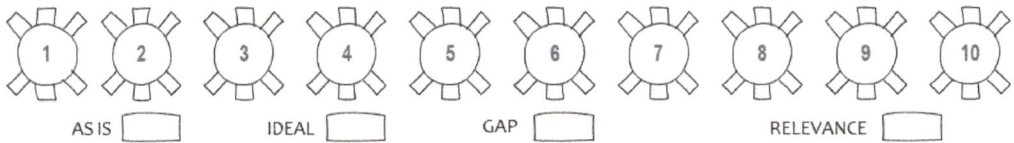

| | | | | | | | | | |
|---|---|---|---|---|---|---|---|---|---|
| 1 | 2 | 3 | 4 | 5 | 6 | 7 | 8 | 9 | 10 |

AS IS [    ]     IDEAL [    ]     GAP [    ]     RELEVANCE [    ]

Do your Sales and Marketing teams fully buy into the segmentation and targeting results and actively use the customer database to execute the sales / marketing strategy? Were they active in the segmentation process and therefore have a stake in the outcome? The adoption and utilization of the segmentation and targeting strategy needs to be adopted by the teams responsible for its execution. Let's analyse it through our three lenses:

## AS IS:

How effectively have the segmentation and targeting results been communicated to and adopted by the Sales and Marketing teams? Is there evidence of "buy-in," such as consistent use of the customer database and alignment of sales and marketing activities with the defined segments? Are there any challenges or resistance to using the new segmentation and targeting approach? How are these challenges addressed? Are there training programs or support resources available to help teams effectively utilize the customer database and implement the strategy? Are there metrics in place to track database usage and alignment of activities?

## IDEAL:

Ideally, there should be full buy-in and active utilization of the segmentation and targeting results by both Sales and Marketing teams. This would involve not only communicating the results but also explaining the rationale behind the segmentation and demonstrating its value in improving sales and marketing effectiveness. There should be ongoing training and support to ensure that teams are proficient in using the customer database and applying the segmentation strategy in their day-to-day activities. Regular feedback mechanisms should be in place to gather input from Sales and Marketing teams and identify areas for improvement in the segmentation and targeting approach. The use of the adoption systems would be high if you catch staff and managers using terms in their day-to-day activities.

## RELEVANCE:

The importance of buy-in and active utilization depends on the complexity of the segmentation strategy and the degree of coordination required between Sales and Marketing. In organisations with complex segmentation or highly integrated sales and marketing efforts, full buy-in and active utilization are crucial for success. In smaller organisations with simpler segmentation or less integrated teams, achieving buy-in might be less challenging, but it's still important to ensure that teams understand and utilize the segmentation strategy effectively. The relevance lens prompts you to consider the specific dynamics of your Sales and Marketing teams and the importance of their alignment for effective strategy execution.

# CUSTOMER TARGETING PRIORITIZATION:

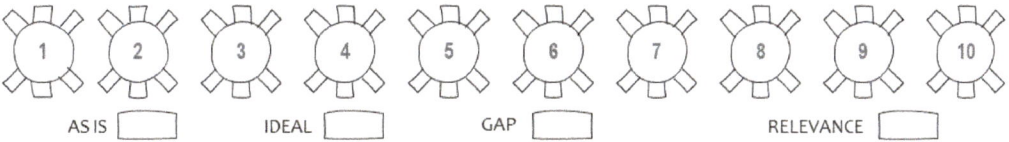

It's important to consider having a defined targeting group in terms of high priority, medium and low priority segments, and also a "No Visit" accounts! I can hear the reps arguing as I type this – yes "No Visit" accounts. Shocking! How can we do such horrible things?

## AS IS:

How does your organisation currently cluster customers into target groups? What criteria are used for clustering (e.g., demographics, industry, size, purchase history)? How many customer segments are currently defined? How are high-/low-priority segments identified within these clusters? How are "not-visited accounts" identified and tracked? Is there a formal process for reviewing and updating these customer clusters? How is this information used to guide sales and marketing efforts?

## IDEAL:

Ideally, your organisation should have a well-defined process for clustering customers into a manageable number of target groups based on relevant and meaningful criteria. This clustering should enable the identification of high-/low-priority segments and not-visited accounts. The criteria for prioritization should be clearly defined and communicated across the organisation. The clustering and prioritization process should be regularly reviewed and updated to reflect changes in the market and customer behaviour. This information should be used to guide sales and marketing efforts, including resource allocation, targeting, and messaging.

## RELEVANCE:

The relevance of customer clustering and prioritization depends on the diversity and complexity of your customer base. For organisations with large and diverse customer bases, effective clustering and prioritization are crucial for efficient resource allocation and targeted marketing efforts. In smaller organisations with more homogenous customer bases, a less formal approach might be sufficient. The relevance lens prompts you to consider how critical it is for your organisation to have a clear and effective customer clustering and prioritization strategy to support your sales and marketing objectives.

# OPTIMAL RESOURCING PER TARGET GROUP:

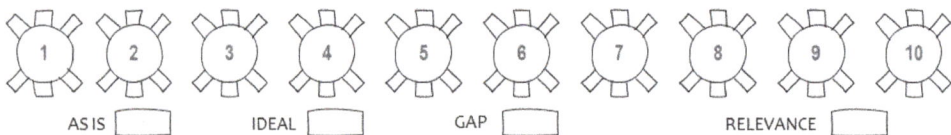

AS IS ☐      IDEAL ☐      GAP ☐      RELEVANCE ☐

Clearly looking into the resourcing required to service each customer target group helps to ensure your resources allocation is not heavy in one group whilst leaving a more important one light. Does your organisation have an optimal visit frequency and resource allocation per target group?

## AS IS:

How does your organisation currently determine visit frequency and resource allocation for different target groups? Are there formal guidelines or processes in place? What factors are considered when determining visit frequency (e.g., customer size, revenue potential, relationship strength, sales cycle length)? How are resources (e.g., sales representatives, budget, time) allocated across different target groups? Are there any tools or systems used to manage and track visit frequency and resource allocation? How effective is the current approach in maximizing sales effectiveness and return on investment?

## IDEAL:

Ideally, your organisation should have a data-driven approach to determining optimal visit frequency and resource allocation per target group that is refined over time. This would involve analysing historical data, market trends, and customer behaviour to identify the most effective visit frequency for each segment. Resource allocation should be optimized to maximize return on investment, ensuring that high-potential customers receive the appropriate level of attention and resources. This could mean a high, medium and low visit groups combined with "Electronic only", "No Regret" or "No Visit" groups. This process should be regularly reviewed and adjusted based on performance data and changing market conditions.

## RELEVANCE:

The importance of defining optimal visit frequency and resource allocation depends on the nature of your business, the characteristics of your target customers, and the resources available. For businesses with limited resources or a large number of customers, efficient resource allocation is crucial. For businesses with complex sales processes or high-value customers, more frequent visits and dedicated resources might be necessary. The relevance lens prompts you to consider how critical it is for your organisation to optimize visit frequency and resource allocation to maximize sales effectiveness and achieve its business objectives.

## GOAL SETTING:

| 1 | 2 | 3 | 4 | 5 | 6 | 7 | 8 | 9 | 10 |

AS IS [ ]    IDEAL [ ]    GAP [ ]    RELEVANCE [ ]

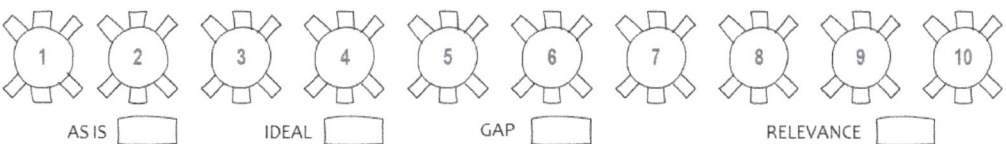

Do you have clear goals for each customer segment and customer for short sales cycle products? This could include aspects like visit frequency, products to offer, etc. For long sales cycle products: customer plans including sales goals and resource/investment levels, products to offer, etc. See the section on Key Accounts for more long sales cycle customers. If you have a three-year sales cycle then the best time to start was three years ago. The second-best time to start is now.

## AS IS:

How does your organisation currently set goals for different customer segments and individual customers? Are these goals differentiated based on sales cycle length? For short sales cycle products, are there specific targets for visit frequency, product offerings, and other relevant metrics? For long sales cycle products, are detailed customer plans developed, including sales goals, resource/investment levels, and recommended product offerings? Are these goals and plans documented, communicated, and tracked effectively? Are there any tools or systems used to manage these goals and plans (e.g., CRM, sales performance management software)? How frequently are these goals and plans reviewed and updated?

## IDEAL:

Ideally, your organisation should have a clear and structured approach to setting goals for different customer segments and individual customers, tailored to the length of the sales cycle. For short sales cycle products, there should be clear targets for key activities like visit frequency, product presentations, and conversion rates. For long sales cycle products, detailed customer plans should be developed, outlining specific sales goals, necessary resources and investments, and recommended product offerings.

These plans should be collaborative, involving input from relevant stakeholders, and should be regularly reviewed and updated to reflect changing customer needs and market conditions. These plans should be managed and tracked within a centralized system. For long cycle sales, consider having 'Specialists' and having the sales representatives maintain "awareness and desire" activities. The sales representatives can then pass the opportunity onto the Specialist for the deep details when the customer is ready.

## RELEVANCE:

The level of detail and formality required for goal setting and planning depends on the complexity of the sales process and the length of the sales cycle. For short sales cycle products, simpler, more activity-based targets might be sufficient. For long sales cycle products, more detailed and strategic customer plans are essential for managing complex relationships and achieving long-term sales goals. The relevance lens prompts you to consider the specific characteristics of your sales cycles and customer relationships when determining the appropriate level of rigor and detail for goal setting and planning.

# CUSTOMER PLANS:

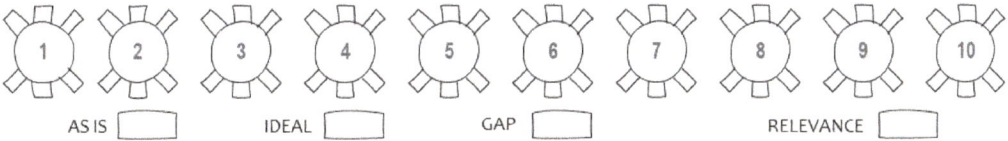

| 1 | 2 | 3 | 4 | 5 | 6 | 7 | 8 | 9 | 10 |

AS IS [ ]     IDEAL [ ]     GAP [ ]     RELEVANCE [ ]

Sales representatives and/or sales managers define individual visit/customer plans that specify work towards the goals?

## AS IS:

How are individual visit/customer plans currently created? Are they developed by sales representatives, sales managers, or collaboratively? Are these plans documented and shared? What types of goals are typically included in these plans (e.g., sales targets, visit frequency, product introductions, relationship building)? Are there specific templates or tools used to create these plans? How are these plans monitored and reviewed? Is there consistent adherence to the planning process across the sales team?

## IDEAL:

Ideally, there should be a consistent and structured process for developing individual visit/customer plans. These plans should be developed collaboratively between sales representatives and their managers, ensuring alignment with overall sales strategy and individual performance goals. Plans should include specific, measurable, achievable, relevant, and time-bound (SMART) goals related to key activities and outcomes. These plans should be documented, readily accessible, and regularly reviewed to track progress and make necessary adjustments. There should be clear guidelines and training provided to ensure consistent implementation of the planning process across the sales team.

## RELEVANCE:

The level of detail and formality required for individual visit/customer plans depends on factors such as the complexity of the sales process, the length of the sales cycle, the value of individual customers, and the size of the sales team. For complex sales or high-value customers, detailed customer plans are essential. For simpler sales or smaller customers, more streamlined visit plans might suffice. The relevance lens prompts you to consider the specific needs of your sales organisation and the importance of structured planning for achieving sales objectives.

## VISIT PLANNING EFFECTIVENESS:

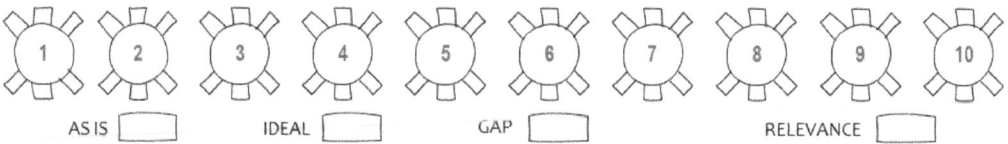

AS IS [     ]     IDEAL [     ]     GAP [     ]          RELEVANCE [     ]

Consider how realistic the plans are of your sales representatives. Do they have realistic targets for the number of visits versus their capacity, with access and geographical issues fully reflected?

## AS IS:

How does your organisation ensure that sales representatives' visit plans are realistic? Are target visit levels based on actual capacity, considering factors like travel time, customer availability, administrative tasks, and other non-selling activities? Are geographical issues, such as travel distances, traffic conditions, and remote locations, fully taken into account? Are there tools or technologies used to optimize visit routes and schedules? How are these plans monitored to ensure they remain realistic and achievable? What happens when unforeseen circumstances (e.g., customer cancellations, emergencies) disrupt planned visits? Are the visits aligned with the customer targeting system? Is the split between prospecting and opportunity management right?

## IDEAL:

Ideally, sales representatives' visit plans should be based on a thorough understanding of their actual capacity and the logistical realities of their territories. This would involve using data and tools to optimize visit routes, minimize travel time, and account for other non-selling activities. Plans should be flexible enough to accommodate unforeseen circumstances and allow for adjustments as needed. There should be regular communication between sales representatives and their managers to ensure that plans remain realistic and achievable. Ideally, there should be a clear and consistently applied method for measuring visit plan compliance. A goal of 80% compliance to the plan is a good one. Keep adding more until you get to about the 80% compliance rate. That seems to be a sweet spot for ensuring the reps are full and having a good plan. When compliance falls below the threshold, there should be a process for identifying the root causes and implementing corrective actions, such as coaching, training, or adjustments to visit plans. The ideal scenario fosters a culture of accountability while also providing support and resources to help sales representatives achieve their targets. There are four aspects here why a rep fails to achieve their planning.

Sales Manager Effectiveness: Distant sales managers, or managers that are acting one level below where you need them to be. The manager who is the "expert" salesperson who loves to jump in and solve the rep's problem or close the deal is in fact not helping the rep.

Knowledge: Does the rep have the right knowledge of the planning process? Do they have the "know-how" to do it?

Skills: Knowing how is one thing but sometimes it's a matter of execution – and execution is different. Coaching is the way to go here.

Motivation: Low motivation, stagnation etc is the final part that affects a rep's ability to plan effectively. A low level of buy in for the process will ultimately create low planning adherence.

The rep should be able to spend ~40% of their time on prospection and 60% on pipeline opportunities and customer care/territory coverage activities.

Prospecting is planned first. Then opportunities, then territory coverage. For all three, the customer targeting "A" segment is prioritized.

## RELEVANCE:

The importance of realistic visit planning depends on the size of the sales territory, the density of customers, and the nature of the sales process. In large territories with dispersed customers, realistic planning is crucial to maximize sales productivity and minimize travel costs. In territories with concentrated customer bases, less complex planning might be sufficient. The relevance lens prompts you to consider the specific geographical and logistical challenges faced by your sales team and the importance of realistic planning for maximizing their effectiveness. Since Covid we have rapidly adopted virtual meeting tools. At first glance this may seem less relevant now than it was pre-Covid. However, I would suggest it's more important now than it was before. As it's easier to visit more people, reps may tend to try and visit everyone. No matter the avenue of visit, prioritization still remains relevant.

## VISIT PLANNING EXECUTION:

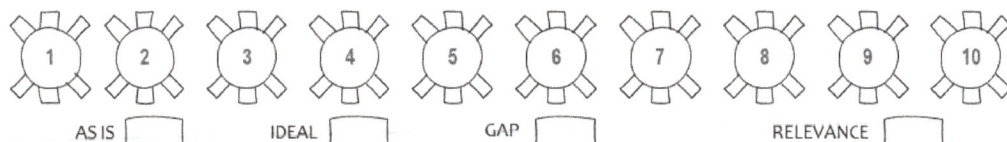

| 1 | 2 | 3 | 4 | 5 | 6 | 7 | 8 | 9 | 10 |

AS IS [ ]    IDEAL [ ]    GAP [ ]    RELEVANCE [ ]

Routinely tracking sales representatives' execution of visit/customer plans (e.g., number of visits per customer segment for short sale cycle products, relationship to key stakeholders for long sale cycle products). After the manager and rep sets the plan, the execution against the plan has thresholds, and follow up on deviations from the plan for improvement.

## AS IS:

How does your organisation currently track sales representatives' execution of visit/customer plans? What specific metrics are tracked (e.g., number of visits, call frequency, meeting duration, key stakeholder interactions)? How is this data collected (e.g., CRM systems, call reports, manual tracking)? Are thresholds or targets set for these metrics? What process is in place for following up on deviations from planned activities or targets? How frequently is this tracking and follow-up conducted? How often does the rep and their manager meet? Is this discussed? What actions are taken when deviations are identified (e.g., coaching, training, performance reviews)?

## IDEAL:

Ideally, there should be a robust system for tracking sales representatives' execution of visit/customer plans.
This system should capture relevant data for both short and long sales cycle products. For cycle products metrics, such as visit frequency per customer, segment and direction (see sales visit canvas in the resourcing and activity level chapter) are valuable. For long cycle products, try key stakeholder interactions, Breadth of interactions within an account and progress against customer plan objectives: Clear thresholds or targets should be established for these metrics, and automated alerts should be triggered when deviations occur. There should be a structured process for following up on deviations, including coaching, training, or other corrective actions. Ideally the system should allow the rep to self-correct. This tracking and follow-up should be conducted regularly and consistently, ideally 1:1 meetings with their manager frequently, e.g. weekly.

## RELEVANCE:

The level of detail and rigor required for tracking visit/customer plan execution depends on the complexity of the sales process, the length of the sales cycle, and the importance of consistent execution. For organisations with complex sales processes or high-value customers, detailed tracking and follow-up are more important. For simpler sales or smaller customers, a less formal approach might be sufficient. The relevance lens prompts you to consider the specific needs of your sales organisation and the importance of consistent plan execution for achieving sales objectives.

# CHAPTER 6:

# Sales Activities

Score this chapter here

| 1 | 2 | 3 | 4 | 5 | 6 | 7 | 8 | 9 | 10 |

AS IS ☐   IDEAL ☐   GAP ☐   RELEVANCE ☐

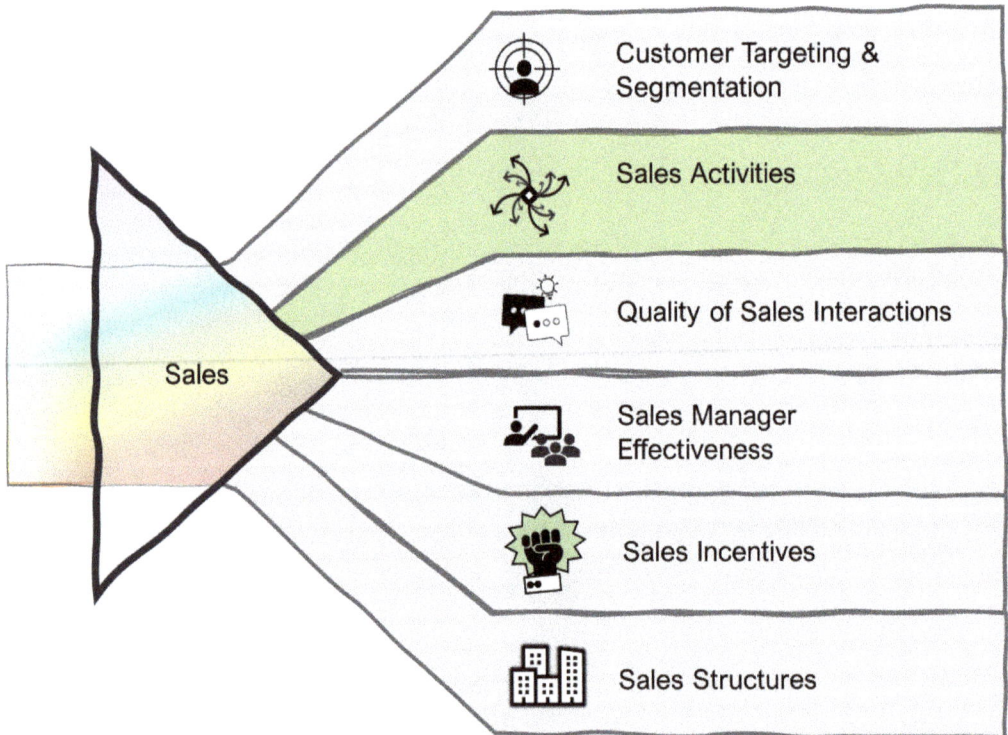

Sales

Customer Targeting & Segmentation

Sales Activities

Quality of Sales Interactions

Sales Manager Effectiveness

Sales Incentives

Sales Structures

# SALES TERRITORY MAKEUP:

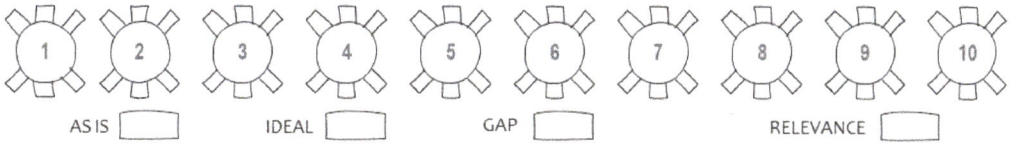

AS IS ⬚  IDEAL ⬚  GAP ⬚  RELEVANCE ⬚

It's surprising how the make-up of a sales territory can affect the sales rep's results. Having appropriately sized territories ensures that they can reach each customer and they are of similar size, and richness of opportunities.

## AS IS:

How are sales territories currently defined and sized? What criteria is used to determine the appropriate size of each territory (e.g., revenue potential, customer density, travel time, sales representative capacity)? Are there any instances of under-resourced territories (i.e., too many customers for a single sales representative)? Are there instances of over-resourced territories (i.e., sales representatives with insufficient customer coverage)? How are these issues identified and addressed (e.g., territory adjustments, rebalancing of sales resources)? Are there any metrics used to assess the effectiveness of territory sizing (e.g., sales productivity per territory, customer satisfaction)?

## IDEAL:

Ideally, sales territories should be sized and staffed to ensure optimal sales coverage while maximizing resource utilization. This would involve a thorough analysis of customer distribution, travel times, and sales representative capacity. Territories should be designed to ensure that all target customers can be reached effectively and efficiently, while avoiding situations where sales representatives are overburdened or underutilized. Regular reviews and adjustments should be made to account for changes in customer base, market conditions, and sales representative performance. The ideal scenario would involve a dynamic approach to territory management that allows for flexibility and adaptation as needed.

## RELEVANCE:

The importance of appropriate sales force and territory sizing depends on several factors, including the size and geography of the market, the distribution of customers, market segment and industry, and the complexity of the sales process. In large territories with dispersed customers, careful planning and resource allocation are crucial to ensure that all customers are adequately covered. Adequate coverage could be as visits to the targeting segments, or use of electronic and light visit mixes to ensure coverage. In smaller territories with concentrated customer bases, over-resourcing might lead to inefficiencies. The relevance lens prompts you to consider the specific characteristics of your market and the impact of territory size and sales force allocation on sales productivity and customer satisfaction.

# SALES FORCE MAKEUP:

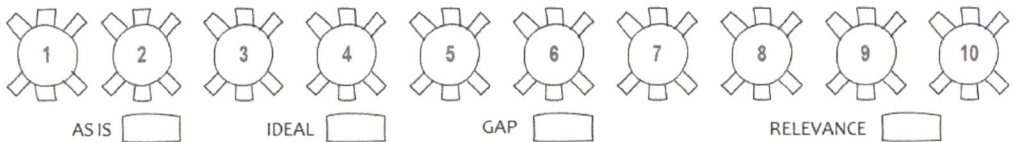

Do you have an optimised sales force? Your sales force size/capacity allows you to spend sufficient time with **priority** customers. The key here is "priority" customers, notice I don't say every customer. Compare your level of resourcing with your competitors.

## AS IS:

How does your organisation currently assess its sales force size and capacity relative to competitors? Is there any formal benchmarking data available on competitor sales force sizes, territory coverage, or customer visit frequency? How do you gather information about competitor sales activities (e.g., industry reports, customer feedback, competitor websites)? How do you define "sufficient time" with priority customers? Are there specific metrics used to track customer interaction time or relationship depth? Does the current sales force capacity allow for adequate coverage of all target customers, especially high-priority accounts, compared to the perceived coverage of competitors? Are there any anecdotal or qualitative insights from customers or the sales team regarding competitor sales activities and engagement levels? Do you have specialists or generalists? How do you determine the right mix between the two?

## IDEAL:

Ideally, your organisation should have a clear understanding of its competitive landscape in terms of sales force capacity and customer engagement. This would involve gathering data on competitor sales force size, territory coverage, and sales strategies. The organisation should define clear metrics for measuring customer interaction time and relationship depth, using these metrics to assess its performance relative to competitors. The ideal scenario is one where the sales force is sized and structured to allow for sufficient time and attention to be dedicated to priority customers, exceeding or at least matching the level of engagement provided by competitors. This ensures that valuable customer relationships are nurtured and that the organisation maintains a competitive edge. For simple, low product complexity then generalists may be sufficient. For higher technical sales or high product complexity, a combination of generalist and specialist roles may be better. For value based sales, economic support models may also be helpful.

## RELEVANCE:

The importance of benchmarking sales force capacity and customer engagement depends on the competitive intensity of the market and the nature of customer relationships. In highly competitive markets where customer relationships are a key differentiator, having a sales force that can dedicate sufficient time to priority customers is crucial. In less competitive markets or where customer relationships are less critical, the focus might be on other factors such as price or product features. The relevance lens prompts you to consider how critical it is for your organisation to maintain a competitive level of customer engagement through appropriate sales force sizing and capacity.

## ACTIVITY LEVELS:

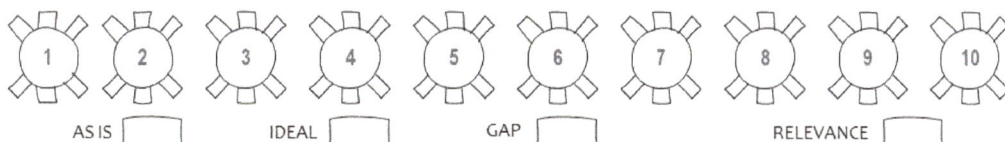

AS IS [     ]     IDEAL [     ]     GAP [     ]     RELEVANCE [     ]

Do you have a targeted activity level for your organisation? There should be a minimum activity level that is acceptable to the organisation. There is a direct correlation between the level of activities and the results of a rep. There are other factors as well that we'll cover later. For now, think about what percentage of sales reps are hitting their activity levels.

# AS IS:

How is "target activity level" defined and measured? What specific activities are tracked (e.g., number of calls, meetings, proposals, demos)? How is the 80% achievement rate calculated? Is this data tracked consistently across all sales representatives and territories? What factors contribute to sales representatives not achieving their target activity levels? Are there any specific training programs, coaching initiatives, or other support mechanisms in place to help representatives improve their performance and hit their numbers? How are these metrics used in performance reviews and compensation decisions? Does missing their numbers affect their sales incentives?

# IDEAL:

Ideally, "target activity levels" should be clearly defined and aligned with overall sales objectives and strategy. The metrics used to track activity should be relevant, measurable, and easily tracked. The 80% achievement rate should be based on data analysis and considered a realistic and challenging target. There should be a system in place to identify and address any performance gaps, including individualized coaching, training, and support. The focus should be on helping all sales representatives reach their full potential and contribute to the company's success. The use of a visit planning canvas may help the rep to analyse their own activities prior to any meeting with their manager.
Below (Figure 17) is a canvas that I use with the reps. Have the rep place the number of activities (or duration or percentage of the week depending upon the rep and circumstance) into each of the boxes and bring it to any sales meeting that they have. Then you can ask them to analyse their activities and what they want to improve upon.

## Figure 17: SALES VISIT CANVAS

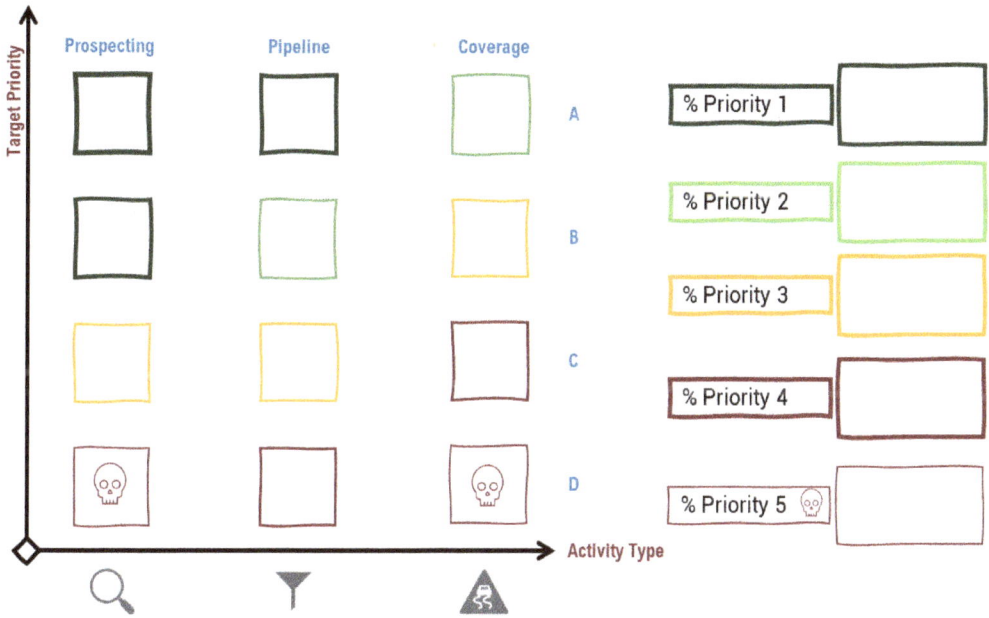

**Target Priority** (vertical axis)

| Prospecting | Pipeline | Coverage | |
|---|---|---|---|
| □ | □ | □ | A |
| □ | □ | □ | B |
| □ | □ | □ | C |
| □ (skull) | □ | □ (skull) | D |

**Activity Type** (horizontal axis)

% Priority 1 □

% Priority 2 □

% Priority 3 □

% Priority 4 □

% Priority 5 (skull) □

# RELEVANCE:

The importance of achieving a specific activity level depends on the sales strategy, the length of the sales cycle, and the nature of the product/service being sold. For example, in a high-volume, transactional sales environment, a higher activity level might be necessary to achieve sales targets. In a complex, consultative sales environment, the focus might be more on the quality of interactions rather than the quantity. The relevance lens prompts you to consider whether the 80% target is appropriate for your specific sales context and what adjustments might be needed based on different sales roles, territories, or product/service offerings. It also emphasizes the importance of understanding the *reasons* behind performance gaps and providing appropriate support.

# CHAPTER 7:

# Quality of Sales Interactions

Score this chapter here

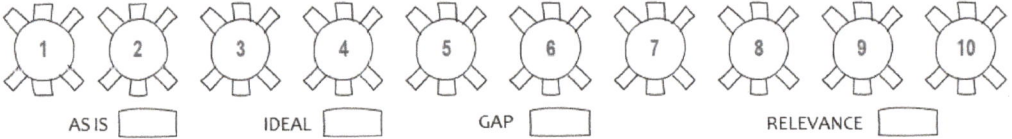

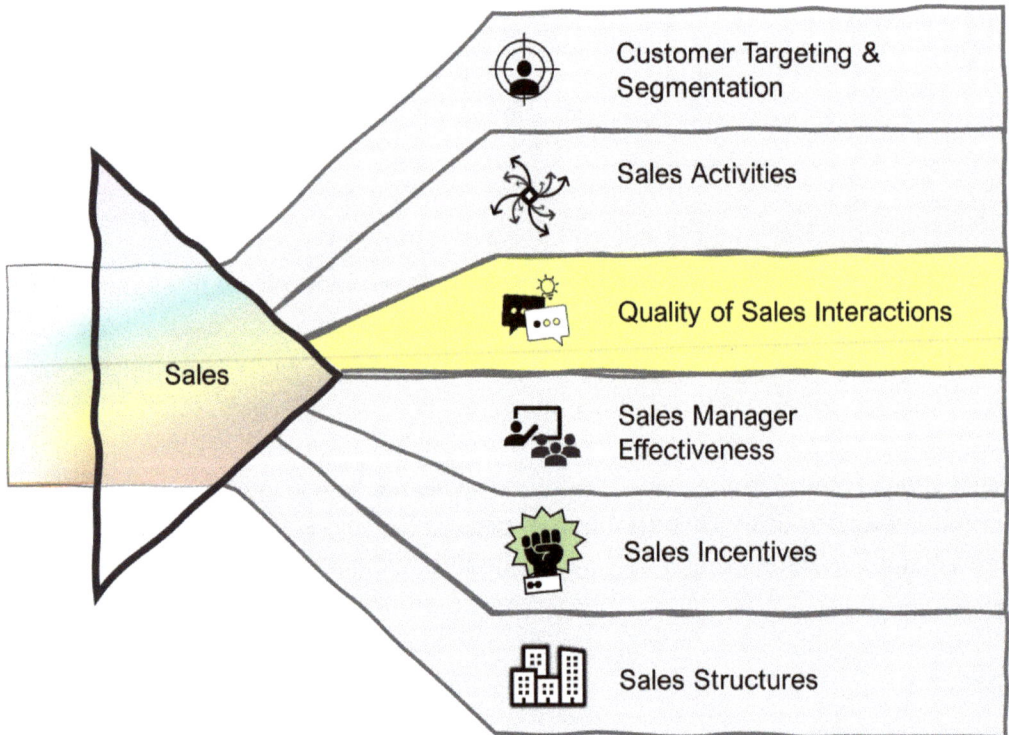

1  2  3  4  5  6  7  8  9  10

AS IS ☐    IDEAL ☐    GAP ☐    RELEVANCE ☐

Customer Targeting & Segmentation

Sales Activities

**Quality of Sales Interactions**

Sales Manager Effectiveness

Sales Incentives

Sales Structures

Sales

# SALES MODELS / PIPELINE & PLAYBOOKS:

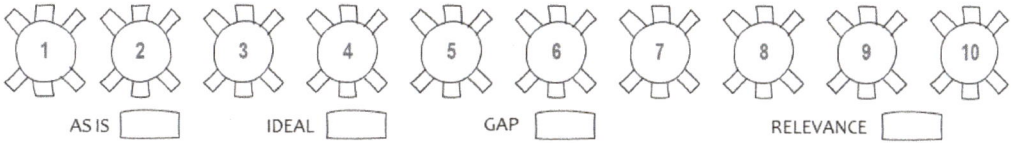

| 1 | 2 | 3 | 4 | 5 | 6 | 7 | 8 | 9 | 10 |

AS IS [    ]          IDEAL [    ]          GAP [    ]          RELEVANCE [    ]

Is there a well-defined selling model that the whole organisation follows? Is it a single model for selling that you're also measuring to ensure your reps are on the same level playing field? Do you have a defined selling/customer engagement model in place? Does it give systematic guidance for visit preparation, execution, and follow-up? For example, a sale model may be: A "SPIN" selling approach (Rackham, 1988) with a four-stage pipeline approach, or a value based sale using "rainmaking conversations" (Doerr, 2011), or DAPA (Mercuri-International, circa 2012) using a six-stage pipeline. All these approaches are based upon a published sales theory that is customised to the businesses situation.

## AS IS:

Is there a documented selling/customer engagement model? Does it provide specific guidance for each stage of the customer interaction: pre-visit preparation (e.g., research, setting objectives), visit execution (e.g., questioning techniques, product demonstrations), and post-visit follow-up (e.g., sending thank-you notes, providing additional information, scheduling next steps)? How consistently is this model applied across the sales team? Are there training programs or resources available to support its implementation? Are there tools or technologies that reinforce the model (e.g., CRM systems with sales playbooks)? How is the effectiveness of the model measured? Are there concrete actions for each stage of the opportunity pipeline?

## IDEAL:

Ideally, there should be a well-defined, documented, and consistently applied selling/customer engagement model that provides clear guidance for all pipeline and milestone stages of the customer interactions. This model should be based on best practices, customer insights, and the organisation's specific sales strategy. It should be regularly reviewed and updated to reflect changing market conditions and customer needs. Training and support should be provided to ensure that all sales representatives are proficient in using the model. The model should be integrated with sales tools and technologies to further reinforce its implementation and effectiveness.

## RELEVANCE:

The importance of a defined selling/customer engagement model depends on the complexity of the sales process, the length of the sales cycle, and the need for consistent customer experiences. In complex sales environments with multiple stakeholders or long sales cycles, a structured model is essential for managing customer interactions effectively. In simpler sales environments, a less formal approach might be sufficient. The relevance lens prompts you to consider the specific characteristics of your sales process and the importance of consistent execution for achieving your sales objectives.

# SALES PROCESS:

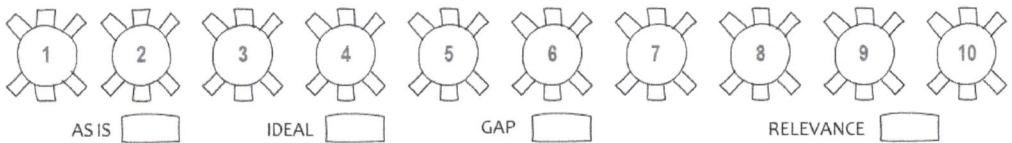

| 1 | 2 | 3 | 4 | 5 | 6 | 7 | 8 | 9 | 10 |

AS IS [    ]    IDEAL [    ]    GAP [    ]    RELEVANCE [    ]

Do the reps have the skills to create customer engagement through a purposeful opening, and by effectively uncovering customer needs and resolving objections raised by the customer?

## AS IS:

How are sales representatives trained on creating customer engagement, uncovering needs, and resolving objections? Are there specific methodologies or frameworks used (e.g., SPIN Selling (Rackham, 1988), Challenger Sale (Adamson, 2011), or solution selling)? How is the effectiveness of these skills assessed (e.g., through role-playing, call monitoring, customer feedback)? Are there ongoing coaching or mentoring programs to reinforce these skills? How are these skills reflected in sales performance metrics (e.g., conversion rates, deal size, customer satisfaction)? Are there specific tools or resources provided to aid in needs uncovering and objection handling (e.g., discovery questions, objection handling guides)?

## IDEAL:

Ideally, sales representatives would be proficient in creating engaging openings, effectively uncovering customer needs through skilful questioning and active listening, and confidently resolving objections using proven techniques. This would involve comprehensive training programs, ongoing coaching, and access to relevant resources and tools. The effectiveness of these skills would be regularly assessed, and feedback would be provided to support continuous improvement. The sales process would be structured to encourage these behaviours and maximize customer engagement.

## RELEVANCE:

The importance of these skills depends on the complexity of the sales process, the length of the sales cycle, and the nature of the customer relationship. In complex sales or when dealing with high-value customers, these skills are crucial for building rapport, understanding customer needs, and overcoming potential barriers to closing deals. In simpler sales environments, while still important, the emphasis might be on other factors, such as product knowledge or pricing. The relevance lens prompts you to consider the specific characteristics of your sales environment and the importance of these engagement and communication skills for achieving your sales objectives.

## SALES TRAINING:

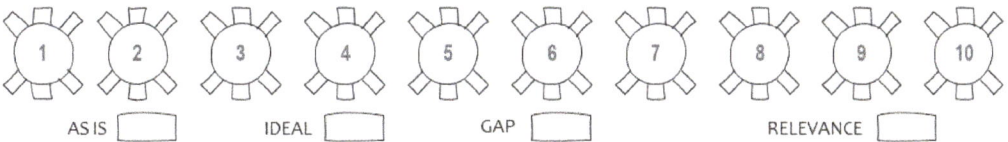

| 1 | 2 | 3 | 4 | 5 | 6 | 7 | 8 | 9 | 10 |

AS IS [     ]          IDEAL [     ]          GAP [     ]                    RELEVANCE [     ]

In this section we will delve into sales training. How well trained are your sales reps? Do they receive training and ongoing support for the sales model and process that we just completed thinking about? Are they trained enough to can outperform your competitors' reps.

## AS IS:

How is training on the selling/customer engagement model conducted and reinforced? What specific metrics are used to measure the effectiveness of sales visits (e.g., conversion rates, average deal size, customer satisfaction, average visit to close ratios)? How is competitor performance assessed (e.g., market share, win rates, customer feedback)? Is there a clear link between training on the model and improved sales performance? Are there ongoing coaching and development programs to reinforce the model and address performance gaps? How is "outperforming competitors" defined and measured? Is there objective data to support this claim? Are your sales managers the sales trainers? How often does training or coaching in the field happen?

## IDEAL:

Ideally, sales representatives would receive comprehensive and ongoing training on the selling/customer engagement model. This training would be reinforced through coaching, mentoring, and practical application. Sales visit effectiveness would be measured using relevant metrics, and performance would be consistently tracked and analysed. The organisation would have a robust system for monitoring competitor performance and benchmarking its own results. "Outperforming competitors" would be based on objective data and clear performance indicators. There would be a strong culture of continuous improvement, with regular reviews of the selling model and training programs to ensure they remain effective and aligned with market needs. Reps would have a way to share successes and incorporate learnings into the model over time.

## RELEVANCE:

The importance of well-trained sales representatives and outperforming competitors depends on the competitive intensity of the market and the complexity of the sales process. In highly competitive markets, having a highly skilled and effective sales force is crucial for success. In less competitive markets, while still important, the emphasis might be on other factors. The relevance lens prompts you to consider how critical it is for your organisation to invest in sales training and development to achieve a competitive advantage and outperform competitors in your specific market.

# DECISION MAKERS:

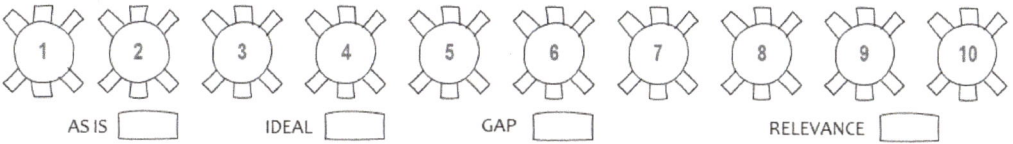

1  2  3  4  5  6  7  8  9  10

AS IS [       ]    IDEAL [       ]    GAP [       ]    RELEVANCE [       ]

In the coming sections we're about to discuss decision makers. For this and future sections a decision maker is the person who makes the call in an opportunity. I also include the term "gate keepers" around this. Coming from the medical diagnostic and devices field, it's almost always a split between who makes the function decision – how the instrument or test works – and the economic decision around how much to pay. In other industries, these are usually the same person. In this book they are treated separately. Keep this in mind as you go through the following sections.

## (ECONOMIC DECISION MAKERS)

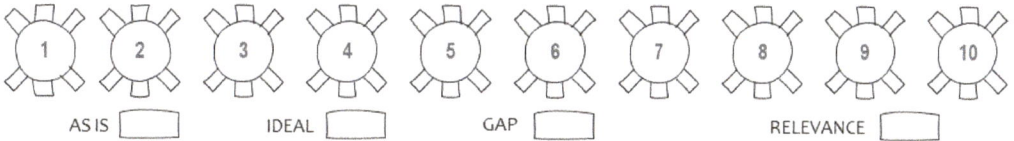

1  2  3  4  5  6  7  8  9  10

AS IS [       ]    IDEAL [       ]    GAP [       ]    RELEVANCE [       ]

How well trained are the reps to effectively sell to the economic decision makers?

# AS IS:

How is training on selling to economic decision-makers conducted? Does the training cover topics like understanding organisational structures, identifying key decision-makers, tailoring communication to different stakeholders, focusing on business value and ROI, and navigating complex buying processes? Are the reps trained on basic financial measures such as ROI, NPV and payback periods? Are the reps able to use these methods to present an interesting case to the economic decision maker?

# IDEAL:

Ideally, sales representatives would receive comprehensive and ongoing training on effectively engaging with economic decision-makers. This training would equip them with the skills to understand the decision-making process within target organisations, identify key stakeholders and their influence, and tailor their messaging to address the economic drivers and business needs of these decision-makers. The reps would be capable of presenting too and be seen as credible by the economic decision makers. Furthermore, they would effectively handle objections and questions, and be able to push back on financial challenges.

# RELEVANCE:

The importance of training sales representatives to sell to economic decision-makers depends on the complexity of the sales process, the size and structure of target organisations, and the value of the deals being pursued. In B2B sales, particularly for high-value or complex solutions, engaging with economic decision-makers is often crucial for closing deals. Even though they're often not the final decider, these individuals often act as gate keepers empowered to say "No" to a deal but without the final "Yes" authority. In simpler sales environments or when dealing with smaller organisations, the focus might be more on engaging with individual users or technical buyers. The relevance lens prompts you to consider the specific characteristics of your target customers and the importance of effectively engaging with economic decision-makers in your sales process.

## (FUNCTIONAL DECISION MAKERS)

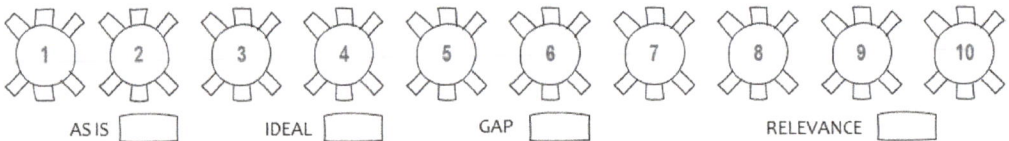

1  2  3  4  5  6  7  8  9  10

AS IS [    ]        IDEAL [    ]        GAP [    ]        RELEVANCE [    ]

How well trained are your sales reps to sell to the functional decision makers? Often before a financial decision can be made, the person on the team that's doing the work will need to push for, or ask for the purchase, by raising the purchase request.

# AS IS:

How is training on selling to functional decision-makers conducted? Does the training cover topics like understanding functional roles and responsibilities, identifying key functional stakeholders, tailoring communication to address specific functional needs and priorities, demonstrating how the product/service solves specific functional problems? Do the reps understand the value proposition as it relates to the functional stakeholders? Can the reps build relationships with functional stakeholders? Are specific methodologies or frameworks used in the sales process that aligns with functional needs.

## IDEAL:

Ideally, sales representatives would receive comprehensive and ongoing training on effectively engaging with functional decision-makers. The sales reps have the skills to understand the specific needs and priorities of different functional roles within target organisations, tailor their messaging to address these needs, and build strong relationships with functional stakeholders. Their training would be practical and interactive, incorporating real-world scenarios and case studies. Its effectiveness would be measured through clear metrics that demonstrate a positive impact on sales outcomes, such as improved stakeholder engagement and faster deal progression. Appropriate proof sources are available and used by the reps to support functional claims and USPs.

## RELEVANCE:

The importance of sales representatives to sell to functional decision-makers depends on the complexity of the sales process, the size and structure of target organisations, and the degree of functional specialization within those organisations. In B2B sales, particularly for solutions that impact multiple functional areas, engaging effectively with functional decision-makers is often crucial for securing buy-in and closing deals. In simpler sales environments or when dealing with smaller organisations, the focus might be more on engaging with a single decision-maker. The relevance lens prompts you to consider the specific characteristics of your target customers and the importance of effectively engaging with functional decision-makers in your sales process.

# VISIT PREPARATION:

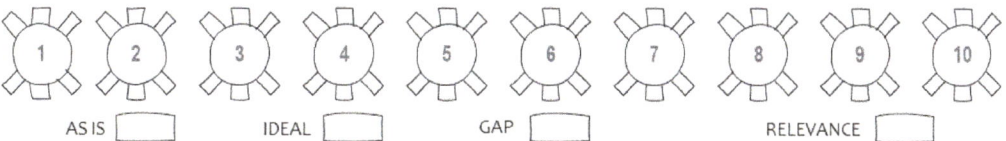

AS IS [        ]    IDEAL [        ]    GAP [        ]    RELEVANCE [        ]

This part is about the preparation for a visit, including review of the last calls, conducting sales analyses as to where this customer is, and setting a clear visit purpose for each visit and reviewing what's happening with the account prior to visiting.

## AS IS:

How do sales representatives currently prepare for customer visits? Is there a standardized process or checklist they follow? Do they routinely review past visit notes and customer history (e.g., previous purchases, interactions, issues)? Do they conduct any sales analysis prior to visits (e.g., sales trends, product performance, competitive information)? Are specific objectives set for each visit, and how are these objectives documented and communicated? Are there tools or technologies used to support visit preparation (e.g., CRM systems, sales enablement platforms)? How consistently is this preparation process followed across the sales team?

## IDEAL:

Ideally, sales representatives would consistently follow a structured process for preparing for each customer visit. This process would include reviewing past visit notes and customer history to understand the customer's current situation and needs. It would also involve conducting relevant sales analysis to identify opportunities and tailor the visit accordingly. Clear and measurable objectives would be set for each visit, ensuring that the sales representative has a clear purpose and focus. This preparation process would be supported by appropriate tools and technologies, such as CRM systems and sales enablement platforms, and would be reinforced through training and coaching.

## RELEVANCE:

The importance of systematic visit preparation depends on the complexity of the sales process, the length of the sales cycle, and the value of individual customers. For complex sales or high-value customers, thorough preparation is essential for maximizing the effectiveness of each visit and minimise the risk of the rep being surprised. Ensuring a structured meeting that the rep has control over: For simpler sales or smaller customers, a less formal approach might be sufficient. The relevance lens prompts you to consider the specific characteristics of your sales environment and the importance of structured preparation for achieving your sales objectives.

# INFLUENCE MAPS:

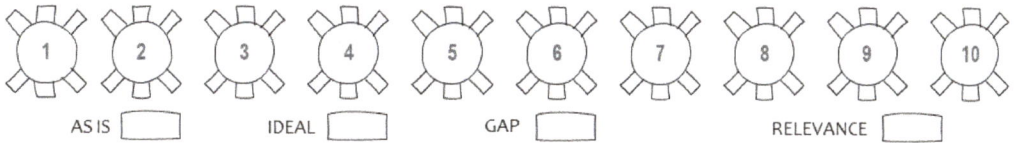

An influence map is a flow diagram showing the stakeholders and influence flows for a customer/market or even an opportunity. Understanding who the stakeholders are and who holds sway over each other can be a powerful tool for understanding the buying behaviours.

**Figure 18:** A Hypothetical Influence Map of an antibiotic selection process by clinicians.

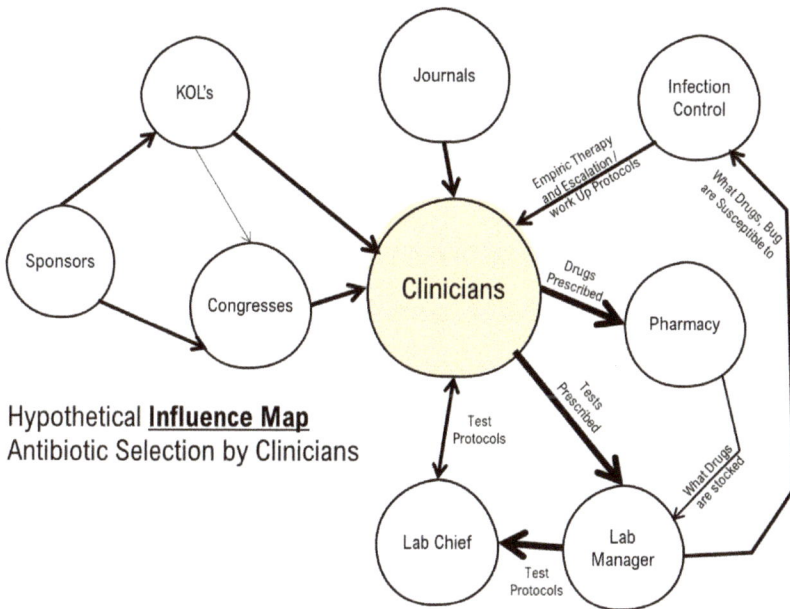

*The larger the circle the larger the decision power, and the thicker the arrow the greater the level of influence over the decision process.*
Are the sales reps both capable of, and actually doing, effective Influence Maps for the purchase influences at their priority customer target segments?

## AS IS:

How do sales representatives currently identify and map purchase influencers as priority customers? Is there a formal process or methodology used for this mapping (e.g., using organisational charts, conducting stakeholder interviews, utilizing relationship mapping tools)? What information is typically captured in the map (e.g., roles, responsibilities, influence levels, relationships between stakeholders)? What is their level of friendliness for your company? How is this information documented and shared within the sales team and with other relevant departments? How consistently is this mapping activity performed across the sales force? How is the effectiveness of this mapping measured in terms of its impact on sales outcomes?

## IDEAL:

Ideally, sales representatives would have a well-defined and consistently applied process for mapping all key purchase influencers as priority customers. This process would involve gathering information from multiple sources to create a comprehensive understanding of the decision-making unit (DMU) or buying centre. The map would clearly identify each influencer's role, level of influence, key concerns, and relationships with other stakeholders and their company. The influence map would show the influencers' personality type (DISC (Geir, 1989)) and potential tactics on how to best deal with them. This information would be documented in a central system (e.g., CRM) and regularly updated to reflect changes in the customer organisation. This mapping would be actively used to inform sales strategies, communication plans, and relationship-building efforts.

## RELEVANCE:

The importance of effectively mapping purchase influencers depends on the complexity of the sales process, the size and structure of target organisations, and the value of the deals being pursued. In B2B sales, particularly for complex solutions or high-value contracts, understanding the dynamics of the DMU is crucial for navigating the sales process and securing buy-in from all (or as many as possible) key stakeholders. In simpler sales environments or when dealing with smaller organisations with fewer decision-makers, the mapping process might be less complex or not relevant. The relevance lens prompts you to consider the specific characteristics of your target customers and the importance of understanding the influence landscape within those organisations.

# DECISION MAKER MESSAGING:

## (FUNCTIONAL DECISION MAKERS)

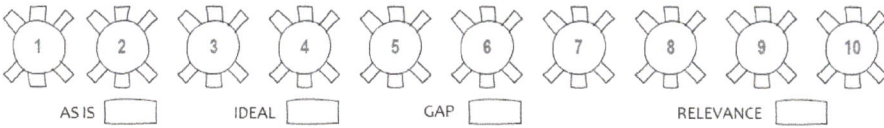

AS IS ☐    IDEAL ☐    GAP ☐    RELEVANCE ☐    Are the salespeople able to effectively provide solutions and deliver core messages for functional decision makers?

## AS IS:

How are sales representatives trained to tailor their solutions and messaging to functional decision-makers? Does training cover understanding different functional roles, their specific needs and priorities, and the language they use? Are there specific tools or resources provided to help sales representatives develop tailored solutions and messaging (e.g., case studies, product demos)? How is the effectiveness of this skill assessed (e.g., through role-playing, customer feedback, win rates within specific functional areas)? Are there ongoing coaching or mentoring programs to reinforce these skills? How is the impact of tailored solutions and messaging measured in terms of sales outcomes (e.g., deal progression, stakeholder buy-in, customer satisfaction within functional teams)?

## IDEAL:

Ideally, sales representatives would be highly skilled at understanding the specific needs and priorities of different functional decision-makers and tailoring their solutions and messaging accordingly. This would involve comprehensive and ongoing training, practical exercises, and access to relevant resources and tools. Sales representatives would be able to effectively communicate the value proposition of their offerings in terms that resonate with each functional area, demonstrating how the solution addresses their specific challenges and contributes to their objectives. The effectiveness of these skills would be regularly assessed, and feedback would be provided to support continuous improvement.

# RELEVANCE:

The importance of tailoring solutions and messaging to functional decision-makers depends on the complexity of the sales process, the size and structure of target organisations, and the degree of functional specialization within those organisations. In B2B sales, particularly for complex solutions that impact multiple functional areas, effectively communicating value to each functional stakeholder is crucial for securing buy-in and closing deals. In simpler sales environments or when dealing with smaller organisations with less functional specialization, the focus might be more on addressing the needs of a single decision-maker or a smaller group of stakeholders. The relevance lens prompts you to consider the specific characteristics of your target customers and the importance of effectively engaging with functional decision-makers by providing tailored solutions and messaging.

# DECISION MAKER MESSAGING:

## (ECONOMIC DECISION MAKERS)

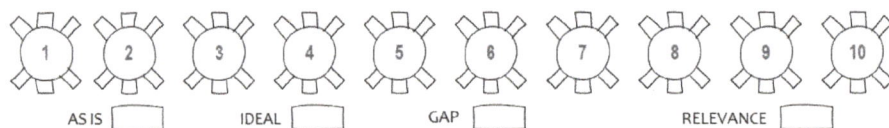

AS IS [    ]   IDEAL [    ]   GAP [    ]   RELEVANCE [    ]

Are the salespeople able to effectively provide solutions and deliver core messages for economic decision makers?

# AS IS:

How are sales representatives trained to tailor their solutions and messaging to economic decision-makers? Does this training focus on understanding financial metrics (ROI, NPV, payback period), business drivers (revenue growth, cost reduction, market share), and strategic priorities of the organisation? Do they have access to – and use – value calculators? Are they able to quantify the value proposition of their offerings in economic terms? Are there specific tools or resources provided to help them develop interesting business cases and presentations for economic buyers? How is the effectiveness of the reps, the tools and the business cases? Do the reps practice through role-playing? Do they review their, deal win rates, and average deal sizes? Are there ongoing coaching or mentoring programs to reinforce these skills? What percentage of deals are lost because of economic reasons? Do you track opportunity loss at stage and what reasons do you categorise lost opportunities?

## IDEAL:

Ideally, sales representatives would be highly proficient at understanding the economic drivers and strategic priorities of economic decision-makers. They would be able to effectively translate the features and benefits of their offerings into quantifiable business value, demonstrating a clear return on investment. They would be skilled at presenting interesting business cases that resonate with the economic buyer's focus on financial metrics and business outcomes. This would be achieved through comprehensive and ongoing training, practical exercises, and access to relevant resources and tools. The effectiveness of these skills would be regularly assessed and reinforced through coaching and feedback.

## RELEVANCE:

The importance of tailoring solutions and messaging to economic decision-makers depends on the complexity of the sale, the size and structure of the customer organisation, and the value of the deal. In B2B sales, particularly for high-value or strategic deals, influencing the economic buyer is often crucial for securing approval and closing the sale. In simpler, transactional sales, the economic buyer might be less directly involved. The relevance lens prompts you to consider the specific characteristics of your target customers and the importance of effectively engaging with economic decision-makers by providing tailored solutions and messaging that clearly demonstrate business value.

## OBJECTION HANDLING:

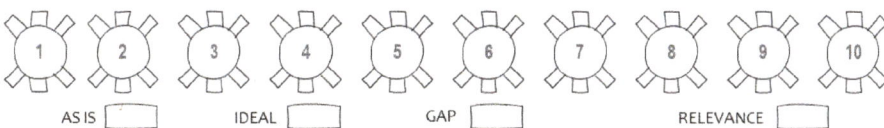

AS IS ☐    IDEAL ☐    GAP ☐    RELEVANCE ☐    How do the sales reps handle the differing types of objections? Do you have the main objections mapped?

## AS IS:

How are sales representatives trained to handle objections? Does the training cover common objections relate to price, features, competition, or timing? Are they taught specific objection handling techniques (e.g., acknowledging the objection, asking clarifying questions, providing evidence or testimonials, reframing the objection)? Are there resources available to help them prepare for and address objections (e.g., objection handling guides, FAQs, case studies)? How is the effectiveness of their objection handling skills assessed (e.g., through role-playing, call monitoring, win/loss analysis)? Is there ongoing coaching or mentoring to reinforce these skills? How is the impact of effective objection handling measured in terms of sales outcomes (e.g., conversion rates, deal size, customer satisfaction)?

## IDEAL:

Ideally, sales representatives would be highly proficient at handling objections, viewing them as opportunities to further understand customer needs and build stronger relationships. They would be equipped with a range of techniques to address different types of objections (Figure 19) effectively, confidently, and professionally. They could anticipate common objections and proactively address them in their presentations. The effectiveness of their objection handling skills would be continuously monitored and improved through ongoing training, coaching, and feedback. They utilize case studies and publications as proof sources for misconception objections.

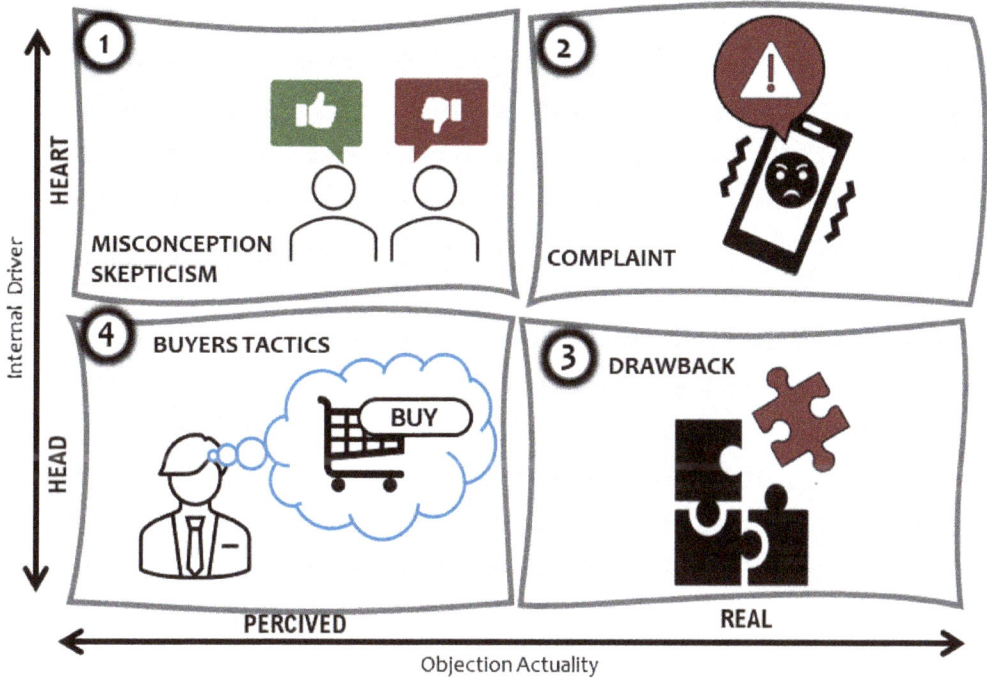

If we examine an objection across either the axis of the underlying driver of the objector, and if the objection is actually valid, we can classify objections into four quadrants (Figure 19 above).

There is a classification system to put objections into classes and objection handling or normative propositions for each class.

E.g.:

**1. Misconceptions/Scepticisms:** Show proof.

**2. Complaints:** Show what action is being taken.

**3. Real Drawback:** Show how it fits into the big picture.

**4. Buyers Tactics:** Go into need discovery and link to benefits.

# RELEVANCE:

The importance of effective objection handling depends on the complexity of the sale, the price point of the product/service, and the level of competition in the market. In complex sales or when dealing with high-value products/services, objections are often a natural part of the buying process. Effectively addressing these objections is crucial for closing deals. In simpler, more transactional sales, objections might be less frequent or less complex. The relevance lens prompts you to consider the specific nature of your sales process and the importance of objection handling for achieving your sales objectives.

# CLOSING:

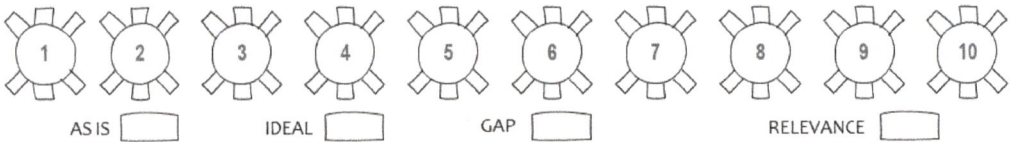

AS IS [　　]　　IDEAL [　　]　　GAP [　　]　　RELEVANCE [　　]

How do your sales representatives handle the closing section of opportunity management. Are they adept in getting a commitment from customers to buy, try, or recommend our products?

## AS IS:

How is "success" defined and measured? Are specific metrics tracked, such as conversion rates (from lead to sale), trial adoption rates, or customer referral rates? Are different types of commitment (buy, try, recommend) weighted differently? Are there specific closing techniques or strategies that are emphasized in sales training? How consistently are these techniques applied across the sales team? What factors contribute to successful commitment versus lost opportunities? Is there analysis done on lost opportunities to understand why commitment was not achieved?

## IDEAL:

Ideally, sales representatives would be highly skilled at guiding customers through the buying process and securing appropriate levels of commitment. This would involve understanding customer needs, building rapport, effectively presenting solutions, addressing objections, and confidently asking for the business (or a trial, or a referral). The focus would be on securing the right type of commitment at the right stage of the sales cycle, maximizing the likelihood of long-term customer relationships and revenue generation. Sales representatives would be equipped with a range of closing techniques and strategies, and they would be adept at adapting their approach to different customer situations. The reps would have a process that reduces resistance and overcomes final objections, making the close simple. The reps would understand that most closing problems are generated by a lack of thoroughness in the needs discovery phase and would incorporate their closing challenges into their discovery phase.

## RELEVANCE:

The importance of securing customer commitment depends on the nature of the product/service, the length of the sales cycle, and the overall sales strategy. For transactional sales, the focus might be on securing immediate purchases. For complex sales, or when introducing new products, securing trials or recommendations might be a more appropriate initial objective. The relevance lens prompts you to consider the specific characteristics of your sales process and the importance of securing different types of commitment for achieving your sales objectives. It is also important to consider what is a realistic expectation of commitment in the marketplace.

## FOLLOW UP:

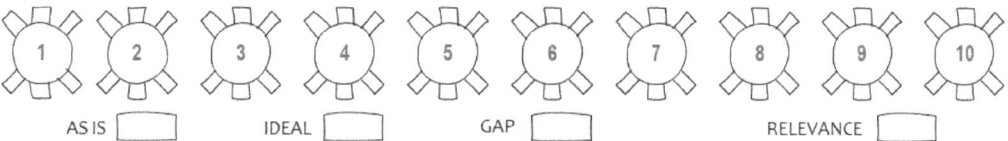

| 1 | 2 | 3 | 4 | 5 | 6 | 7 | 8 | 9 | 10 |

AS IS [     ]          IDEAL [     ]          GAP [     ]          RELEVANCE [     ]

Sales reps can perform post-visit analyses, and document the visit, the findings, set next visit objectives, and ensure an appropriate follow-up.

## AS IS:

How consistently do sales representatives conduct post-visit analyses? What information is documented (e.g., key discussion points, customer feedback, competitive intelligence, actions)? Are there standardized templates or tools used for this documentation (e.g., CRM systems, call reports)? How are next visit objectives set, and are they clearly documented? What constitutes "appropriate follow-up," and how is it ensured (e.g., sending thank-you notes, providing requested information, scheduling follow-up meetings)? How is the effectiveness of post-visit analysis and follow-up measured in terms of sales outcomes? Is there managerial oversight or coaching related to post-visit activities?

## IDEAL:

Ideally, post-visit analysis would be a standard practice for all sales representatives, consistently performed after every customer interaction. This analysis would involve documenting key findings, updating customer profiles in the CRM system, setting clear and measurable objectives for the next visit, and ensuring timely and appropriate follow-up. This process would be supported by user-friendly tools and technologies and reinforced through regular coaching and training. The focus would be on using post-visit analysis to improve sales effectiveness, strengthen customer relationships, and drive future sales opportunities. Next steps are agreed by the reps and the customer/prospect at the sales visit and clear follow up objectives that are time bound are in place.

## RELEVANCE:

The importance of routine post-visit analysis depends on the complexity of the sales process, the length of the sales cycle, and the importance of ongoing customer relationship management. In complex sales or when dealing with high-value customers, thorough post-visit analysis is crucial for maintaining momentum, ensuring effective follow-up, and maximizing the likelihood of closing deals. In simpler sales environments, a less formal approach might be sufficient. The relevance lens prompts you to consider the specific characteristics of your sales process and the importance of post-visit activities for achieving your sales objectives.

# CHAPTER 8:

# Sales Manager Effectiveness

Score this chapter here

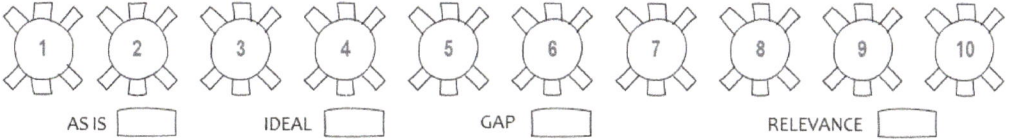

AS IS ☐   IDEAL ☐   GAP ☐   RELEVANCE ☐

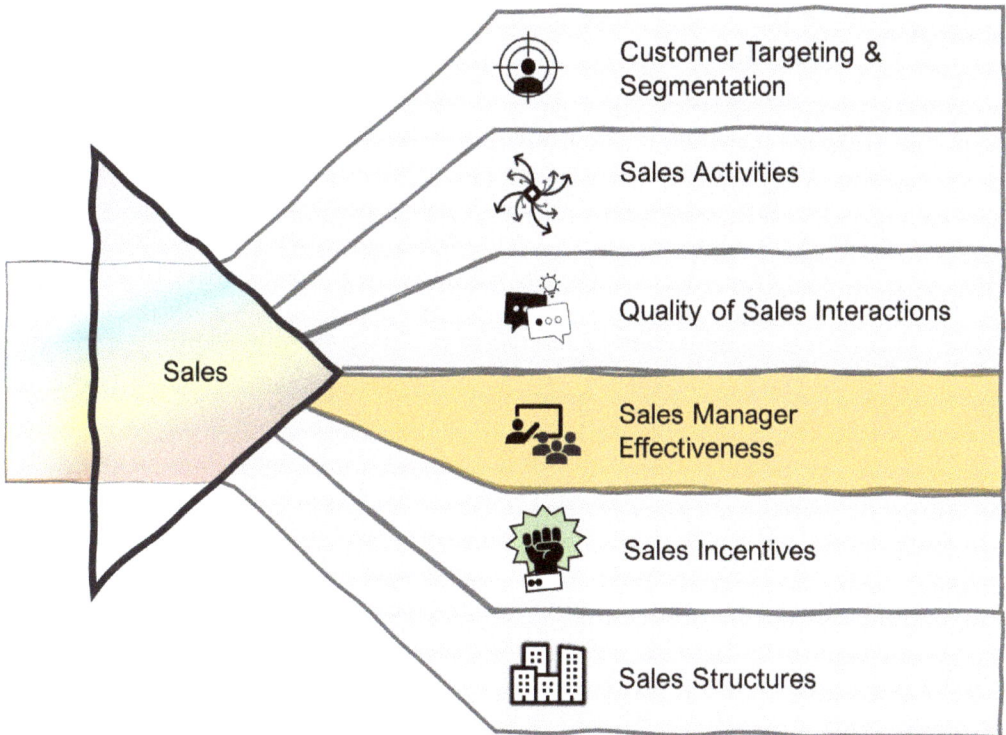

Customer Targeting & Segmentation

Sales Activities

Quality of Sales Interactions

Sales Manager Effectiveness

Sales Incentives

Sales Structures

Sales

# SALES MANAGER ROLE:

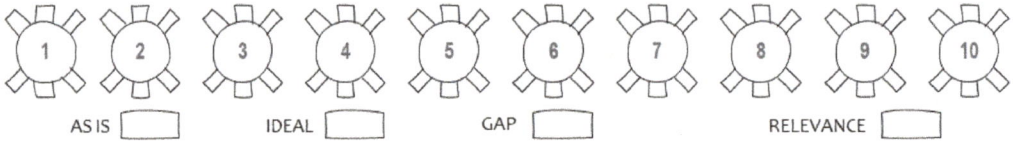

| | | | | | | | | | |
|---|---|---|---|---|---|---|---|---|---|
| 1 | 2 | 3 | 4 | 5 | 6 | 7 | 8 | 9 | 10 |

AS IS [      ]     IDEAL [      ]     GAP [      ]     RELEVANCE [      ]

This area is about how the role of a sales manager is understood and lived in practice.

The role of the sales manager is often misunderstood, not only from one company to the next but also within a company. Here is my take on it – the number one job of a sales manager is to help plan the reps' activities. This is closely followed by gathering intelligence and coaching their reps. Then comes all the admin and management tasks.

## AS IS:

Is there a clearly defined job description for sales managers? Does it outline their key responsibilities, such as coaching and mentoring sales representatives, setting sales targets, managing sales territories, monitoring performance, and providing feedback? How well do sales managers understand their roles and responsibilities? How consistently do they perform these responsibilities in practice? Are there any gaps between the defined role and the actual performance of sales managers? Are there training or development programs in place to support sales managers in fulfilling their roles effectively? How is the effectiveness of sales managers measured (e.g., team performance, individual sales representative performance, employee satisfaction, quota achievement, budget achievement or growth)?

## IDEAL:

Ideally, the role of a sales manager would be clearly defined, well-communicated, and consistently executed. Sales managers would be seen as effective leaders, coaches, and mentors, responsible for developing their teams, driving sales performance, and ensuring alignment with overall sales strategy. They would possess strong leadership, communication, and coaching skills, and they would be provided with the necessary resources and support to succeed in their roles. Their effectiveness would be measured using relevant metrics that reflect their impact on team performance and overall sales outcomes. Sales managers should have clear priorities.

The Commercial Excellence Playbook

## RELEVANCE:

The importance of a well-defined and effectively executed sales manager role depends on the size and structure of the sales organisation, the complexity of the sales process, and the importance of effective sales leadership. In larger sales organisations or those with complex sales processes, strong Sales Management is crucial for driving performance and ensuring consistency in sales execution. In smaller organisations, the role might be less formalized, but effective leadership and coaching are still essential. The relevance lens prompts you to consider the specific needs of your sales organisation and the importance of effective Sales Management for achieving your sales objectives.

## MANAGER FIELD TIME:

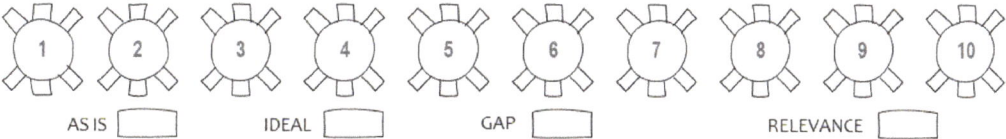

How much time do your sales managers spend in the field?

## AS IS:

How is the allocation of Sales Managers' time currently tracked and measured? Is there a formal system for tracking time spent in the field versus other activities (e.g., administrative tasks, reporting, meetings)? What constitutes "joint sales visits" and "active coaching"? Are there specific coaching methodologies or frameworks used? How is the effectiveness of field coaching measured (e.g., through improved sales representative performance, increased deal sizes, improved conversion rates)? What other demands are placed on sales managers' time, and how does this affect their ability to spend 60% of their time in the field?

## IDEAL:

Ideally, sales managers would dedicate a significant portion of their time to field coaching and joint sales visits, with the specific percentage based on data and analysis of what drives the best performance outcomes. "Active coaching" would involve structured observation, feedback, and development plans tailored to individual sales representatives' needs. The impact of field coaching would be measured through clear performance metrics. The balance between field time and other responsibilities would be carefully managed to ensure that sales managers can effectively support their teams while also fulfilling other essential duties. Just as important is what sales managers should not be doing. They should not be doing the job of the sales rep whilst on the field, e.g. closing deals.

## RELEVANCE:

The optimal allocation of sales managers' time depends on factors such as the complexity of the sales process, the experience level of the sales team, and the company's sales strategy. In situations where sales representatives require significant coaching and development, or when dealing with complex sales cycles, a higher percentage of field time might be necessary. In situations where sales representatives are more experienced, or the sales process is simpler, a lower percentage might be sufficient. In these cases, are the senior reps being promoted? Given manager tasks? What is the career progression for the manager? The relevance lens prompts you to consider the specific needs of your sales team and the impact of field coaching on sales performance. It's important to justify the 60% figure with data and analysis rather than treating it as a fixed target.

## SALES COACHING:

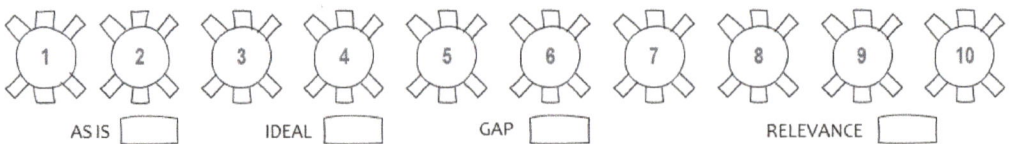

| 1 | 2 | 3 | 4 | 5 | 6 | 7 | 8 | 9 | 10 |

AS IS [    ]    IDEAL [    ]    GAP [    ]    RELEVANCE [    ]

If planning is the number one job, then coaching in the field is number two.

# AS IS:

Is there a documented coaching methodology? What specific coaching techniques or frameworks are used (e.g., GROW model, situational coaching (Whitmore, 2011))? How are sales managers trained on this methodology? Is coaching provided regularly and consistently? How is the quality and effectiveness of the coaching assessed (e.g., through feedback from sales representatives, observation of coaching sessions, improvement in sales performance metrics)? Are there tools or resources provided to support the coaching process (e.g., coaching guides, performance dashboards)? How is coaching linked to performance reviews and development plans?

# IDEAL:

Ideally, sales managers would be equipped with a clearly defined and proven coaching methodology that is based on best practices and tailored to the specific needs of the sales team. They would receive thorough training on this methodology and be provided with ongoing support and resources to effectively implement it. Coaching would be conducted regularly and consistently, focusing on specific skills and behaviours that drive sales performance. The quality and effectiveness of the coaching would be monitored and evaluated, with feedback mechanisms in place to ensure ongoing improvement.

# RELEVANCE:

The importance of high-quality coaching based on a defined methodology depends on the size and the experience level of the sales team, and the organisation's focus on continuous improvement. In situations where sales representatives require significant development or when dealing with complex sales cycles, high-quality coaching is crucial for driving performance and achieving sales objectives. In simpler sales environments or when dealing with highly experienced sales representatives, the need for formal coaching might be less pronounced. However, even in these situations, some level of coaching and feedback can be beneficial. The relevance lens prompts you to consider the specific needs of your sales team and the importance of effective coaching for maximizing their performance.

# SALES MANAGER TRAINING:

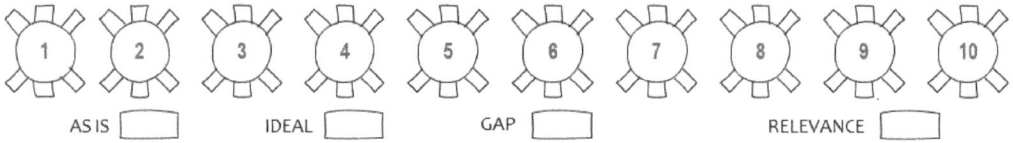

| 1 | 2 | 3 | 4 | 5 | 6 | 7 | 8 | 9 | 10 |

AS IS [          ]    IDEAL [          ]    GAP [          ]    RELEVANCE [          ]

## AS IS:

What specific topics are covered in the sales manager training program (e.g., coaching skills, performance management, sales planning, territory management, leadership development, financial management, legal and compliance)? What training methods are used (e.g., classroom training, online modules, workshops, simulations, mentoring, on-the-job training)? How frequently is training conducted (e.g., onboarding for new managers, regular refreshers, training on new management techniques or company initiatives)? How is the effectiveness of the training program evaluated (e.g., through knowledge assessments, skills assessments, 360-degree feedback, team performance metrics, feedback from sales representatives and senior management)? Are there mechanisms for updating the training program to reflect changing market conditions, sales strategies, or management best practices?

## IDEAL:

Ideally, the sales manager training program would be comprehensive, covering all essential aspects of the sales manager role and aligned with the organisation's sales strategy and leadership development framework. It would utilize a variety of engaging and effective training methods, incorporating both theoretical and practical components. Training would be ongoing, with regular refreshers and updates to ensure that sales managers stay current with the latest management techniques, market trends, and company initiatives. The effectiveness of the training program would be regularly evaluated using a combination of quantitative and qualitative data, and feedback would be used to continuously improve the program. The program would also foster a community of practice among sales managers, encouraging peer learning and knowledge sharing. The program must include, how to help the sales rep plan. How to coach on the field, territory set up and management, customer targeting and sale training skills (TTT).

# RELEVANCE:

The importance of an effective training program for sales managers depends on the complexity of the sales management role, the rate of change in the market, and the organisation's focus on sales performance and leadership development. In organisations with complex sales structures, diverse product portfolios, or rapidly changing markets, a robust training program for sales managers is essential for equipping them with the necessary skills and knowledge to lead their teams effectively. In simpler sales environments or in more stable markets, while still important, the emphasis might be less pronounced. The relevance lens prompts you to consider the specific demands placed on your sales managers and the impact of their effectiveness on overall sales performance and business outcomes.

# SALES MANAGER ENGAGEMENT:

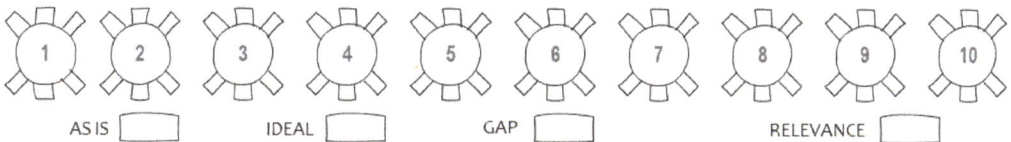

| 1 | 2 | 3 | 4 | 5 | 6 | 7 | 8 | 9 | 10 |

AS IS [      ]     IDEAL [      ]     GAP [      ]     RELEVANCE [      ]

Engaged managers actively promote teamwork and harmony, bringing up the entire team.

# AS IS:

How is the engagement of sales managers currently assessed? Are there specific leadership competencies or behaviours that are emphasized (e.g., communication, motivation, coaching, conflict resolution)? How is teamwork promoted within the sales team (e.g., regular team meetings, collaborative projects, shared goals)? Are there any metrics used to measure team cohesion or collaboration (e.g., team sales performance, employee satisfaction surveys)? What is the turnover rates for individual sales managers? What is the turnover rate for the sales managers' level? Are there any observable behaviours that indicate effective leadership and teamwork (e.g., open communication, mutual support, shared learning)? Are there any instances where leadership or teamwork is lacking, and how are these issues addressed? Is senior management messaging getting through the sales managers to the frontline reps? Is this messaging consistent?

## IDEAL:

Ideally, sales managers would be seen as strong and effective leaders who inspire, motivate, and develop their teams. They would actively foster a culture of teamwork, collaboration, and mutual support. This would involve clear communication, shared goals, and opportunities for team members to learn from each other. Sales managers would be adept at recognizing and addressing individual strengths and weaknesses, fostering a positive and productive team environment.

## RELEVANCE:

The importance of effective leadership and teamwork depends on the size and structure of the sales organisation, the complexity of the sales process, and the importance of collaboration in achieving sales objectives. In larger sales organisations or those with complex sales processes that require cross-functional collaboration, strong leadership and teamwork are crucial. In smaller organisations or those with simpler sales processes, while still important, the emphasis might be less pronounced. The relevance lens prompts you to consider the specific needs of your sales organisation and the impact of leadership and teamwork on overall sales performance.

## REP PERFORMANCE AND DEVELOPMENT:

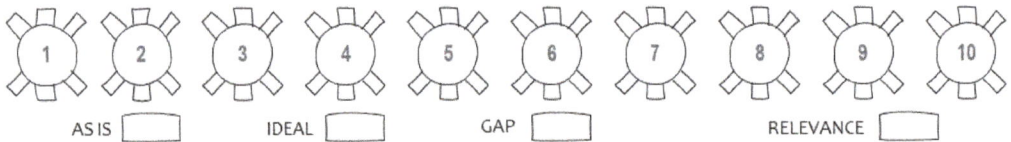

| 1 | 2 | 3 | 4 | 5 | 6 | 7 | 8 | 9 | 10 |

AS IS _____   IDEAL _____   GAP _____   RELEVANCE _____

Engaged sales managers should be obsessed with their reps' performance and development. They can't close all the deals anymore – they have to work through their reps. This means getting the most out of them and cutting those without the ability early.

# AS IS:

How do sales managers currently manage sales representative performance? Are there formal performance reviews, regular feedback sessions, and documented performance improvement/development plans? What metrics are used to evaluate performance (e.g., sales revenue, conversion rates, activity levels, customer satisfaction)? How are development needs identified (e.g., through performance reviews, skills assessments, observation of sales activities)? What development opportunities are provided (e.g., training programs, coaching, mentoring, stretch assignments)? How is the effectiveness of performance management and development activities measured (e.g., through improved sales performance, increased skill levels, employee retention)? Are performance management and development processes consistently applied across all sales teams?

# IDEAL:

Ideally, sales managers would be highly effective at managing sales representative performance and fostering their professional development. This would involve a structured and ongoing process of setting clear performance expectations, providing regular feedback and coaching, identifying development needs, and providing relevant development opportunities. Performance management would be data-driven, using relevant metrics to track progress and identify areas for improvement. Development activities would be tailored to individual needs and aligned with career goals. The overall focus would be on maximizing the potential of each sales representative and driving continuous improvement in sales performance.

# RELEVANCE:

The importance of effective performance management and development depends on the complexity of the sales role, the experience level of the sales team, and the organisation's focus on talent development. In organisations with complex sales processes or where sales representatives require specialized skills, effective performance management and development are crucial for maximizing sales effectiveness. In simpler sales environments or when dealing with highly experienced sales representatives, while still important, the emphasis might be less pronounced. The relevance lens prompts you to consider the specific needs of your sales organisation and the impact of performance management and development on overall sales success.

## TERRITORY PLANNING:

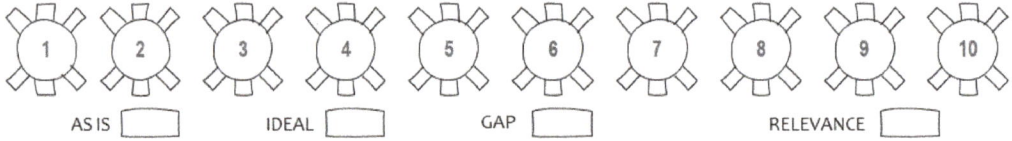

AS IS [     ]     IDEAL [     ]     GAP [     ]     RELEVANCE [     ]

How do sales managers plan out their territories. Are they having their own small business plans. A territory plan is more than just a visit plan.

## AS IS:

How are territory business plans currently developed? Are there standardized templates or processes used? What key elements are included in these plans (e.g., territory analysis, sales targets, key account plans, competitive analysis, marketing activities, resource allocation, market Intelligence and proof source gathering)? Are these plans aligned with the overall sales strategy and company objectives? How are these plans reviewed and approved? How frequently are they updated? Are there tools or technologies used to support the planning process (e.g., CRM systems, sales planning software)? How is the effectiveness of these plans measured (e.g., through achievement of sales targets, market share growth, customer acquisition)?

## IDEAL:

Ideally, sales managers would be proficient at developing comprehensive and effective business plans for their territories. These plans would be based on a thorough analysis of the territory, including customer segmentation, market trends, competitive landscape, and historical performance. The plans would include specific, measurable, achievable, relevant, and time-bound (SMART) objectives, along with clear strategies and tactics for achieving those objectives. These plans would be aligned with the overall sales strategy and company objectives and would be regularly reviewed and updated to reflect changing market conditions.

The Commercial Excellence Playbook

## RELEVANCE:

The importance of effective territory business planning depends on factors such as the size and complexity of the sales territories, the diversity of the customer base, and the competitive intensity of the market. In larger territories with diverse customer bases, detailed business plans are crucial for maximizing sales effectiveness and resource allocation. In smaller territories or when dealing with a more homogenous customer base, a less complex planning process might be sufficient. The relevance lens prompts you to consider the specific characteristics of your sales territories and the importance of effective planning for achieving your sales objectives.

# TERRITORY PERFORMANCE:

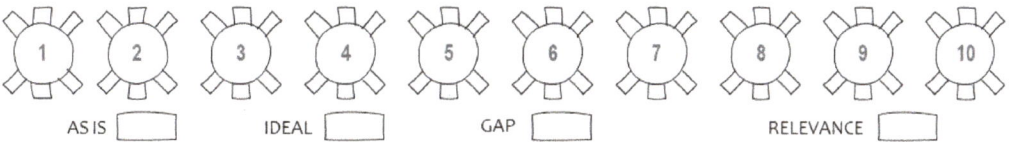

Thinking about each of the territories and their performance. How is the performance monitored by the territory manager, are they initiating proper actions to maintain the course.

## AS IS:

How do sales managers currently monitor regional business performance? What metrics are tracked (e.g., sales revenue, market share, customer acquisition cost, customer retention, sales cycle length)? How frequently is performance monitored (e.g., weekly, monthly, quarterly)? What tools or technologies are used to track and analyse performance data (e.g., CRM systems, sales dashboards, reporting tools)? What process is in place for identifying performance deviations or underperformance? What types of corrective actions are typically initiated (e.g., coaching, training, territory adjustments, changes in sales strategy)? How is the effectiveness of these corrective actions measured?

## IDEAL:

Ideally, sales managers would have access to real-time performance data and utilize robust analytical tools to monitor regional business performance effectively. They would be proactive in identifying potential issues and initiating timely corrective actions. These actions would be based on data analysis and tailored to the specific needs of the region and the sales team. There would be a clear process for documenting corrective actions and tracking their impact on performance. The focus would be on continuous improvement and proactive problem-solving.

## RELEVANCE:

The importance of effective performance monitoring and corrective action depends on the size and complexity of the sales organisation, the volatility of the market, and the importance of achieving sales targets. In larger organisations with geographically dispersed sales teams or in rapidly changing markets, close monitoring and swift corrective action are important. In smaller organisations or in more stable markets, the need for frequent monitoring and intervention might be less pronounced. The relevance lens prompts you to consider the specific characteristics of your sales organisation and the importance of effective performance management for achieving your sales objectives.

# CHAPTER 9:

# Sales Incentives

Score this chapter here

1  2  3  4  5  6  7  8  9  10

AS IS [        ]    IDEAL [        ]    GAP [        ]    RELEVANCE [        ]

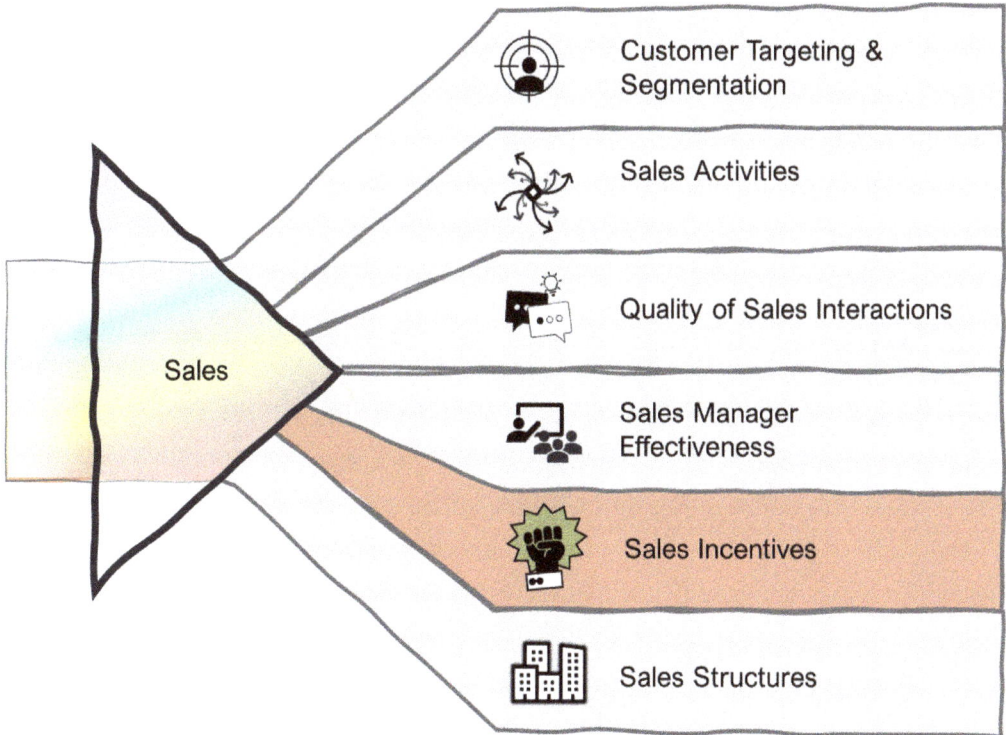

Customer Targeting & Segmentation

Sales Activities

Quality of Sales Interactions

Sales Manager Effectiveness

Sales Incentives

Sales Structures

Sales

# GOAL SETTING:

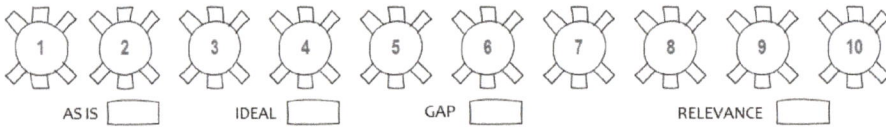

| | | | | | | | | | |
|---|---|---|---|---|---|---|---|---|---|
| 1 | 2 | 3 | 4 | 5 | 6 | 7 | 8 | 9 | 10 |

AS IS [　　]    IDEAL [　　]    GAP [　　]    RELEVANCE [　　]

Setting of aligned goals from the top that are cascaded throughout the entire organisation. Each territory has a quota and goals that are linkable to the overarching company strategy.

## AS IS:

How are goals/quotas currently set? Is there a formal process that involves both top-down target setting (driven by overall company objectives) and bottom-up forecasting (based on territory-level analysis)? How are top-down targets cascaded down through different levels of the sales organisation (e.g., from national to regional to individual)? How are bottom-up estimates generated (e.g., based on historical data, market analysis, sales representative input)? How are these top-down targets and bottom-up estimates reconciled to arrive at final quotas? What tools or technologies are used to support this process (e.g., sales planning software, CRM systems)? How frequently is this process conducted (e.g., annually, quarterly)? How effective is this process in setting realistic and achievable goals/quotas?

## IDEAL:

Ideally, the goal-setting/quota process would be a collaborative and iterative process that effectively integrates both top-down strategic objectives and bottom-up market realities. Top-down targets are clear, communicated and aligned with overall company goals. Bottom-up estimates would be based on accurate data and realistic assessments of the opportunity in each territory, incorporating input from sales representatives and sales managers. The reconciliation process would be transparent and data-driven, ensuring that final quotas are both challenging and attainable. This process is supported by the appropriate tools and technologies and regularly reviewed and improved.

## RELEVANCE:

The importance of a structured goal-setting/quota process depends on the size and complexity of the sales organisation, the diversity of the product/service portfolio, and the volatility of the market. In larger organisations with complex sales structures or in rapidly changing markets, a robust and well-defined process serves well to set realistic and motivating goals. In smaller organisations or in more stable markets, a less formal approach might be sufficient. The relevance lens prompts you to consider the specific characteristics of your sales organisation and the importance of a balanced top-down/bottom-up approach for setting effective sales targets.

# GOAL PRACTICALITY:

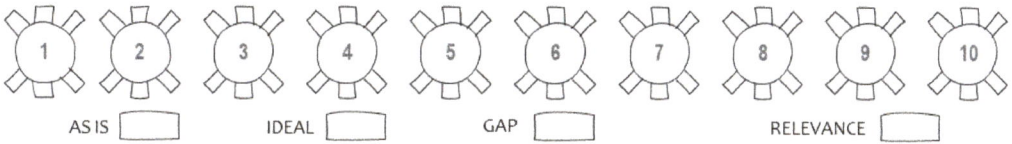

AS IS [ ]    IDEAL [ ]    GAP [ ]    RELEVANCE [ ]

Goals that are achievable, realistic and yet challenging and fair work as motivation for the sales reps. Goals that aren't have the opposite effect.

## AS IS:

How is a sales representative's perception of goal fairness and achievability currently assessed? Are the achievability of goals discussed during regular feedback sessions/loops, or one-on-one meetings? What is the current level of satisfaction among sales representatives regarding their goals? Are there specific concerns or recurring themes related to goal setting? How are these concerns addressed? Is there a process for adjusting goals if they are unfair or unachievable? How does management ensure that goals are both challenging enough to motivate performance and realistic enough to be attainable? How often do goals get missed by more than 10%?

## IDEAL:

Ideally, there would be open communication and a collaborative approach to goal setting, ensuring that sales representatives feel their input is valued and that their goals are fair and achievable. There would be a high level of trust and transparency between management and sales representatives regarding the goal-setting process. Goals would be data-driven, based on realistic assessments of market opportunity and individual capabilities. Regular feedback mechanisms would be in place to monitor perceptions of goal fairness and make adjustments as needed. Goals would include a mixture of existing, new and stretch targets.

## RELEVANCE:

The importance of sales representatives perceiving their goals as challenging but fair and achievable depends on the company culture, the sales compensation plan, and the overall management style. When sales representatives feel their goals are unattainable, it can lead to demotivation, decreased performance, and even turnover. On the other hand, if goals are perceived as too easy, it can lead to complacency and underperformance. The relevance lens prompts you to consider the impact of goal perception on sales representative motivation and performance within your specific organisational context. It emphasizes the importance of striking a balance between setting challenging goals that drive performance and ensuring that those goals are perceived as fair and achievable to maintain motivation and engagement.

## GOAL MONITORING:

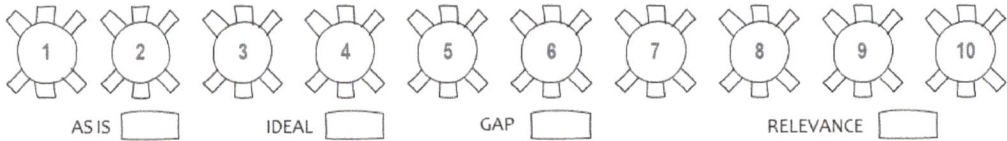

| AS IS | IDEAL | GAP | RELEVANCE |

Everyone has worked in a place where you start the year sitting down with your manager, setting your goals, and then nothing happens until the middle year check-up...and you find out that you haven't moved towards these goals at all. The role of a sales manager is to document reviews and implement formal development plans for each of his/her reps.

## AS IS:

How frequently are goals reviewed? Are they both for regional sales managers and sales representatives? What is the format of these reviews (e.g., written evaluations, verbal feedback, self-assessments)? What metrics and criteria are used to evaluate performance? How are these reviews documented (e.g., in performance management systems, HR files)? Are individual development plans (IDPs) created because of these reviews? What is the process for creating IDPs, and what types of development activities are included (e.g., training, coaching, mentoring, stretch assignments)? How are IDPs tracked and monitored? How are these processes linked to compensation, promotion, and other HR decisions?

## IDEAL:

Ideally, there would be a formal and consistent process for performance review and development for both sales managers and sales representatives. This would involve regular (e.g. monthly) reviews that are based on clear goals, expectations and relevant metrics. These reviews would be documented (The level of detail would vary depending upon the rep's goal and achievement levels) and used to identify development needs and create individualized development plans. IDPs would be specific, measurable, achievable, relevant, and time-bound (SMART). They are actively tracked and monitored to ensure progress. The process would be transparent and fair, providing opportunities for feedback and two-way communication and frequent.

## RELEVANCE:

The importance of goal monitoring and development processes depends on the number and performance levels of the sales organisation. In larger organisations or where sales roles require specialized skills, a more formal processes maybe essential for ensuring consistency, fairness, and effective development. In smaller organisations, a less formal but more frequent, approach might be sufficient. The relevance lens prompts you to consider the specific needs of your sales organisation and the impact of performance management and development on overall sales effectiveness, employee retention, and overall business achievement.

## SALES INCENTIVE PLANS (SIP):

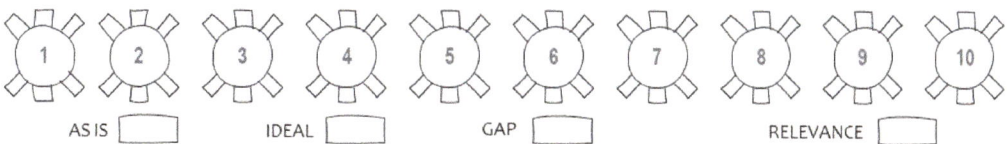

AS IS [    ]    IDEAL [    ]    GAP [    ]    RELEVANCE [    ]

A transparent system communicated that includes multiple aspects including salary, bonuses, benefits and non-monetary components.

## AS IS:

How is the compensation and incentive system currently communicated to sales representatives and sales managers? Are all components (base salary, bonus structure, benefits, non-monetary rewards) clearly documented and easily accessible (e.g., in employee handbooks, online portals, compensation statements)? Are there regular opportunities for employees to ask questions and receive clarification about the system? How is the communication of changes to the compensation and incentive system handled? Is there a process for addressing discrepancies or concerns related to compensation? How is the effectiveness of the communication measured (e.g., through employee surveys, feedback sessions)?

## IDEAL:

Ideally, the compensation and incentive system would be communicated clearly, concisely, and in an easily understandable manner. All components are documented and readily accessible and calculable to all employees. It would reward for their contribution to the overall company achievement, being linked to the business success. Alignment with the customer targeting system and have an accelerator to ensure that upon budget achievement nothing was held back for future budgets. There would be regular opportunities for employees to ask questions and receive personalized explanations. Any changes to the system would be communicated proactively and transparently, with sufficient time for employees to understand the implications. The communication would foster trust and confidence in the fairness and integrity of the system.

## SPECIAL NOTE:

Compensation statements, sales incentive plans, employee handbooks etc are all ideal entry points for an enterprise AI, or GPT from a large language model. At the time of writing, this is just at the beginning of becoming mainstream. Loading these manuals into a large language model can help employees chat with a personalised Company AI which can provide answers and calculate out potential earning systems. This is a simple way for the company to start to learn how to utilize AI tools.

## RELEVANCE:

The importance of transparent communication of the compensation and incentive system depends on the complexity of the system, the company culture, and the importance of attracting and retaining top sales talent. As well as the contribution a good rep makes to the achievement of sales revenue targets, in organisations with complex compensation structures or where incentives play a significant role in motivating and achieving performance, a clear and transparent SIP is crucial. In simpler organisations there may be less need for a complicated integrated SIP. The relevance lens prompts you to consider the specific needs of your sales organisation and the impact of driving aligned sales activities.

## INCENTIVE ATTAINMENT:

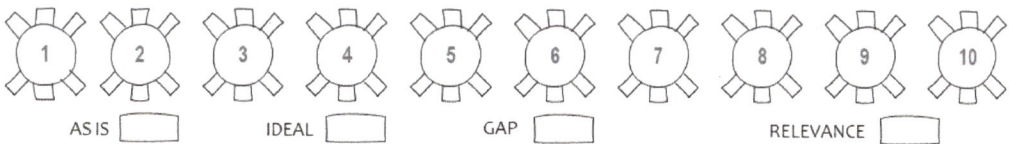

| 1 | 2 | 3 | 4 | 5 | 6 | 7 | 8 | 9 | 10 |

AS IS [      ]     IDEAL [      ]     GAP [      ]     RELEVANCE [      ]

## AS IS:

How is the bonus system structured? What percentage of bonus attainment is currently tied to quantitative result targets versus activity targets? Are these percentages clearly defined and communicated to the sales team? What specific metrics are used for both result and activity targets? Is there a clear rationale for the chosen weighting? How is the effectiveness of the bonus structure evaluated to motivate desired behaviours and achieving business objectives? Are there any unintended consequences of the current weighting (e.g., focusing on short-term gains at the expense of long-term customer relationships)? Does everyone achieve 100% of their SIP? Is this every year? Do the reps bringing in more for the organisation achieve a higher level of compensation from the SIP?

## IDEAL:

Ideally, the bonus system would primarily reward results that contribute to the overall business strategy. At least 80% (or an appropriate percentage based on analysis) of bonus attainment should be linked to quantitative result targets, such as sales growth, profit contribution, market share gains, or customer retention. Activity targets, while potentially useful for monitoring effort, should play a smaller role in bonus calculations. The bonus system should be designed to encourage behaviours that drive long-term sustainable growth and customer value. It should include accelerators to:

**1.** Ensure budget achievement.

**2.** Not stop or hold back when/if budget is achieved. Ensuring that the company has buffers for those territories that miss their budgets.

A simple three-step plan may include the following:

**Figure 20:** SIP Accelerator Curve

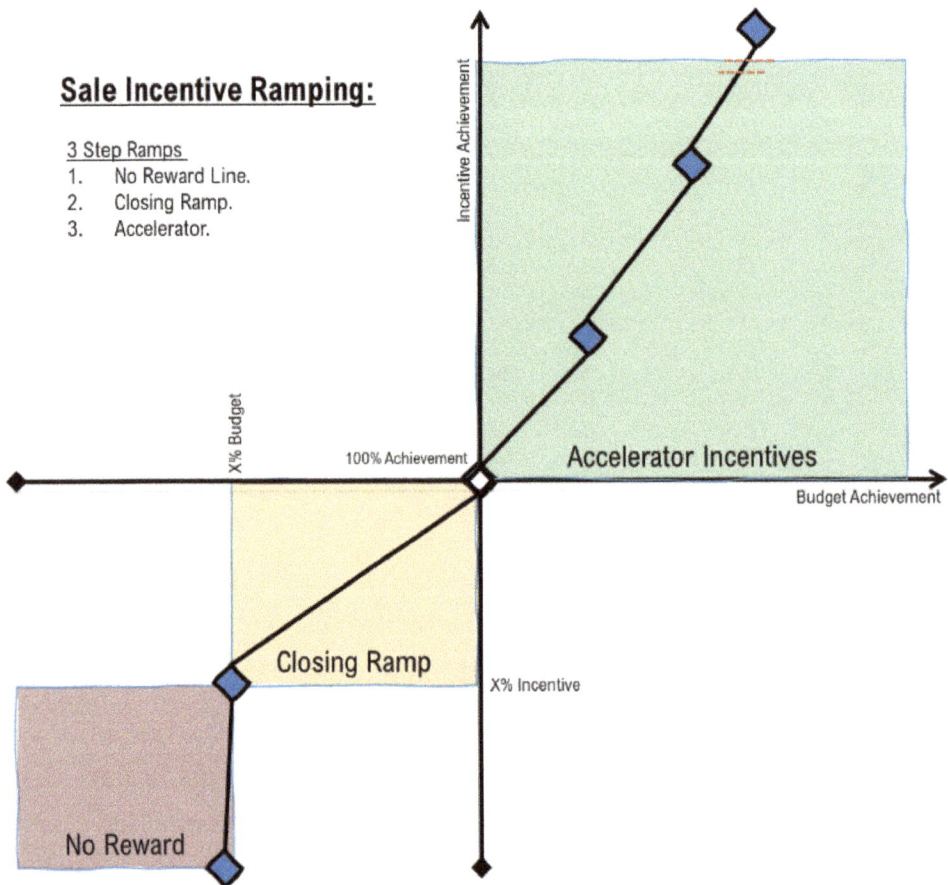

**Sale Incentive Ramping:**

3 Step Ramps
1.   No Reward Line.
2.   Closing Ramp.
3.   Accelerator.

Incentive Achievement

X% Budget

100% Achievement

Accelerator Incentives

Budget Achievement

Closing Ramp

X% Incentive

No Reward

In my experience some overachieving reps will stop or slow down when they have achieved their budgets to hold reserves to ensure they achieve next year's targets. You want to ensure that every rep brings everything to the table every year.

# RELEVANCE:

The appropriate weighting of result versus activity targets depends on the specific sales strategy, the length of the sales cycle, and the complexity of the sales role. In sales environments where results are directly and quickly influenced by individual sales representative actions (e.g., transactional sales), a higher weighting on result targets might be appropriate. In longer sales cycles or when team selling is involved, a greater emphasis on activity targets or a more balanced approach might be necessary. The relevance lens prompts you to consider the specific characteristics of your sales environment and the impact of the bonus structure on sales representative motivation and the achievement of business objectives. It also highlights the importance of aligning incentives with the desired long-term strategic outcomes.

# CHAPTER 10:

# Sales Structures

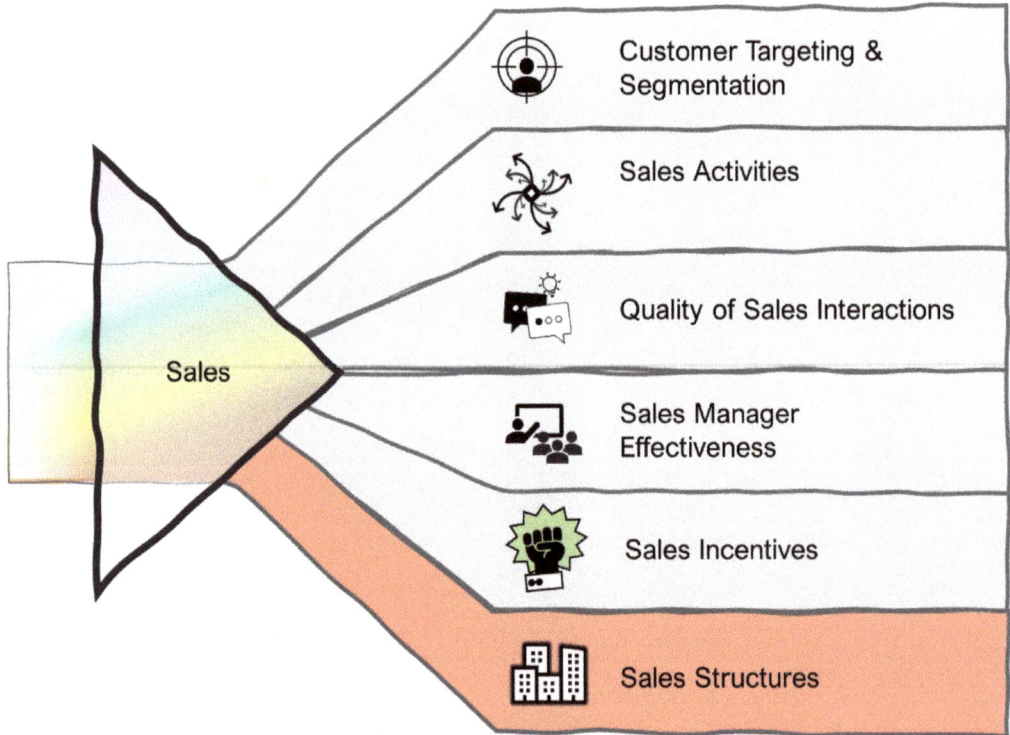

# SALES TEAM STRUCTURE:

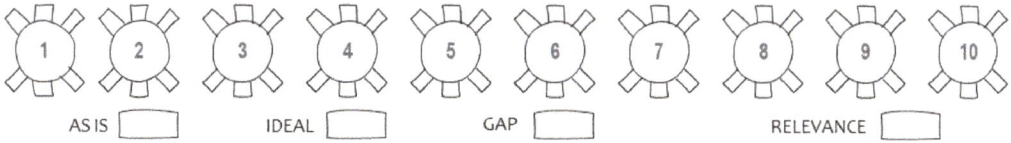

AS IS [　　]     IDEAL [　　]     GAP [　　]     RELEVANCE [　　]

## AS IS:

How is your sales force currently structured? Are roles and responsibilities clearly defined and communicated? Are there any overlaps or gaps in responsibilities? How is coordination achieved between different sales roles or teams that interact with the same customer (e.g., account managers, product specialists, inside sales, technical sales)? How are synergies across product groups leveraged (e.g., cross-selling, bundled offerings)? Is there a clear rationale for using contract sales organisations (CSOs) or co-promotion partners, and how is their performance monitored and evaluated? How well does the current structure support the sales strategy and meet the needs of the market?

## IDEAL:

Ideally, the sales force structure is aligned with the specific characteristics of the market, the complexity of the product/service portfolio, and the overall sales strategy. Roles and responsibilities are clearly defined, with minimal overlap or gaps. There would be effective coordination mechanisms to ensure seamless customer interactions and leverage synergies across product groups. The use of CSOs or co-promotion partners would be strategically justified and carefully managed to maximize effectiveness and return on investment. The structure would be adaptable to changes in the market or business strategy.

## RELEVANCE:

The importance of an effectively structured sales force depends on factors such as the size and complexity of the market, the diversity of the customer base, and the competitive landscape. In large and complex markets with diverse customer needs, a well-structured sales force is crucial for achieving sales objectives. This is similar for technical or value based sales where sales may require a team. In smaller or more homogenous markets, a simpler structure might be sufficient. The relevance lens prompts you to consider the specific characteristics of your market and the impact of sales force structure on sales effectiveness and customer satisfaction.

# SALES RESOURCE DEPLOYMENT CRITERIA:

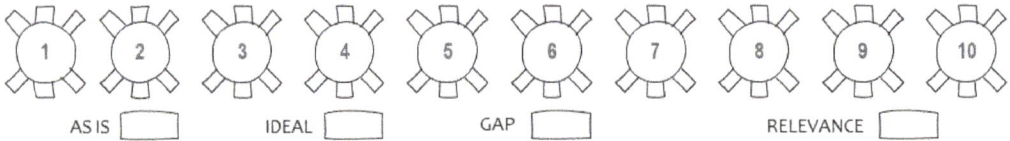

AS IS [    ]     IDEAL [    ]     GAP [    ]     RELEVANCE [    ]

## AS IS:

Reflect on your current approach to using sales agents versus direct staff. Are the criteria for choosing one over the other clearly defined? Or are these decisions made on an ad-hoc basis? If you use sales agents, how effectively are they managed? Are they provided with clear targets, regular coaching, and performance feedback? Are their incentives aligned with your overall sales strategy? Honestly evaluating these aspects will highlight areas for improvement in your agent management strategy.

## IDEAL:

Ideally, the decision to use sales agents or direct staff should be based on a clear strategic rationale, considering factors like market coverage, cost-effectiveness, and specialized expertise. If you utilize sales agents, they are treated as an extension of your sales team, receiving proper onboarding, training, and ongoing support. This includes clear segmentation and targeting guidelines, defined activity levels, regular coaching, performance management, and appropriate incentives that motivate them to achieve shared goals.

## RELEVANCE:

Effectively managing sales agents is crucial for maximizing their contribution to your sales efforts. Using agents can be a cost-effective way to expand market reach or access specialized expertise. However, simply hiring agents without proper management will likely yield disappointing results. This area is highly relevant if you currently use or are considering using sales agents. Effective management, including clear criteria for deployment and a robust support system, is essential for maximizing their ROI and achieving your sales objectives.

# Section Conclusion

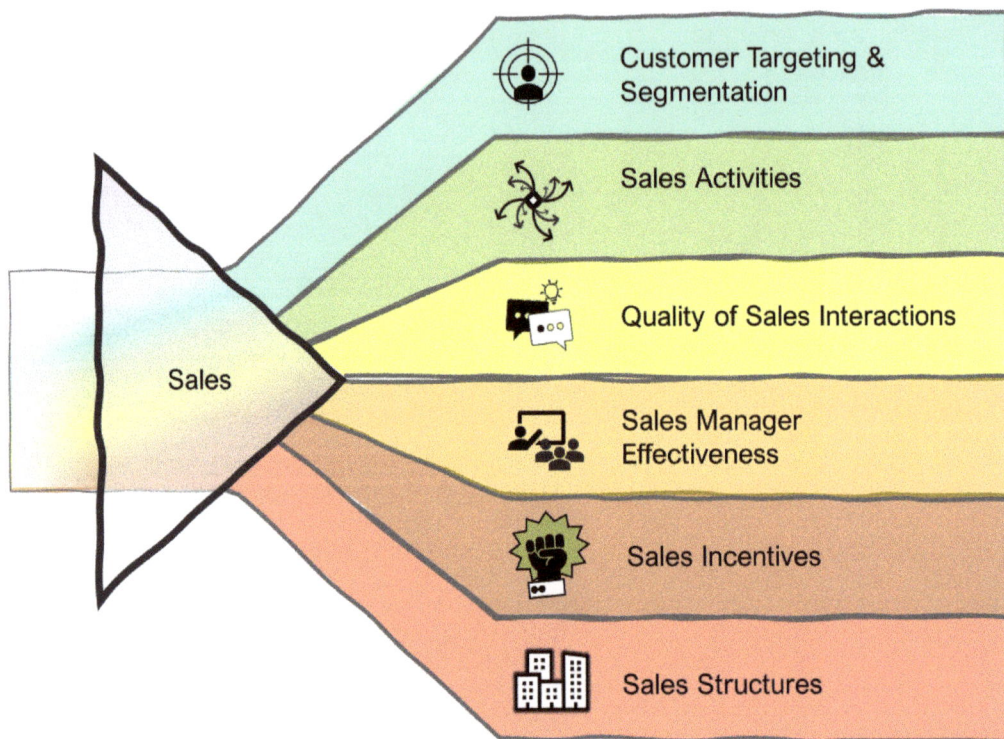

Customer Targeting & Segmentation

Sales Activities

Quality of Sales Interactions

Sales Manager Effectiveness

Sales Incentives

Sales Structures

Sales

**Transfer the ratings at the beginning of each chapter here:**

| Chapter | AS IS | Ideal | Gap | Relevance |
|---|---|---|---|---|
| Customer Targeting | | | | |
| Sales Direction | | | | |
| Quality of Interactions | | | | |
| Sales Manager Effectiveness | | | | |
| Sales Incentives | | | | |
| Sales Structures | | | | |

Is there one particular area that is better or worse than the others?

Plot the chapters into the strategy box plot.

# SALES BOX PLOT:

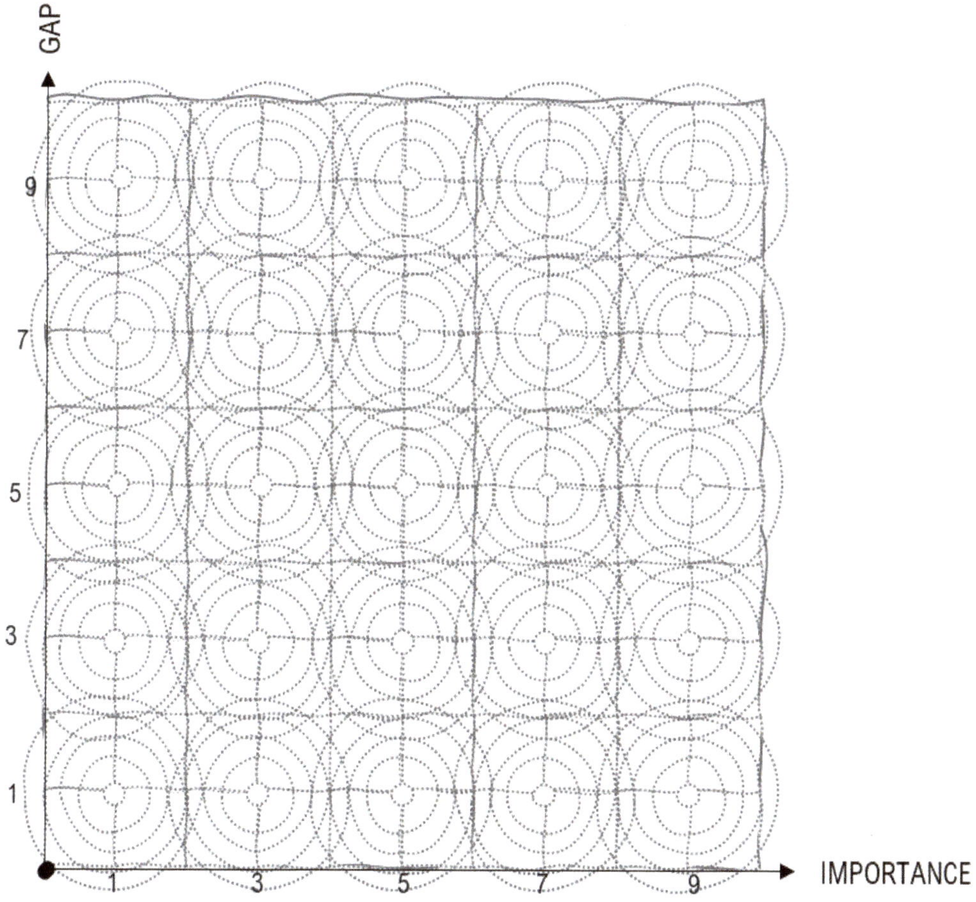
GAP
9
7
5
3
1
1
3
5
7
9
IMPORTANCE

# SALES OVERALL EVALUATION:

Looking at the box plot what is your assessment of Sales?

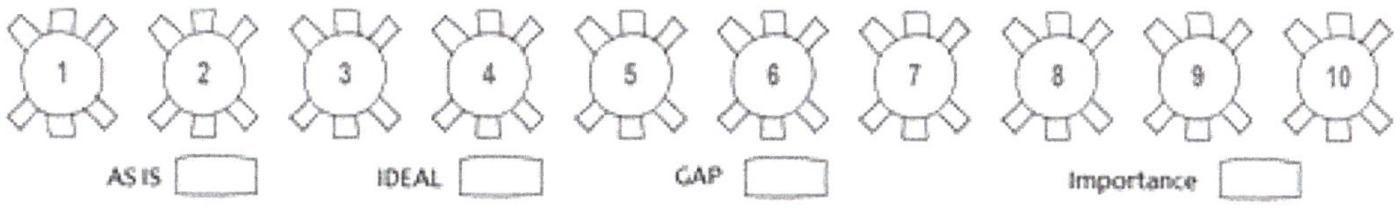
1
2
3
4
5
6
7
8
9
10
AS IS
IDEAL
GAP
Importance

# SECTION 3: MARKETING

The Demand Creator and

Lead Generation Machine

Strategy

Sales

Marketing

Key Accounts

Services

Channel Management

Finance & Pricing

Are your marketing efforts a beacon of brilliance or a dim flicker in a crowded marketplace? In today's digital age, effective marketing isn't just about broadcasting your message—it's about creating meaningful connections with your target audience. This chapter challenges you to critically examine your marketing strategies, brand positioning, and customer engagement tactics. Are you truly leveraging data-driven insights to drive your marketing decisions, or are you relying on outdated assumptions? Let's explore how to align your marketing initiatives with your overall business strategy, ensuring that every campaign not only captures attention but also drives measurable business results in an increasingly competitive landscape.

In this section we will look at how the business conducts its marketing activities. To do this we will break it down into five spectrum areas:

**Figure 21:** The 5 Wavelengths of Marketing

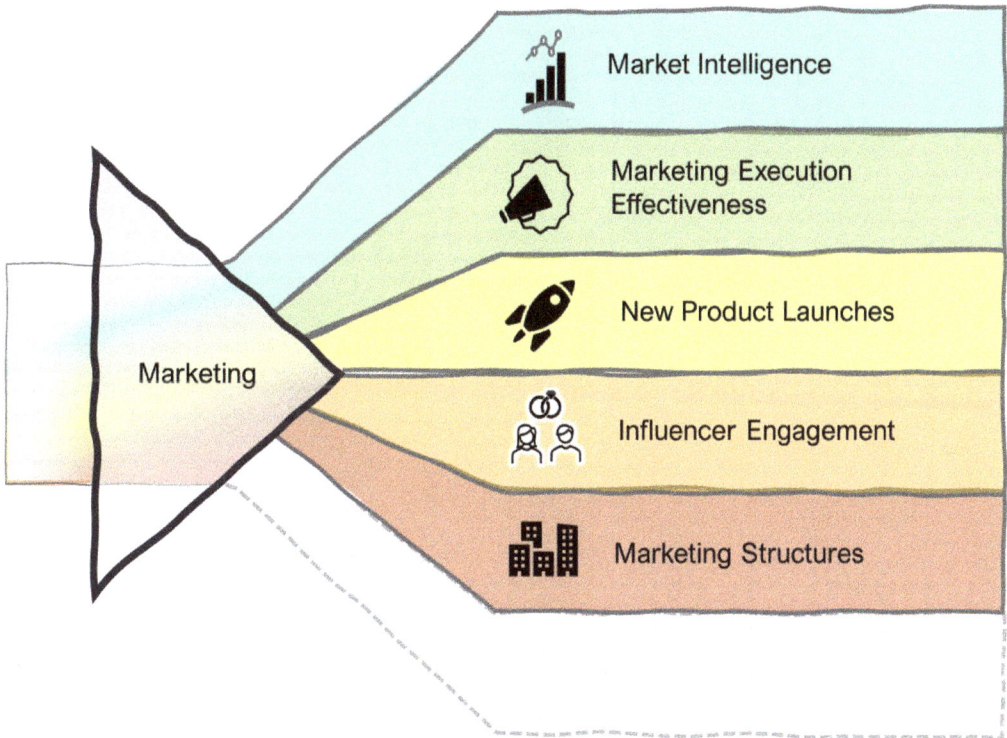

# CHAPTER 11:

# Market Intelligence

Score this chapter here

| 1 | 2 | 3 | 4 | 5 | 6 | 7 | 8 | 9 | 10 |

AS IS [     ]     IDEAL [     ]     GAP [     ]     RELEVANCE [     ]

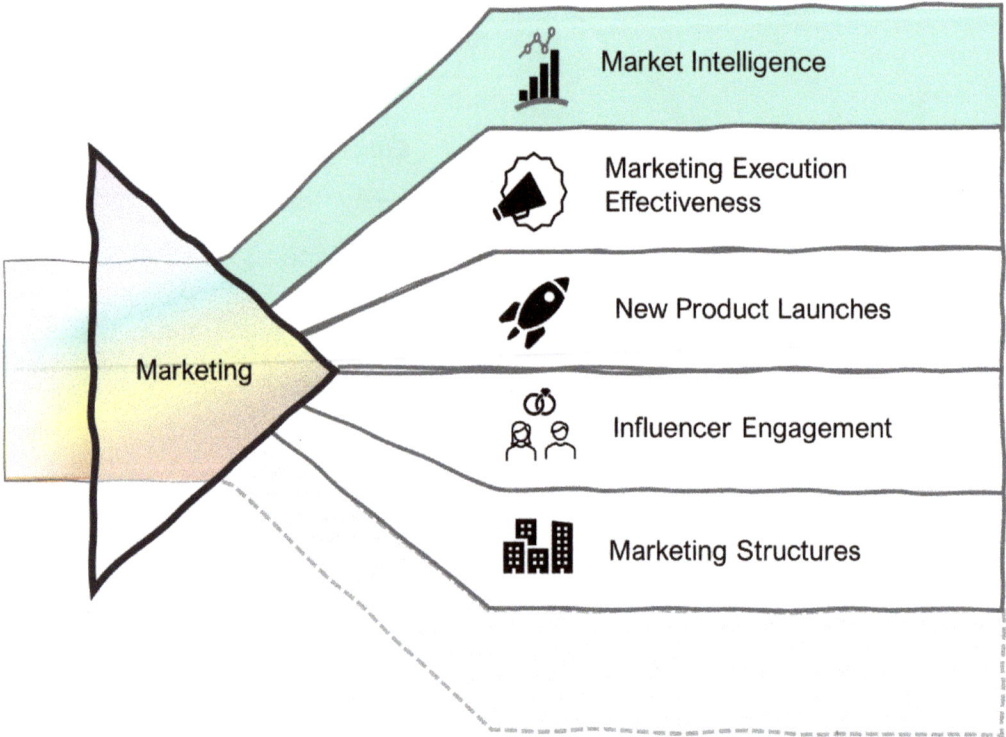

- Market Intelligence
- Marketing Execution Effectiveness
- New Product Launches
- Influencer Engagement
- Marketing Structures

Marketing

In this chapter we will look at how the organisation gains its understanding of what is happening in the marketplace, what its competitors are doing, and how it incorporates these learnings into driving the business.

# MARKET AND COMPETITIVE INTELLIGENCE:

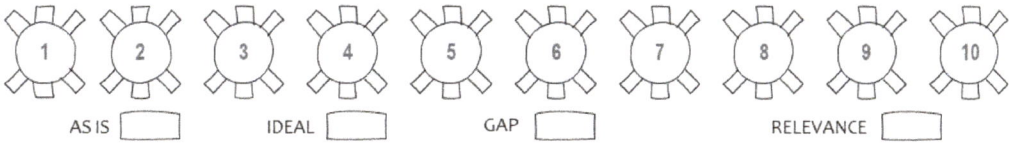

Table with positions 1-10, each labeled.

AS IS [    ]     IDEAL [    ]     GAP [    ]     RELEVANCE [    ]

## AS IS:

Consider your current understanding of your market. Do you have concrete data on market size and growth, or are your estimates based on assumptions? Do you accurately track your own and your competitors' market share? How well do you understand your competitors' strategies, positioning, and marketing activities? Are you aware of their strengths, weaknesses, and potential vulnerabilities? Honestly assessing your knowledge in these areas will reveal potential blind spots. How does the business find data on its competitors? Are there paid reports available? Are competitors public companies where financial statements and annual reports are available? Are there other sources of information such as customers, KOLs etc?

## IDEAL:

In an ideal scenario, you possess a deep and data-driven understanding of your market environment. This includes accurate information on market size, growth trends, and competitive dynamics. You have a clear picture of your own and your competitors' market share and share of mind. You understand your competitors' strategies, target audiences, and marketing tactics. This comprehensive understanding allows you to anticipate market changes, identify opportunities, and develop effective competitive strategies.

## RELEVANCE:

A thorough understanding of your market and competitive landscape is essential for making informed business decisions. This knowledge is crucial for identifying growth opportunities and staying ahead of the competition. If you lack accurate market data or a clear understanding of your competitors, this statement is highly relevant. Investing in market research and competitive analysis will provide valuable insights to guide your marketing and sales efforts.

# COMPETITIVE DIFFERENTIATION:

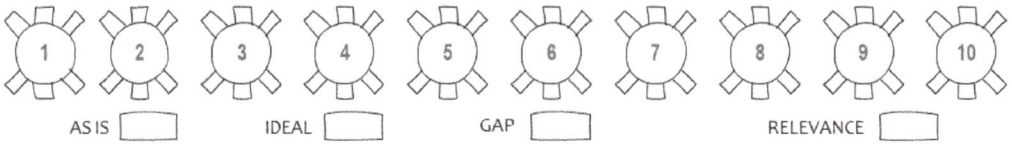

AS IS [ ]   IDEAL [ ]   GAP [ ]   RELEVANCE [ ]

## AS IS:

How well can you articulate the unique value proposition (UVP) of your products? Can you clearly explain how they differ from the competition in terms of features, benefits, and overall value? Do you understand how your competitors position their products in the market? Are you aware of their strategies for countering your marketing messages? Evaluating these aspects will reveal potential weaknesses in your competitive positioning.

## IDEAL:

Ideally, you have a crystal-clear understanding of your product differentiation and your competitors' marketing strategies. You can articulate your unique value proposition (UVP) concisely and persuasively. You understand how your competitors position their products and how they attempt to counter your marketing efforts. This knowledge allows you to develop effective marketing messages that highlight your key differentiators and resonate with your target audience.

## RELEVANCE:

Clear product differentiation is essential for standing out in a crowded marketplace. Effectively communicating your unique value proposition can be a key for driving of growth. If you struggle to articulate how your products are different or if you are unaware of your competitors' marketing tactics, this area is highly relevant. Investing in understanding your differentiation and competitive marketing strategies will improve your messaging and market positioning.

# CUSTOMER-CENTRIC MARKETING AND SALES ALIGNMENT:

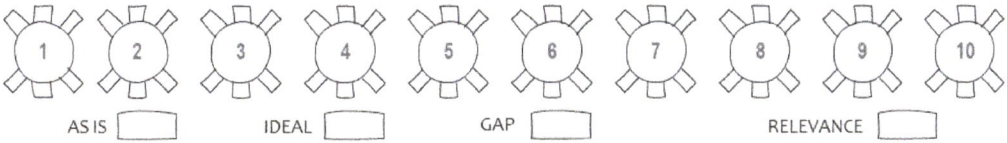

AS IS [_____]  IDEAL [_____]  GAP [_____]  RELEVANCE [_____]

## AS IS:

Consider your understanding of your customers' buying journey. Do you know the steps they take from initial awareness to final purchase? Do you know who is involved in the decision-making process? Does your marketing and sales process align with this customer journey? Evaluating these aspects will reveal potential gaps in your customer understanding.

## IDEAL:

Ideally, you have a deep understanding of your customers' purchasing process and the individuals involved in the decision-making unit. Your marketing and sales processes is tailored to address each stage of the customer journey, engaging with the relevant decision-makers. This ensures that your messaging is timely, relevant, and persuasive.

## RELEVANCE:

Understanding the customer's purchasing process is crucial for effective marketing and sales. Tailoring your approach to the specific needs of your target audience can significantly improve conversion rates. If you lack a clear understanding of the customer journey or the decision-making unit, this area is highly relevant. Investing in customer research will provide valuable insights to optimize your marketing and sales processes.

# CUSTOMER DRIVEN PROCESS ALIGNMENT:

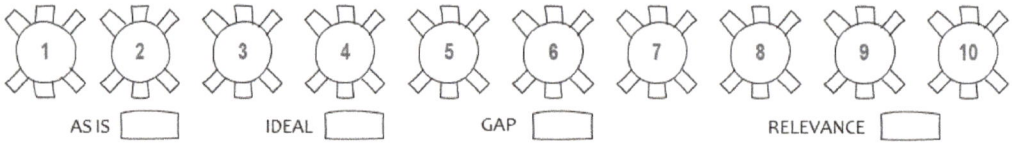

AS IS [ ]    IDEAL [ ]    GAP [ ]    RELEVANCE [ ]

## AS IS:

How well do you understand the internal workings of your key customers' organisations? Do you know their internal approval processes, timelines, and the roles of different stakeholders? Does your internal coordination align with these customer processes? Evaluating these aspects will highlight potential areas for improvement in your customer relationship management.

## IDEAL:

Ideally, your marketing and sales processes are aligned with the internal decision-making processes of your key customers. You understand their timelines, approval hierarchies, and the responsibilities of different stakeholders. Your internal teams are effectively coordinated to ensure a seamless and efficient experience for your customers.

## RELEVANCE:

Aligning with your customers' internal processes can significantly improve your chances of closing deals and building strong relationships. Understanding and adapting to the specific needs of key repeat customers is essential for long-term success. If you lack insights into your customers' internal workings or if your internal coordination is lacking, this area is highly relevant. Investing in understanding your key customers' organisational structures and processes will improve your sales effectiveness and customer satisfaction. For micro businesses this may be for a small number of high repeat sales. For business that have low or no repeat products this may also affect the relevance (either up or down).

# ACTIONABLE MARKET SEGMENTATIONS:

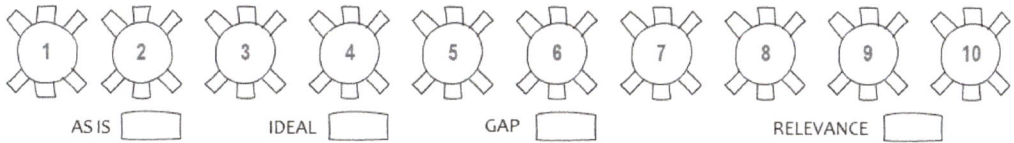

1  2  3  4  5  6  7  8  9  10

AS IS [　]　　IDEAL [　]　　GAP [　]　　RELEVANCE [　]

## AS IS:

Consider your current market segmentation. Are your segments clearly defined and differentiated? Are they based on relevant criteria such as demographics, needs, or behaviours? Are the sizes of these segments accurately estimated? Does your segmentation effectively guide your commercial activities? Evaluating these aspects will reveal potential weaknesses in your segmentation strategy.

## IDEAL:

Ideally, you have a well-defined and actionable market segmentation that clusters prospects into distinct and clearly sized segments. These segments are based on relevant criteria and provide valuable insights to guide your marketing, sales, and product development efforts. This segmentation allows you to tailor your messaging, offerings, and strategies to the specific needs of each segment. Depending upon your industry they may be product / feature / demographic / disease state / ego or character or even professional segments. Ideally within a market segment the customer targeting segmentation can be used to further narrow and target messaging.

## RELEVANCE:

Effective customer segmentation is essential for targeting your marketing and sales efforts effectively. Focusing on specific customer segments can significantly improve ROI. If your segmentation is weak or non-existent, this area is highly relevant. Investing in developing a robust customer segmentation strategy will improve your targeting and resource allocation.

# DEPARTMENTAL SEGMENTATION ALIGNMENT:

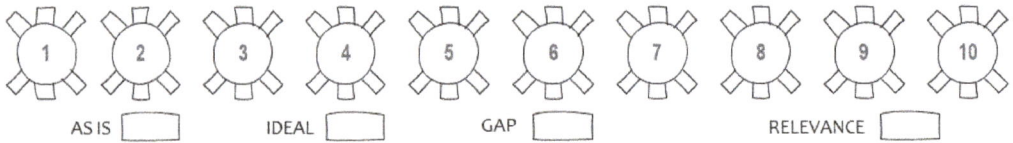

| 1 | 2 | 3 | 4 | 5 | 6 | 7 | 8 | 9 | 10 |

AS IS [    ]    IDEAL [    ]    GAP [    ]    RELEVANCE [    ]

## AS IS:

Consider how your customer segmentation is used across different departments. Is there a shared understanding and consistent application of the segmentation across Sales, Key Account Management, Marketing, Pricing, and Remote Selling Teams? Or are there discrepancies and inconsistencies in how the segments are defined and used? Evaluating this alignment will highlight potential areas for improved cross-functional collaboration.

## IDEAL:

In the ideal scenario, your customer segmentation is fully aligned across all relevant departments. Sales, Key Account Management, Marketing, Pricing, and Remote Selling Teams share a common understanding of the segments and use them consistently to guide their activities. This alignment ensures a coordinated and consistent customer experience.

## RELEVANCE:

Alignment across departments is crucial for maximizing the effectiveness of your customer segmentation. For micro businesses this may not be relevant as the teams are likely to be 1-2 people. Ensuring that all customer-facing teams agree is important for delivering a consistent brand experience and maximizing sales effectiveness. For businesses over the $50 million turnover range this area can be a source of improvements and more relevant. If there are discrepancies in how the segmentation is used across departments, this area is highly relevant. Investing in cross-functional communication and training will improve alignment and optimize your commercial activities.

# PRODUCT OFFERING TARGETS AND MESSAGING:

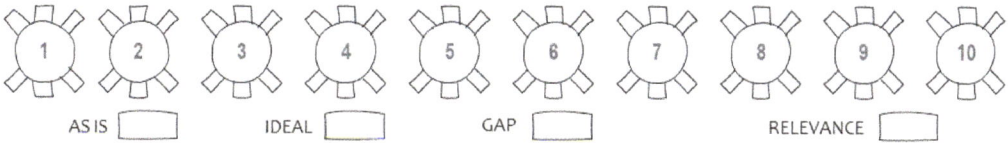

AS IS [        ]    IDEAL [        ]    GAP [        ]    RELEVANCE [        ]

## AS IS:

Does your customer segmentation effectively guide your product offerings and messaging? Does it help you understand which products and solutions are most relevant to each segment? Does it inform your messaging strategy, including how you position your offerings against competitors? Evaluating these aspects will reveal potential gaps in how your segmentation is used to drive commercial activities.

## IDEAL:

Ideally, your customer segmentation provides clear guidance on which products and solutions to offer to each segment and how to tailor your messaging accordingly. It also informs your competitive messaging strategy, including how to "counter-sell" competitors' products. This ensures that your marketing and sales efforts are targeted, relevant, and persuasive.

## RELEVANCE:

Using your segmentation to guide product offerings and messaging is essential for maximizing the impact of your marketing and sales efforts. For micro businesses this may be of higher importance because of the cost to acquire each new customer and that customer will make a bigger impact relative to the business's size. Tailoring your approach to specific customer needs and preferences can significantly improve conversion rates. If your segmentation does not effectively inform your product and messaging strategies, this area is highly relevant. Investing in developing a more actionable segmentation will improve your targeting and commercial effectiveness.

# ACTIONABLE INSIGHTS THROUGH STRATEGIC TOOLS:

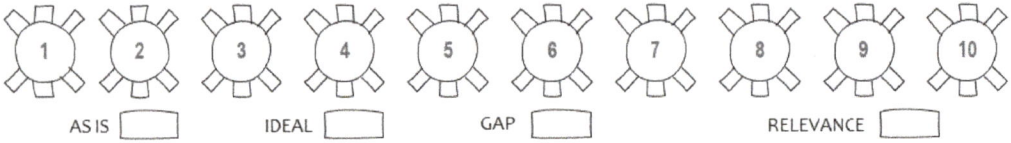

AS IS [ ]    IDEAL [ ]    GAP [ ]    RELEVANCE [ ]

## AS IS:

Consider how you currently synthesize customer, market, and internal insights. Do you use a structured framework or tool, such as a SWOT analysis? Or are these insights scattered across different documents and presentations? How actionable are the insights you generate? Reflecting on these questions will reveal potential gaps in your insight management process. When customers or prospects ask for something how is this captured? Does marketing have access to customer groups? Or focus groups? How are these groups used to improve marketing, messaging and new products or services?

## IDEAL:

Ideally, you will have a system that captures customer insights and stores them for analysis and processing. You will have a system to analyse, improve and beta test marketing activities and messaging. This process will be linked into the new product development and strategic processes of the business.

## RELEVANCE:

Effectively summarizing and utilizing insights is crucial for developing sound product strategies. Having a clear and actionable overview of the market and competitive landscape is essential for making informed decisions. If you lack a structured approach to summarizing insights, this area is highly relevant. If you can draw strategic incites, craft better messaging from focus or customer groups this area is important for the business.

# INSIGHT-DRIVEN PRODUCT STRATEGIES:

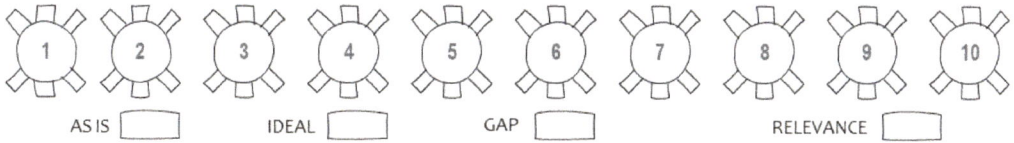

AS IS [ ]    IDEAL [ ]    GAP [ ]    RELEVANCE [ ]

## AS IS:

How well do your product strategies reflect customer and market realities? Are they based on solid data and insights, or are they driven by internal assumptions or opinions? Do you regularly analyse market size and growth, customer needs and drivers, and competitor activities to inform your product decisions? Evaluating these aspects will reveal potential gaps in your product strategy development process.

## IDEAL:

Ideally, your product strategies are firmly rooted in deep customer and market insights. This includes a thorough understanding of market size and growth, customer needs and pain points, and competitors' strategies and positioning. This data-driven approach ensures that your product development efforts are aligned with market demand and customer needs.

## RELEVANCE:

Basing product strategies on solid insights is crucial for developing successful products. Understanding customer needs and market dynamics is essential for achieving product-market fit and driving growth. If your product strategies are not based on robust data and insights, this area is highly relevant. Investing in market research and customer analysis will improve your product development success rate.

# MARKETING STRATEGY PLANNING:

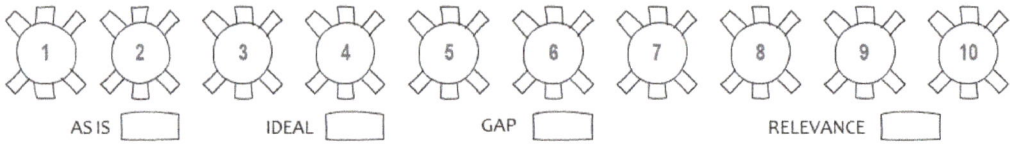

| 1 | 2 | 3 | 4 | 5 | 6 | 7 | 8 | 9 | 10 |

AS IS [ ]    IDEAL [ ]    GAP [ ]    RELEVANCE [ ]

## AS IS:

Consider your current marketing planning process. Is it a systematic and structured process, or is it more ad-hoc and reactive? Do you develop formal marketing strategies and objectives regularly, at least annually? Do you follow a marketing process or strategy? Is it published? Evaluating these aspects will reveal potential gaps in your marketing planning process.

## IDEAL:

Ideally, you have a well-defined and systematic marketing planning process that takes place at least annually. This process involves setting clear marketing objectives, developing strategies to achieve those objectives, and allocating resources effectively. This structured approach ensures that your marketing efforts are aligned with your overall business goals. The approach is based upon a proven marketing methodology. Outcomes from the marketing planning are used as inputs into other departments such as sales, Key Accounts, R&D and Services. The marketing strategy as a clear link between marketing and the sales process and links to the business objectives from Strategy. This would include an objective for both the business and marketing, a source of the volume, segment, targeting and positioning which flow into the 4P's as seen in the "Big Picture" marketing process (Dapena-Baron C. N., 2015) which is the best I've seen.

## RELEVANCE:

A systematic marketing planning process is crucial for maximizing the effectiveness of your marketing investments. Having a clear marketing plan is essential for achieving sustainable growth. If your marketing planning is ad-hoc or infrequent, this area is highly relevant. Implementing a structured planning process will improve your marketing effectiveness and ROI.

# PRODUCT AND VALUE PROPOSITION:

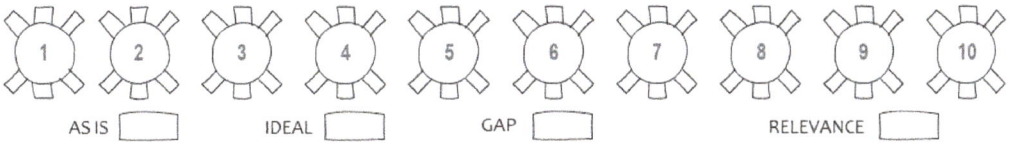

AS IS [    ]   IDEAL [    ]   GAP [    ]   RELEVANCE [    ]

## AS IS:

How clearly defined is the positioning of your products and services? Can you articulate their unique value proposition (UVP) in a concise and interesting way? How well does this positioning differentiate you from the competition? Evaluating these aspects will reveal potential weaknesses in your brand and product positioning.

## IDEAL:

Ideally, the positioning of your products and services is clearly defined, simple and widely understood, both internally and externally. You can articulate their UVP in an interesting way that resonates with your target audience and clearly differentiates you from the competition. The UVP is simple yet powerful. It's linked to the products features allowing the prospect or customer to easily see or draw a value conclusion.

## RELEVANCE:

Clear product and service positioning is essential for attracting and retaining customers. A strong and differentiated positioning can be a key driver of growth. If your positioning is unclear or weak, this area is highly relevant. Investing in defining and communicating your value proposition will improve your brand recognition and market share.

# VALUE PROOFS:

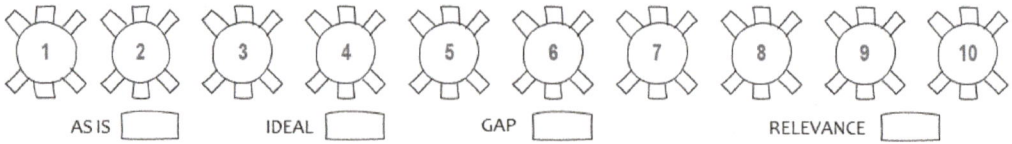

| | | | |
|---|---|---|---|
| AS IS | IDEAL | GAP | RELEVANCE |

Prospects are sceptical. They need proof sources to confirm the benefits that you provide so they can draw what benefit it is for them.

## AS IS:

How well do you substantiate the positioning of your products and services? Do you have clear value proofs, such as clinical outcomes, economic data, customer testimonials, patient stories or competitive comparisons, to support your claims? Or are your positioning areas based on assumptions or marketing hype? Evaluating these aspects will reveal potential weaknesses in your value communication.

## IDEAL:

Ideally, you substantiate the positioning of your products and services with robust value proofs, including relevant data such as clinical outcomes (if applicable), economic considerations, customer testimonials, patient stories and clear comparisons to the competition. These proofs are published and peer reviewed or challenge tested, ideally by independent authorities. For the medical device and diagnostic industry this is usually scientific journals. This data-driven approach enhances credibility and strengthens your value proposition.

## RELEVANCE:

Substantiating your positioning with clear value proofs is essential for building trust and credibility with your target audience. Demonstrating the value of your offerings is crucial for winning customers and gaining market share. If you lack strong value proofs, this area is highly relevant. Investing in gathering and presenting interesting data will significantly strengthen your marketing and sales efforts.

# CHAPTER 12:

# Marketing Execution Effectiveness

1   2   3   4   5   6   7   8   9   10

AS IS [        ]        IDEAL [        ]        GAP [        ]        RELEVANCE [        ]

Market Intelligence

Marketing Execution Effectiveness

New Product Launches

Influencer Engagement

Marketing Structures

Marketing

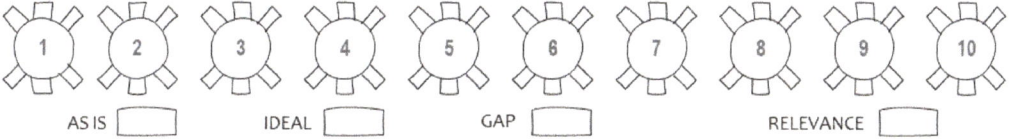

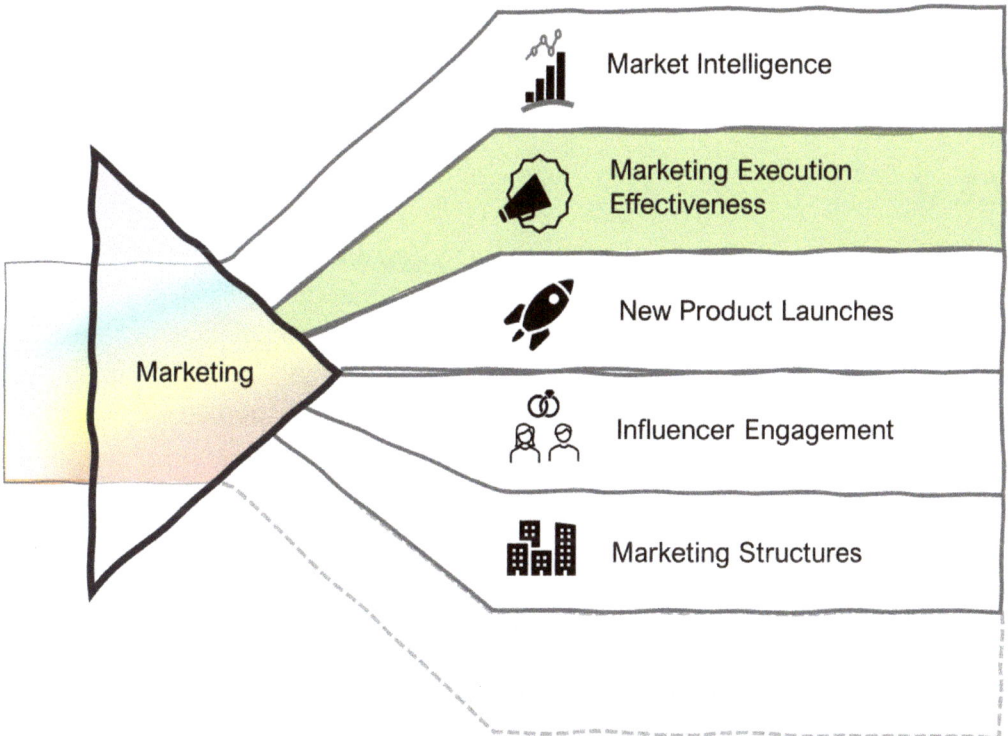

*In this chapter we will examine how the organisation executes its marketing activities.*

# SYSTEMATIC RESOURCE ALLOCATION AND OPTIMIZATION:

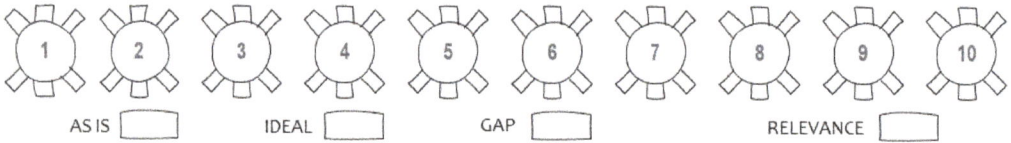

AS IS [ ]    IDEAL [ ]    GAP [ ]    RELEVANCE [ ]

## AS IS:

How do you currently allocate your commercial resources, including marketing field force deployment and promotional budget? Is it a systematic process with regular reviews and adjustments, or is it more ad-hoc and reactive? Do you have a documented plan that outlines how resources are allocated and why? Reflecting on these questions will reveal potential gaps in your marketing resource allocation process? Is your marketing spend / time / effort even across marketing areas (trade events, advertising, lead generation, marketing intel) or is one area taking more of the resources?

## IDEAL:

Ideally, you have a well-defined process for systematically planning and optimizing your commercial resource allocation at least annually. This process involves analysing market trends, customer needs, and competitive dynamics to determine the most effective deployment of your marketing field force and allocation of your promotional budget. This ensures that resources are used efficiently and effectively to achieve your commercial objectives.

## RELEVANCE:

Effective resource allocation is crucial for maximizing your return on investment in commercial activities. Optimizing resource allocation can significantly affect profitability and growth. If your current process is not systematic or regular, this area is highly relevant. Implementing a structured planning process will improve your resource utilization and commercial effectiveness.

# DATA-DRIVEN MARKETING EFFECTIVENESS:

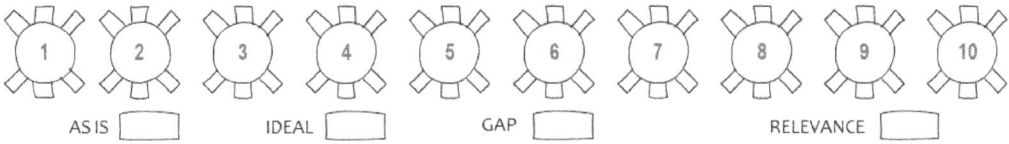

| 1 | 2 | 3 | 4 | 5 | 6 | 7 | 8 | 9 | 10 |

AS IS [        ]          IDEAL [        ]          GAP [        ]          RELEVANCE [        ]

## AS IS:

How do you currently measure the effectiveness of your marketing activities? Do you have systems in place to track key metrics and analyse the impact of different campaigns and initiatives? Or is your understanding of marketing effectiveness based on anecdotal evidence or gut feelings? Evaluating these aspects will reveal potential gaps in your marketing measurement and analysis? Can you truly calculate an ROI for marketing activities?

## IDEAL:

Ideally, you have a robust system for tracking and analysing the impact of your marketing activities. This includes defining clear key performance indicators (KPIs), implementing tracking mechanisms, and regularly analysing the data to understand what's working and what's not.

## RELEVANCE:

Measuring marketing effectiveness is essential for demonstrating ROI and making informed decisions about future investments. ROI is very difficult to measure. Over longer-term sales cycles linking marketing activities to a successful sales can be difficult. However, measuring the spend and movement through the lead generation areas Awareness Interest Desire (AID) can help narrow the gap. Demonstrating the value of marketing activities is crucial for securing resources and achieving growth objectives. If you lack a systematic approach to tracking marketing impact, this area is highly relevant. Implementing a robust measurement system will improve your marketing accountability and effectiveness.

# DIGITAL MARKETING ADOPTION:

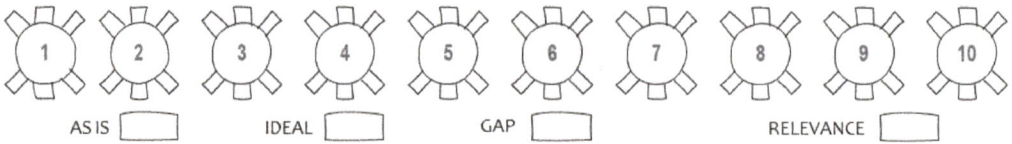

AS IS [        ]    IDEAL [        ]    GAP [        ]    RELEVANCE [        ]

Are you still printing? If so, why?

## AS IS:

Consider your current investment in digital marketing. Are you allocating sufficient resources to leverage digital channels and reach your target audience online? Are you keeping up with the latest digital marketing trends and technologies? Or are you relying primarily on traditional marketing methods? Evaluating these aspects will reveal potential gaps in your digital marketing strategy.

## IDEAL:

Ideally, you are investing strategically in digital marketing opportunities, allocating sufficient resources to leverage the most effective digital channels for reaching your target audience. This includes staying up-to-date with the latest trends and technologies and adapting your digital marketing strategy accordingly.

## RELEVANCE:

In today's digital landscape, investing in digital marketing is essential for reaching customers and achieving marketing objectives. A strong digital presence is crucial for competing effectively. If you are underinvesting in digital marketing, this area is highly relevant. Increasing your investment in digital channels can significantly improve your reach, engagement, and overall marketing effectiveness.

# STRATEGIC MARKETING CAMPAIGN EXECUTION AND MONITORING:

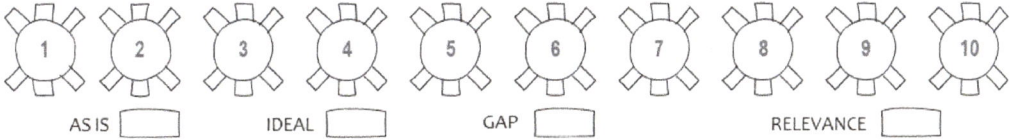

AS IS [ ]    IDEAL [ ]    GAP [ ]    RELEVANCE [ ]

## AS IS:

How do you currently plan and execute your marketing campaigns? Is there a structured process in place, including clear objectives, timelines, and responsibilities? Are the campaigns linked to your marketing objectives? Are they aligned with your UVP? Do you routinely track progress against key performance indicators (KPIs)? Do you have a process for implementing countermeasures if campaigns are not performing as expected? Evaluating these aspects will reveal potential gaps in your campaign management process.

## IDEAL:

Ideally, you have a well-defined process for planning, executing, and monitoring your marketing campaigns. This includes setting clear objectives, establishing timelines and responsibilities, tracking progress against KPIs, and implementing countermeasures as needed. This data-driven approach ensures that campaigns are executed effectively, and that performance is continuously optimized and aligned with the company UVP and marketing objectives.

## RELEVANCE:

Effective campaign management is crucial for maximizing the impact of your marketing investments. Well-planned and executed campaigns can significantly drive brand awareness, lead generation, and sales. If your campaign management process is ad-hoc, rather than systematic, then this area is highly relevant. Implementing a structured approach will improve your campaign effectiveness and ROI.

# SYSTEMATIC PRODUCT TACTICAL EXECUTION:

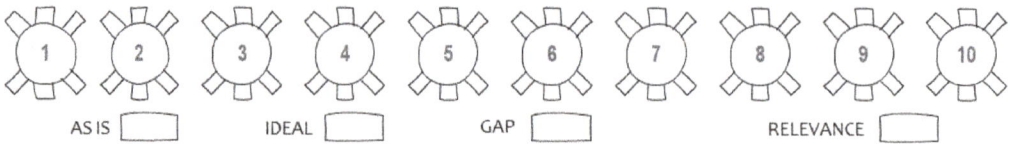

AS IS [ ]   IDEAL [ ]   GAP [ ]   RELEVANCE [ ]

This section is to reflect upon the tactics that you use within your organisation for marketing the products. For this section, tactics are defined as the method used to highlight a feature or benefit that solves the problem for example they could be: Loss aversion or fear. They could be shock or playing to a group's ego (especially good when dealing with doctors). Or focusing on improvement or more with less.

## AS IS:

How are your marketing tactics developed? Are they part of a broader product planning and strategy process? Is there a clear purpose and alignment to the UVP for the tactics? Or are tactics developed in isolation or reactively? Evaluating these aspects will reveal potential gaps in your tactical execution. Is there a bias to one type of tactic? E.g., loss aversion, shock, fear, ego or improvement.

## IDEAL:

Ideally, your marketing tactics are developed as an integral part of a systematic product planning and strategy process. The UVP and benefits drive the type of tactics that are used in the execution. This ensures that tactics are aligned with overall product objectives and contribute to achieving strategic goals. There are clear implementation timelines and assigned responsibilities, ensuring that tactics are executed effectively and efficiently.

## RELEVANCE:

Aligning marketing tactics with overall product strategy is crucial for maximizing their impact. A well-coordinated approach to tactical planning and execution is essential for achieving marketing objectives and driving business growth. If your tactics are not developed within a strategic framework, this area is highly relevant. Implementing a systematic planning process will improve the

146

effectiveness of your marketing efforts and contribute to achieving your business goals.

# LEAD MANAGEMENT:

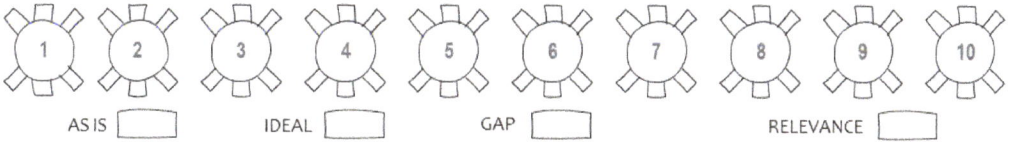

| 1 | 2 | 3 | 4 | 5 | 6 | 7 | 8 | 9 | 10 |

AS IS [  ]    IDEAL [  ]    GAP [  ]    RELEVANCE [  ]

Having a system that tracks all leads, efficiently distributes leads to sales, to ensure that every lead is captured and followed up.

## AS IS:

How does your organisation currently manage leads? Are there systems in place to track all leads from various sources (e.g., website forms, marketing campaigns, referrals)? How are leads qualified and prioritized? How efficiently are leads distributed to the appropriate sales representatives? What metrics are used to track lead response times, conversion rates, and overall lead management effectiveness? Are there any bottlenecks or inefficiencies in the current lead management process?

## IDEAL:

Ideally, your organisation should have a robust and efficient lead management process. This would involve a system for capturing and tracking all leads from various sources. Leads should be promptly qualified and prioritized based on their potential value and fit with the target customer profile. Qualified leads should be efficiently distributed to the appropriate sales representatives, ensuring timely follow-up and maximizing conversion rates. The lead management process should be continuously monitored and optimized based on key metrics such as lead response times, conversion rates, and customer acquisition cost.

# RELEVANCE:

The importance of effective lead management depends on the volume of leads generated, the complexity of the sales process, and the organisation's reliance on lead generation activities. For organisations with high-volume lead generation or complex sales cycles, a robust lead management system is crucial for maximizing sales productivity and return on investment. In smaller organisations with simpler sales processes, a less formal approach might be sufficient. The relevance lens prompts you to consider the specific needs and challenges of your organisation in terms of lead generation and management.

# CHAPTER 13:

# New Product Launches

---

1  2  3  4  5  6  7  8  9  10

AS IS ☐    IDEAL ☐    GAP ☐    RELEVANCE ☐

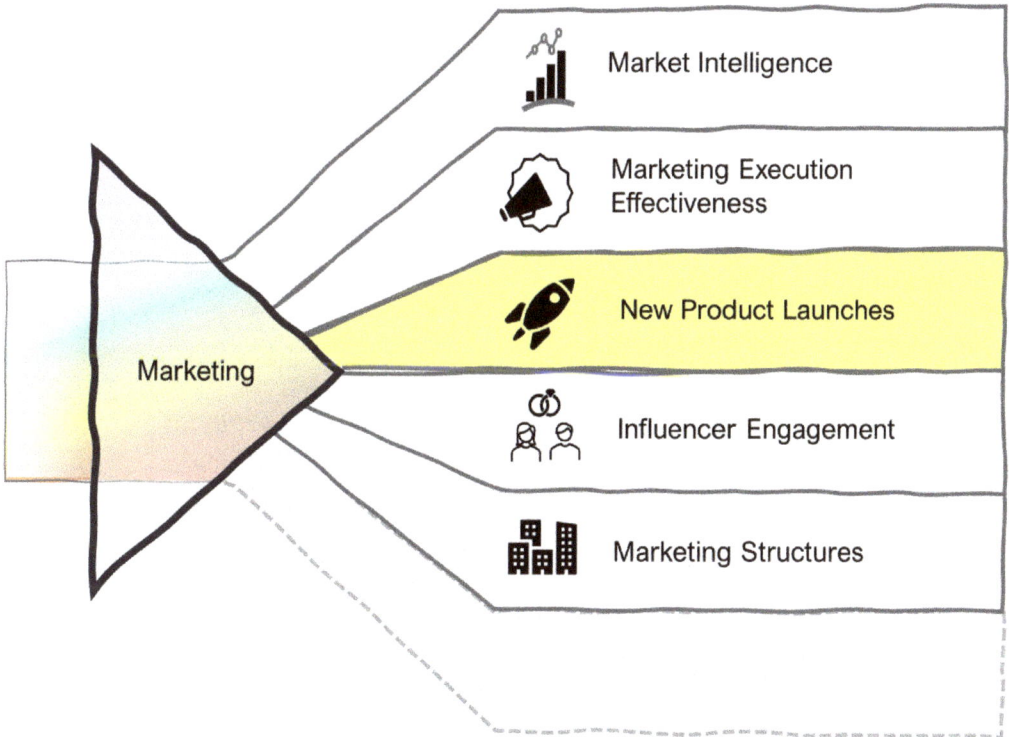

Market Intelligence

Marketing Execution Effectiveness

New Product Launches

Marketing

Influencer Engagement

Marketing Structures

# PROACTIVE AND COMPREHENSIVE LAUNCH PLANNING:

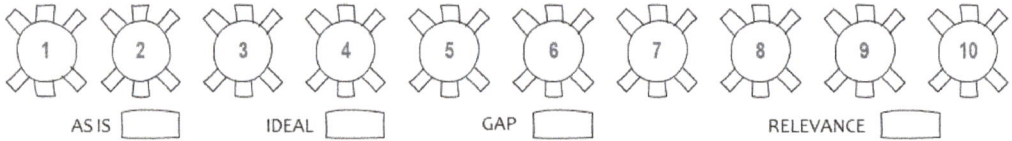

1 2 3 4 5 6 7 8 9 10

AS IS [____]    IDEAL [____]    GAP [____]    RELEVANCE [____]

## AS IS:

Think about your past product launches. How far in advance were detailed launch plans developed? Were these plans comprehensive, covering all key aspects of the launch? Or were they developed closer to the launch date, potentially leading to rushed execution and missed opportunities? Reflecting on this timeline will reveal potential areas for improvement in your launch planning process.

## IDEAL:

Ideally, detailed and comprehensive launch plans are developed 9-12 months prior to launch. This allows sufficient time for thorough planning, coordination, and execution across all relevant departments and local organisations. Collection of proof sources, testimonials and initial feedback can be incorporated, ideally with multiple iterations of the plan prior to its launch. The process of challenge testing launch planning activities is ingrained and all participants take this as process and can separate their own self-worth away from the challenges.

## RELEVANCE:

Early and comprehensive planning is crucial for successful product launches. A well-executed launch can significantly affect market penetration and revenue generation. If your launch planning process is rushed or inadequate, this area is highly relevant. Implementing a longer planning horizon will improve your launch execution and increase your chances of success.

# IN-DEPTH MARKET AND CUSTOMER ANALYSIS FOR PRODUCT LAUNCHES:

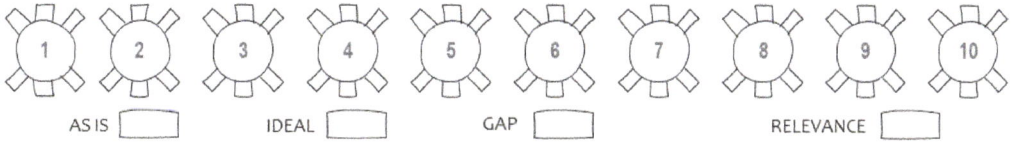

AS IS ☐   IDEAL ☐   GAP ☐   RELEVANCE ☐

## AS IS:

Before launching a new product, how thoroughly do you analyse the market and gain customer insights? Do you have a clear understanding of the market potential, competitive landscape, customer buying process, and target segments? Or are these analyses less comprehensive, potentially leading to misaligned product positioning and marketing messages? Evaluating these aspects will reveal potential gaps in your pre-launch research.

## IDEAL:

Ideally, for every launch product, you conduct a thorough market analysis, including market potential and competitive landscape, and gain a deep understanding of the customer buying process and target segments. This data-driven approach ensures that your product launch is aligned with market demand and customer needs.

## RELEVANCE:

Comprehensive market and customer understanding is essential for successful product launches. Accurate market insights and customer understanding can significantly improve product adoption and market share. If your pre-launch research is inadequate, this area is highly relevant. Investing in thorough market and customer analysis will improve your launch success rate.

# PRODUCT LAUNCH VALUE POSITION & KEY MESSAGES:

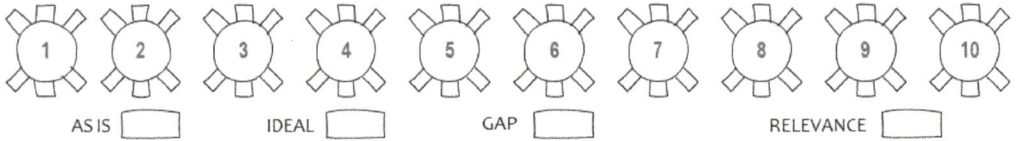

AS IS [ ]     IDEAL [ ]     GAP [ ]          RELEVANCE [ ]

## AS IS:

Before launching a new product, how clearly do you define its value proposition, product positioning, proof sources, key objections and key messages? Are these elements well-defined and consistently communicated across all marketing and sales materials? Or are they less clear, potentially leading to confusion among customers and inconsistent messaging?

## IDEAL:

Ideally, for every launch product, you clearly define the value proposition, product positioning, and key messages. You have proof sources available to support the value proposition and clear anticipated objections and methods to support the sale staff to handle objections. These elements are concise, interesting, and consistently communicated across all channels, ensuring that customers understand the unique benefits of your product.

## RELEVANCE:

A clear and interesting value proposition is essential for attracting customers and driving product adoption. Effectively communicating the value of new products is crucial for achieving launch success. If your value proposition or messaging is unclear, this area is highly relevant. If you get a large number of similar objections from this or previous launches this area is important to deep dive into. Investing in defining and communicating your value proposition will improve your product's market reception.

# COLLABORATIVE MARKET ENTRY PLANNING AND PRICING STRATEGY:

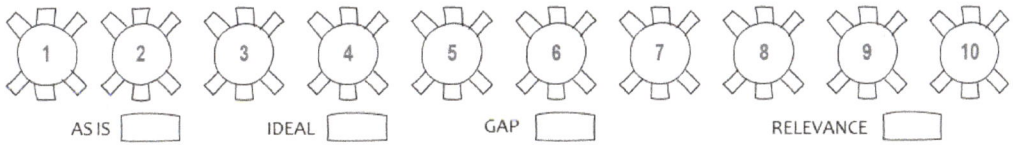

AS IS [ ]    IDEAL [ ]    GAP [ ]    RELEVANCE [ ]

## AS IS:

How closely do you collaborate with market access, health economics, and reimbursement experts during the product launch process? Do you develop a comprehensive market entry plan, including value/impact studies (if required) and a robust pricing strategy? Or is this collaboration less effective, or non-existent, potentially leading to challenges with market access, reimbursement and pricing issues related to your value proposition? Evaluating these aspects will reveal potential gaps in your market access strategy.

## IDEAL:

Ideally, you collaborate closely with market access, health economics, and reimbursement experts to develop a comprehensive market entry plan, including value/impact studies (if required) and a robust pricing and re-imbursement strategy. This collaboration ensures that your product launch is aligned with market access requirements and reimbursement policies.

## RELEVANCE:

Effective market access and reimbursement strategies are crucial for successful product launches, especially in regulated industries. Navigating market access and reimbursement complexities can be challenging but essential for achieving commercial success. If your collaboration with these experts is lacking, this area is highly relevant. Investing in a robust market access strategy will improve your product's market penetration and speed.

# KOL (INFLUENCER) ENGAGEMENT:

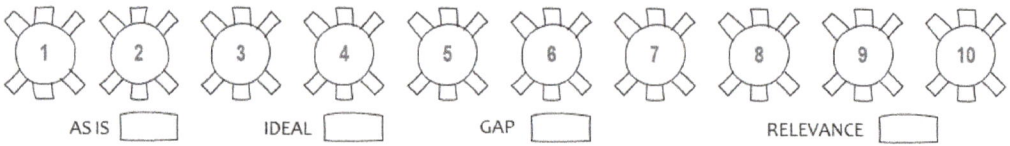

AS IS [    ]    IDEAL [    ]    GAP [    ]    RELEVANCE [    ]

This section is specifically to refer to the Key Opinion Leaders (KOL) at the launch of a new product.

## AS IS:

How effectively do you engage with key opinion leaders (KOLs) and relevant stakeholders to gain endorsements for your launch products? Do you have a clear strategy for identifying, engaging, and building relationships with these key influencers as early adopters? Or is this engagement less structured? Do you have advisory boards that are pre-launch advocates? Evaluating these aspects will reveal potential gaps in your influencer engagement strategy.

## IDEAL:

Ideally, you have a well-defined strategy for engaging with KOLs and relevant stakeholders to secure endorsements for your launch products. This includes identifying key influencers, building strong relationships, and effectively communicating the value proposition of your products. Potentially they are the source of the value proofs or heavily involved in creating the proofs.

## RELEVANCE:

Engaging with KOLs and stakeholders can significantly enhance the credibility and visibility of your launch products. Securing endorsements from respected figures in your industry can be a powerful driver of new product adoption.

# NEW LAUNCH SALES TRAINING:

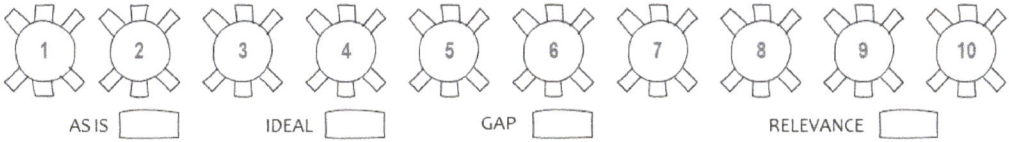

AS IS ▭    IDEAL ▭    GAP ▭    RELEVANCE ▭

## AS IS:

How effectively do you train and mobilize your sales force on new launch products? Do they receive comprehensive training on the product's features, benefits, value proposition, common objections and how to use proof sources? Are they equipped to effectively communicate this information to customers? Is the training aligner with the sales methodology, market and customer targeting segmentations? Evaluating these aspects will reveal potential gaps in your sales force training.

## IDEAL:

Ideally, your sales force receives comprehensive training on all aspects of the launch product, including its features, benefits, value proposition, competitive advantages, objection handling, the use of proof sources and incentives? The reps are equipped with the necessary tools and resources to effectively communicate this information to customers and drive sales. The training would be aligned with the selling methodologies, marketing and customer targeting segmentations.

## RELEVANCE:

A well-trained and mobilized sales force is crucial for driving early adoption of new products. Equipping your sales team with the necessary knowledge and skills is essential for achieving launch success. If your sales force training is inadequate, this area is highly relevant. Investing in comprehensive sales training will improve your product's market penetration

# NEW LAUNCH RESOURCE ALLOCATION:

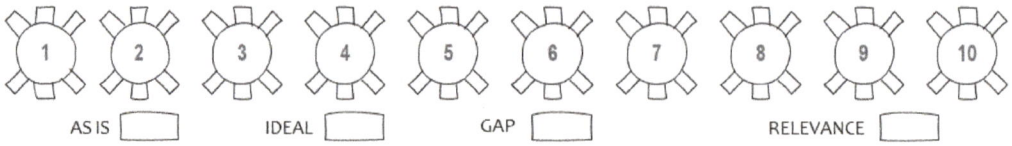

| 1 | 2 | 3 | 4 | 5 | 6 | 7 | 8 | 9 | 10 |

AS IS [＿＿]    IDEAL [＿＿]    GAP [＿＿]    RELEVANCE [＿＿]

## AS IS:

How efficiently do you ramp up the necessary resources for product launches? Are there often delays in securing resources or completing key launch activities? Or is the resource allocation process well-managed, ensuring timely execution of launch plans? Evaluating these aspects will reveal potential bottlenecks in your launch execution.

## IDEAL:

Ideally, you efficiently ramp up the required resources for launch, minimizing delays and ensuring timely execution of all launch activities. This includes securing necessary funding, personnel, and other resources well before the launch date.

## RELEVANCE:

Efficient resource management is crucial for a smooth and successful product launch. Avoiding delays and ensuring timely execution is essential for maximizing the impact of your launch efforts. If you frequently experience delays in resource allocation, this area is highly relevant. Implementing a more efficient resource management process will improve your launch execution.

# EFFECTIVE MARKETING AND CHANNEL STRATEGY FOR PRODUCT LAUNCH:

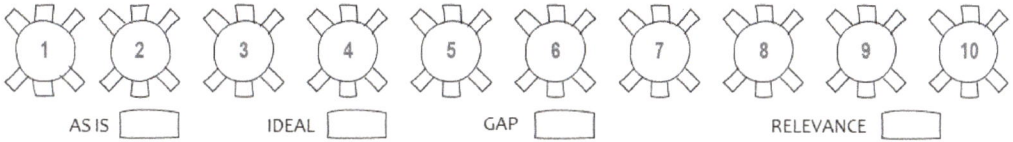

| 1 | 2 | 3 | 4 | 5 | 6 | 7 | 8 | 9 | 10 |

AS IS [ ]    IDEAL [ ]    GAP [ ]    RELEVANCE [ ]

## AS IS:

How do you determine the optimal marketing and channel mix for your launch products? Do you carefully consider the target audience, market dynamics, and competitive landscape when selecting marketing channels? Or is the channel selection less strategic? Do you launch in selected geographies? Only via direct sales or only via distribution first? Why did you select this approach? Evaluating these aspects will reveal potential gaps in your channel strategy.

## IDEAL:

Ideally, you bring your launch products successfully to market by carefully considering the optimal marketing and channel mix. This involves analysing the target audience, market dynamics, and competitive landscape to select the most effective channels for reaching your target audience and achieving your marketing objectives.

## RELEVANCE:

Selecting the right marketing and channel mix is crucial for maximizing the reach and impact of your launch efforts. Reaching the target audience effectively is essential for driving product adoption and achieving launch success. If your channel strategy is not optimized, this area is highly relevant. Investing in developing a more strategic channel mix will improve your reach and marketing effectiveness.

# DEMAND AND SUPPLY PLANNING FOR NEW PRODUCTS:

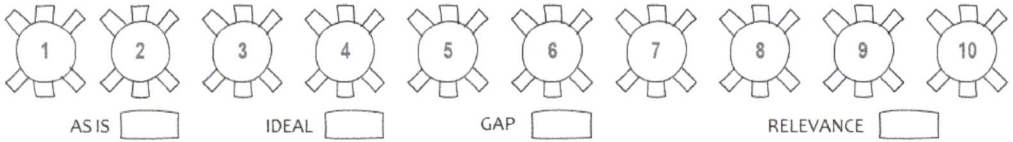

AS IS [___]   IDEAL [___]   GAP [___]   RELEVANCE [___]

## AS IS:

How robust is your supply management plan for new product launches? Is it based on detailed demand forecasts, production planning, and efficient distribution logistics? Or is the supply chain management less coordinated, potentially leading to stockouts or overstocking? Consider how accurate your past demand forecasts have been and how effectively you've managed production and distribution during launches. Evaluating these aspects will reveal potential weaknesses in your supply chain management.

## IDEAL:

Ideally, you have a clear and robust supply management plan for new product launches, based on detailed demand forecasts, well-coordinated production planning, and efficient distribution logistics. This plan should be developed well before the launch and regularly updated as needed. It ensures that you can meet customer demand without experiencing costly stockouts or overstocking, maximizing revenue and minimizing waste. Ideally the business will have a scenario plan for 10% achievement as well as 1000% achievement.

## RELEVANCE:

Effective supply chain management is crucial for ensuring product availability and meeting customer demand during a launch, whilst minimising any potential stock losses, over stock and cash flow problems. Efficient supply chain management is essential for scaling production and distribution effectively. If your supply management forecasting is weak or reactive, this area is highly relevant. Investing in a robust supply chain plan will minimize disruptions and maximize your launch success.

158                                          The Commercial Excellence Playbook

# LEADING AND LAGGING LAUNCH KPI'S:

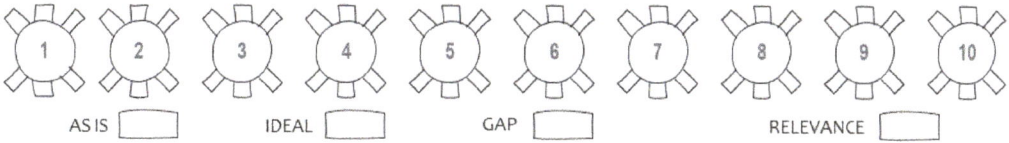

AS IS ⬚  IDEAL ⬚  GAP ⬚  RELEVANCE ⬚

## AS IS:

How do you monitor the progress of your product launches? Do you have a well-defined set of Key Performance Indicators (KPIs), including both leading and lagging indicators? Do you regularly track these KPIs and analyse the data to identify potential issues? Do you have a process for taking corrective actions when necessary? Reflecting on your past launches and how you tracked their performance will highlight potential gaps in your launch monitoring process.

## IDEAL:

Ideally, you closely monitor the launch through a well-defined set of KPIs, including both leading indicators (predictive measures like website traffic or lead generation) and lagging indicators (outcome measures like sales revenue or market share). You have a system for regularly tracking these KPIs, analysing the data, and taking corrective actions promptly when needed. This data-driven approach allows you to identify and address potential issues early on, maximizing the chances of a successful launch.

## RELEVANCE:

Closely monitoring the launch and taking corrective actions is essential for maximizing its success. Effectively tracking launch performance and adapting to changing market conditions is crucial for achieving launch growth objectives and adoption. If your launch monitoring process is weak or reactive, this area is highly relevant.

# CHAPTER 14:

# Influencer Engagement

Score this chapter here

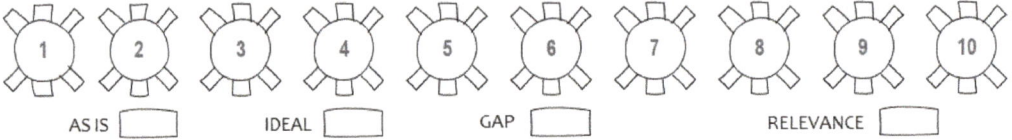

AS IS [        ]    IDEAL [        ]    GAP [        ]    RELEVANCE [        ]

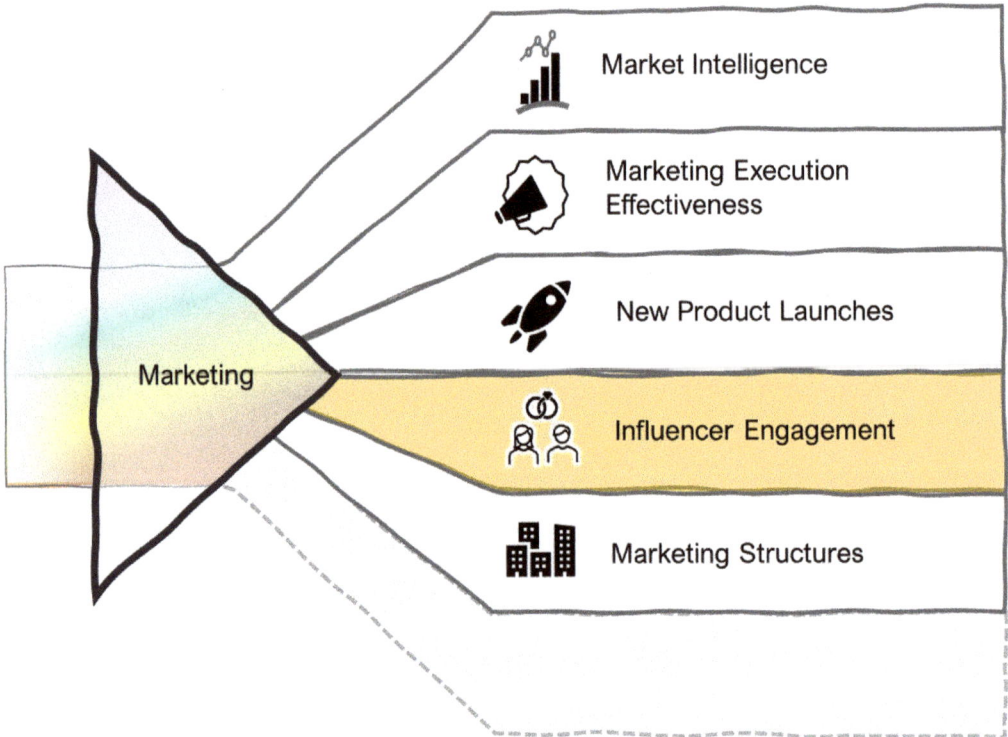

Marketing

Market Intelligence

Marketing Execution Effectiveness

New Product Launches

Influencer Engagement

Marketing Structures

# KOL STRATEGY ALIGNMENT:

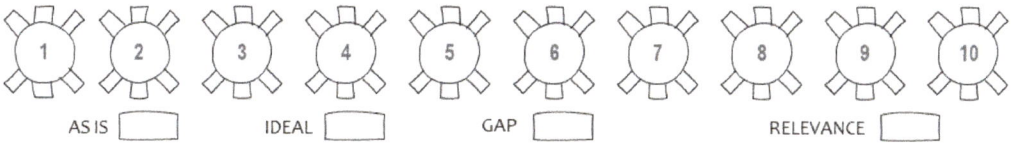

| | | | | | | | | | |
|---|---|---|---|---|---|---|---|---|---|
| 1 | 2 | 3 | 4 | 5 | 6 | 7 | 8 | 9 | 10 |

AS IS [        ]     IDEAL [        ]     GAP [        ]     RELEVANCE [        ]

## AS IS:

Consider your current Key Opinion Leader (KOL) strategy. Is it clearly documented and understood by all relevant departments? Is there a coordinated approach or method to KOL engagement across Sales, Key Account Management, Distributor Management, Marketing, Market Access, Pricing and Tendering, Service, and Medical teams? Or do these departments operate in silos, potentially leading to duplicated efforts or conflicting messages? Evaluating the level of alignment will reveal potential gaps in your KOL strategy.

## IDEAL:

Ideally, your KOL strategy is clearly defined, documented, and fully aligned with all relevant departments. This ensures a coordinated and consistent approach to KOL engagement, maximizing the impact of your efforts and avoiding duplication of resources. All teams understand their roles and responsibilities in the KOL engagement process.

## RELEVANCE:

A well-defined and aligned KOL strategy is crucial for maximizing the influence of these key stakeholders. Effective KOL engagement can significantly enhance credibility, drive product adoption, and support market access. If your KOL strategy lacks clarity or alignment, this area is highly relevant. Investing in developing a coordinated KOL strategy will improve your stakeholder engagement and its impact on your business.

# KOL DATA MANAGEMENT:

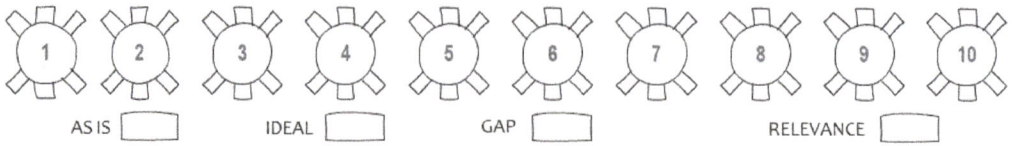

| 1 | 2 | 3 | 4 | 5 | 6 | 7 | 8 | 9 | 10 |

AS IS [ ]    IDEAL [ ]    GAP [ ]    RELEVANCE [ ]

## AS IS:

How do you currently manage information about KOLs? Do you systematically collect data on their importance, influence, activities, publications and networks? Is this information readily accessible to all relevant departments in a central database? Or is it scattered across different files and systems, making it difficult to access and utilize effectively?

## IDEAL:

Ideally, you have a robust system for regularly and systematically collecting relevant data on KOLs. This data, including their importance, influence, activities, publications, interactions and influence networks and specialities. This ensures that everyone has access to the most up-to-date information, facilitating informed decision-making and coordinated engagement.

## RELEVANCE:

Effective KOL data management will maximize the value of your KOL relationships. Having a centralized database of KOL information can significantly improve efficiency and collaboration across departments. If your KOL data is not managed effectively, or non-existent, this area is highly relevant. How do influencers impact purchase decisions? How do influencers impart their credibility? Investing in a central database and a systematic data collection process will improve your KOL engagement and its impact on your business.

# STRATEGIC ENGAGEMENT OF KOLS:

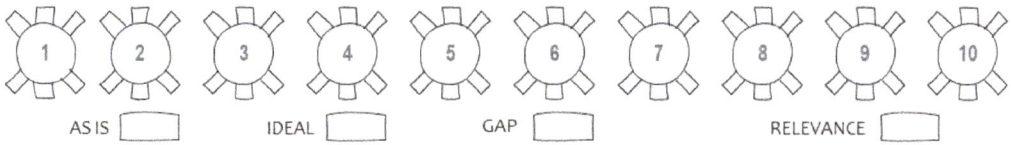

AS IS ☐   IDEAL ☐   GAP ☐   RELEVANCE ☐

## AS IS:

How do you currently engage with KOLs? Do you have individual engagement plans tailored to each KOL's specific interests and expertise? Do you utilize various engagement methods, such as advisory boards, speaking engagements, and collaborative research projects? Or is your engagement less structured? Evaluating your KOL engagement approach will reveal potential gaps in your engagement strategy.

## IDEAL:

Ideally, you systematically develop and actively engage KOLs through individual engagement plans tailored to their specific needs and expertise. This includes utilizing a range of engagement methods, such as advisory boards, speaking engagements, publications, and collaborative research projects. This personalized and multifaceted approach fosters strong, long-term relationships with KOLs.

## RELEVANCE:

Systematic and personalized KOL engagement is crucial for building strong and mutually beneficial relationships. Developing strong KOL relationships can significantly enhance credibility and support market access. If your KOL engagement is not structured or personalized, this area is relevant. Investing in developing individual engagement plans and utilizing diverse engagement methods will improve your KOL relationships and their impact on your business.

# GOAL SETTING FOR KOLS:

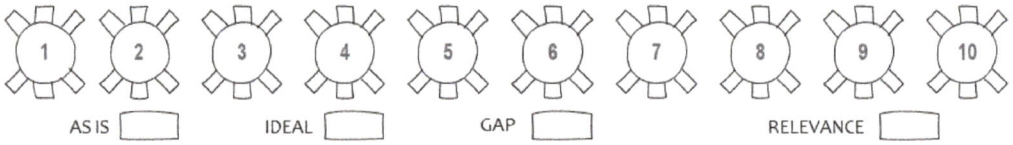

AS IS [ ]    IDEAL [ ]    GAP [ ]    RELEVANCE [ ]

## AS IS:

How do you measure the effectiveness of your KOL management activities? Do you have defined KPIs for KOL engagement, including clear responsibilities and concrete countermeasures in case of deviation from targets? Or is your evaluation of KOL activities less formal?

## IDEAL:

Ideally, you have defined and tracked KPIs for your KOL management activities. These KPIs include clear responsibilities for achieving targets and concrete countermeasures to be taken if deviations occur. This data-driven approach allows you to monitor the effectiveness of your KOL engagement, identify areas for improvement, and ensure that your efforts are aligned with your overall business objectives.

## RELEVANCE:

Measuring and managing KOL performance is essential for maximizing the ROI of your KOL investments. Demonstrating the value of KOL engagement is crucial for justifying resource allocation from other areas and ensuring the achieving business objectives. If you do not have defined KPIs for KOL management, this area is relevant. Implementing a robust performance measurement system will improve your KOL engagement and its impact on your business.

# CHAPTER 15:

# Marketing Structures

Score this chapter here

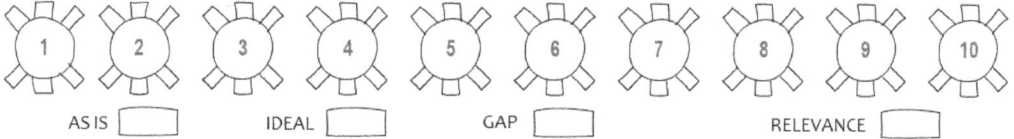

| 1 | 2 | 3 | 4 | 5 | 6 | 7 | 8 | 9 | 10 |

AS IS [        ]        IDEAL [        ]        GAP [        ]        RELEVANCE [        ]

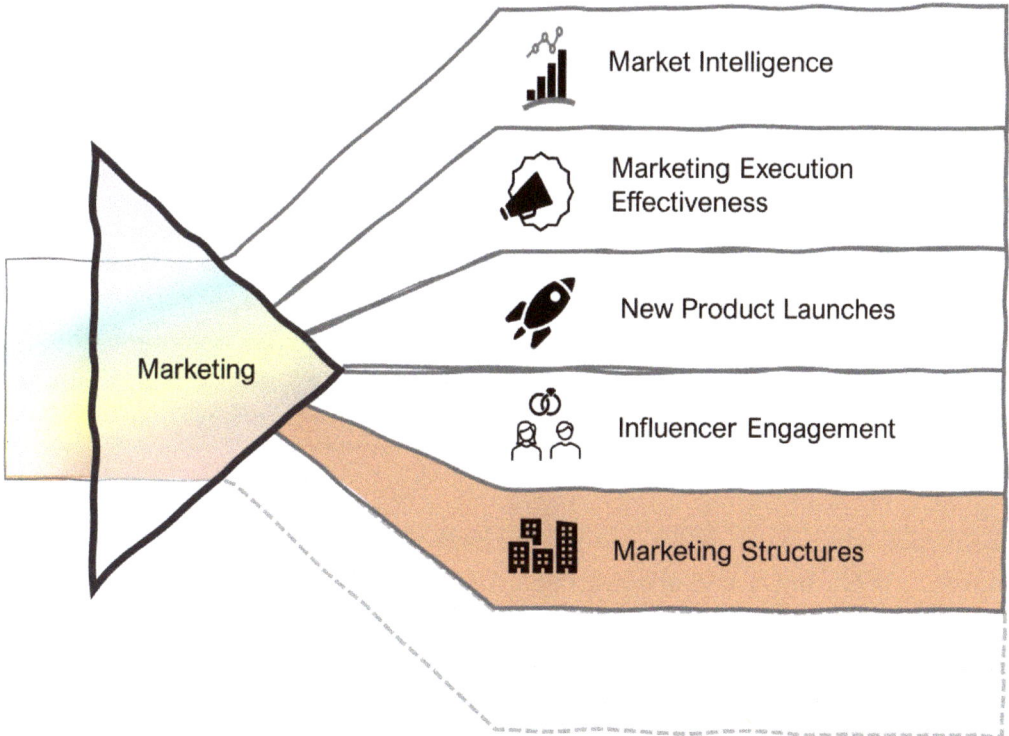

Marketing

- Market Intelligence
- Marketing Execution Effectiveness
- New Product Launches
- Influencer Engagement
- Marketing Structures

# MARKETING ROLES AND RESPONSIBILITIES:

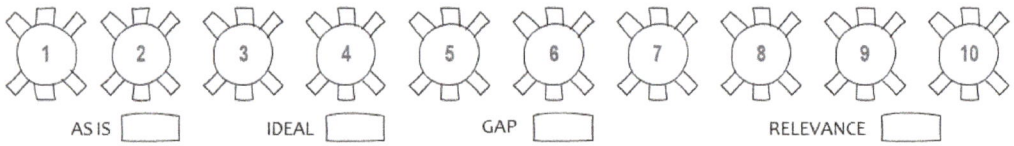

AS IS [ ]     IDEAL [ ]     GAP [ ]     RELEVANCE [ ]

## AS IS:

Consider the structure of your marketing organisation. Are roles and responsibilities clearly defined across corporate, regional, and local teams? Are there instances of overlapping responsibilities or duplicated efforts? Are synergies between teams actively leveraged? Or do teams operate in silos, potentially leading to inefficiencies? Evaluating these aspects will reveal potential gaps in your marketing organisation structure.

## IDEAL:

Ideally, your corporate, regional, and local marketing teams have clearly defined roles and responsibilities that maximize synergies and minimize unnecessary duplications. This ensures efficient resource allocation and a coordinated approach to marketing activities. Each team understands its specific contribution to the overall marketing strategy. The structure allows the global strategy to be translated into regional targets and adjusted for local market specifies.

## RELEVANCE:

Clear roles and responsibilities within the marketing organisation are crucial for maximizing efficiency and effectiveness. Optimizing marketing resources is essential for achieving growth objectives. If your marketing organisation lacks clarity or coordination, this area is highly relevant. Investing in defining clear roles and responsibilities will improve your marketing efficiency and impact.

# MARKETING DEPARTMENT ALIGNMENT:

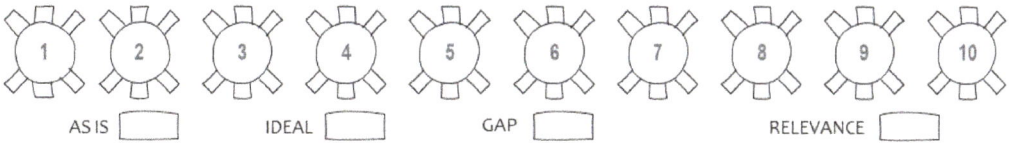

| 1 | 2 | 3 | 4 | 5 | 6 | 7 | 8 | 9 | 10 |

AS IS [　　] IDEAL [　　] GAP [　　] RELEVANCE [　　]

## AS IS:

Consider the level of support provided by your corporate marketing team to regional and local marketing activities. Is this support sufficient to meet the needs of local teams? Does it include guidance, resources, and best practices? Or is the support lacking, potentially hindering the effectiveness of local marketing efforts? Evaluating this support structure will reveal potential gaps in your corporate-local marketing collaboration.

## IDEAL:

Ideally, the corporate marketing team provides sufficient support to regional and local marketing activities. The regional teams act as mediators between global and local teams. Providing both execution and alignment support and resources: This includes providing strategic guidance, sharing best practices, offering resources and tools, and facilitating communication and collaboration. This support empowers local teams to execute effective marketing campaigns tailored to their specific market needs.

## RELEVANCE:

Effective support from corporate marketing is crucial for empowering local teams and maximizing the impact of regional and local marketing activities. Strong corporate support can significantly enhance the effectiveness of local marketing efforts. If your corporate support for local marketing is lacking, then this area is highly relevant. Investing in strengthening the corporate support structure will improve the overall effectiveness of your marketing organisation.

# MARKETING STRUCTURE OPTIMIZATION:

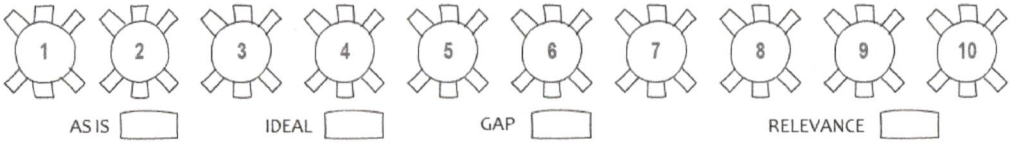

| 1 | 2 | 3 | 4 | 5 | 6 | 7 | 8 | 9 | 10 |

AS IS [ ]    IDEAL [ ]    GAP [ ]    RELEVANCE [ ]

## AS IS:

Consider the structure and size of your global, regional, and local marketing functions. Do they align with the priorities of your product portfolio? Are resources allocated appropriately based on the strategic importance and potential of each product? Or are resources distributed unevenly, potentially neglecting key products or overinvesting in less important ones? Evaluating this alignment will reveal potential gaps in your marketing resource allocation.

## IDEAL:

Ideally, the structure and size of your local marketing functions directly reflect the priorities of your product portfolio. Resources are allocated strategically based on the importance and potential of each product, ensuring that key products receive the necessary marketing support. There is an embracing of AI to optimize workflows and speed "messaging testing" etc.

## RELEVANCE:

Aligning marketing resources with product portfolio priorities is crucial for maximizing ROI. Focusing resources on key products is essential for driving growth and achieving business objectives. If your marketing resources are not aligned with product priorities, this area is highly relevant. Investing in aligning your marketing structure and resource allocation with your product portfolio will improve your marketing effectiveness.

# INTERDEPARTMENTAL COLLABORATION:

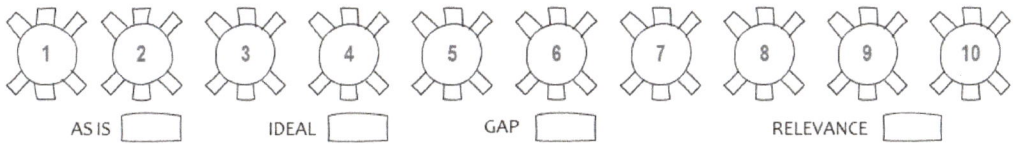

| 1 | 2 | 3 | 4 | 5 | 6 | 7 | 8 | 9 | 10 |

AS IS [　　]　　IDEAL [　　]　　GAP [　　]　　RELEVANCE [　　]

## AS IS:

Consider the role of your product, brand and market managers in driving interdepartmental collaboration. Do they effectively facilitate communication and collaboration between different departments, such as Sales, Key Account Management, Marketing, and others? Do they utilize cross-functional product teams to ensure alignment and coordination? Or is collaboration lacking, potentially leading to miscommunication and inefficiencies? Evaluating these aspects will reveal potential gaps in your cross-functional collaboration.

## IDEAL:

Ideally, your product, brand and marketing managers are effective drivers of interdepartmental collaboration. They actively facilitate communication and collaboration between different departments through cross-functional product teams. This ensures that all relevant perspectives are considered and that product strategies are aligned with overall business objectives.

## RELEVANCE:

Effective interdepartmental collaboration is crucial for successful product management. Strong cross-functional collaboration can significantly improve product development, launch, and marketing effectiveness. If collaboration is lacking, this area is highly relevant. Investing in empowering product managers to drive interdepartmental collaboration will improve your product management effectiveness.

# MARKETING FIELD EXECUTION:

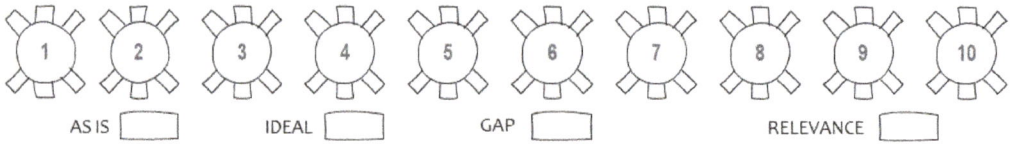

| 1 | 2 | 3 | 4 | 5 | 6 | 7 | 8 | 9 | 10 |

AS IS [ ]    IDEAL [ ]    GAP [ ]    RELEVANCE [ ]

## AS IS:

Consider how much time your local marketing personnel spend in the field interacting with customers and sales teams. Do they dedicate sufficient time to collecting first-hand customer feedback and understanding sales force needs? Or are they primarily office-bound, potentially missing valuable insights from the field? Why don't they spend more time in the field? Is it because of resourcing, or knowledge, skills or motivation? Is it as simple as management don't ask or drive this type of activity? Are there no feedback systems to capture the insights and this leads to them being seen as less valuable? Evaluating this field engagement will reveal potential gaps in your customer and sales force understanding.

## IDEAL:

Ideally, your local product managers dedicate sufficient time to field activities, such as visiting customers, attending sales meetings, and interacting with sales teams. This allows them to collect first-hand customer feedback, understand sales force needs, and gain valuable market insights. A suggested benchmark could be around 20% of their time, but this will vary by industry and business model. There is a feedback mechanism that incorporates insights into corporate and a 360° feedback loop. Local teams know that their insights have been incorporated and are considered at a corporate level (even if the outcome was not favourable).

## RELEVANCE:

Direct customer and sales force interaction is crucial for effective product management. Understanding customer needs and sales force challenges is essential for developing successful products and marketing strategies. If your product managers are not spending enough time in the field, this area is highly relevant. Encouraging and enabling field engagement will improve your product and marketing effectiveness.

# PRODUCT / BRAND / MARKET MANAGER

# EXPERTISE:

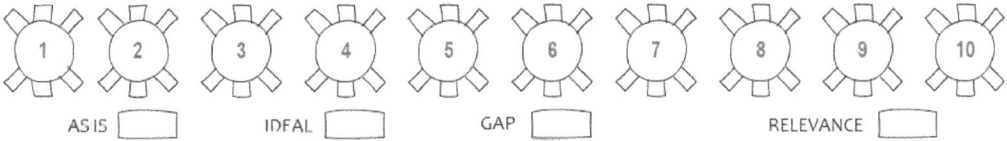

AS IS [　　]    IDEAL [　　]    GAP [　　]    RELEVANCE [　　]

## AS IS:

Consider the skills, experience, and functional understanding of your product managers. Do they possess the necessary expertise to effectively drive your marketing agenda? Are they proficient in market analysis, product positioning, marketing strategy development, and cross-functional collaboration? Are they all trained on the same methodologies? Could you pick a manager from one country/territory and place them in another? What would happen – and why? Evaluating these aspects will reveal potential gaps in your product management capabilities.

## IDEAL:

Ideally, your product managers possess the optimal skills, experience, and deep functional understanding to effectively drive your marketing agenda. This includes expertise in market analysis, product positioning, marketing strategy development, cross-functional collaboration, and customer understanding. You could give cross pollination assignments without the need to re-train methodologies, allowing them to rapidly gain full effectiveness in the new territory.

## RELEVANCE:

Skilled and experienced product managers are crucial for driving successful marketing outcomes. Having strong product management capabilities is essential for achieving marketing objectives and driving business growth. If your product managers lack the necessary skills or experience, this area is highly relevant. Investing in their training and development will improve your marketing effectiveness and overall business performance.

# Section Conclusion

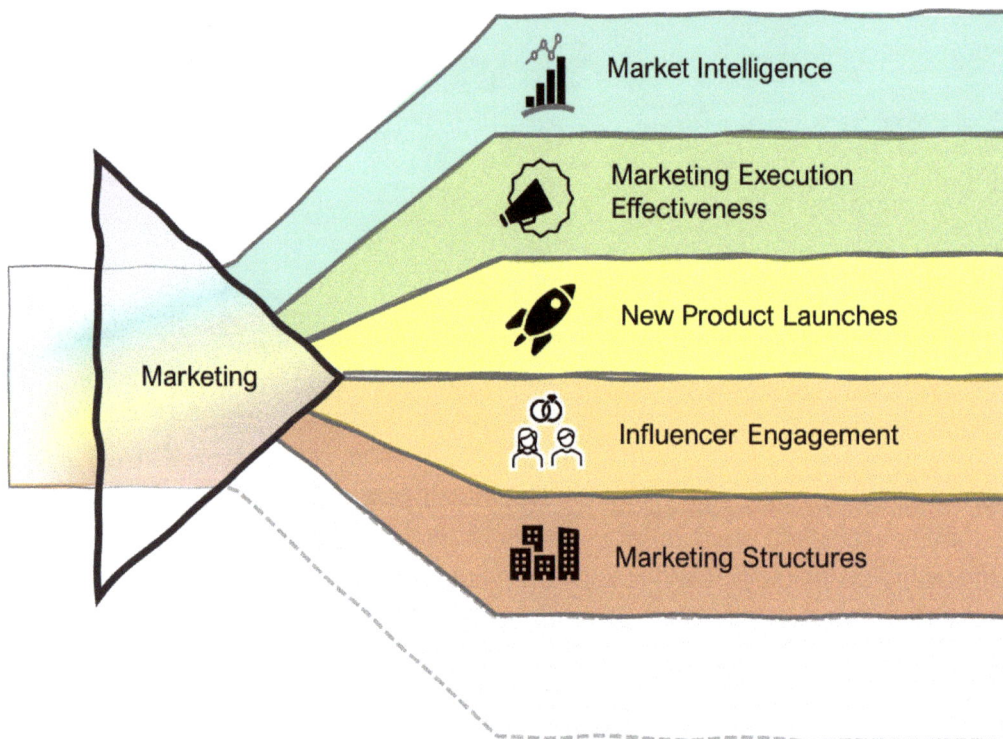

Market Intelligence

Marketing Execution Effectiveness

New Product Launches

Influencer Engagement

Marketing Structures

Marketing

**Transfer the ratings at the beginning of each chapter here:**

| Chapter | AS IS | Ideal | Gap | Relevance |
|---|---|---|---|---|
| Market Intelligence | | | | |
| Marketing Execution Effectiveness | | | | |
| New Product Launches | | | | |
| Influencer Engagement | | | | |
| Marketing Structures | | | | |

Is there one area that is better or worse than the others?

# MARKETING PLOT:

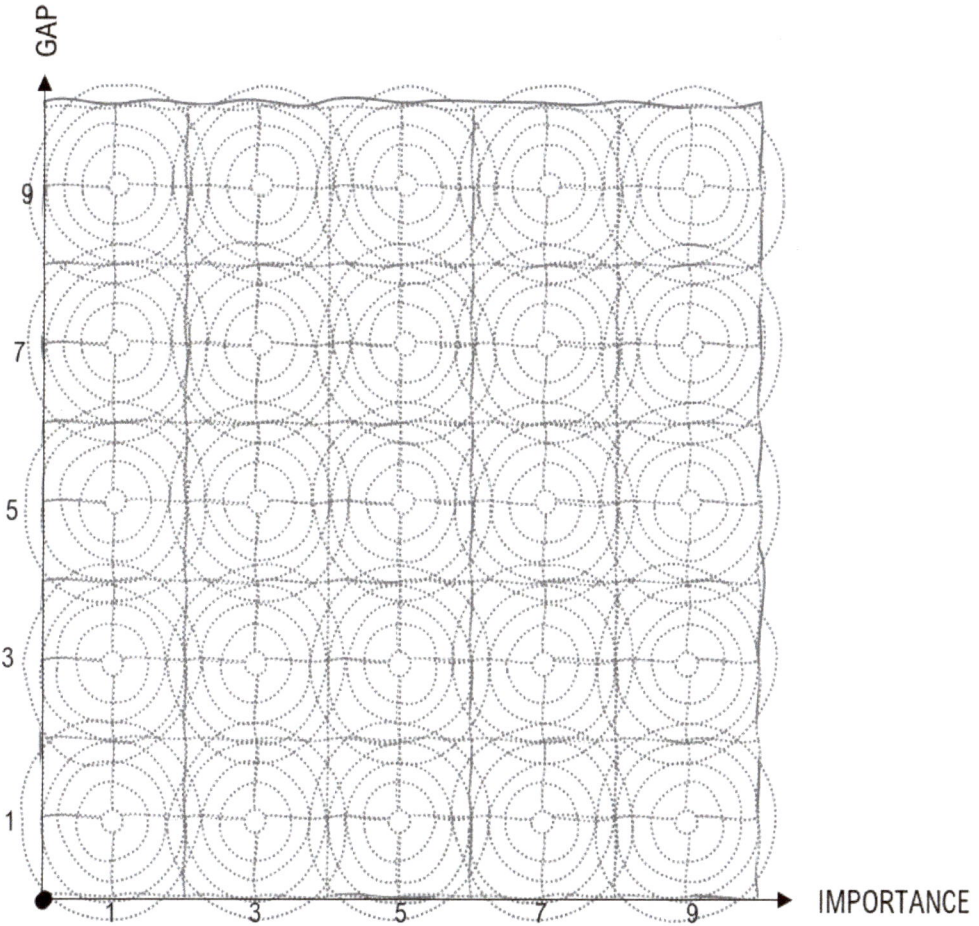

Looking at the box plot what is your assessment of Marketing?

# OVERALL EVALUATION:

AS IS [        ]    IDEAL [        ]    GAP [        ]    RELEVANCE [        ]

# SECTION 4: KEY ACCOUNTS

Strategic Customer Relationship Management

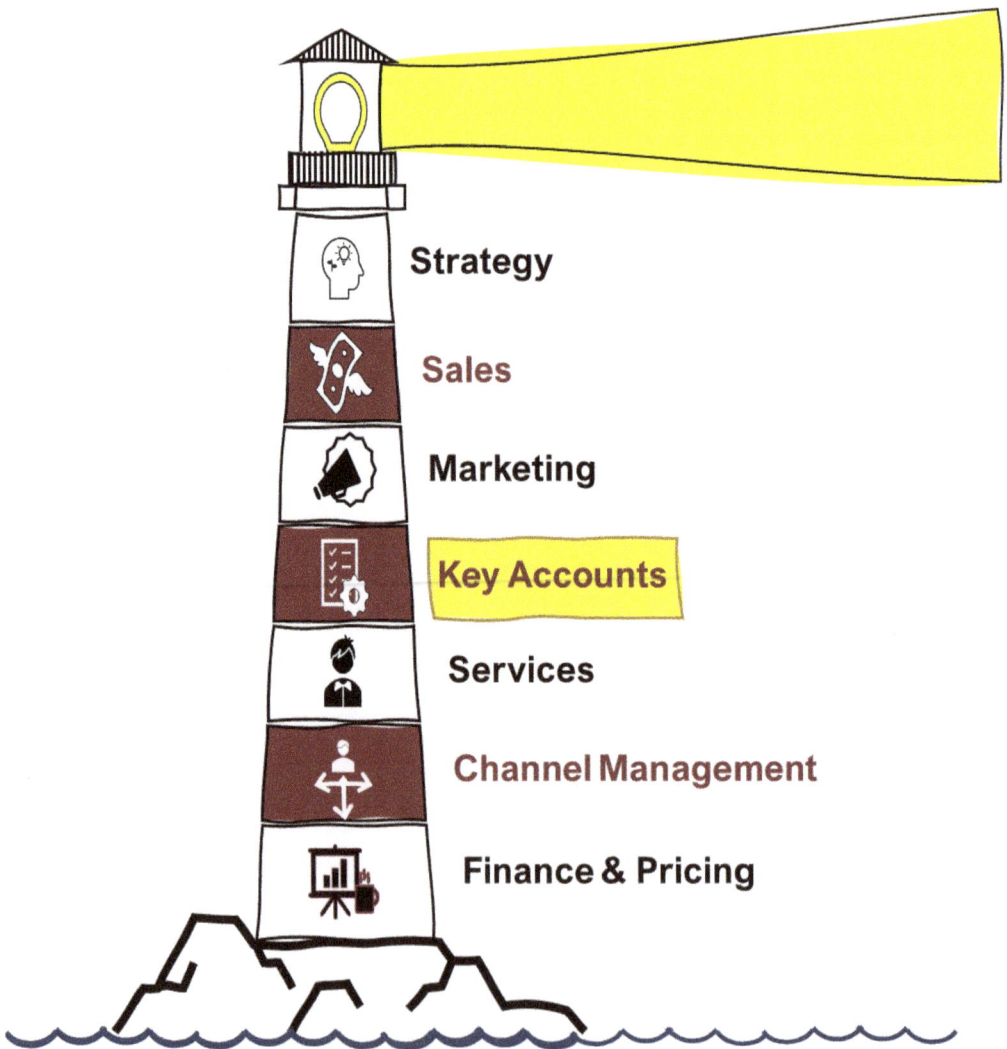

Strategy

Sales

Marketing

Key Accounts

Services

Channel Management

Finance & Pricing

Are your most valuable clients receiving the VIP treatment they deserve, or are they just another entry in your database? In today's relationship-driven business world, strategic key account management is not a luxury—it's a necessity for sustainable growth. This chapter challenges you to critically examine your approach to your most significant customers. Are you truly leveraging these partnerships to drive mutual value, or are you leaving untapped potential on the table? Let's explore how to transform your key account strategies from transactional to transformational, ensuring that your most important relationships are nurtured, protected, and primed for long-term success.

In this section we will look through the spectrum of Key Accounts examining five wavelengths:

**Figure 22:** The 5 Wavelengths of Key Accounts

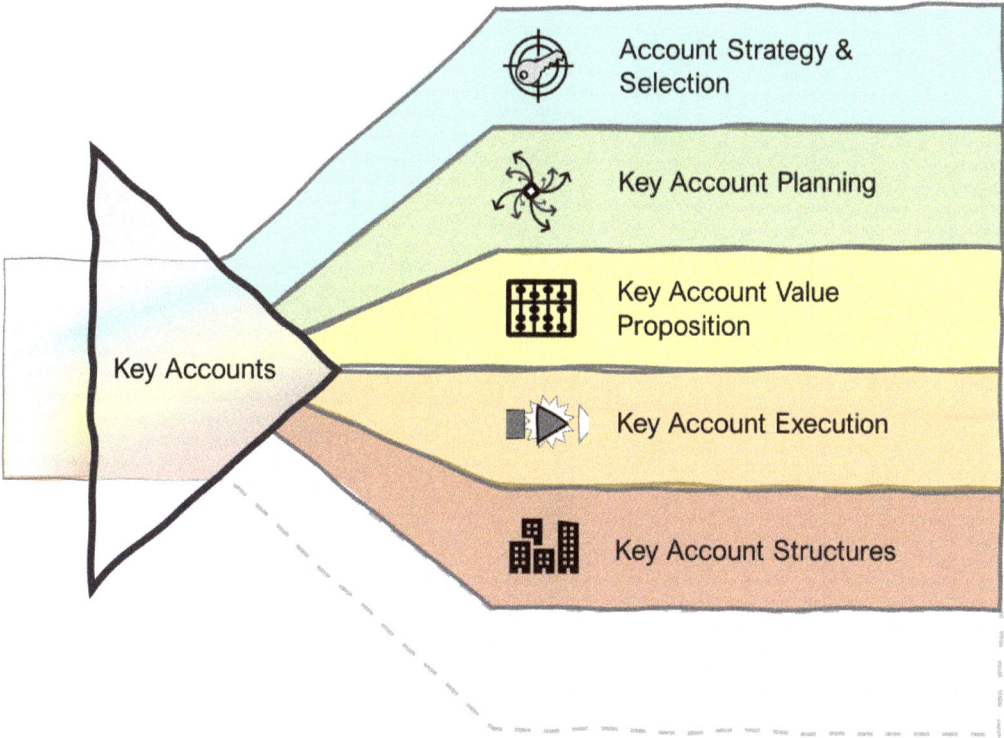

Personally, I look at key accounts a little differently than most. For me a key account represents an account with aligned, values, strategy, mission, values or financial success. We both know that the relationship is needed, and we both actively engage with each other. Where the engagement is only one-sided, then for me, they are NOT a key account. This concept is illustrated in figure 23 below. There needs to be a desire to engage in the process for it to be a true key account. We may be a key supplier for them, or they may be strategically important for our growth, but they are not a key account.

Without engagement on both sides, KAM processes won't have the incremental payback. There would not be sufficient gain to manage them using the KA processes.

A question to ask yourself is: "If I was seeking to be vertically integrated would I want this key account to buy my company? Or would I want to buy them?" Could these accounts become part of an 'exit' strategy for the business's owners? Again, if the answer is no, they are likely not a key account. They may be key for our business, but we are not key for theirs. Here, the relationship will always be one-sided – and with you as the subordinate. If this is the case, I'd personally invest the resources elsewhere.

**Figure 23:** KA Suitability

NB: If Customer only they are your Key Supplier. If supplier only they are your strategic customer and "Don't Engage" means do not engage in a Key Account Management process as it's unlikely to provide a return on your investment.

The Commercial Excellence Playbook

# CHAPTER 16:

# Key Account Strategy & Selection

Score this chapter here

| 1 | 2 | 3 | 4 | 5 | 6 | 7 | 8 | 9 | 10 |

AS IS ☐     IDEAL ☐     GAP ☐     RELEVANCE ☐

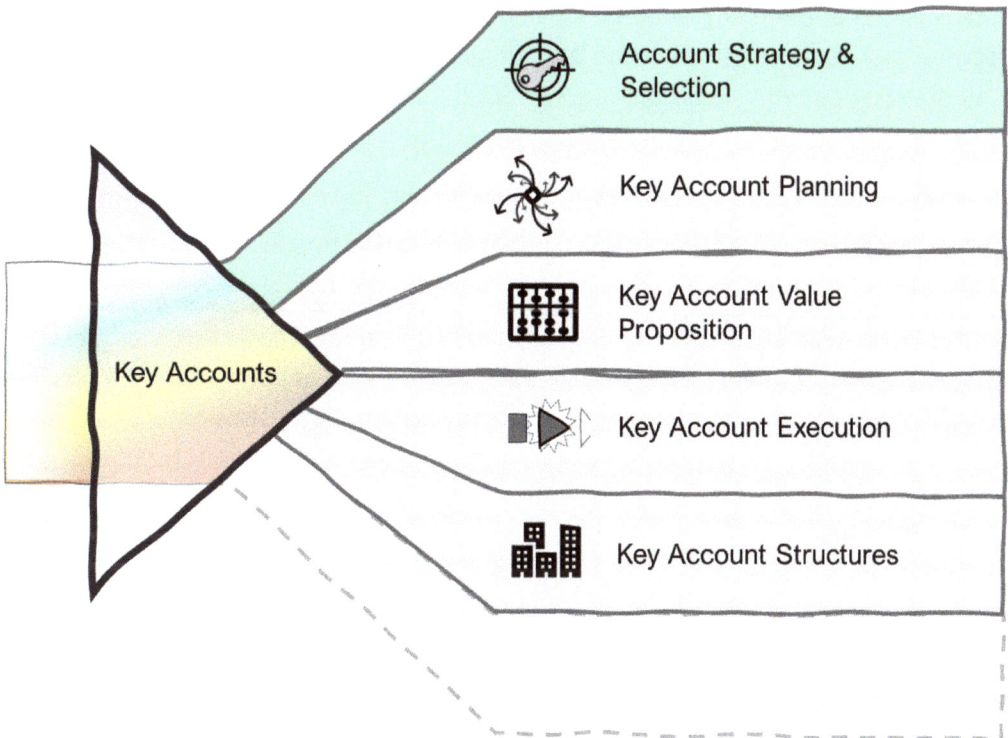

- Account Strategy & Selection
- Key Account Planning
- Key Account Value Proposition
- Key Account Execution
- Key Account Structures

Key Accounts

# CUSTOMER-DRIVEN KEY ACCOUNT MANAGEMENT (KAM) STRATEGY:

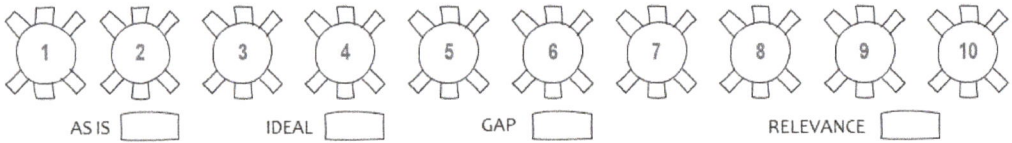

```
1   2   3   4   5   6   7   8   9   10
```

AS IS [ ]          IDEAL [ ]          GAP [ ]          RELEVANCE [ ]

## AS IS:

Consider the foundation of your KAM strategy. Is it built upon a deep understanding of your key accounts, including their performance, competitive landscape, and the broader market context? Does your strategy incorporate growth and a future mindset? Or is it based on more general assumptions or historical data? How well do you understand the specific needs, challenges, and opportunities of each key account? Evaluating these aspects will reveal potential gaps in your customer knowledge and its application to your KAM strategy. Is your strategy based upon a proven key account methodology? Such as Miller Heiman's LAMP (Large Account Management) (Miller Heiman, 1991).

## IDEAL:

Ideally, your KAM strategy is firmly grounded in deep customer knowledge. This includes a thorough understanding of each key account's performance, their competitive situation, and the overall market structure and development. Your KAM strategy incorporates both securing today and building the future. This data-driven approach ensures that your KAM strategy is tailored to the specific needs and opportunities of each key account. Ideally the use of a framework for key account planning such as the Gold Sheet (Miller Heiman, 1991) method. This method is in place, understood and followed.

## RELEVANCE:

Basing your KAM strategy on deep customer knowledge is crucial for maximizing its effectiveness. Understanding the nuances of your key accounts is essential for building strong relationships and driving profitable growth. If your KAM strategy is not based on robust customer insights, this area is highly relevant. Investing in gathering and analysing customer data and using it in a KA framework will significantly improve your KAM effectiveness.

# KA STRATEGY ALIGNMENT:

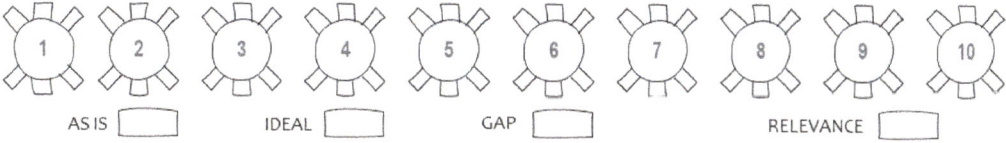

## AS IS:

Consider the level of alignment of your KAM strategy across different departments. Is there a shared understanding and consistent application of the strategy across marketing, sales, pricing, market access, and services? Or are there discrepancies and inconsistencies in how the KAM strategy is implemented? Evaluating this alignment will highlight potential areas for improved cross-functional collaboration.

## IDEAL:

Ideally, your KAM strategy is fully aligned across all relevant departments. Marketing, sales, pricing, market access, and services teams share a common strategic understanding and work together seamlessly to execute it. This cross-functional alignment ensures a consistent and coordinated approach to managing key accounts.

## RELEVANCE:

Cross-functional alignment is crucial for maximizing the effectiveness of your KAM strategy. Ensuring that all customer-facing teams agree is essential for delivering a consistent customer experience and maximizing account penetration. If there are discrepancies in how the KAM strategy is implemented across departments, this area is highly relevant. Investing in cross-functional communication and training will improve alignment and optimize your KAM activities.

# KA SELECTION:

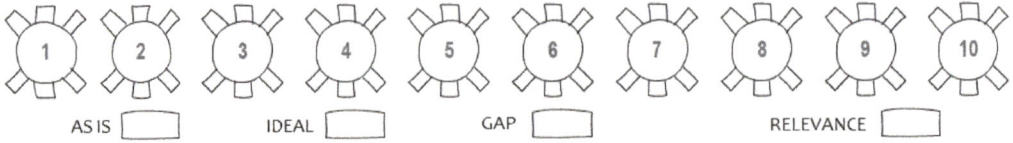

AS IS [ ]   IDEAL [ ]   GAP [ ]   RELEVANCE [ ]

## AS IS:

Consider the criteria you used to select key accounts for your KAM program. Do these criteria include factors like future sales potential and the account's openness to partnership? Or are other factors, such as current revenue or historical relationships, prioritized? Evaluating your selection criteria will reveal potential gaps in your account selection process.

## IDEAL:

Ideally, your KAM program has well-defined selection criteria that include future sales potential and the account's openness to a collaborative partnership and secure existing reviews of today. This balancing act should not balance! A clear priority should be visible either secure today or grow tomorrow (market penetration) – not both. This balancing ensures that you are focusing your resources on accounts that offer the greatest potential for long-term growth and mutually beneficial relationships.

## RELEVANCE:

Using appropriate selection criteria is crucial for maximizing the ROI of your KAM program. Focusing on accounts with high growth potential and a willingness to partner is essential for achieving long-term success. If your selection criteria are not aligned with these objectives, this area is ready for reflection. Refining your selection criteria will improve the effectiveness of your KAM program.

# UNIFIED KEY ACCOUNT MANAGEMENT:

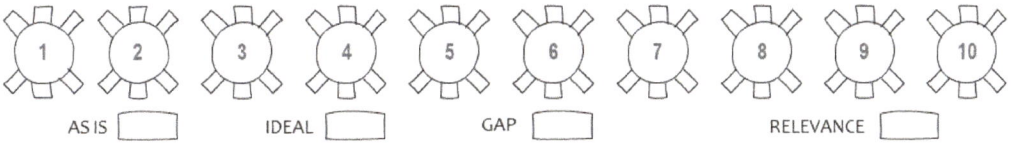

```
1   2   3   4   5   6   7   8   9   10

AS IS [    ]   IDEAL [    ]   GAP [    ]   RELEVANCE [    ]
```

## AS IS:

How is your list of key accounts managed and shared within your organisation?
Is there a single, unified list that is accessible to all relevant departments? Or
are there multiple, potentially conflicting lists circulating within different teams?
Evaluating your account list management will reveal potential gaps in your
internal communication and coordination. Do you need layered key accounts?
For global, regional and local? How do you ensure alignment? Do you have
clear criteria for each? Can key accounts have more than one category? For
example, a global key account with local subs having local key accounts?

## IDEAL:

Ideally, your KAM program has a single, unified list of key accounts that is
shared across the entire organisation. This ensures that everyone is working
from the same information and that there is no confusion about which accounts
are being managed under the KAM program. They may have multiple KA
classifications.

## RELEVANCE:

Having a single, shared list of key accounts is crucial for ensuring consistent
and coordinated account management. Avoiding confusion and duplication of
effort is essential for maximizing efficiency and effectiveness. If there are
multiple KAM lists within your organisation, this area is highly relevant.
Implementing a single, shared list will improve internal communication and
coordination.

# STANDARDIZED KEY ACCOUNT SELECTION AND ONBOARDING:

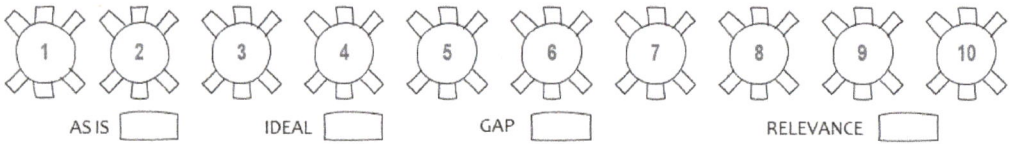

AS IS [ ]    IDEAL [ ]    GAP [ ]    RELEVANCE [ ]

## AS IS:

Consider your process for selecting and onboarding key accounts. Is it a documented and reproducible process? Does it explicitly consider the importance of the account relative to the rest of the market? Or is the process more informal and ad hoc? Are you utilizing a proven methodology or do you have your own bespoke methods? How do you onboard new key accounts? Do they know that they are a key account? Have they dedicated resources to make the collaboration work? Or is it one-sided? Evaluating your selection and onboarding process will reveal potential gaps in your KAM program management.

## IDEAL:

Ideally, you have a documented and reproducible process for selecting and onboarding key accounts. This process includes clear criteria for evaluating the importance of the account relative to the overall market and ensures a consistent and effective onboarding experience for new key accounts. Most published KAM programs incorporate the right tools to make good assessments. The onboarding process has commitment and resourcing from the key account and your own business to make the relationships work.

## RELEVANCE:

A documented and reproducible process for selection and onboarding is crucial for ensuring consistency and efficiency in your KAM program. Having a clear process for managing key accounts is essential for scaling the program effectively. If your selection and onboarding process is informal or undocumented, this area is highly relevant. Implementing a documented process will improve the consistency and effectiveness of your KAM program.

182

# KA LIST REVIEWS:

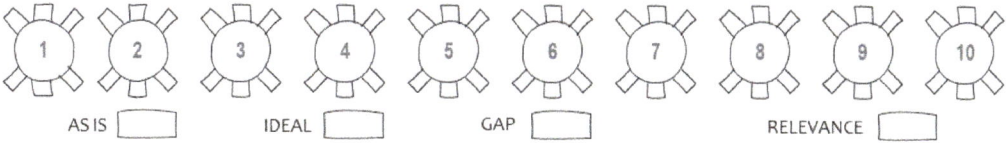

AS IS [          ]    IDEAL [          ]    GAP [          ]    RELEVANCE [          ]

## AS IS:

How frequently and systematically do you review your list of key accounts? Is there a documented and reproducible process for adding and removing accounts from the list? Where has the relationship lapsed? Is the KA still committed to your organisation? Has new market potential emerged? Do the existing KAs still have the same value to your organisation? Or is the review process less formal, potentially leading to outdated account lists and misallocation of resources? Evaluating your account review process will reveal potential gaps in your KAM program management.

## IDEAL:

Ideally, your key accounts are reviewed at regular intervals using a documented and reproducible process. This process includes clear criteria for adding and removing accounts from the list, ensuring that your KAM program remains focused on the most strategic and valuable accounts.

## RELEVANCE:

Regular review of your key account list is crucial for ensuring that your KAM program remains aligned with your business objectives and changing market dynamics. Adapting your KAM program to changing market conditions is essential for maintaining a competitive edge. If your account review process is infrequent or undocumented, this area is highly relevant. Implementing a regular and documented review process will improve the effectiveness and relevance of your KAM program.

# CHAPTER 17:

# Key Account Planning

Score this chapter here

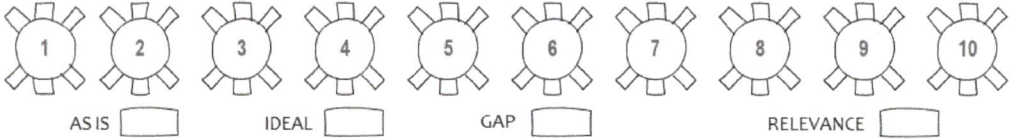

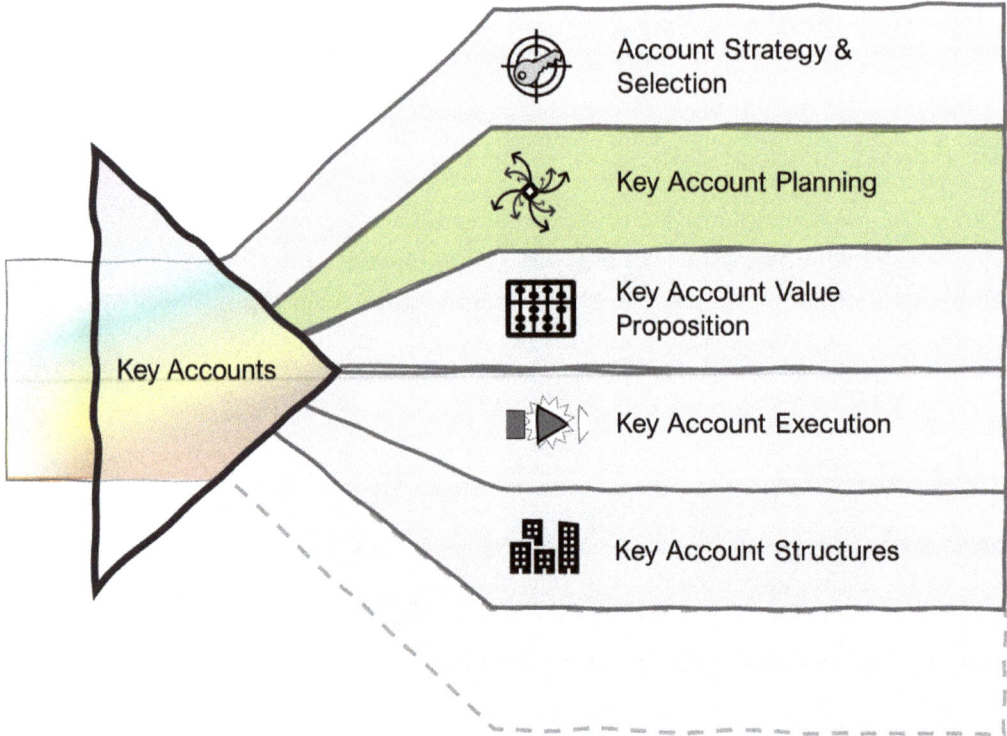

1  2  3  4  5  6  7  8  9  10

AS IS [        ]    IDEAL [        ]    GAP [        ]    RELEVANCE [        ]

⊕  Account Strategy & Selection

※  Key Account Planning

🧮  Key Account Value Proposition

▶  Key Account Execution

🏢  Key Account Structures

Key Accounts

# KEY ACCOUNT PLANS:

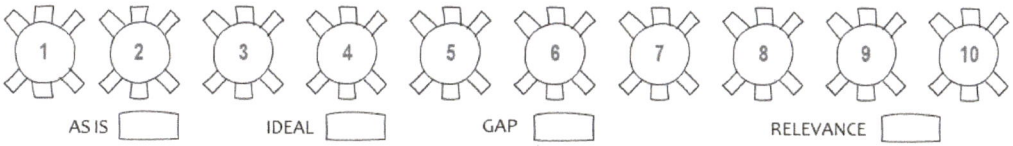

AS IS [___]     IDEAL [___]     GAP [___]     RELEVANCE [___]

## AS IS:

Consider your current approach to planning for key accounts. Do you develop formal, annual key account plans for each key account? Or is planning less structured, perhaps relying on informal discussions or ad-hoc strategies? Do your plans include where you are on the Buy Sell Hierarchy (Miller Heiman, 1991) and the level of the relationships with the key personnel? The joint objectives, as well as your own objectives? Does it have influence within the company and your plans to expand that span? Evaluating your planning process will reveal potential gaps in your account management approach.

How do your plans fall into figure 24 below? Are they all in one area? or on one side?

**Figure 24:** Four Aspects of Key Account Planning

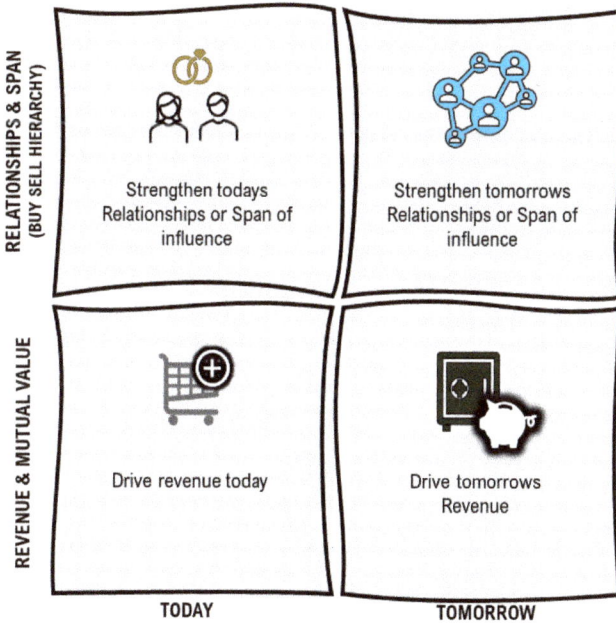

## IDEAL:

Ideally, each key account has a documented annual key account plan. This plan outlines specific objectives, strategies, and action plans for the coming year, providing a roadmap for managing and growing the account. The plans include how to increase joint value between both companies? Actions and goals towards improving the buy sell hierarchy (Miller Heiman, 1991) and growing the influence and span within the key account.

## RELEVANCE:

Having a formal key account plan is crucial for providing focus and direction to your KAM efforts. Structured planning is essential for maximizing the value of key account relationships. If you do not have annual key account plans, this area is highly relevant. Implementing formal planning will improve your account management effectiveness, enable accountability and adjustments.

# COMPREHENSIVE DATA COLLECTION FOR KEY ACCOUNTS:

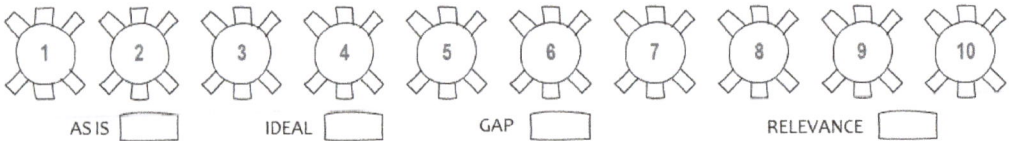

AS IS [ ]    IDEAL [ ]    GAP [ ]    RELEVANCE [ ]

## AS IS:

What information does your KAM program collect and analyse for each key account? Do you systematically gather data on their strategy, requirements, sales potential, share of wallet, competitor activities, decision structures, and internal and market relationships? Or is your data collection less comprehensive? Where do you store the data? Is it confirmed by second sources or trusted from the primary source? Do you utilize multiple data sources? Company report? Annual reports? Market data? Sales visits? Internal stakeholders? Evaluating your data collection process will reveal potential gaps in your customer understanding.

## IDEAL:

Ideally, your KAM program collects and analyses comprehensive data on each key account, including their strategy, requirements, sales potential, share of wallet, competitor activities, decision structures, and internal and market relationships. This data-driven approach provides a deep understanding of each account, enabling you to develop tailored strategies and maximize account value.

## RELEVANCE:

Comprehensive customer data is crucial for developing effective KAM strategies. Understanding the nuances of your key accounts is essential for building strong relationships and driving profitable growth. If your data collection is incomplete, or single sourced this area is relevant. Investing in gathering and analysing comprehensive customer data will significantly improve your KAM effectiveness.

## KA DECISION MAKER IDENTIFICATION:

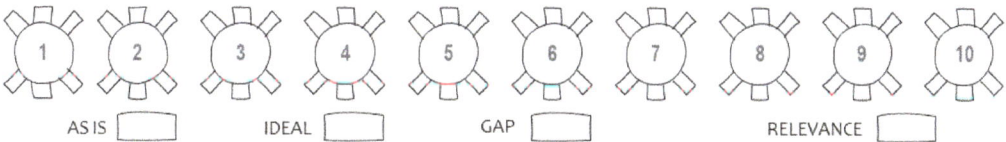

AS IS     IDEAL     GAP     RELEVANCE

## AS IS:

How well does your KAM process identify the key decision-makers and influencers within each key account? Do you have a clear understanding of the account's organisational structure and the roles of different stakeholders? Does the account have separate decision makers for financial and technical / functional decisions? What is their decision hierarchy? How do you identify who is a gate keeper and who are the real decision makers? What criteria do they use to decide? What influence can you have over the criteria? Decision makers and gate keepers? Or is your understanding less precise, potentially hindering your ability to influence purchasing decisions? Evaluating your understanding of the decision-making unit will reveal potential gaps in your account knowledge.

## IDEAL:

Ideally, your KAM process effectively identifies the key decision-makers and influencers within each key account. This includes understanding their roles, responsibilities, and influence within the organisation. This knowledge allows you to tailor your communication and engagement strategies to effectively influence purchasing decisions. Both technical and financial deciders are considered, and influencers are known. Each of the decision makers' personalities, goal, needs and wants are known. The decision criteria is understood as well as your influence over the criteria.

## RELEVANCE:

Identifying key decision-makers and influencers is crucial for navigating the account's organisational structure and influencing purchasing decisions. Understanding the decision-making unit is essential for the smooth closing of deals and building strong relationships. If you lack a clear understanding of these key stakeholders, this area is relevant. Investing in mapping the decision-making unit will improve your account penetration and sales effectiveness whilst also increasing loyalty to your own company.

## IDENTIFICATION OF UNMET NEEDS:

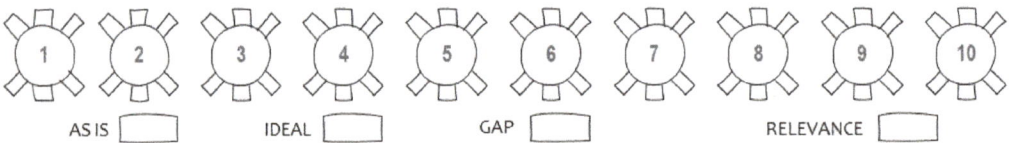

| 1 | 2 | 3 | 4 | 5 | 6 | 7 | 8 | 9 | 10 |

AS IS [ ]    IDEAL [ ]    GAP [ ]    RELEVANCE [ ]

## AS IS:

How does your KAM program identify the real unmet needs of your key accounts? Do you have a structured process for uncovering these needs, perhaps through direct interaction, surveys, or data analysis? Or is your understanding of their needs based on assumptions or general market trends? Evaluating your needs identification process will reveal potential gaps in your customer understanding.

## IDEAL:

Ideally, your KAM program has a well-defined process for identifying the real unmet needs of your key accounts. Understanding their goals and ambitions and the associated avenue of how they will achieve them. This process involves actively seeking customer feedback, conducting thorough needs assessments, and analysing data to uncover hidden needs and opportunities. This deep understanding of customer needs allows you to develop tailored solutions and strengthen customer relationships.

## RELEVANCE:

Identifying and addressing unmet customer needs is needed for building strong relationships and driving customer loyalty. Understanding and addressing the specific needs of key accounts is essential for maximizing account value. If your needs identification process is weak, this area is highly relevant. Investing in a robust needs assessment process will improve your ability to provide valuable solutions and strengthen customer relationships.

# KEY ACCOUNT OBJECTIVE SETTING:

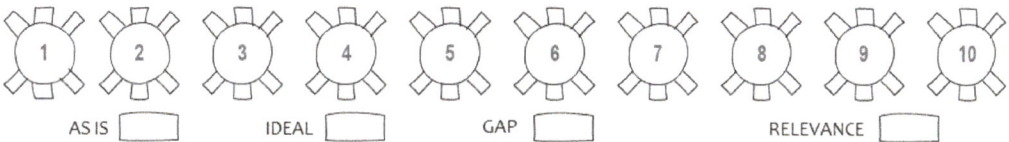

AS IS [ ]   IDEAL [ ]   GAP [ ]   RELEVANCE [ ]

## AS IS:

Are the objectives in your key account plans SMART (Specific, Measurable, Achievable, Relevant, and Time-bound)? Do these objectives encompass key areas such as relationship development, strategic partnership development, cross-selling opportunities, and integrated services? Or are the objectives less defined? How do you measure progress and ultimate success? Evaluating your objective setting process will reveal potential gaps in your planning.

## IDEAL:

Ideally, your key account plans have SMART objectives for each key account, covering key areas such as relationship development, strategic partnership development, cross-selling opportunities, progressing the buy / sell hierarchy and integrated services. This ensures that your efforts are focused on achieving measurable results and maximizing account value. Ideally, the objectives will fall into: Revenue Today, Revenue Tomorrow, Buy Sell Hierarchy Improvement Today and Buy Sell Hierarchy Improvement Tomorrow.

## RELEVANCE:

SMART objectives are crucial for providing focus and direction to your KAM efforts and measuring progress effectively. Setting clear and measurable objectives is essential for maximizing the ROI of your KAM program.

# CROSS-FUNCTIONAL COLLABORATION IN KA PLANNING:

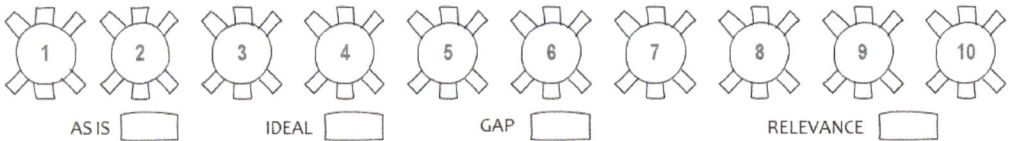

AS IS ☐     IDEAL ☐     GAP ☐     RELEVANCE ☐

## AS IS:

How inclusive is your KAM planning process? Do you actively involve representatives from sales, marketing, service, and other relevant functions? Or is the planning process conducted primarily within the KAM team, potentially missing valuable perspectives and insights? Evaluating your planning process will reveal potential gaps in your cross-functional collaboration.

## IDEAL:

Ideally, your KAM planning process is highly collaborative, actively involving representatives from sales, marketing, service, and other relevant functions. This cross-functional collaboration ensures that all relevant perspectives are considered and that the key account plans are aligned with overall business objectives.

# RELEVANCE:

Cross-functional involvement in KAM planning is crucial for ensuring alignment and maximizing the effectiveness of your account management efforts. Involving all relevant stakeholders is essential for delivering a consistent customer experience and achieving account growth objectives. If your planning process is not inclusive, this area is highly relevant. Investing in cross-functional collaboration will improve your planning and execution.

# CHAPTER 18:

# Key Account Value Proposition

Score this chapter here

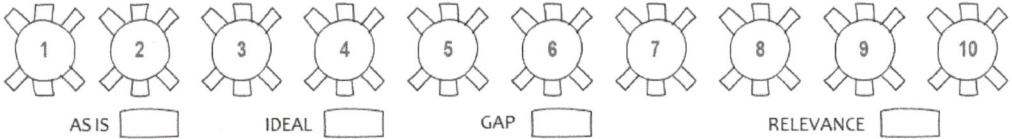

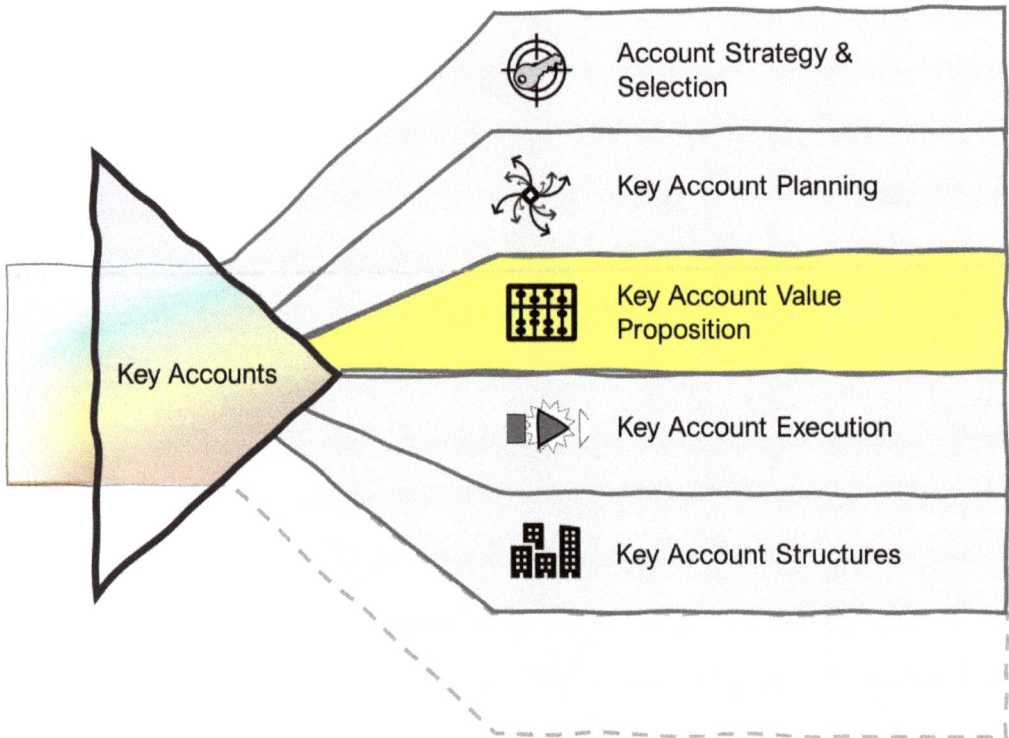

1  2  3  4  5  6  7  8  9  10

AS IS [    ]     IDEAL [    ]     GAP [    ]     RELEVANCE [    ]

- Account Strategy & Selection
- Key Account Planning
- Key Account Value Proposition
- Key Account Execution
- Key Account Structures

Key Accounts

# TAILORING KA APPROACHES:

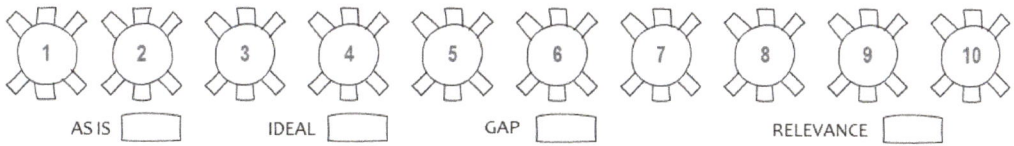

AS IS [ ]    IDEAL [ ]    GAP [ ]    RELEVANCE [ ]

## AS IS:

Consider your current approach to managing key accounts. Do your KAMs develop tailored strategies for each account based on specific insights gathered about that customer? Does your KA approach understand how you add value to the KA's organisation? Is that value aligned with their strategy? Their mission? Their values? How does what you offer make the KA revenue or profit? Can you link your offering directly to their overarching strategy? Or is there a more standardized approach used across all key accounts? How effectively are customer insights used to identify opportunities for profitable growth? Evaluating these aspects will reveal potential gaps in your account-specific strategy development.

## IDEAL:

Ideally, your KAMs develop individualized approaches for each key account, leveraging the specific insights gathered about that customer to drive profitable growth for both entities. The value you provide their organisation is liked to their purpose, mission and revenue / profit generation. This personalized approach ensures that your strategies are tailored to the unique needs and opportunities of each account, maximizing value creation and strengthening customer relationships.

## RELEVANCE:

A tailored approach is crucial for maximizing the value of key account relationships. If you cannot link your value proposition to their strategy, revenue or profit, they may be a key account for you – but you're not strategic for them. Understanding the nuances of each key account and developing customized strategies will drive profitable growth by linking what you provide directly to their strategy. If your approach is standardized, this area is highly relevant. Investing in developing individualized approaches will improve your account management effectiveness, drive greater profitability and loyalty.

# KA VALUE PROPOSITION FORMULATION:

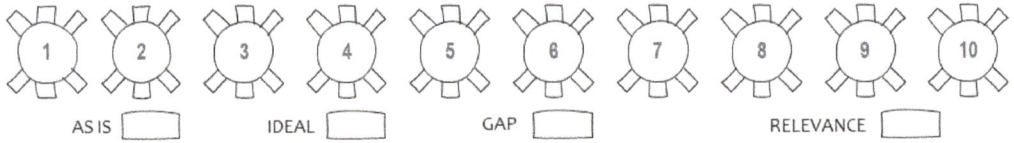

| 1 | 2 | 3 | 4 | 5 | 6 | 7 | 8 | 9 | 10 |

AS IS [        ]    IDEAL [        ]    GAP [        ]    RELEVANCE [        ]

## AS IS:

How is your KAM value proposition used in practice? Does your KAM program effectively utilize this value proposition to tailor solutions and enable joint value creation programs with key accounts? Or is the value proposition more of a theoretical concept, not actively applied in customer interactions? Does the KA know what your value proposition is? How it relates to their business, mission, strategy, etc? Do they help in crafting the value proposition? Evaluating how your value proposition is implemented will reveal potential gaps in its practical application.

## IDEAL:

Ideally, your KAM program actively utilizes the KAM value proposition to tailor solutions and enable joint value creation programs with key accounts. The KA understand your value proposition and actively engages with your organisation. This ensures that your offerings are aligned with customer needs and that you are working collaboratively to achieve mutual benefits.

## RELEVANCE:

Effectively, utilizing your KAM value proposition is crucial for building strong partnerships and driving mutual value creation. Demonstrating and delivering on your value proposition is essential for building trust and securing long-term relationships. If your value proposition is not actively used to tailor solutions and enable joint programs, this area is relevant. Investing in training and tools to support its implementation will improve your KAM effectiveness.

# KA VALUE CALCULATORS:

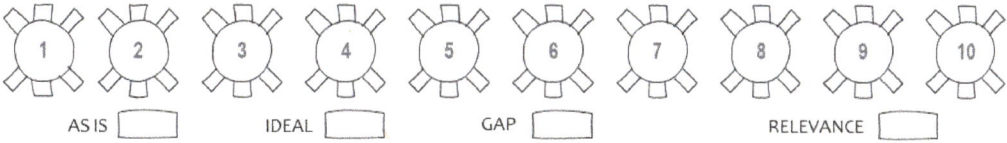

AS IS ☐    IDEAL ☐    GAP ☐    RELEVANCE ☐

## AS IS:

What tools and resources are available to your KAMs to support the creation of unique solutions and joint value creation programs? Or are the same tools used for the rest of the organisation? Do they have access to appropriate marketing materials, cost-benefit calculators, and other analytical tools? Are they tailored to the KA value proposition? Or are they lacking the necessary resources to effectively demonstrate value and develop interesting proposals? Evaluating the availability of these tools will reveal potential gaps in your KAM support infrastructure.

## IDEAL:

Ideally, your KAMs have access to a suite of appropriate marketing materials and cost-benefit calculators to enable them to create **unique** solutions and **joint** value creation programs. These tools empower them to effectively demonstrate the value of your offerings and develop interesting proposals that resonate with key accounts.

## RELEVANCE:

Providing the right tools and resources is crucial for empowering your KAMs to create value and build strong partnerships. Equipping your KAMs with the necessary tools is essential for maximizing their effectiveness and driving profitable growth. If your KAMs lack access to appropriate tools, or only generic tools, this area is relevant. Investing in providing these resources will improve their ability to create value and strengthen customer relationships.

# KA VALUE PROPOSITION TRAINING:

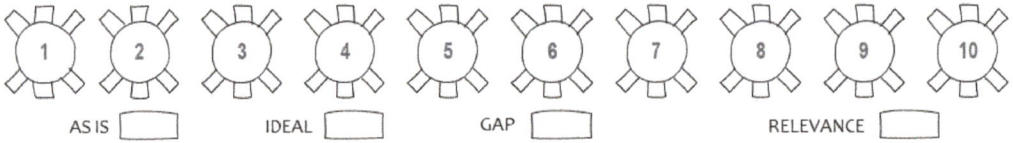

AS IS [ ]     IDEAL [ ]     GAP [ ]     RELEVANCE [ ]

## AS IS:

How well-trained is your commercial organisation on your KAM value proposition? Do all relevant team members understand the key messages and how to effectively communicate them to key accounts? Or is there inconsistency in understanding and application of the value proposition? Evaluating the level of training will reveal potential gaps in your internal communication and training efforts.

## IDEAL:

Ideally, your entire commercial organisation is well-trained in your KAM value proposition. This ensures that everyone understands the key messages and can effectively communicate them to key accounts, creating a consistent and interesting customer experience.

## RELEVANCE:

Consistent communication of your KAM value proposition is crucial for building a strong brand and establishing credibility with key accounts. Ensuring that all customer-facing teams are aligned with the value proposition will maximize its impact. If your commercial organisation is not adequately trained, this area is relevant. Investing in training will improve communication consistency and strengthen your customer relationships.

# VALUE ADDED SERVICES FOR KA'S:

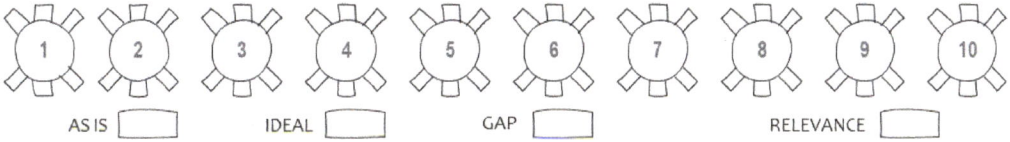

| 1 | 2 | 3 | 4 | 5 | 6 | 7 | 8 | 9 | 10 |

AS IS [ ]   IDEAL [ ]   GAP [ ]   RELEVANCE [ ]

## AS IS:

Consider how your value-added services contribute to the sales in your KAs? Do they demonstrably enhance your ability to win or increase share within the accounts? Or are the services offered more than an afterthought, with limited impact on core product sales? Evaluating the connection between your services and core product sales will reveal potential gaps in both your service strategy and your key account strategy.

## IDEAL:

Ideally, your value-added services directly and significantly enhance your ability to improve the value of your core product offerings. They act as a differentiator, strengthening relationships with key accounts, ultimately driving sales of your core products.

## RELEVANCE:

Aligning value-added services with the value of your core product sales is crucial for maximizing their impact on the key accounts. Strategically designed services can be a powerful differentiator in competitive markets. If your services are not effectively contributing to core product sales, this area is highly relevant. Investing in aligning your service offerings with core product strategies will improve your overall market share and profitability.

# CHAPTER 19:

# Key Account Execution

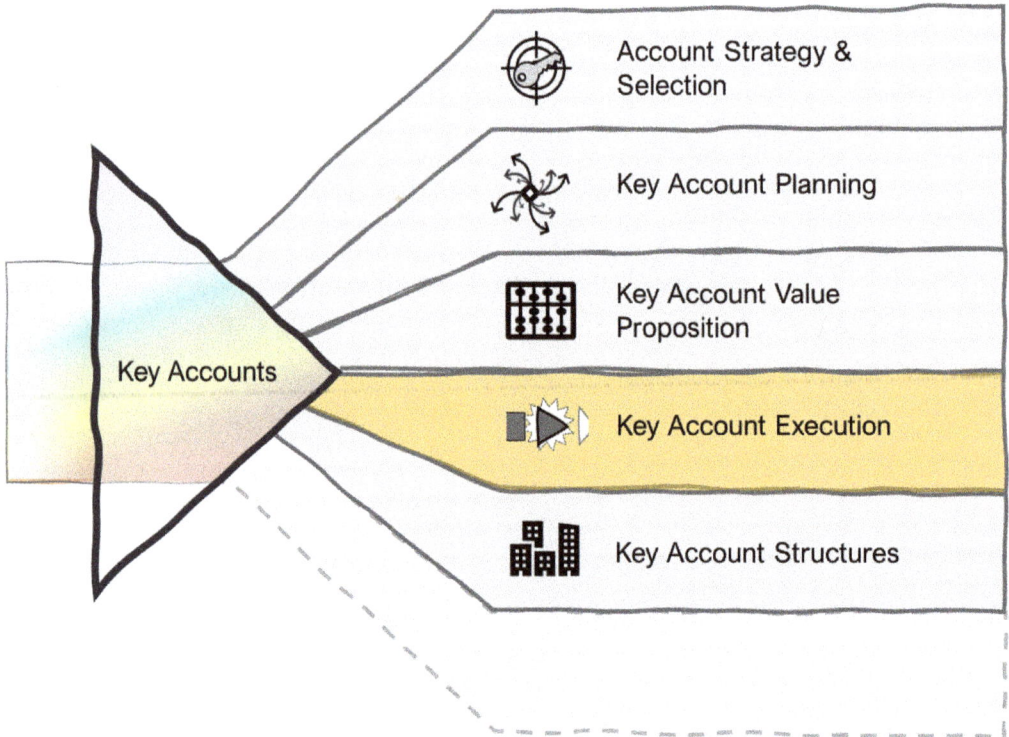

- Account Strategy & Selection
- Key Account Planning
- Key Account Value Proposition
- Key Accounts
- Key Account Execution
- Key Account Structures

# LONG TERM KAS:

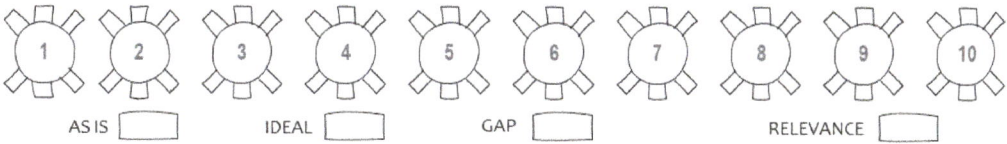

AS IS [ ]   IDEAL [ ]   GAP [ ]   RELEVANCE [ ]

## AS IS:

Consider the nature of your relationships with key accounts. Are they based on short-term transactions, or do they demonstrate characteristics of sustainable, long-term partnerships? Do you have evidence of strong customer loyalty, repeat business, and proactive communication? Evaluating the longevity and strength of your key account relationships will reveal potential gaps in your relationship management. Potentially highlighting one-sided relationships – look more deeply here. Are you providing value for them? What about the value they provide for you? Do you receive more benefit from the program that it costs? In terms of revenue, time, complexity?

## IDEAL:

Ideally, your key accounts have sustainable, long-term relationships with your organisation. These relationships are characterized by mutual trust, open communication, and a shared commitment to achieving mutual success. They extend beyond transactional interactions and involve ongoing collaboration and value creation.

## RELEVANCE:

Building sustainable long-term relationships with key accounts is crucial for securing predictable revenue streams and maximizing customer lifetime value. Strong key account relationships can be a significant driver of stability and growth. If your key account relationships are primarily transactional, this area is highly relevant. Investing in building stronger relationships will improve customer loyalty and long-term profitable.

# KA KPI TRACKING:

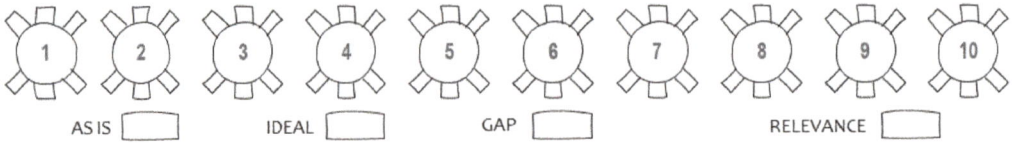

AS IS [ ]    IDEAL [ ]    GAP [ ]    RELEVANCE [ ]

## AS IS:

How do you track the performance of your key accounts? Do you have a defined process for monitoring progress against targets and identifying performance gaps? How are the KPIs used? What does an increase or drop in a measure allow you to do? What actions can you take that move the measure? Are corrective actions taken promptly when needed? Or is performance monitoring less structured, potentially leading to missed opportunities for improvement? Evaluating your performance tracking process will reveal potential gaps in your account management execution.

## IDEAL:

Ideally, your KAM program has a robust process for tracking key account performance against pre-defined targets. This process includes regular monitoring, data analysis, and prompt corrective actions to address any performance gaps. The measures chosen are chosen because the levers to change the KPI are known and well understood. this data-driven approach ensures that you are proactively managing account performance and maximizing results.

## RELEVANCE:

Effective performance tracking and gap management are crucial for achieving key account objectives. Actively managing account performance is essential for maximizing ROI and driving growth. If your performance tracking is weak or reactive, this area is relevant. Implementing a robust tracking and gap management process will improve your account management execution and results, avoiding wasted time and resources.

# KA PROFIT MEASUREMENT:

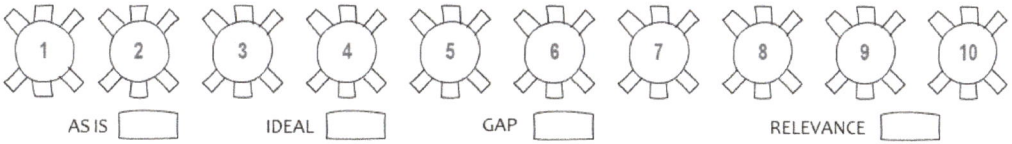

AS IS [ ]    IDEAL [ ]    GAP [ ]    RELEVANCE [ ]

## AS IS:

How do you measure the profitability of each key account? Is profitability measured regularly, and are resources allocated based on account profitability? Or is profitability analysis less frequent or less integrated with resource allocation decisions? Evaluating your profitability measurement and resource allocation will reveal potential gaps in your account management effectiveness.

## IDEAL:

Ideally, your KAM program measures the profitability of each key account regularly. This data is then used to inform resource allocation decisions, ensuring that resources are deployed strategically to maximize overall profitability.

## RELEVANCE:

Measuring and managing key account profitability is crucial for maximizing ROI and ensuring the long-term sustainability of your KAM program. Understanding account profitability is essential for making informed business decisions. If profitability is not measured regularly or effectively linked to resource allocation, this area is highly relevant. Implementing a robust profitability measurement and resource allocation process will improve your account management effectiveness and profitability.

**NOTE:** We will cover this concept more in the finance and pricing sections.

# EFFICIENT EXECUTIVE ACCESS:

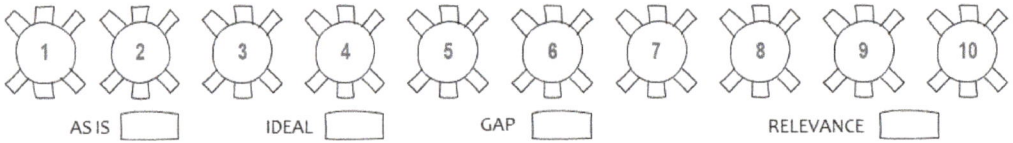

| 1 | 2 | 3 | 4 | 5 | 6 | 7 | 8 | 9 | 10 |

AS IS [　　]     IDEAL [　　]     GAP [　　]       RELEVANCE [　　]

## AS IS:

How easily can your key account managers secure meetings or appointments with executives within key accounts? Are they able to access decision-makers in a timely manner? Or are there challenges in gaining access, potentially hindering their ability to build strong relationships and influence decisions? Evaluating your access to key decision-makers will reveal potential gaps in your relationship management.

## IDEAL:

Ideally, your key account managers can secure meetings and appointments with key executives within key accounts in an appropriately short time frame. This demonstrates strong relationships and facilitates effective communication and collaboration.

## RELEVANCE:

Access to key executives is crucial for building strong relationships and influencing strategic decisions within key accounts. Having strong executive-level relationships can be a significant driver of long-term success. If your KAMs are struggling to gain access to key decision-makers, this area is highly relevant. Investing in building stronger relationships at all levels within key accounts will improve your influence and account penetration.

# FEEDBACK-LOOPS FOR KEY ACCOUNTS:

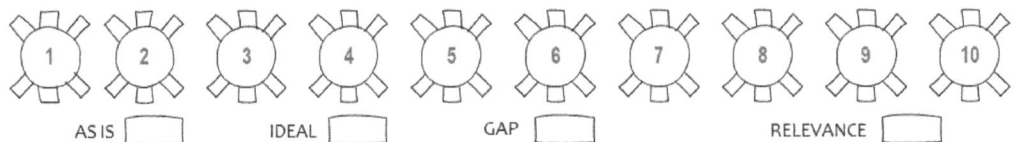

| 1 | 2 | 3 | 4 | 5 | 6 | 7 | 8 | 9 | 10 |

AS IS [　　]     IDEAL [　　]     GAP [　　]       RELEVANCE [　　]

## AS IS:

How frequently do you solicit feedback from your key accounts on your KAM process and their account plans? Is this feedback actively sought and used to improve your approach? Or is feedback collection less frequently or less effectively integrated into your planning and execution? Evaluating your feedback collection process will reveal potential gaps in your continuous improvement efforts.

## IDEAL:

Ideally, your key accounts regularly provide feedback on your KAM process and their account plans, especially during joint development of the value proposition and plan updates. This feedback is actively solicited, carefully considered, and used to continuously improve your KAM approach and strengthen customer relationships.

## RELEVANCE:

Regularly seeking and acting upon customer feedback is crucial for ensuring that your KAM program is aligned with their needs and expectations. Actively listening to your key accounts is essential for building strong partnerships and driving mutual success. They are more likely to give you the "brutal truth". If you are not regularly seeking feedback, this area is highly relevant. Implementing a robust feedback collection and analysis process will improve your KAM effectiveness and strengthen customer relationships.

# CHAPTER 20:

# Key Account Structures

1  2  3  4  5  6  7  8  9  10

AS IS ☐   IDEAL ☐   GAP ☐   RELEVANCE ☐

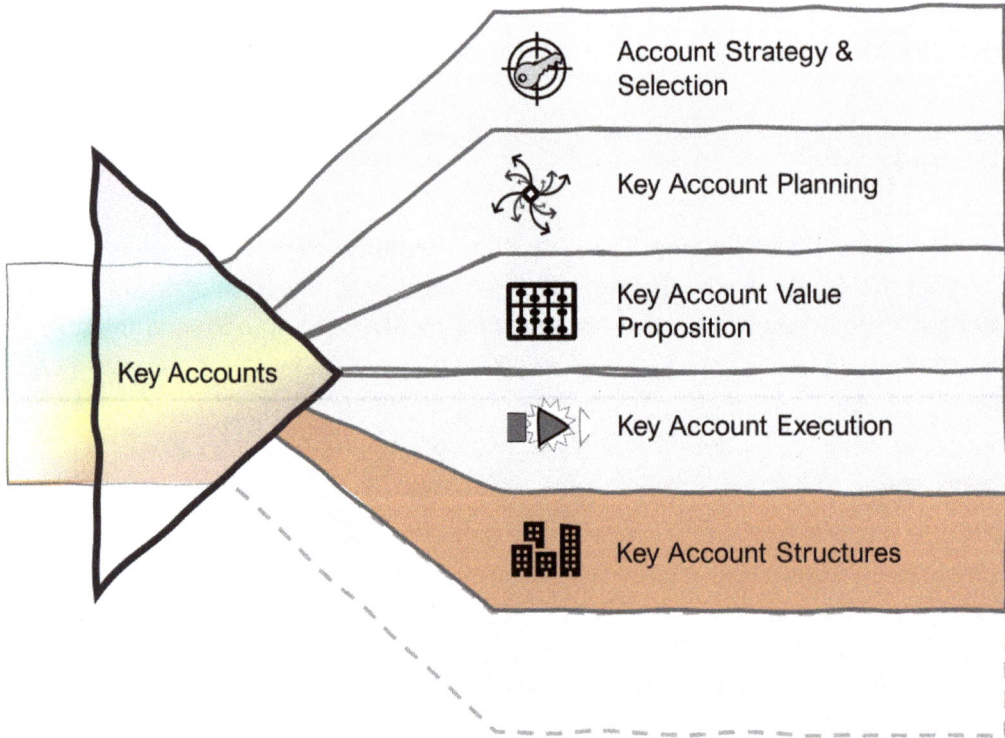

- Account Strategy & Selection
- Key Account Planning
- Key Account Value Proposition
- Key Account Execution
- Key Account Structures

Key Accounts

# KA MANAGEMENT RESOURCES:

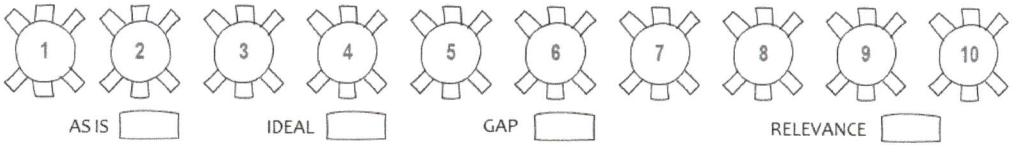

| 1 | 2 | 3 | 4 | 5 | 6 | 7 | 8 | 9 | 10 |

AS IS [       ]       IDEAL [       ]       GAP [       ]       RELEVANCE [       ]

## AS IS:

Consider the skills and experience of your current KAM team. Do they possess the necessary competencies to effectively manage key accounts and meet their specific needs? Are there any skill gaps that need to be addressed through training or recruitment? Is any lack of skills made up for by extra people, time, money? How many KAs do your accounts people manage? Does this number of accounts give them sufficient time to deep dive into each account? With the thorough analysis, are they able to complete a true gold sheet (Miller Heiman, 1991)? Evaluating the capabilities and workload of your KAM team will reveal potential gaps in your talent management.

## IDEAL:

Ideally, you have a team of highly skilled and experienced key account managers who possess the necessary competencies to effectively manage key accounts and meet their diverse needs. This includes strong relationship-building skills, commercial acumen, strategic thinking, and deep product/service knowledge. They will be handling the number of accounts that allow proper planning and execution of your key account processes. Drawing upon sales and marketing resources support and integrations.

## RELEVANCE:

Having the right talent in your KAM team is crucial for maximizing the effectiveness of your KAM program. If your KAM team lacks the necessary skills or experience, this area is highly relevant. Investing in talent development will

improve your account management effectiveness.

# Take a breath and really think about
# <u>KEY ACCOUNTS</u> here!!

I know many, many people who are called Key Account Managers who are not performing the "role" of a Key Account Manager. Often, upon reflection, you'll conclude that they are salespeople with nice titles. If that is the case, revisit the sales section of this book with this new insight.

## KA MANAGER EMPOWERMENT:

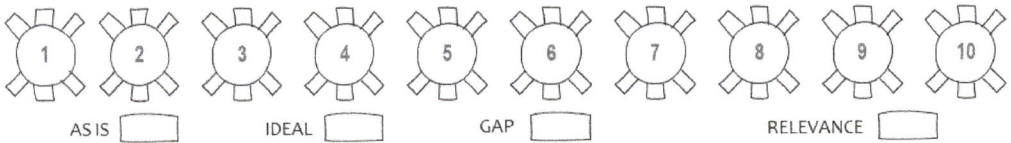

AS IS [    ]    IDEAL [    ]    GAP [    ]    RELEVANCE [    ]

## AS IS:

Consider the level of empowerment given to your Key Account Managers. Are they authorized to make decisions related to their key accounts, or do they need to seek approval for most actions? Does this level of empowerment enable them to respond quickly and effectively to customer needs? Has the account ever thought "if I'm a key account this would be sorted already?" Evaluating the level of empowerment will reveal potential bottlenecks in your decision-making processes.

## IDEAL:

Ideally, your dedicated Key Account Managers are fully empowered to make the right decisions related to their key accounts. This empowers them to act quickly, respond effectively to customer needs, and build stronger relationships. Clear guidelines and boundaries should be established to ensure accountability and alignment with overall business strategy. They can gather the needed support from other departments to execute actions.

## RELEVANCE:

Empowering KAMs is crucial for enabling them to act quickly and effectively in managing their accounts. Empowering KAMs to make timely decisions can significantly improve customer satisfaction and drive sales. If your KAMs lack sufficient empowerment, this area is highly relevant. Investing in clear guidelines and levels of accountability will improve their effectiveness and responsiveness.

## KA SUPPORT MECHANISMS:

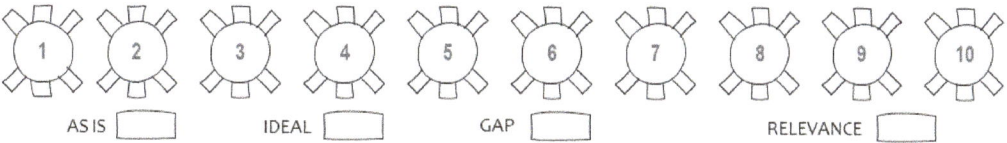

| | | | |
|---|---|---|---|
| AS IS | IDEAL | GAP | RELEVANCE |

## AS IS:

Consider the level of support provided by senior executives to your Key Account Managers. Are senior leaders actively involved in key account relationships, providing guidance, resources, and access to their networks? Or is executive support less visible, potentially limiting the influence and effectiveness of your KAMs? Evaluating the level of executive support will reveal potential gaps in your leadership commitment to KAM.

## IDEAL:

Ideally, your Key Account Managers receive strong and visible support from senior executives. This includes regular communication, strategic guidance, access to executive networks, and active involvement in key account interactions. This demonstrates a strong commitment to KAM and empowers KAMs to build stronger relationships at all levels within key accounts.

## RELEVANCE:

Strong executive support is vital for demonstrating the importance of KAM within your organisation and enhancing the credibility of your KAMs with key accounts. Visible executive support can be a significant differentiator in building strong partnerships. If executive support is lacking, this area is highly relevant. Investing in increasing executive involvement will strengthen your KAM program and its impact.

# KA GOVERNANCE:

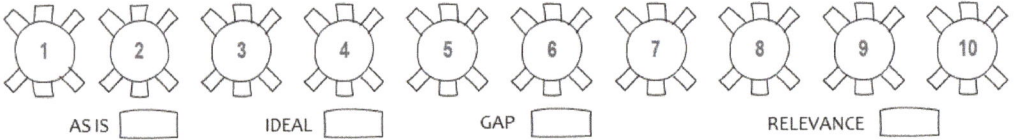

AS IS [　　]    IDEAL [　　]    GAP [　　]    RELEVANCE [　　]

## AS IS:

Consider the governance model that guides decision-making related to key accounts. Are decisions made based on the overall interest of the company, or are they influenced by departmental silos or individual preferences? Who can call or name an account a "key account?" Is there a clear process for resolving conflicts and ensuring alignment with strategic objectives? Evaluating your governance model will reveal potential gaps in your decision-making processes.

## IDEAL:

Ideally, you have a robust governance model in place that ensures decisions related to key accounts are made based on the overall interest of the company. This model includes clear decision-making authority, escalation paths for resolving conflicts, and mechanisms for ensuring alignment with strategic objectives.

## RELEVANCE:

A strong governance model is crucial for ensuring that KAM decisions are aligned with overall business strategy and maximize company value. Effective governance is essential for managing complex key account relationships and driving profitable growth. If your governance model is weak or unclear, this area is relevant. Investing in developing a robust governance model will improve your decision-making, ensure alignment with strategic objectives, and avoid duplication of efforts.

     The Commercial Excellence Playbook

# KA ROLES & RESPONSIBILITIES:

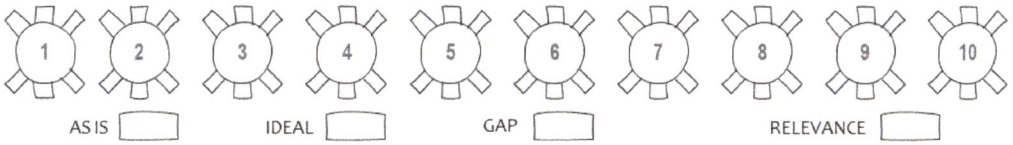

| 1 | 2 | 3 | 4 | 5 | 6 | 7 | 8 | 9 | 10 |

AS IS [ ]    IDEAL [ ]    GAP [ ]    RELEVANCE [ ]

## AS IS:

How effectively does your KAM organisation interact with other departments within your company? Are roles and responsibilities clearly defined, facilitating smooth communication and collaboration? Or are there instances of miscommunication, duplicated efforts, or conflicting priorities? Evaluating cross-functional interaction will reveal potential gaps in your internal collaboration.

## IDEAL:

Ideally, your KAM organisation interacts seamlessly with other departments, with clear roles and responsibilities defined for each function. This facilitates effective communication, collaboration, and coordination, ensuring that all teams work together effectively to support key account relationships.

## RELEVANCE:

Effective cross-functional collaboration is crucial for maximizing the effectiveness of your KAM program. Strong internal collaboration is essential for delivering a consistent customer experience and achieving account growth objectives. If cross-functional interaction is weak, this area is highly relevant. Investing in improving communication and collaboration will strengthen your KAM program.

# KAM INTERDEPARTMENTAL SUPPORT:

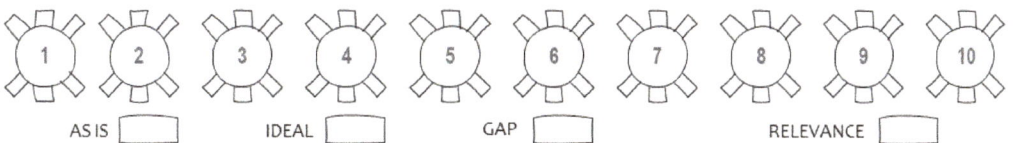

| 1 | 2 | 3 | 4 | 5 | 6 | 7 | 8 | 9 | 10 |

AS IS [ ]    IDEAL [ ]    GAP [ ]    RELEVANCE [ ]

## AS IS:

Consider the level of support provided to your KAMs by other departments, such as Sales, Marketing, Supply Chain, and others. Do these departments provide timely and effective support to help KAMs manage their accounts? Or are there instances of delays, miscommunication, or lack of support? Evaluating the level of support provided to KAMs will reveal potential gaps in your internal support structure.

## IDEAL:

Ideally, your KAMs receive strong and consistent support from all relevant departments within your organisation. This includes timely responses to requests, proactive communication, and effective collaboration to address customer needs and achieve account objectives. The interfaces between KA, sales and marketing are smooth and the work is performed as a team.

## RELEVANCE:

Strong internal support is crucial for empowering KAMs to effectively manage their accounts and build strong customer relationships. Providing adequate support to KAMs is essential for maximizing their effectiveness and driving profitable growth. If support from other departments is lacking, this area is highly relevant. Investing in improving internal support structures will strengthen your KAM program.

## KA INFLUENCE MAPPING:

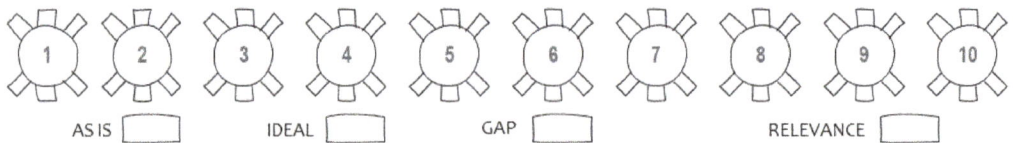

AS IS [ ]    IDEAL [ ]    GAP [ ]    RELEVANCE [ ]

## AS IS:

How well do your KAMs understand the internal dynamics and key stakeholders within each key account? Do they maintain relationship and influence maps to track key contacts, their roles, and their level of influence within the account? Or is their understanding less structured, potentially hindering their ability to navigate the account's organisational structure and influence decisions? Evaluating the use of relationship mapping will reveal potential gaps in your account knowledge.

## IDEAL:

Ideally, your KAMs maintain up-to-date relationship and influence maps for each key account. These maps clearly identify key contacts, their roles, their level of influence, and the relationships between them. This provides a valuable tool for navigating the account's organisational structure and effectively influencing decisions.

## RELEVANCE:

Having a clear understanding of the internal dynamics and key stakeholders within each key account is crucial for building strong relationships and influencing purchasing decisions. Effective relationship mapping can significantly improve account penetration and sales effectiveness. If your KAMs are not utilizing relationship maps, this area is highly relevant. Encouraging and training them on relationship mapping will improve their ability to navigate key accounts and drive results.

# Section Conclusion

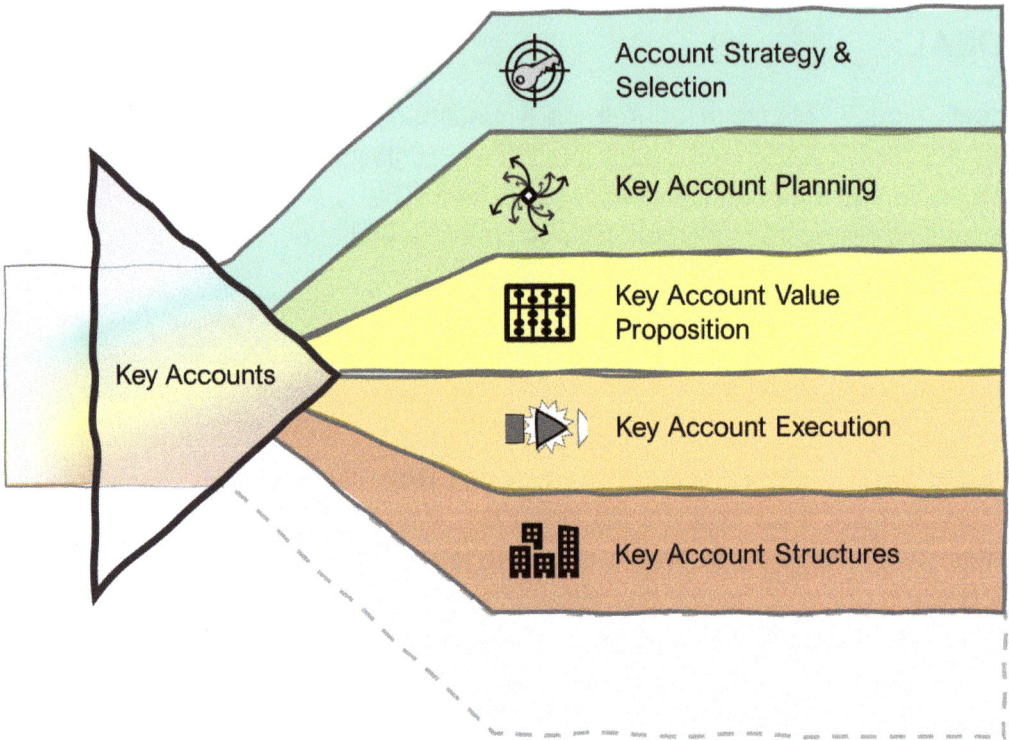

Account Strategy & Selection

Key Account Planning

Key Account Value Proposition

Key Account Execution

Key Account Structures

Key Accounts

**Transfer the ratings at the beginning of each chapter here:**

| Chapter | AS IS | Ideal | Gap | Relevance |
|---|---|---|---|---|
| Account Strategy & Selection | | | | |
| Key Account Planning | | | | |
| KA Value Proposition | | | | |
| KA Execution | | | | |
| KA Structures | | | | |

Is there one area that is better or worse than the others?

Plot the chapters into the strategy box plot.

# KEY ACCOUNT PLOT:

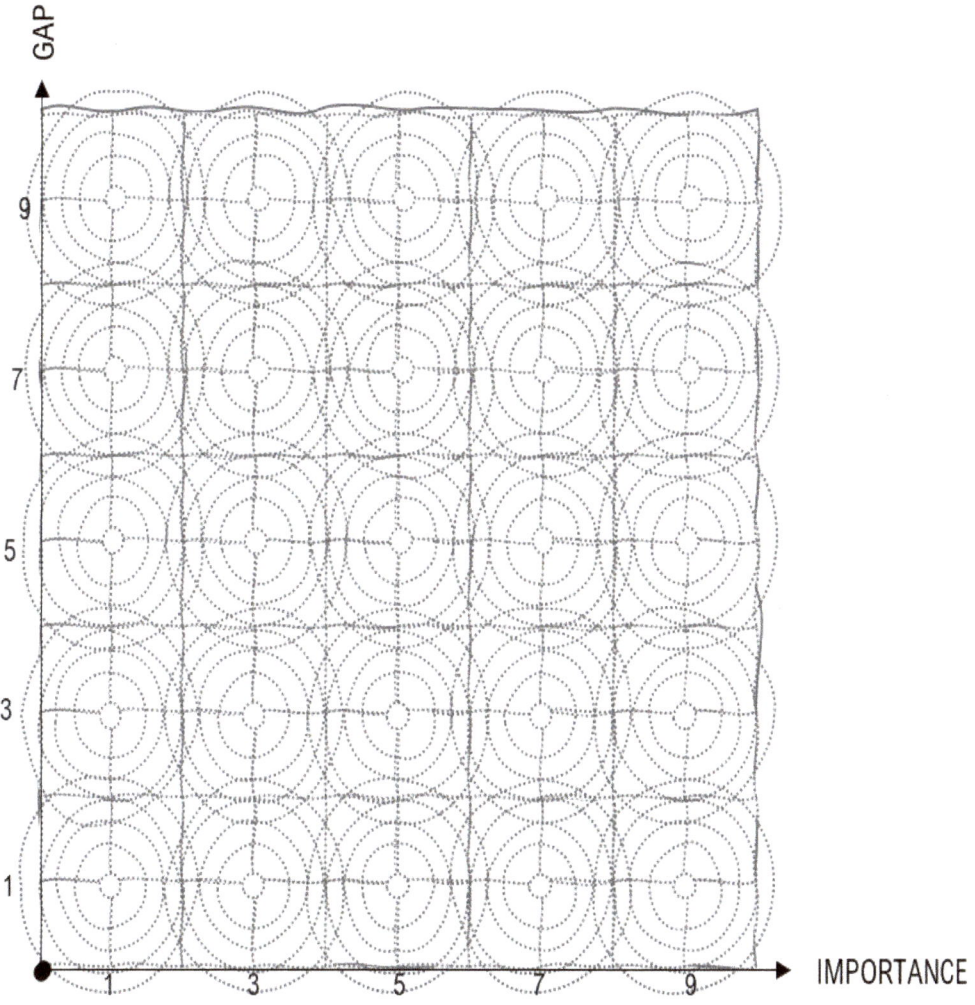

## OVERALL EVALUATION:

AS IS [ ]    IDEAL [ ]    GAP [ ]    RELEVANCE [ ]

Looking at the box plot what is your assessment of key accounts?

# SECTION 5: SERVICE

Strategy

Sales

Marketing

Key Accounts

Services

Channel Management

Finance & Pricing

Are your services a source of customer delight or a necessary evil? In today's experience-driven economy, exceptional service isn't just about fixing problems—it's about creating advocates for your brand. This chapter challenges you to critically examine your service offerings, customer support processes, and value-added initiatives. Are you truly leveraging your services to differentiate your business and drive customer loyalty, or are you merely meeting basic expectations? Let's explore how to transform your service operations from a cost centre to a strategic asset, ensuring that every customer interaction reinforces your value proposition and strengthens your market position

Let's examine services through the following five wavelengths.

**Figure 25:** The 5 Wavelengths of Services

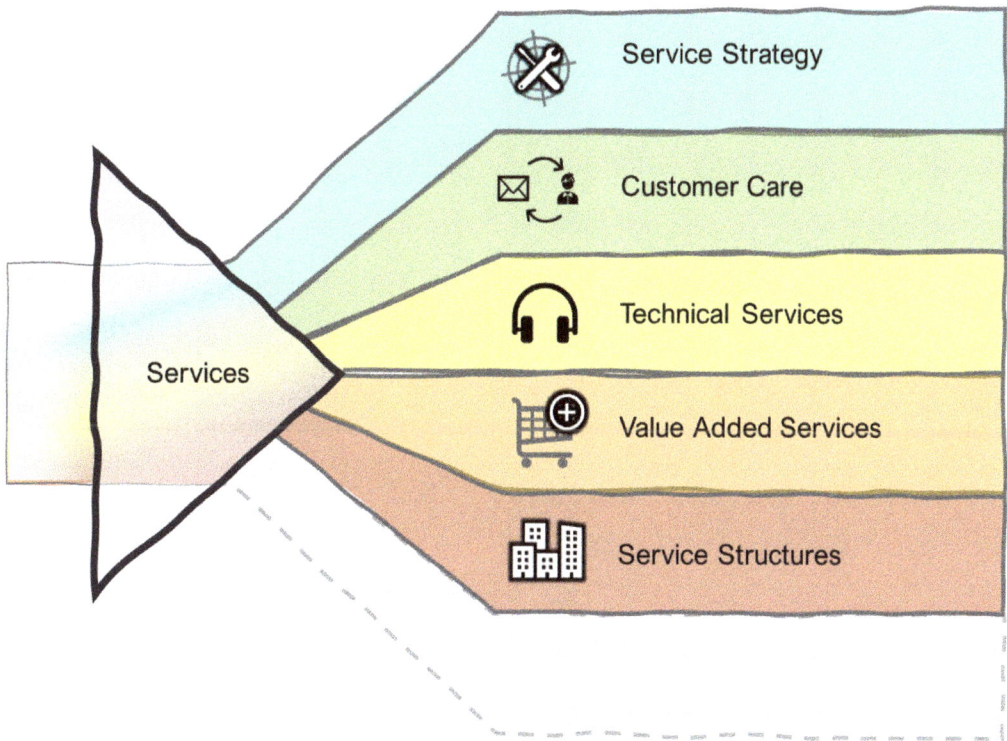

Services

- Service Strategy
- Customer Care
- Technical Services
- Value Added Services
- Service Structures

# CHAPTER 21:

# Service Strategy

Score this chapter here

| 1 | 2 | 3 | 4 | 5 | 6 | 7 | 8 | 9 | 10 |

AS IS [ ]    IDEAL [ ]    GAP [ ]    RELEVANCE [ ]

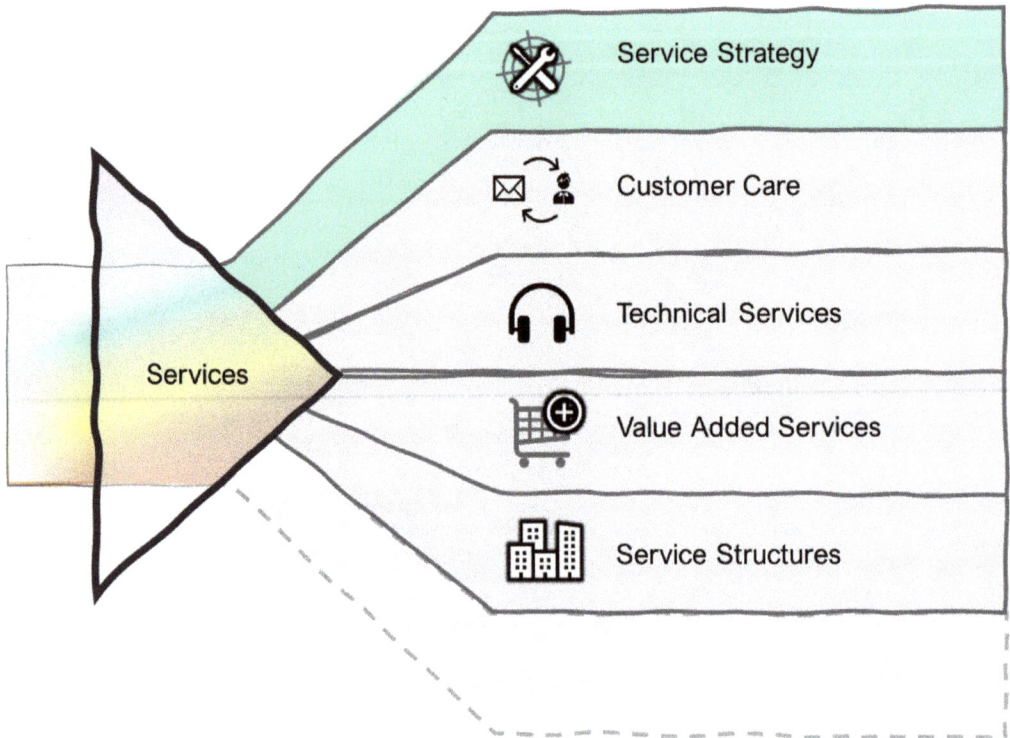

Services

- ⚒ Service Strategy
- ✉ Customer Care
- 🎧 Technical Services
- 🛒 Value Added Services
- 🏢 Service Structures

# SERVICE STRATEGY ALIGNMENT:

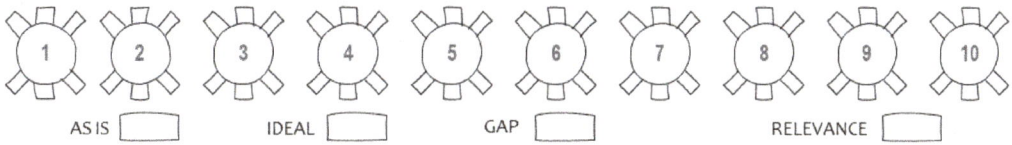

AS IS [ ]   IDEAL [ ]   GAP [ ]   RELEVANCE [ ]

## AS IS:

Consider your current service strategy. Does it have clearly defined objectives that are understood by all relevant departments? Is the strategy aligned across departments such as Sales, Marketing, Operations, and Customer Support? Were services implemented as a part of a deliberate plan or ad hoc response to customer needs as the organisation grew? Does your strategic plan have services as a key part? Are services seen as a revenue stream or cost centre? Or are there inconsistencies in understanding and implementation, potentially leading to fragmented service delivery? Evaluating the clarity and alignment of your service strategy will reveal potential gaps in your strategic planning and cross-functional collaboration.

## IDEAL:

Ideally, your service strategy has clear, measurable objectives that are fully aligned across all relevant departments. This ensures that everyone is working towards the same goals and that service delivery is consistent and effective. These objectives should be linked to overall business goals and contribute to achieving strategic priorities.

## RELEVANCE:

A clear and aligned service strategy is crucial for maximizing the impact of your service offerings. A well-defined service strategy can be a significant differentiator in competitive markets. If your service strategy lacks clarity or alignment, this area is relevant. Investing in developing a clear and aligned strategy will improve your service delivery and its contribution to your business.

# CUSTOMER CENTRIC SERVICE STRATEGY:

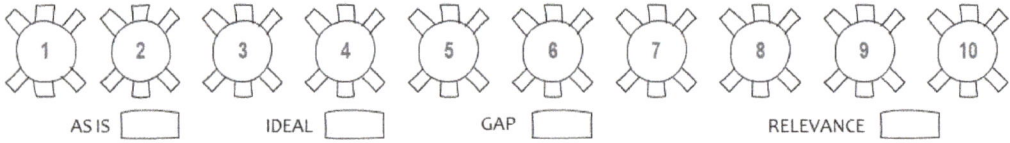

AS IS [ ]    IDEAL [ ]    GAP [ ]    RELEVANCE [ ]

## AS IS:

How well does your service strategy reflect your customers' needs and expectations? Does it clearly articulate the role of service offerings in attracting new customers and retaining existing ones? Or is the strategy more internally focused, potentially missing opportunities to leverage service as a key differentiator? Evaluating the customer-centricity of your service strategy will reveal potential gaps in your customer understanding and service value proposition.

## IDEAL:

Ideally, your overall service strategy is deeply rooted in a thorough understanding of your customers' needs and expectations. It clearly articulates the role of service offerings in both winning new business and retaining existing customers. This customer-centric approach ensures that your services are aligned with customer needs and contribute to achieving business objectives.

## RELEVANCE:

A customer-centric service strategy is crucial for maximizing the impact of your service offerings on customer satisfaction and loyalty. Understanding customer needs and leveraging service as a differentiator can be a significant driver of growth and profitability. If your service strategy is not sufficiently customer-focused, this area is highly relevant. Investing in understanding customer needs and developing a customer-centric service strategy will improve customer satisfaction, loyalty, and business performance.

# COMPREHENSIVE SERVICE STRATEGY TO LEVERAGE MARKET OPPORTUNITIES:

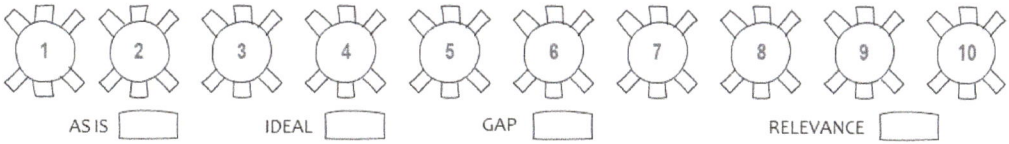

| 1 | 2 | 3 | 4 | 5 | 6 | 7 | 8 | 9 | 10 |

AS IS [      ]     IDEAL [      ]     GAP [      ]          RELEVANCE [      ]

## AS IS:

Consider your current service strategy and how it addresses the various service areas mentioned. How effectively does your current service model leverage market opportunities across customer care (order-to-cash, returns, complaints), technical services (implementation, maintenance, fault correction), education (training, operational support), and value-added services (beyond-the-product solutions, consulting)? Are these areas addressed comprehensively, or are there gaps in your service offering? Are these services integrated and aligned, or do they operate in silos? How well do these services contribute to winning new business and retaining existing customers? Do you have clear metrics to track the performance of each service area? Evaluating these aspects will reveal potential gaps in your overall service strategy and execution.

## IDEAL:

Ideally, your service strategy effectively leverages market opportunities by defining an optimal service model that comprehensively addresses all key service areas. This includes: robust customer care processes that ensure smooth order-to-cash, efficient returns handling, and effective complaint resolution; comprehensive technical services that provide seamless implementation, proactive maintenance, and rapid emergency fault correction; valuable education and training programs that empower customers to effectively use your products and optimize their operations; and interesting value-added services that offer beyond-the-product solutions and consulting, positioning you as a trusted partner. These services are seamlessly integrated, creating a cohesive and interesting customer experience that drives customer satisfaction, loyalty, and business growth.

## RELEVANCE:

A comprehensive and market-focused service strategy is crucial for maximizing business opportunities and achieving sustainable growth, especially for businesses in the $20-50 million range. By effectively addressing all key service areas, you can differentiate yourself from competitors, attract new customers, and build strong, long-term relationships with existing ones. If your current service strategy has gaps in any of these areas—customer care, technical services, education, or value-added services—this area is highly relevant. Investing in developing a comprehensive and integrated service model will significantly enhance your competitiveness, customer satisfaction, and overall business performance. By offering a full spectrum of services, from basic support to advanced consulting, you position yourself as a true partner, capable of addressing a wider range of customer needs and driving mutual success.

# COMPETITION SERVICE OFFERING
# COMPREHENSION:

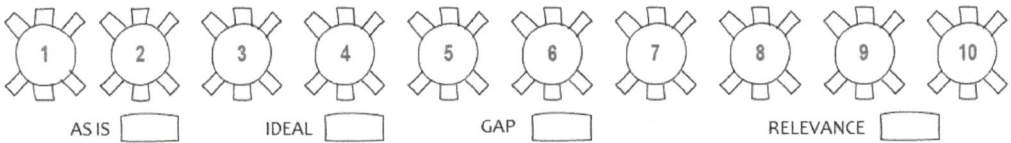

AS IS [     ]    IDEAL [     ]    GAP [     ]    RELEVANCE [     ]

## AS IS:

How well do you understand your competitors' service offerings? Do you have a clear picture of the services they provide, their strengths and weaknesses, and their pricing strategies? Are you actively monitoring changes in their service offerings and identifying opportunities to differentiate your own services? What are they offering that differs from yours? Why are they offering that? Or is your understanding of the competitive landscape less comprehensive, potentially leading to missed opportunities for differentiation? Evaluating your competitive intelligence in the service domain will reveal potential gaps in your competitive analysis.

## IDEAL:

Ideally, you have a deep and comprehensive understanding of your competitors' service offerings. This includes detailed knowledge of their service portfolio, pricing, service levels, customer satisfaction ratings, and any other relevant metrics. You actively monitor their activities and identify opportunities to differentiate your services based on factors such as service quality, speed, expertise, innovation, or value-added offerings. This knowledge allows you to develop an interesting service value proposition that sets you apart from the competition.

## RELEVANCE:

Understanding your competitors' service offerings is crucial for developing a competitive service strategy and winning market share. Differentiating your services can be a powerful driver of growth and customer loyalty. If your understanding of the competitive landscape is weak, this area is highly relevant. Investing in competitive intelligence will enable you to develop a more interesting service value proposition and gain a competitive edge.

# SERVICE OFFERING AS A REVENUE GROWTH DRIVER:

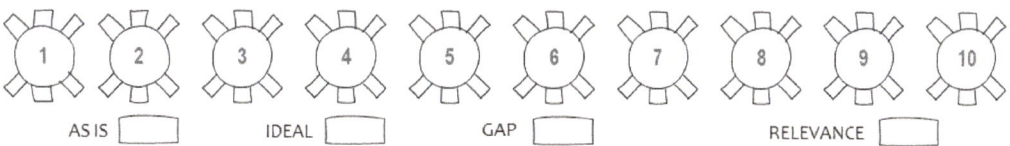

AS IS    IDEAL    GAP    RELEVANCE

## AS IS:

How do you view your service offerings from a financial perspective? Are they considered a cost centre, a necessary expense, or a potential revenue stream? Do you have a clear strategy for monetizing your services and contributing to overall profitability? Or is the focus primarily on providing support, with less emphasis on revenue generation? Evaluating your service monetization strategy will reveal potential gaps in your service business model.

## IDEAL:

Ideally, you consider your service offering as an important additional source of revenue that contributes significantly to growth and profitability. You have a clear and well-defined strategy for monetizing your services, whether through direct fees, service contracts, bundled offerings, or other revenue models. You actively track service revenue and profitability and consider service offerings as a key driver of business growth.

## RELEVANCE:

Monetizing your service offerings can significantly enhance your profitability and create a more sustainable business model. Developing a profitable service business can be a key driver of growth and long-term success. If your service offerings are not effectively monetized, this area is highly relevant. Investing in developing a robust service business model will improve your profitability and overall business performance. By treating services as a profit centre, you can unlock new revenue streams, enhance customer loyalty, and create a more resilient and valuable business.

# CHAPTER 22:

# Customer Care

Score this chapter here

1  2  3  4  5  6  7  8  9  10

AS IS [    ]    IDEAL [    ]    GAP [    ]    RELEVANCE [    ]

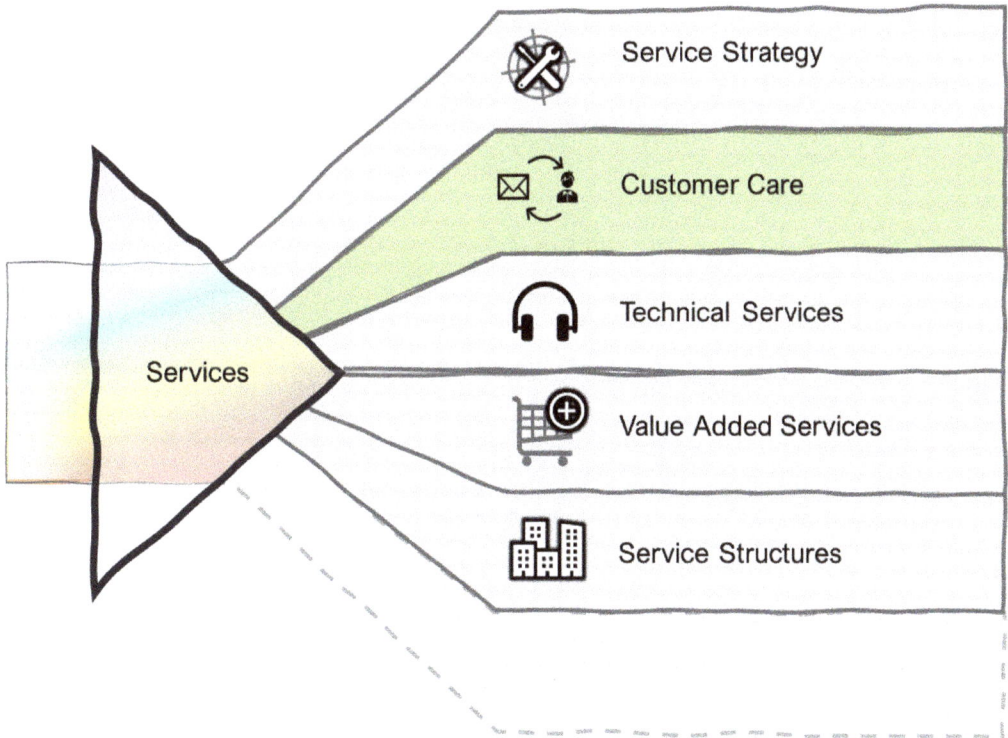

Service Strategy

Customer Care

Technical Services

Value Added Services

Service Structures

Services

# CUSTOMER SERVICE AS A COMPETITIVE ADVANTAGE:

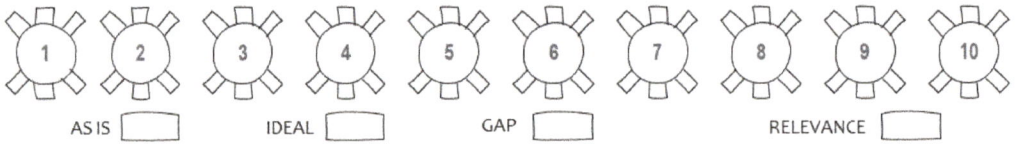

AS IS [ ]   IDEAL [ ]   GAP [ ]   RELEVANCE [ ]

## AS IS:

Consider your basic customer service experience. Does it truly make it easier for customers to do business with you compared to your competitors? Are processes straightforward, communication clear, and issues resolved efficiently? Are your agents easy to get in contract with? Can they handle complaints well? Or are there friction points that create frustration for customers? Evaluating your basic customer service will reveal potential gaps in your customer experience.

## IDEAL:

Ideally, your basic customer service is a key differentiator, making it significantly easier for customers to do business with you than with your competitors. This includes streamlined processes, clear communication, prompt issue resolution, and a customer-centric approach that anticipates and addresses customer needs proactively.

## RELEVANCE:

Making it easy to do business with you is crucial for attracting and retaining customers. Exceptional basic customer service can be a powerful competitive advantage. If your basic customer service is not significantly better than your competitors', this area is highly relevant. Investing in improving basic customer service will enhance customer satisfaction, loyalty, and ultimately drive business growth.

# EFFICIENT AND CONSISTENT SERVICE PROCESSES:

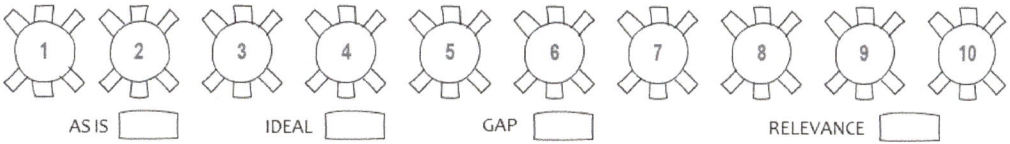

| 1 | 2 | 3 | 4 | 5 | 6 | 7 | 8 | 9 | 10 |

AS IS [        ]    IDEAL [        ]    GAP [        ]    RELEVANCE [        ]

## AS IS:

Consider your service processes. Are they well-documented, lean, and consistently followed across all relevant departments? Are they regularly reviewed and updated to ensure efficiency and effectiveness? Or are processes less formal, potentially leading to inconsistencies and inefficiencies in service delivery? Evaluating your service processes will reveal potential gaps in your operational efficiency.

## IDEAL:

Ideally, you have well-documented lean service processes in place that are consistently followed across all relevant departments. These processes are regularly reviewed and updated to ensure optimal efficiency and effectiveness, enabling seamless end-to-end execution and consistent service delivery. Agents can easily find the relevant information and build upon the process as new insights are learnt.

## RELEVANCE:

Well-defined and consistently followed processes are crucial for efficient and effective service delivery. Streamlined processes can significantly improve operational efficiency and reduce costs. This is even more important if your services are still seen as a cost centre rather than a revenue stream. If your service processes are not well-documented or consistently followed, this area is highly relevant. Investing in documenting, streamlining, and enforcing consistent processes will improve your service delivery and operational efficiency.

# POTENTIAL BASED TIERED SERVICE OFFERINGS:

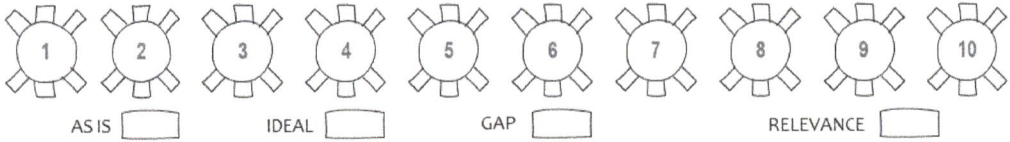

AS IS [____]    IDEAL [____]    GAP [____]    RELEVANCE [____]

## AS IS:

Consider your customer care service offering. Do you offer different levels of service based on customer segmentation and potential value? Or is there a one-size-fits-all approach to service delivery? Does everyone get the same offering? Same time spent? Same access level to support (Level 1/2/3 etc)? Is it time bound? Or do they get unlimited services? Evaluating your service tiring will reveal potential gaps in your customer segmentation and service personalization.

## IDEAL:

Ideally, you have a tiered customer care service offering that varies processes and service levels based on customer segmentation and potential value. This allows you to provide higher levels of service to your most valuable customers, maximizing their satisfaction and loyalty, while still providing efficient service to other customer segments. I've often found that the customers needing and utilizing services the most are usually not purchasing much and aren't your key accounts.

## RELEVANCE:

Tiered service offerings are crucial for maximizing customer satisfaction and optimizing resource allocation. Tailoring service levels to customer value can significantly improve customer retention and profitability. If you do not have a tiered service offering, this area is highly relevant. Implementing a tiered approach will improve your customer satisfaction and resource allocation.

The Commercial Excellence Playbook

# SERVICE OPERATING MODEL:

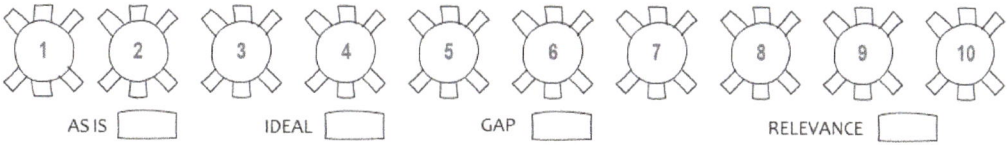

AS IS [ ]    IDEAL [ ]    GAP [ ]    RELEVANCE [ ]

## AS IS:

Consider your customer care operating model. Do you leverage low-cost solutions and online approaches where feasible? Are your internal operations efficient and streamlined? Do you send an expert to the customer? Or does the customer's equipment come to you? How often are service people on the field? Is this balanced? Too much or lacking? Or are there opportunities to reduce costs and improve efficiency? Evaluating your operating model will reveal potential gaps in your cost management and operational efficiency.

## IDEAL:

Ideally, you have an efficient operating model for customer care, leveraging low-cost solutions, online approaches where feasible, and streamlined internal operations. Field work is limited to where it's needed and prioritised for higher value customers. Potentially utilizing the customer targeting system for prioritization. Or potentially those customers who are lower down the targeting segmentation but have service contracts. This ensures that you are providing high-quality service at a reasonable cost, maximizing profitability and resource utilization.

## RELEVANCE:

An efficient operating model is crucial for managing customer care costs and maximizing profitability. Optimizing operational efficiency is essential for maintaining competitiveness. If your operating model is not efficient, this area is relevant. Investing in streamlining operations and leveraging technology will improve your cost management and profitability.

# INNOVATIVE SERVICE OFFERING THROUGH DIGITAL SOLUTIONS:

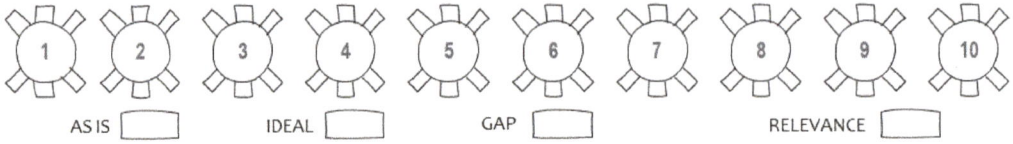

AS IS ☐    IDEAL ☐    GAP ☐    RELEVANCE ☐

## AS IS:

Consider the technology used to support your customer care operations. Do you leverage state-of-the-art digital solutions, such as EDI ordering, online catalogues, and communication platforms? Are you integrating AI agents into your service organisation? Utilizing an enterprise GPT for service efficiency? Do you have your manuals loaded into a GPT where your service tech's can ask questions of the AI? Or are your systems outdated, potentially hindering efficiency and customer experience? Evaluating your technology infrastructure will reveal potential gaps in your digital enablement.

## IDEAL:

Ideally, you provide an innovative service offering enabled by state-of-the-art digital solutions, such as EDI ordering, online catalogues, and seamless communication platforms between customer care, sales representatives, and customers. The business will be utilizing an AI model that allows customer service integration. You may also potentially have an enterprise copy AI that's pre-coded with the service manuals, fault trees and big data from your service records so it can be utilized as an "ask anything" system available to the field service personnel.

## RELEVANCE:

Leveraging technology is crucial for providing efficient and innovative customer care. Investing in digital solutions can significantly improve customer experience and operational efficiency. If your technology infrastructure is outdated, this area is highly relevant. Investing in modern digital solutions will improve your customer care effectiveness and competitiveness. Having a programmed AI source that lists the policies, procedures and failure modes to integrate into the service offering can be a strategic advantage. AI will be rapidly adopted into the mainstream therefore this area will be one of the first that is integrated – making this section extremely relevant at this point in history.

# CUSTOMER SERVICE AGENT TRAINING:

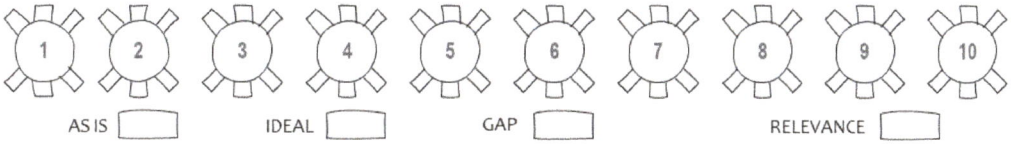

| 1 | 2 | 3 | 4 | 5 | 6 | 7 | 8 | 9 | 10 |

AS IS [ ]   IDEAL [ ]   GAP [ ]   RELEVANCE [ ]

## AS IS:

Consider the training provided to your customer service agents. Are they effectively trained in customer engagement skills, such as telephone etiquette, objection handling, and account data analysis? Or are there gaps in their training, potentially affecting customer interactions and service quality? Evaluating your training programs will reveal potential gaps in your agent capabilities.

## IDEAL:

Ideally, your customer service agents receive comprehensive training in customer engagement skills, including telephone etiquette, objection handling, account data analysis, and effective communication techniques. This ensures that they are equipped to provide high-quality service and build strong customer relationships.

## RELEVANCE:

Well-trained customer service agents are crucial for providing excellent customer care. Investing in agent training can significantly improve customer satisfaction and loyalty. If your agent training is inadequate, this area is highly relevant. Investing in comprehensive training programs will improve your customer service quality and effectiveness.
**NOTE:** At the time of writing, AI is just starting to gain mainstream traction. Training of agents on how to best utilize and prompt engineering tools will rapidly become the norm.

# CUSTOMER SATISFACTION:

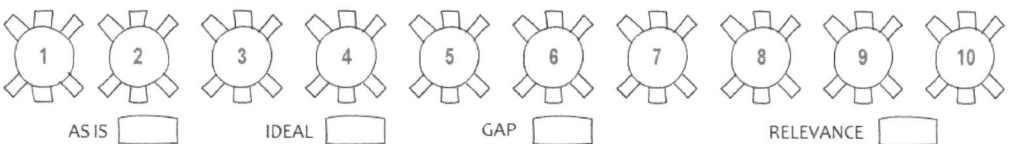

| 1 | 2 | 3 | 4 | 5 | 6 | 7 | 8 | 9 | 10 |

AS IS [ ]   IDEAL [ ]   GAP [ ]   RELEVANCE [ ]

## AS IS:

How do you monitor customer satisfaction and other relevant KPIs? Do you have systems in place to collect customer feedback and track key metrics, such as on-time-in-full delivery, Net Promoter Score (NPS) (Reichheld, 2006) and reachability? Or is your performance monitoring less systematic, potentially missing opportunities for improvement? Evaluating your performance monitoring will reveal potential gaps in your data collection and analysis.

## IDEAL:

Ideally, you monitor overall customer satisfaction and other relevant KPIs, such as on-time-in-full delivery, NPS reachability, first-call resolution, and customer effort score. You have systems in place to collect customer feedback and track this metrics regularly, enabling you to identify areas for improvement and continuously enhance the customer experience. If you're in a regulated industry, you will use the annual survey requirement here. Ideally, you will also understand if the customer is a Hostage or an Apostle from HBR's Improvements on the NPS model as seen in figure 26 below.

**Figure 26:** Hostages and Apostle Model Adaptation

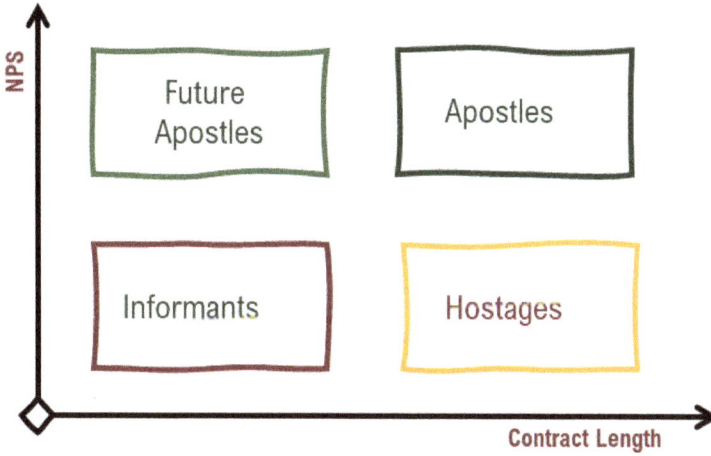

# RELEVANCE:

Monitoring customer satisfaction and relevant KPIs is crucial for continuously improving your customer care operations. Data-driven performance monitoring is essential for optimizing service delivery and maximizing customer loyalty. If your performance monitoring is weak, this area is highly relevant. Implementing a robust monitoring system will improve your ability to identify areas for improvement and enhance the customer experience.

# CHAPTER 23:

# Technical Services

Score this chapter here

1  2  3  4  5  6  7  8  9  10

AS IS ____   IDEAL ____   GAP ____   RELEVANCE ____

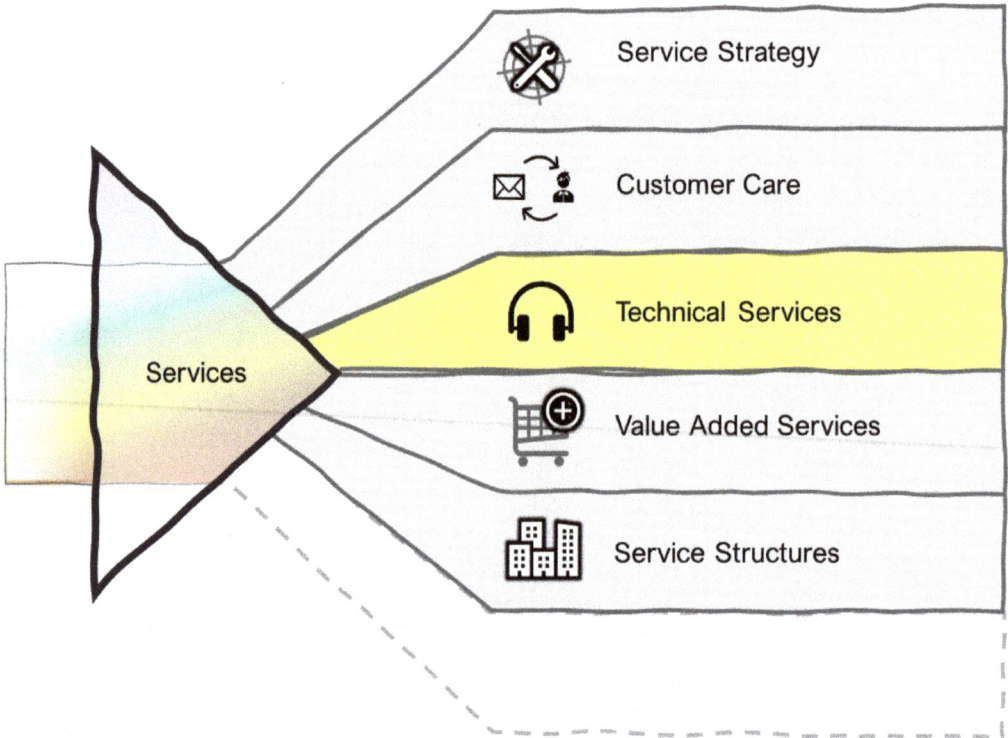

Service Strategy

Customer Care

Technical Services

Services

Value Added Services

Service Structures

# TECHNICAL SERVICES ORGANISATION:

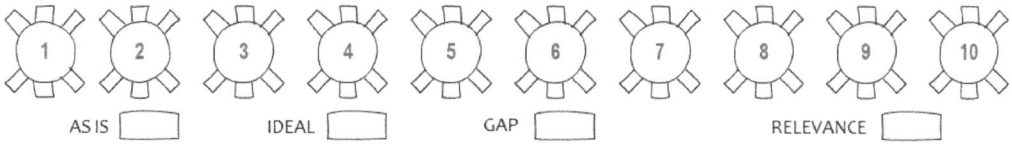

AS IS [ ]  IDEAL [ ]  GAP [ ]  RELEVANCE [ ]

## AS IS:

Consider your Technical Service delivery organisation. Is it recognized by your customers for its superior capabilities compared to the competition? Do you have data or testimonials to support this claim? Or is this perception based on internal assumptions? Are Technical Services based solely on existing customers or are they also used as proof sources to for the sales process? (E.g. Demos). Evaluating customer perception of your technical services will reveal potential gaps in your service delivery and competitive differentiation.

## IDEAL:

Ideally, you have a strong Technical Service delivery organisation that is widely recognized by your customers for its superior capabilities compared to the competition. This recognition is based on demonstrable performance, positive customer feedback, and a clear track record of exceeding customer expectations. Technical Services play a two-fold role:

**1.** Presales as technical experts.

**2.** Post sales as service support.

## RELEVANCE:

Having a strong and recognized Technical Service organisation is crucial for building customer loyalty and gaining a competitive advantage. Superior technical service can be a key differentiator. If your technical services are not perceived as superior, this area is highly relevant. Investing in improving your technical service capabilities and communicating those improvements to customers will enhance your reputation and competitiveness.

# SERVICE LEVEL ACHIEVEMENT:

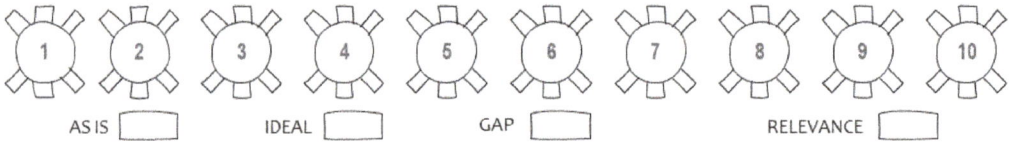

AS IS [    ]    IDEAL [    ]    GAP [    ]    RELEVANCE [    ]

## AS IS:

Consider your service level ambitions. Do you consistently achieve the service levels you have set for your technical services? Are these service levels clearly defined and measurable? Or are there frequent deviations from your targets, potentially affecting customer satisfaction? Evaluating your service level performance will reveal potential gaps in your service delivery and performance management.

## IDEAL:

Ideally, you consistently achieve your service level ambitions across all key metrics, such as response time, resolution time, first-time fix rate, MTBF and others. These ambitions are clearly defined, measurable, and aligned with or exceed the customer expectations.

## RELEVANCE:

Achieving your service level ambitions is crucial for meeting customer expectations and maintaining high service quality. Consistent service delivery is essential for building customer trust and loyalty. If you are not consistently achieving your service level ambitions, this area is highly relevant. Investing in improving your service delivery processes and performance management will enhance customer satisfaction and strengthen your reputation.

# CONTINUOUS IMPROVEMENT OF SERVICE PROCESSES:

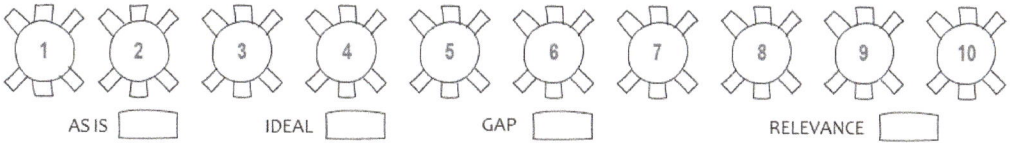

AS IS ☐    IDEAL ☐    GAP ☐    RELEVANCE ☐

## AS IS:

Consider the processes you have in place for implementation, maintenance, and fault correction. Are these processes well-documented, lean, and consistently followed? Do you have a system for capturing feedback from sales representatives and using it to continuously improve these processes? Or are processes less formal, potentially leading to inconsistencies and inefficiencies? Evaluating your service processes and continuous improvement efforts will reveal potential gaps in your operational efficiency.

## IDEAL:

Ideally, you have well-documented, lean processes in place for implementation, maintenance, and fault correction. These processes are continuously reviewed and improved based on feedback from sales representatives, customer feedback, and internal learning. This continuous improvement cycle ensures optimal efficiency and effectiveness in your service delivery.

## RELEVANCE:

Well-defined and continuously improved processes are crucial for efficient and effective technical service delivery. Streamlined processes can significantly improve operational efficiency and reduce costs. If your service processes are not well-documented or continuously improved, this area is highly relevant. Investing in documenting, streamlining, and continuously improving your processes will enhance your service delivery and operational efficiency.

# TIERED SERVICE OFFERINGS:

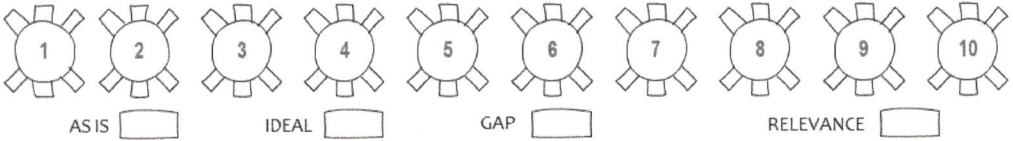

AS IS [    ]    IDEAL [    ]    GAP [    ]    RELEVANCE [    ]

## AS IS:

Consider your technical service offering. Do you offer different tiers of service with varying prices based on service levels, such as response time, coverage hours, or included services? Does it prioritize preventative maintenance over reactive break-fix approaches? Do you use a tiered response model to prioritize and allocate resources efficiently? Are dispatching processes optimized to minimize response times? Or are there opportunities to improve efficiency and reduce costs? Or is there a one-size-fits-all approach to pricing and service delivery? Evaluating your service tiering and pricing strategy will reveal potential gaps in your service value proposition and revenue generation.

## IDEAL:

Ideally, you have a tiered service offering that provides customers with different service levels at varying price points. This allows customers to choose the service level that best meets their needs and budget, while also maximizing your revenue potential. You will have an efficient operating model for your technical services that emphasizes preventative maintenance, uses a tiered response model for efficient resource allocation, and optimizes dispatching processes to minimize response times. This proactive approach minimizes downtime for customers, reduces costs, and improves overall service efficiency

## RELEVANCE:

A tiered service offering is crucial for providing flexibility to customers and maximizing revenue generation. Offering different service levels can attract a wider range of customers and increase profitability. If you do not have a tiered service offering, this area is highly relevant. Implementing a tiered approach will improve your customer satisfaction and revenue generation.

# TECH SERVICES CUSTOMER SATISFACTION:

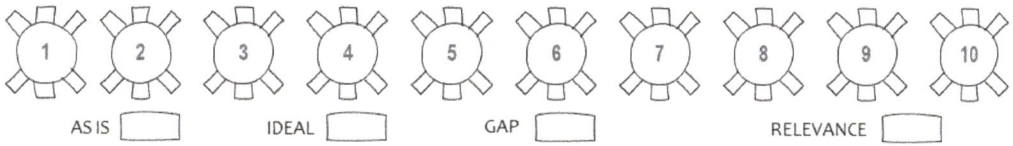

| 1 | 2 | 3 | 4 | 5 | 6 | 7 | 8 | 9 | 10 |

AS IS [      ]     IDEAL [      ]     GAP [      ]          RELEVANCE [      ]

## AS IS:

How do you monitor customer satisfaction with your technical services? Do you track relevant KPIs such as mean time between failure (MTBF), response time, and first-time resolution rate? Do you have post intervention surveys? Do services have an NPS or equivalent measure? Or is your performance monitoring less systematic, potentially missing opportunities for improvement? Evaluating your performance monitoring will reveal potential gaps in your data collection and analysis.

## IDEAL:

Ideally, you monitor customer satisfaction with your technical services through regular surveys, feedback mechanisms, and tracking of relevant KPIs such as MTBF, response time, first-time resolution rate, NPS and customer effort score. This data-driven approach allows you to identify areas for improvement and continuously enhance the customer experience.

## RELEVANCE:

Monitoring customer satisfaction and relevant KPIs is crucial for continuously improving your technical services. Data-driven performance monitoring is essential for optimizing service delivery and maximizing customer loyalty. If your performance monitoring is weak, this area is highly relevant. Implementing a robust monitoring system will improve your ability to identify areas for improvement and enhance the customer experience.

# TECH SERVICES REVENUE GENERATION:

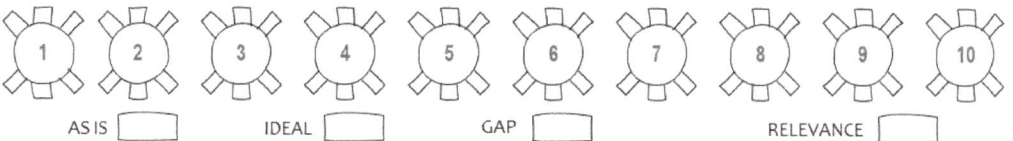

| 1 | 2 | 3 | 4 | 5 | 6 | 7 | 8 | 9 | 10 |

AS IS [      ]     IDEAL [      ]     GAP [      ]          RELEVANCE [      ]

## AS IS:

How do you measure the financial performance of your technical services? Are you able to generate appropriate revenues and profits from these services? Do you have a clear pricing strategy and cost management process? Or is the financial performance of your technical services less clear, potentially limiting their contribution to overall profitability? Evaluating your financial performance will reveal potential gaps in your service business model.

## IDEAL:

Ideally, you have a clear and effective strategy for generating appropriate revenues and profits from your technical services. This includes a well-defined pricing strategy, efficient cost management, and a focus on maximizing customer value.

## RELEVANCE:

Generating appropriate revenues and profits from technical services is crucial for their long-term sustainability and contribution to your business. Developing a profitable service business can be a key driver of growth. If your technical services are not generating appropriate revenues and profits, this area is highly relevant. Investing in developing a robust service business model will improve their profitability and overall business performance.

# SERVICE CONTRACTING:

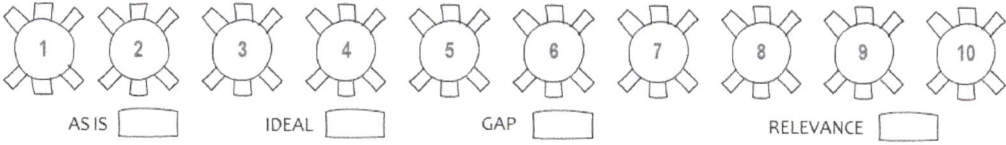

| 1 | 2 | 3 | 4 | 5 | 6 | 7 | 8 | 9 | 10 |

AS IS [ ]    IDEAL [ ]    GAP [ ]    RELEVANCE [ ]

## AS IS:

What percentage of your customers that are covered by technical service contracts? Is it a high percentage (e.g., >50%), demonstrating strong customer engagement and recurring revenue streams? Or is the coverage lower, potentially indicating missed opportunities for service revenue and customer retention? Evaluating your contract coverage will reveal potential gaps in your service sales and customer engagement.

## IDEAL:

Ideally, you have technical service contracts covering a high percentage (e.g., >50%) of your customer or equipment base. This demonstrates strong customer engagement, provides predictable recurring revenue streams, and strengthens customer relationships.

## RELEVANCE:

High contract coverage is crucial for generating recurring revenue and building strong customer relationships. Maximizing contract coverage can significantly improve revenue stability and profitability. If your contract coverage is low, this area is highly relevant. Investing in improving your service sales and customer engagement will increase your contract coverage and strengthen your business.

# CHAPTER 24:

# Value Added Services

Score this chapter here

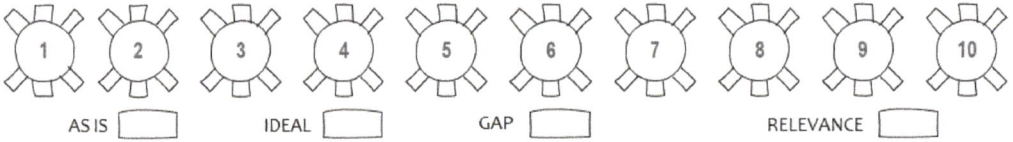

AS IS ☐    IDEAL ☐    GAP ☐    RELEVANCE ☐

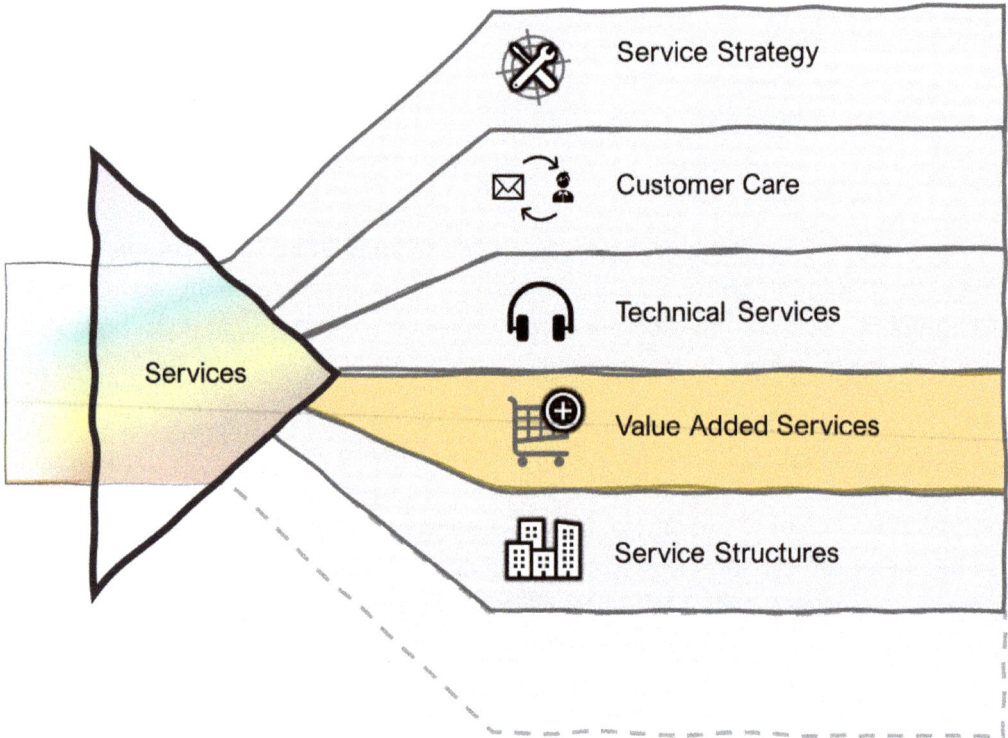

- Service Strategy
- Customer Care
- Technical Services
- Value Added Services
- Service Structures

Services

# SERVICES TO REDUCE OPERATIONAL COSTS FOR CUSTOMERS:

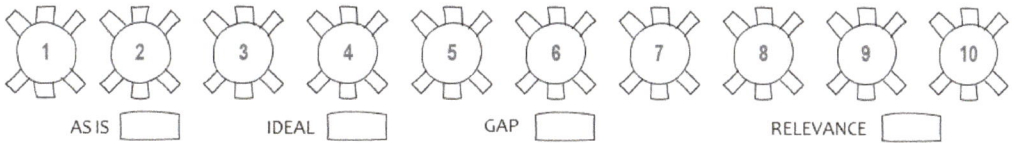

| 1 | 2 | 3 | 4 | 5 | 6 | 7 | 8 | 9 | 10 |
|---|---|---|---|---|---|---|---|---|----|

AS IS ☐   IDEAL ☐   GAP ☐   RELEVANCE ☐

## AS IS:

What types of services do you offer to help customers reduce their operational costs? Do these services address key areas such as process simplification, inventory management, patient flow optimization (if applicable), or facility layout? Or are the services offered less focused on cost reduction, potentially limiting their appeal to cost-conscious customers? Evaluating the focus of your services will reveal potential gaps in their value proposition.

## IDEAL:

Ideally, you offer a range of services specifically designed to help customers reduce their operational costs. These services address key areas relevant to their business, such as process simplification, inventory management, patient flow optimization (if applicable), or facility layout, demonstrating a clear commitment to helping them improve efficiency and profitability. Ideally the benefit allows greater revenue for your company either through consulting fees or increase sales because you're increasing the customers throughput.

## RELEVANCE:

Offering services that directly address customer pain points, such as operational costs, is brilliant for building strong relationships and demonstrating value. Helping customers improve efficiency and reduce costs can be a powerful differentiator. If your services won't increase throughput by breaking the accounts or if you can't capture revenue from consulting fees this area may not be of high important to the organisation If your services are not effectively addressing these needs, this area is highly relevant. Investing in developing services that directly affect customer operational costs will enhance their value and attractiveness.

# PARTNER OF CHOICE POSITIONING:

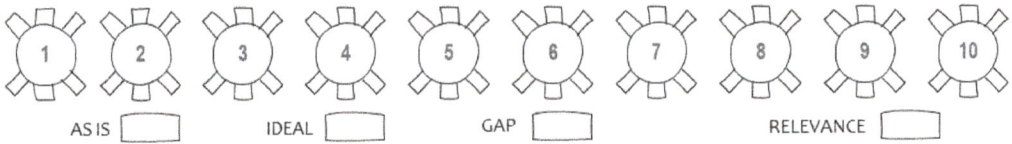

| | | | | | | | | | |
|---|---|---|---|---|---|---|---|---|---|
| 1 | 2 | 3 | 4 | 5 | 6 | 7 | 8 | 9 | 10 |

AS IS [ ]     IDEAL [ ]     GAP [ ]     RELEVANCE [ ]

## AS IS:

How do your value-added services impact your customer relationships? Do they position you as a trusted partner, rather than just a vendor? Or are the services offered in a more transactional manner, with limited impact on building long-term relationships? Evaluating the impact of your services on customer relationships will reveal potential gaps in your partnership strategy.

## IDEAL:

Ideally, your value-added services play a key role in positioning you as a "partner of choice" for your customers. They demonstrate a deep understanding of customer needs and a commitment to helping them achieve their business objectives, fostering strong, long-term relationships built on trust and mutual value creation.

## RELEVANCE:

Positioning yourself as a partner of choice is excellent for building long-term customer loyalty and securing repeat business. Building strong partnerships with key customers can be a significant driver of sustainable growth. If your services are not effectively positioning you as a partner, this area is highly relevant. Investing in developing services that foster deeper customer relationships will improve customer loyalty and drive long-term value.

The Commercial Excellence Playbook

# VALUE-ADDED SERVICES AS A COMPETITIVE ADVANTAGE:

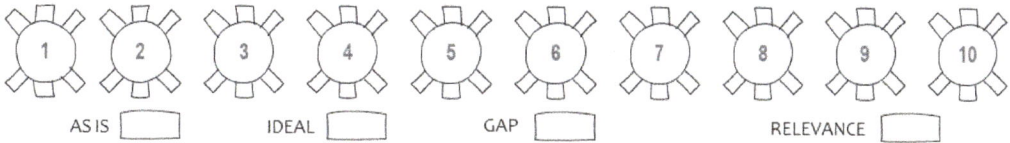

## AS IS:

Consider your Value-Added Services (VAS) delivery organisation. Is it recognized by your customers as a "partner of choice" because of superior capabilities compared to competitors? Do you have concrete evidence, such as testimonials, case studies, or high customer satisfaction scores, to support this claim? Or is this perception based on internal assumptions? Evaluating customer perception of your VAS delivery will reveal potential gaps in your service delivery and competitive differentiation.

## IDEAL:

Ideally, you have a strong VAS delivery organisation that is consistently recognized by customers as their "partner of choice." This recognition stems from demonstrable superior capabilities, a proven track record of delivering value, and strong, collaborative relationships with customers. You have tangible evidence to support this claim, showcasing the positive impact of your VAS on customer outcomes.

## RELEVANCE:

Being recognized as a "partner of choice" is crucial for building strong, long-term customer relationships and securing repeat business. Strong VAS can be a key differentiator and a source of competitive advantage. If your organisation is not perceived as a partner of choice, this area is highly relevant. Investing in enhancing your VAS capabilities, improving customer communication, and focusing on collaborative partnerships will strengthen your customer relationships and drive business growth.

# SERVICES SUPPORTING CUSTOMER NEEDS:

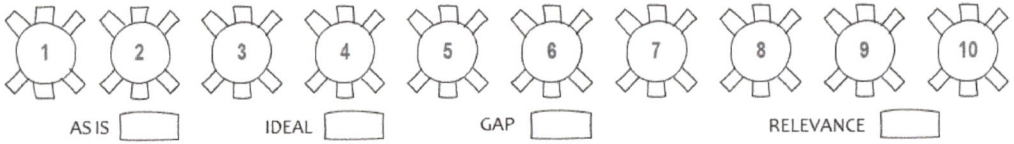

| 1 | 2 | 3 | 4 | 5 | 6 | 7 | 8 | 9 | 10 |

AS IS ☐   IDEAL ☐   GAP ☐   RELEVANCE ☐

## AS IS:

Consider the types of VAS you offer. Do they directly support customers in delivering their value to their customer base? If you're in diagnostics or medical devices, does the offer support in areas such as outcome measurement programs, training and education in improved procedures or patient management, and patient pathway enhancement? Or are your Value Added Services less focused on these critical aspects of care delivery? Evaluating the focus of your VAS will reveal potential gaps in their value proposition and relevance to customer needs.

## IDEAL:

Ideally, you offer a comprehensive suite of VAS specifically designed to support customers in delivering a higher quality of care. This includes services such as support in outcome measurement programs, training and education in improved interventional procedures or patient management, and patient pathway enhancement education programs. These services directly address customer needs and contribute to improved patient outcomes.

## RELEVANCE:

Offering VAS that directly support improved quality of care is crucial for building strong relationships with healthcare providers and demonstrating a commitment to patient well-being. For businesses in the $20-50 million range serving the healthcare sector, this focus can be a significant differentiator. If your VAS are not effectively supporting quality of care initiatives, this area is highly relevant. Investing in developing and delivering such services will enhance your value proposition and strengthen your relationships with healthcare customers.

# VALUE ADDED SERVICES REVENUE GENERATION:

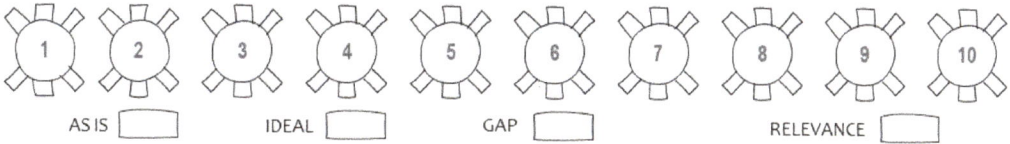

AS IS [ ]  IDEAL [ ]  GAP [ ]  RELEVANCE [ ]

## AS IS:

How do you measure the financial performance of your VAS? Are you able to generate appropriate revenues and profits from these services? Do you have a clear pricing strategy and cost management process for your VAS? Or is the financial performance less clear, potentially limiting their contribution to overall profitability? Evaluating your financial performance will reveal potential gaps in your VAS business model.

## IDEAL:

Ideally, you have a clear and effective strategy for generating appropriate revenues and profits from your VAS. This includes a well-defined pricing strategy that reflects the value delivered to customers, efficient cost management, and a focus on maximizing profitability.

## RELEVANCE:

Generating appropriate revenues and profits from VAS IS crucial for their long-term sustainability and contribution to your business. Developing a profitable VAS business can be a key driver of growth and profitability. If your VAS are not generating appropriate revenues and profits, this area is highly relevant. Investing in developing a robust VAS business model, including pricing and cost management, will improve their financial performance and overall business success.

# CHAPTER 25:

# Service Structures

Score this chapter here

| 1 | 2 | 3 | 4 | 5 | 6 | 7 | 8 | 9 | 10 |

AS IS [        ]    IDEAL [        ]    GAP [        ]    RELEVANCE [        ]

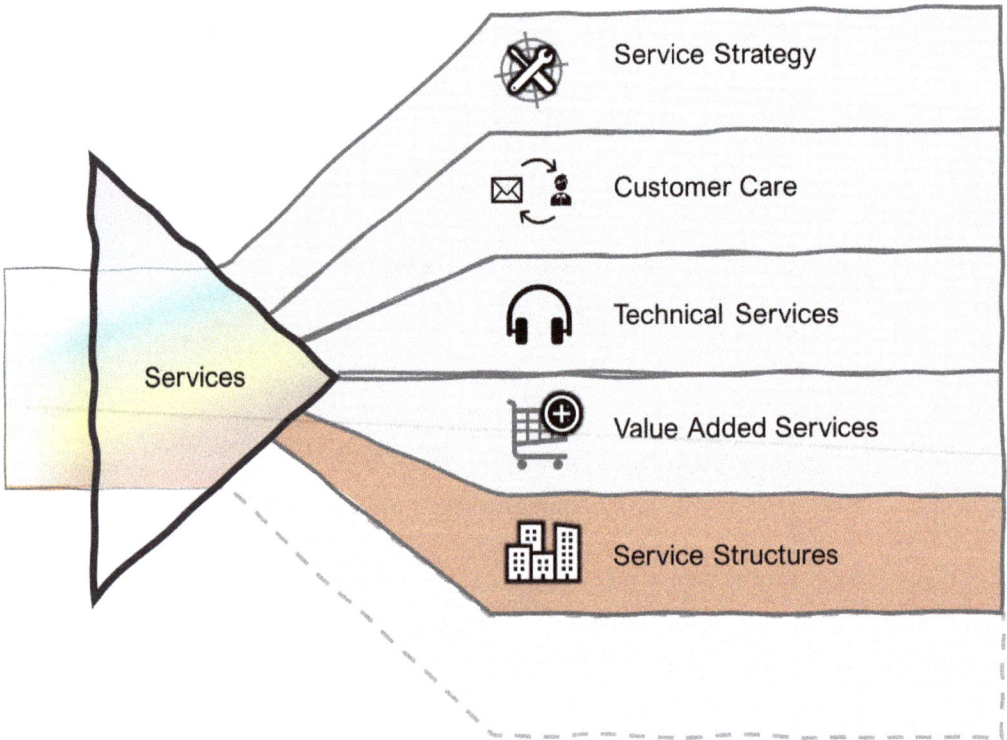

Services

- Service Strategy
- Customer Care
- Technical Services
- Value Added Services
- Service Structures

# SERVICE RESOURCING:

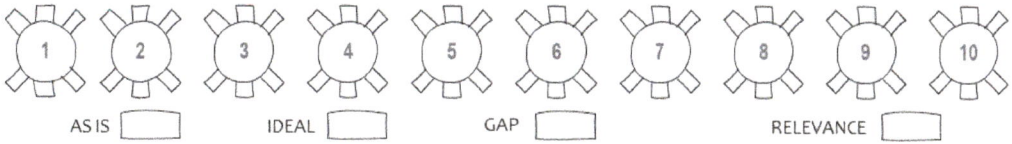

| 1 | 2 | 3 | 4 | 5 | 6 | 7 | 8 | 9 | 10 |

AS IS [        ]        IDEAL [        ]        GAP [        ]        RELEVANCE [        ]

## AS IS:

Consider the current staffing levels within your service department. Reflect on whether you have sufficient personnel to effectively serve your target customer base. Are service teams consistently overloaded, leading to delays in response times or reduced service quality? Or are there periods of underutilization, indicating potential overstaffing? Consider metrics such as customer-to-service-personnel ratios, average handling times, and customer wait times. Analysing these factors will reveal potential gaps in your service department's capacity planning.

## IDEAL:

Ideally, your service department is staffed at a level that enables it to effectively cover your target customer base without compromising service quality or employee well-being. This involves a proactive approach to capacity planning, taking into account factors such as customer growth projections, service demand fluctuations, and employee workload. The goal is to maintain optimal staffing levels that ensure timely and efficient service delivery while also preventing employee burnout.

## RELEVANCE:

Adequate staffing within the service department is crucial for meeting customer expectations and maintaining high service quality. Having the right number of service personnel is essential for scaling operations and supporting business growth. If your service department is understaffed, this area is highly relevant. Investing in appropriate staffing levels will improve customer satisfaction, reduce employee stress, and enhance overall service effectiveness.

# EXPERTISE AND CAPABILITY IN EXECUTING SERVICE STRATEGY:

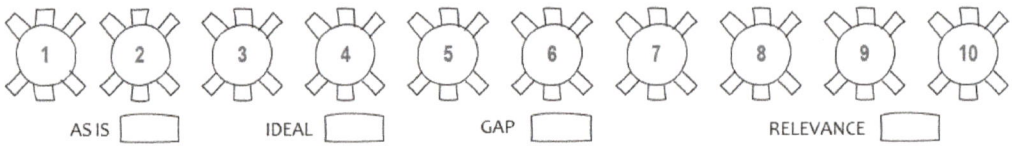

AS IS [ ]     IDEAL [ ]     GAP [ ]     RELEVANCE [ ]

## AS IS:

Consider the skills, experience, and functional knowledge of your service team members. Reflect on whether they possess the necessary competencies to fully execute your service strategy and meet evolving customer needs. Are there any skill gaps that need to be addressed through training or recruitment? Do team members have a deep understanding of your products/services, customer needs, and industry best practices? Evaluating these aspects will reveal potential gaps in your service team's capabilities.

## IDEAL:

Ideally, your service team members possess the optimal mix of skills, experience, and deep functional understanding required to fully and successfully execute your service strategy. This includes technical expertise, strong communication skills, problem-solving abilities, and a customer-centric mindset. Ongoing training and development programs should be in place to ensure that team members stay up to date with the latest technologies, industry trends, and best practices.

## RELEVANCE:

Having a highly skilled and knowledgeable service team is essential for delivering exceptional service and achieving strategic objectives. Investing in talent development within the service department can be a significant differentiator. If your service team lacks the necessary skills or experience, this area is highly relevant. Investing in training and development will improve service quality, enhance customer satisfaction, and drive business growth.

# SERVICE COMPETITIVE ADVANTAGES:

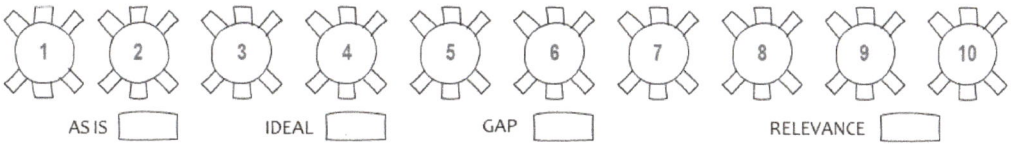

AS IS [     ]     IDEAL [     ]     GAP [     ]     RELEVANCE [     ]

## AS IS:

Consider how your service performance compares to that of your competitors. Reflect on whether you are consistently delivering superior service because of either better training programs for your service personnel or higher retention rates of experienced team members, or both. Do you actively compare your service metrics (e.g., customer satisfaction, resolution times) with those of your competitors? If you cannot clearly demonstrate a competitive advantage in service delivery, this area warrants further investigation.

## IDEAL:

Ideally, your organisation consistently delivers superior service compared to competitors, either through more effective training programs that equip service personnel with advanced skills and knowledge, or through higher retention rates of experienced service team members who possess invaluable institutional knowledge and customer relationships, or ideally both. This competitive edge in service delivery should be demonstrable through metrics, customer feedback, and market recognition.

## RELEVANCE:

Delivering superior service is a powerful differentiator in competitive markets. Achieving a competitive advantage through better training or better retention of experienced service personnel can significantly enhance customer loyalty and drive business growth. If you cannot confidently claim to provide better service than competitors, this area is highly relevant. Investing in training programs or employee retention strategies can improve your service delivery and strengthen your competitive position.

# SERVICE IT TOOLS:

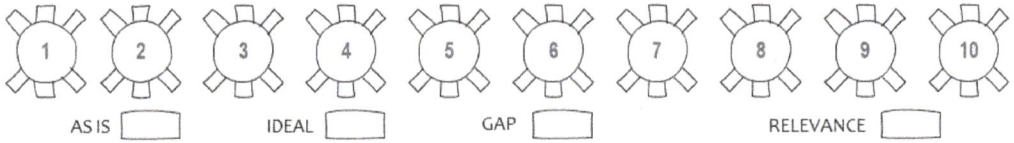

```
  1    2    3    4    5    6    7    8    9   10
```

AS IS [        ]    IDEAL [        ]    GAP [        ]    RELEVANCE [        ]

## AS IS:

Consider the IT tools and systems used by your customer service organisation. Reflect on whether these tools optimally support their daily activities and enable them to provide efficient and effective service. Are your systems integrated, user-friendly, and regularly updated? Or are there gaps in functionality, usability, or integration that hinder service delivery? Evaluating your IT infrastructure will reveal potential gaps in your technology enablement. Do you utilize AI to gain insights?

## IDEAL:

Ideally, your customer service organisation is equipped with state-of-the-art IT tools that fully support their operations and enable them to provide seamless and efficient service. These tools should be integrated, user-friendly, and regularly updated to meet evolving customer needs and technological advancements. This includes CRM systems, knowledge bases, ticketing systems, communication platforms, and other relevant technologies.

## RELEVANCE:

Optimally supporting your customer service organisation with effective IT tools is crucial for maximizing efficiency and enhancing customer experience. Investing in appropriate technology can significantly improve service delivery and reduce costs. If your IT tools are not optimally supporting your customer service organisation, this area is highly relevant. Investing in upgrading or integrating your systems will improve efficiency, enhance customer experience, and drive business growth.

# SERVICE STRUCTURE:

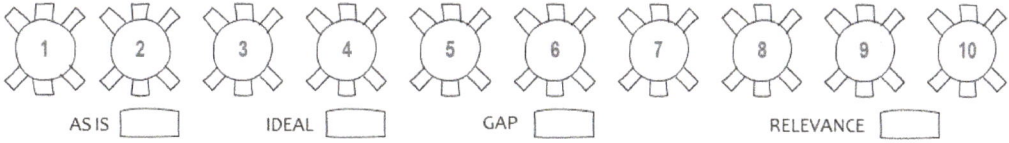

AS IS [____]    IDEAL [____]    GAP [____]    RELEVANCE [____]

## AS IS:

Consider the structure of your service organisation. Reflect on whether the current structure effectively supports your service strategy and customer needs. Are roles and responsibilities clearly defined? Is there effective communication and collaboration between different service teams and departments? Or are there inefficiencies, bottlenecks, or communication breakdowns because of structural issues? Evaluating your organisational structure will reveal potential gaps in your operational efficiency and service delivery.

## IDEAL:

Ideally, your service organisation is structured in a way that effectively supports your service strategy and customer needs. This involves clearly defined roles and responsibilities, efficient workflows, effective communication channels, and seamless collaboration between different service teams and departments. The structure should be flexible enough to adapt to changing business needs and customer demands.

## RELEVANCE:

An effective organisational structure is crucial for efficient and effective service delivery. Optimizing your service organisation's structure can significantly improve operational efficiency and customer satisfaction. If your service organisation is not structured effectively, this area is highly relevant. Investing in restructuring or streamlining your service organisation will improve efficiency, enhance communication, and drive better service outcomes.

# SERVICES ROLES AND RESPONSIBILITIES:

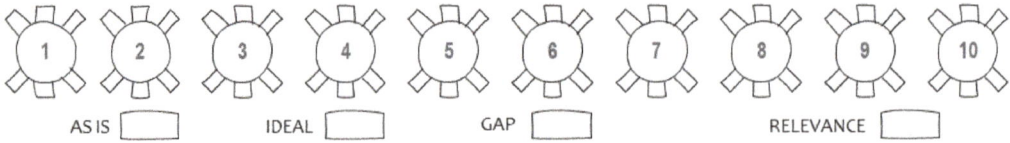

| | | | | | | | | | |
|---|---|---|---|---|---|---|---|---|---|
| 1 | 2 | 3 | 4 | 5 | 6 | 7 | 8 | 9 | 10 |

AS IS [ ]    IDEAL [ ]    GAP [ ]    RELEVANCE [ ]

## AS IS:

Consider the roles, responsibilities, and interfaces within your service function. Reflect on whether all relevant parties clearly defined and understood these. Is there effective collaboration between the service function and other departments, such as the sales team? Or are there ambiguities, overlaps, or communication breakdowns that hinder effective service delivery? Evaluating the clarity of roles, responsibilities, and interfaces will reveal potential gaps in your internal communication and collaboration.

## IDEAL:

Ideally, your service function has clearly defined roles, responsibilities, and interfaces with other departments, particularly the sales team. This ensures seamless communication, efficient workflows, and a coordinated approach to serving customers. Documented processes and communication protocols should be in place to facilitate effective collaboration and prevent misunderstandings.

## RELEVANCE:

Clearly defined roles, responsibilities, and interfaces are crucial for effective service delivery and cross-functional collaboration. Clear communication and collaboration between service and sales teams, and other relevant functions, are essential for maximizing customer satisfaction and driving business growth. If these aspects are not clearly defined, this area is highly relevant. Investing in clarifying roles, responsibilities, and interfaces will improve communication, enhance collaboration, and drive better service outcomes.

# Section Conclusion

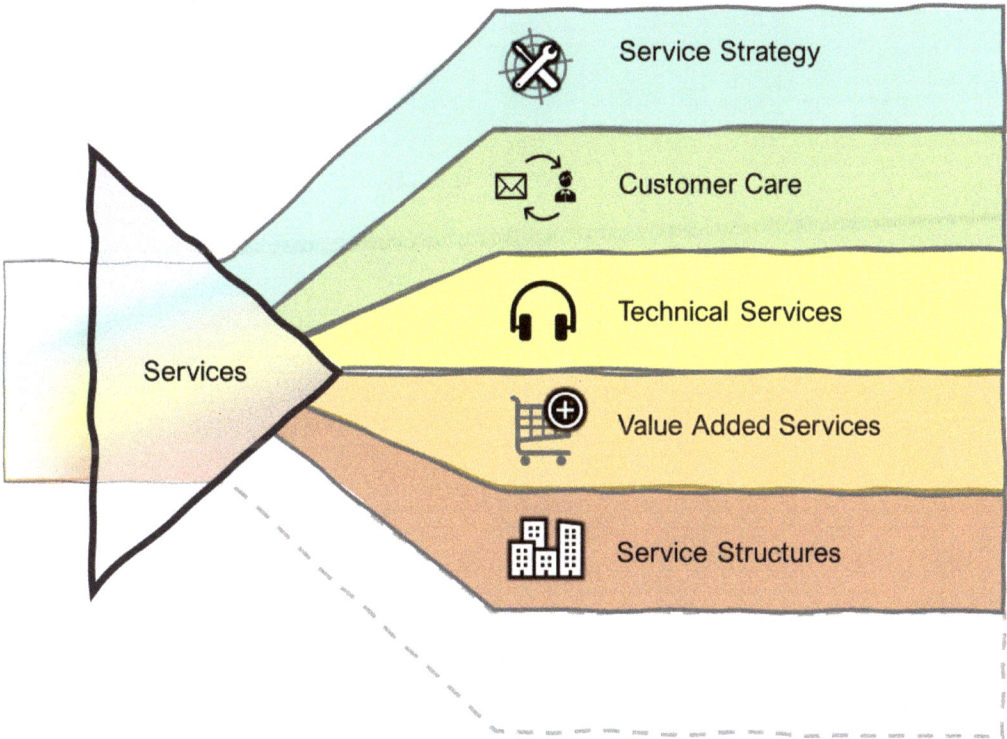

Service Strategy

Customer Care

Technical Services

Value Added Services

Service Structures

Services

**Transfer the ratings at the beginning of each chapter here:**

| Chapter | AS IS | Ideal | Gap | Relevance |
|---|---|---|---|---|
| Service Strategy | | | | |
| Customer Care | | | | |
| Technical Services | | | | |
| Value Added Services | | | | |
| Service Structures | | | | |

Is there one area that is better or worse than the others?
Plot the chapters into the strategy box plot.

# SERVICES PLOT:

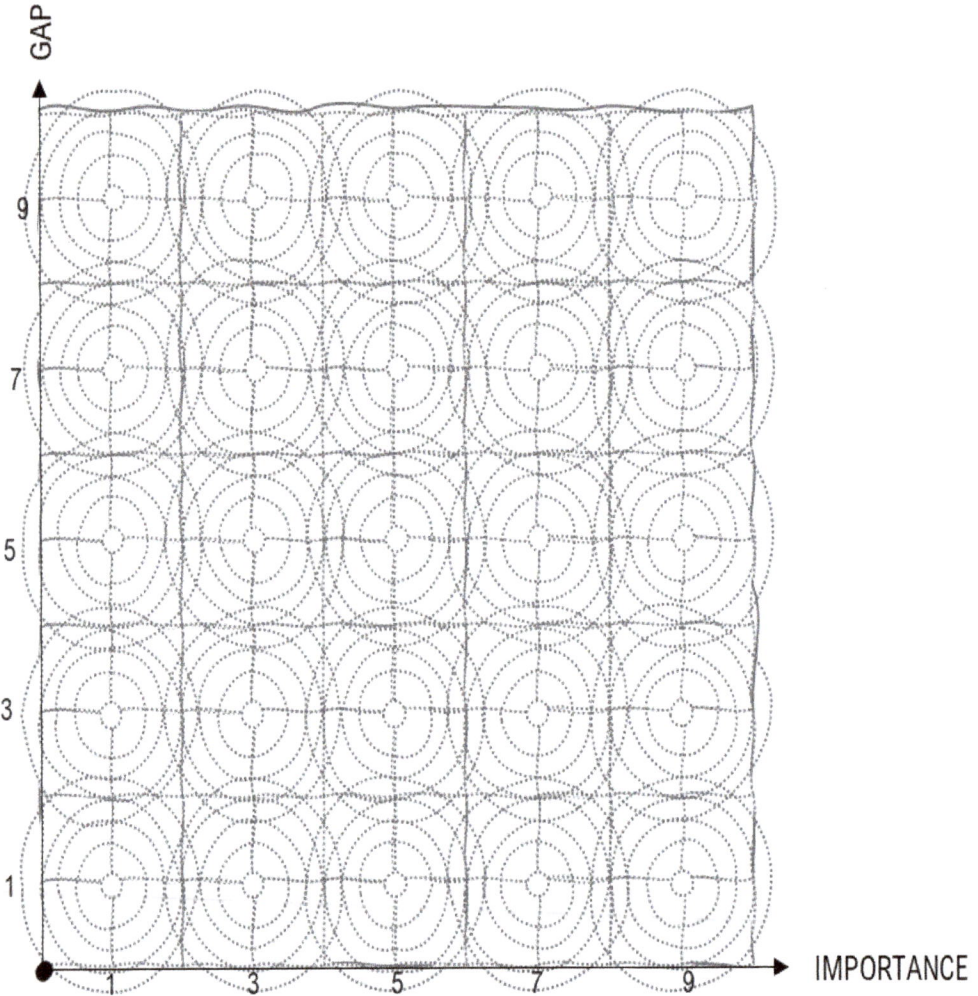

Looking at the box plot, what is your assessment of services?

# OVERALL EVALUATION:

AS IS [          ]    IDEAL [          ]    GAP [          ]    RELEVANCE [          ]

# SECTION 6:
# CHANNEL
# MANAGEMENT

Market Reach Optimization

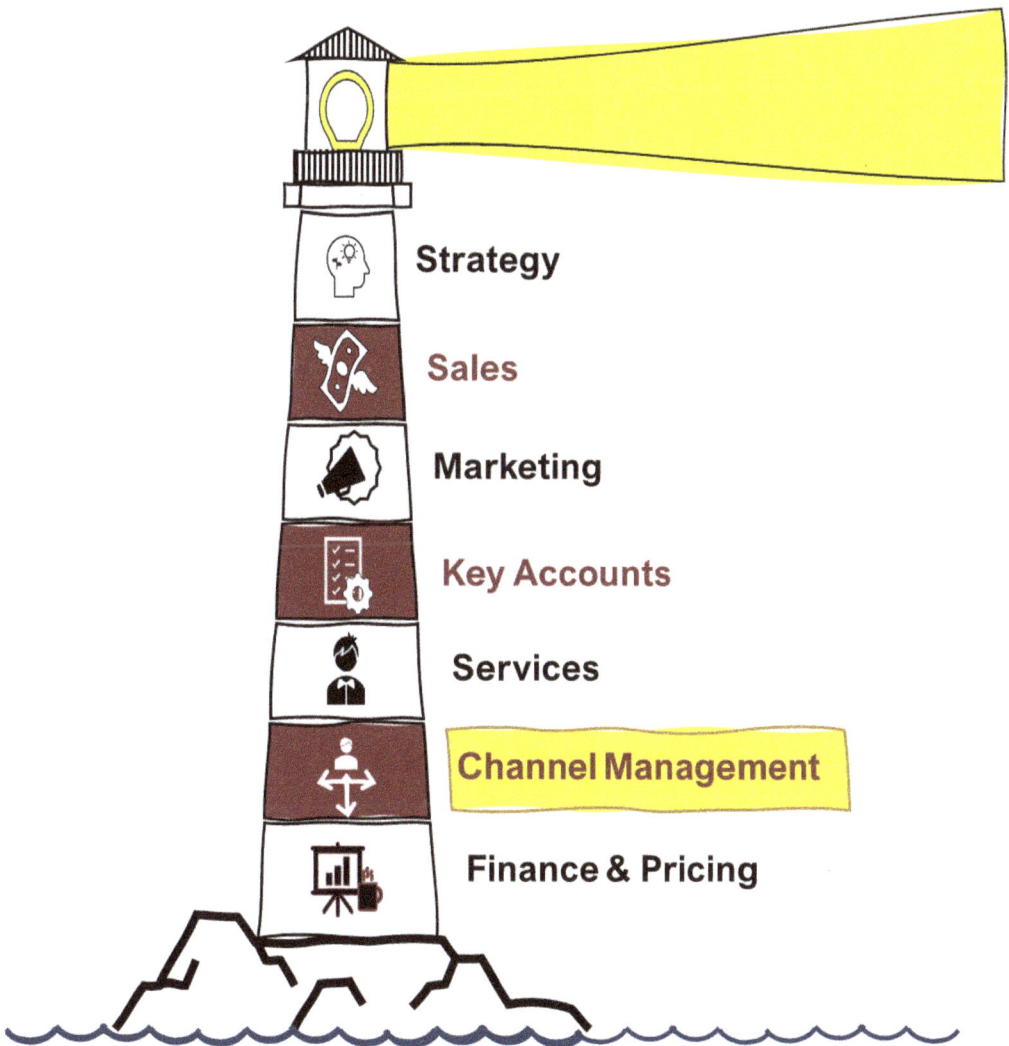

Strategy

Sales

Marketing

Key Accounts

Services

Channel Management

Finance & Pricing

Are your distribution channels a well-oiled machine or a tangled web of inefficiencies? In today's global marketplace, effective channel management isn't just about moving products—it's about creating seamless pathways for your customers. This chapter challenges you to critically examine your go-to-market strategies, partner relationships, and distribution networks. Are you truly optimizing your channels to maximize reach and profitability, or are you missing opportunities in emerging markets? Let's explore how to transform your channel management from a logistical necessity into a strategic advantage, ensuring that your products and services are not just available, but positioned for success in every market you serve.

In this section, we will look through the following four wavelengths of channel management as shown in figure 27.

**Figure 27:** The 4 Wavelengths of Channel Management

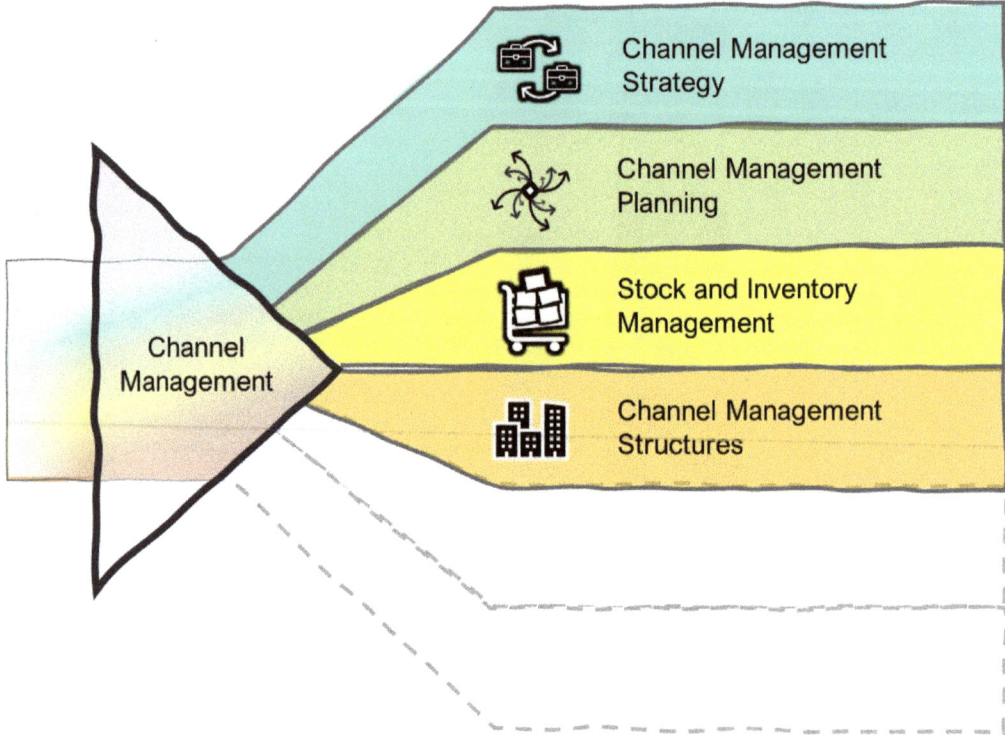

Channel Management

Channel Management Strategy

Channel Management Planning

Stock and Inventory Management

Channel Management Structures

# CHAPTER 26:

# Channel Management Strategy & Selection

Score this chapter here

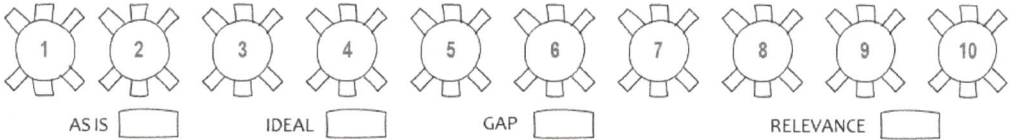

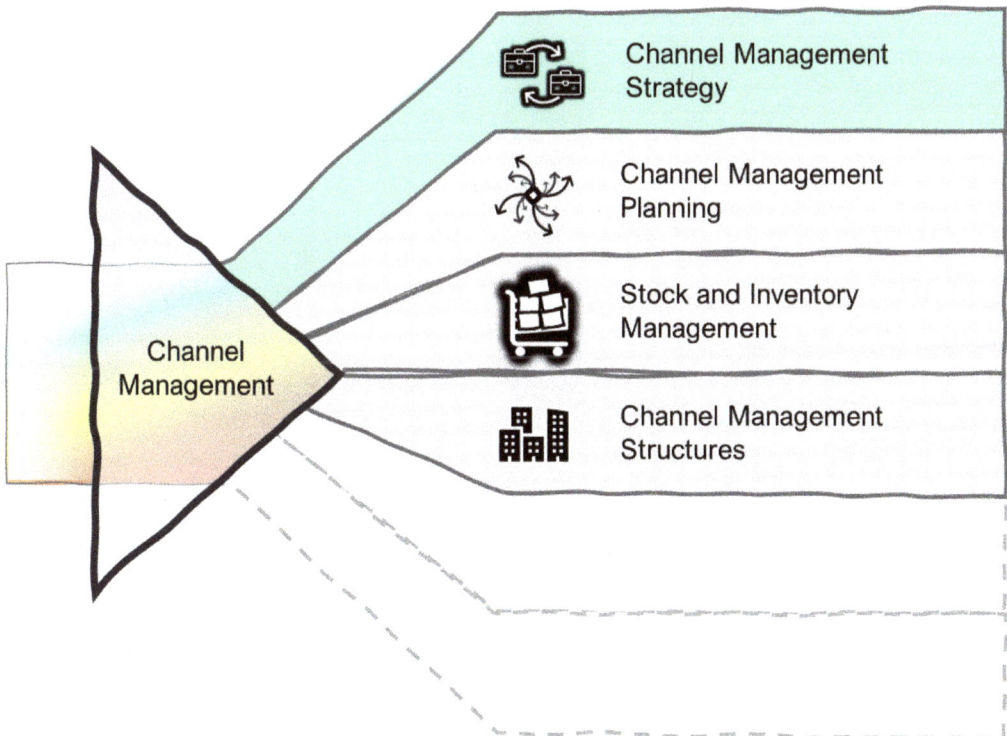

| 1 | 2 | 3 | 4 | 5 | 6 | 7 | 8 | 9 | 10 |

AS IS [ ]   IDEAL [ ]   GAP [ ]   RELEVANCE [ ]

Channel Management
- Channel Management Strategy
- Channel Management Planning
- Stock and Inventory Management
- Channel Management Structures

# CUSTOMER-FOCUSED CHANNEL AND DISTRIBUTION MANAGEMENT STRATEGY:

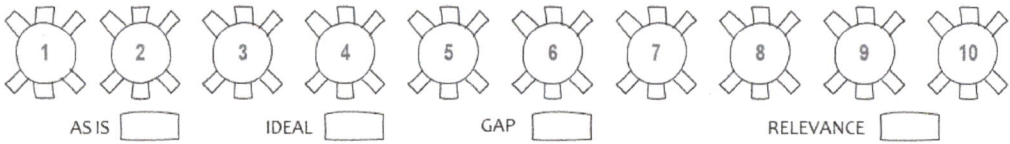

| 1 | 2 | 3 | 4 | 5 | 6 | 7 | 8 | 9 | 10 |

AS IS [     ]     IDEAL [     ]     GAP [     ]     RELEVANCE [     ]

## AS IS:

Consider your current Channel/Distribution Management strategy. Reflect on how well it addresses the needs of your end customers. Why do you have channel partners? Does that season still hold true? Is the strategy based on thorough market insights, including market structure and development, major accounts, account performance, cash flow, profitability and the competitive landscape? Or are these considerations less central to your channel strategy? Evaluating the reasons for having partners will reveal potential gaps in its effectiveness.

## IDEAL:

Ideally, you have a comprehensive Channel/Distribution Management strategy that is firmly grounded in a deep understanding of end-customer needs and robust market insights. This strategy should be based on thorough research and analysis of the market structure and its development, a clear understanding of major accounts and their performance, and a comprehensive assessment of the competitive situation. The strategy should consider access to the decision makers, the number of levels until the end customer, the market norms, including your standing in it and the size of the market. Your ability to serve the territory, the amount of margin that is captured versus losses and your understanding of the marketplace. This customer-centric and data-driven approach ensures that your channel and distribution efforts are aligned with market demand and customer expectations.

## RELEVANCE:

A customer-centric and data-driven Channel/Distribution Management strategy is crucial for maximizing reach, efficiency, and customer satisfaction. A well-defined strategy can be a significant driver of growth and market share.

# CROSS-FUNCTIONAL ALIGNMENT IN CHANNEL AND DISTRIBUTION MANAGEMENT:

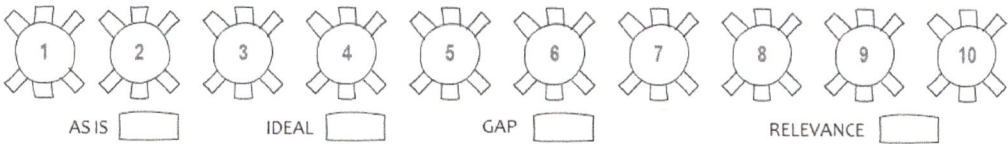

## AS IS:

Consider the alignment of your Channel/Distribution Management strategy across different departments and business units you are marketing working for both direct and indirect channels? Does your sales training allow for managing sales reps through influence rather than direct management? Reflect on whether there is a shared understanding and consistent implementation of the strategy across Marketing, Sales, Pricing, Market Access, and Services. Or are there discrepancies or conflicting priorities between departments, potentially leading to inefficiencies and a fragmented customer experience? Evaluating cross-functional alignment will reveal potential gaps.

## IDEAL:

Ideally, your Channel/Distribution Management strategy is fully aligned across all relevant departments and business units. This means that Marketing, Sales, Pricing, Market Access, and Services operate with a shared understanding of the strategy and work together seamlessly to execute it. This cross-functional alignment ensures a consistent and coordinated approach to channel management, maximizing efficiency, and delivering a unified customer experience.

## RELEVANCE:

Cross-functional alignment is crucial for maximizing the effectiveness of your Channel/Distribution Management strategy. Ensuring that all customer-facing teams agree is essential for delivering a consistent brand experience and maximizing channel performance. If there are discrepancies or conflicting priorities between departments, this area is relevant. How much of the overall revenue comes from indirect sales? Do your teams spend their efforts proportionally to this split? Investing in improved communication and collaboration between departments will enhance alignment and optimize your channel management efforts.

## CHANNEL PARTNER SELECTION:

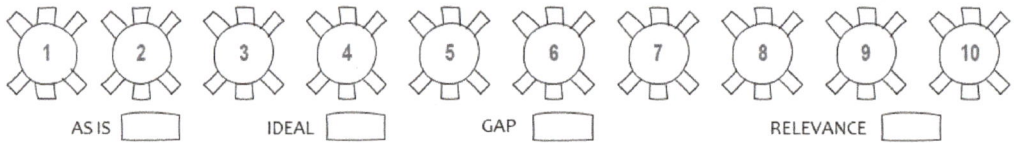

AS IS [ ]   IDEAL [ ]   GAP [ ]   RELEVANCE [ ]

## AS IS:

Consider the criteria you used to select distributors. Reflect on whether your selection process considers factors beyond just revenue generation, such as the distributor's openness to partnership, their willingness to share end-customer information, and their strategic fit within the target market. Why do you have a partner? Why not direct? Or is the selection process primarily focused on revenue potential, potentially overlooking other important qualitative factors? Evaluating your distributor selection criteria will reveal potential gaps in your channel partner selection process.

## IDEAL:

Ideally, you have well-defined and comprehensive selection criteria for distributors that go beyond revenue considerations. These criteria should include factors such as the distributor's openness to a collaborative partnership, their willingness and capability to share valuable end-customer information, their strategic fit within the target market and their financial stability, logistical capabilities, and market knowledge. Internal factors such as market knowledge, regulatory factors, cash flow considerations. Consideration to the customers' business supply needs and how the distributors' product ranging, and their completeness of offer should also be reflected in the selection decision. This holistic approach ensures that you select distributors who are not only capable of generating revenue but are also aligned with your business objectives and committed to building long-term, mutually beneficial relationships.

## RELEVANCE:

Using comprehensive selection criteria is crucial for building a strong and effective distribution network. Choosing the right distributors can significantly affect market reach, customer satisfaction, and overall channel performance. If your selection criteria are too narrowly focused on revenue, this area is highly relevant. Expanding your criteria to include qualitative factors will help you select distributors who are better aligned with your business objectives and more likely to contribute to long-term success.

# CHAPTER 27:

# Channel Management Planning

Score this chapter here

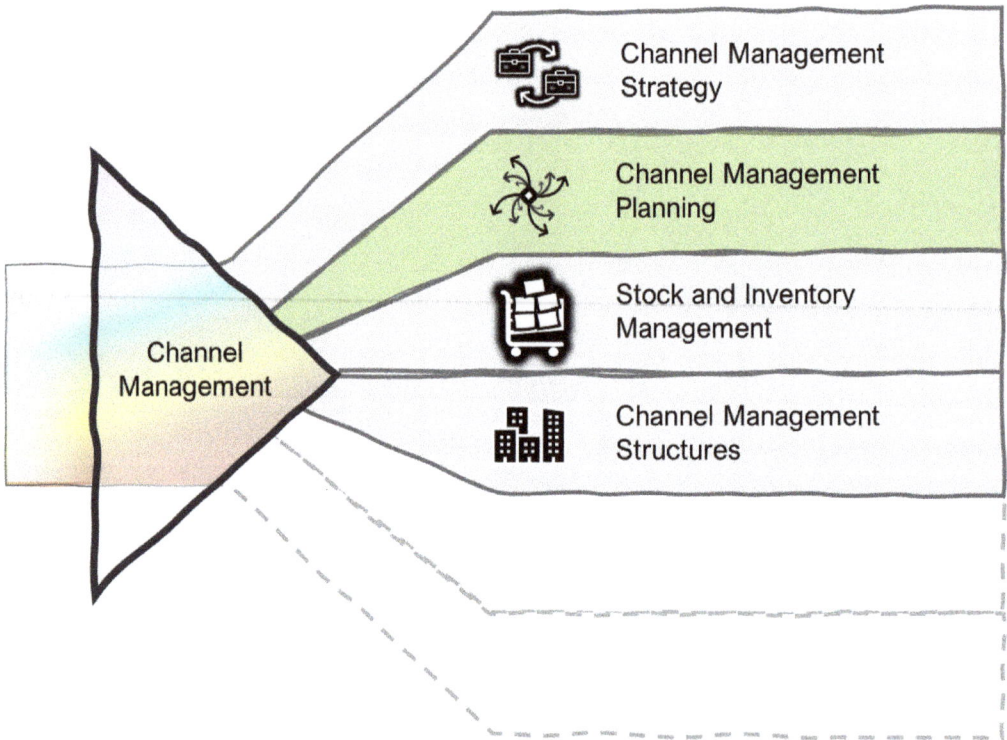

AS IS ☐   IDEAL ☐   GAP ☐   RELEVANCE ☐

Channel Management Strategy

Channel Management Planning

Stock and Inventory Management

Channel Management Structures

Channel Management

# CHANNEL MANAGEMENT PLANNING:

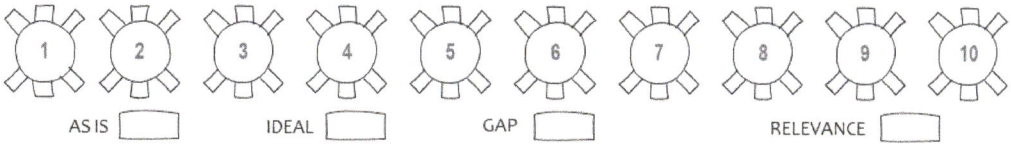

| 1 | 2 | 3 | 4 | 5 | 6 | 7 | 8 | 9 | 10 |

AS IS ☐   IDEAL ☐   GAP ☐   RELEVANCE ☐

## AS IS:

Consider your current approach to Channel Management planning. Do you as the principle have dedicated business plans for the distributor's territory? Do they include sales, marketing, service and delivery aspects? Who is developing the plan? Is it you as the principle by yourself? Or the distributor or jointly developed? Reflect on whether you have a systematic process in place that is conducted at least annually. Is this process documented, structured, and consistently followed? Or is planning more ad hoc and reactive, potentially leading to missed opportunities and inefficiencies? Evaluating the regularity and structure of your planning process will reveal potential gaps in your channel management approach.

## IDEAL:

Ideally, you conduct a systematic Channel Management planning process at least annually. This process should be documented, structured, and consistently followed, involving relevant stakeholders from different departments of both the distributor and the principal. This should shift as the principle becomes more active in the market. In the beginning, there may be little the principle can provide for the local market and should act more than corporate support. However, as we move more into a hybrid model, there will be a natural progression into the principle and distributor working together on developing the plans. The planning should include a thorough review of past performance, an analysis of market trends and competitive dynamics, and the development of clear objectives and action plans for the upcoming year.

## RELEVANCE:

A systematic annual planning process is crucial for effective Channel Management. A well-defined planning process can significantly improve channel performance and drive business growth. If your planning process is not systematic or conducted regularly, this area is highly relevant. Implementing a structured annual planning process will improve your channel management effectiveness and lead to better business outcomes.

# CHANNEL PARTNER OBJECTIVES:

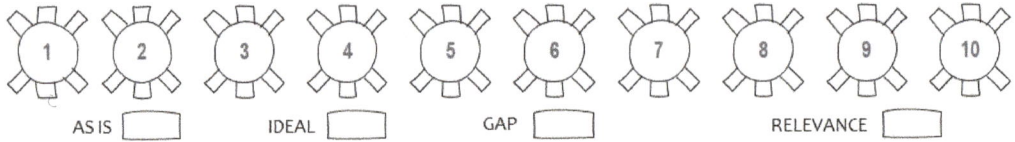

## AS IS:

Consider how you set objectives and define actions with your channel partners. Reflect on whether these objectives and actions are realistic and tailored to specific target groups. Are they developed in collaboration with your partners, taking into account their capabilities and market knowledge? Or are they imposed top-down, potentially leading to misalignment and reduced partner engagement? Evaluating your objective-setting process will reveal potential gaps in your partner collaboration.

## IDEAL:

Ideally, you set realistic objectives and define specific actions in close collaboration with your channel partners, tailoring them to the unique characteristics of each target group. This collaborative approach ensures that objectives are achievable, actions are effective, and partners are fully engaged.

## RELEVANCE:

Setting realistic and tailored objectives is crucial for motivating channel partners and achieving desired outcomes. Effective collaboration with partners is essential for maximizing channel performance. If your objective-setting process is not collaborative or does not consider target group specifics, this area is highly relevant. Investing in closer collaboration with your partners will improve their engagement and drive better results.

# COLLABORATIVE PARTNERSHIPS:

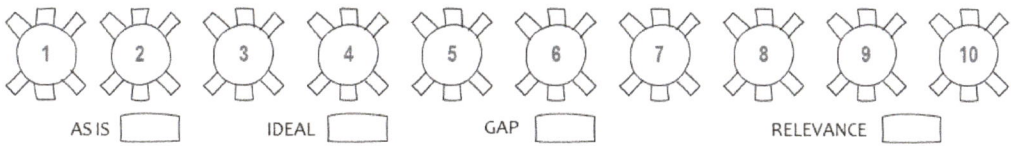

AS IS [ ]   IDEAL [ ]   GAP [ ]   RELEVANCE [ ]

## AS IS:

Consider the nature of your relationships with key channel partners. Reflect on whether you have established close partnerships characterized by mutual trust and open communication. Does this partnership include a regular and systematic exchange of information, such as revenue, profitability, target customer profiles, and end-customer insights? Or is communication more transactional and limited, potentially hindering mutual understanding and collaboration? Evaluating your partner relationships will reveal potential gaps in your partner collaboration.

## IDEAL:

Ideally, you have established close partnerships with your key channel partners, built on mutual trust, open communication, and a regular exchange of valuable information. The channel partner will trust the principle is there to help the business and not take over. Where there is a lack of trust there is usually a lack of information sharing. This includes sharing data on revenue, profitability, target customer profiles, and end-customer insights. This transparency and information sharing fosters a strong collaborative environment and enables partners to work together effectively to achieve shared goals.

## RELEVANCE:

Close partnerships and mutual information exchange are crucial for maximizing channel performance and achieving mutual success. Strong partner relationships can be a significant driver of growth and market share. If your partner relationships are not characterized by open communication and information sharing, this area is highly relevant. Investing in building stronger partnerships will improve channel performance and drive better business outcomes.

# CHANNEL PARTNER KPI'S:

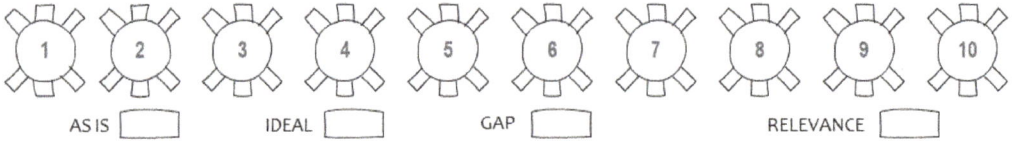

| 1 | 2 | 3 | 4 | 5 | 6 | 7 | 8 | 9 | 10 |

AS IS [ ]     IDEAL [ ]     GAP [ ]     RELEVANCE [ ]

## AS IS:

Consider how you monitor the performance of your channel partners. Reflect on whether you have a regular and systematic process for tracking their performance against agreed-upon targets. Do you have clear metrics and reporting mechanisms in place? Are corrective actions taken promptly when deviations occur? Or is performance monitoring less structured?

## IDEAL:

Ideally, you have a robust system for regularly and systematically tracking your channel partners' performance against targets. This system should include clear metrics, regular reporting, and a well-defined process for taking corrective actions when deviations occur. This proactive approach ensures that partner performance is consistently monitored and that any issues are addressed promptly.

## RELEVANCE:

Regular performance monitoring and proactive intervention are important for maximizing channel effectiveness and achieving desired outcomes. Effective performance management is essential for optimizing channel performance. If your performance monitoring is weak or reactive, or if you have troubled relationships with your partners. This area is highly relevant. Implementing a robust tracking and intervention system will improve channel performance and drive better results.

# INCENTIVE SYSTEMS FOR CHANNEL PARTNERS:

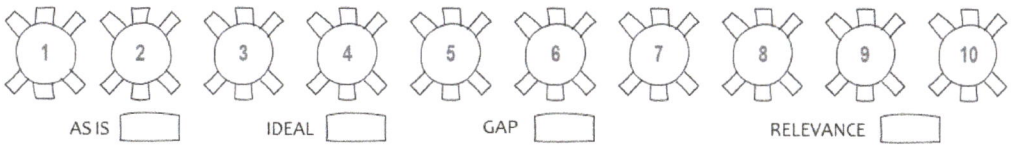

AS IS ☐   IDEAL ☐   GAP ☐   RELEVANCE ☐

## AS IS:

Consider your reward system for channel partners. Reflect on whether this system effectively aligns their incentives with your overall business strategy. Do partners feel motivated to achieve the desired outcomes? Or are there misalignments that lead to partners prioritizing their own interests over your strategic objectives? Are the incentive systems robust? Do they include both financial and non-financial components? Are the financial components discounts or retrospective discounts? When are these financial aspects achieved – upon ordering or upon completion of an annual cycle, or a mix? For the non-financial aspects do they include things like meeting participation and marketing activities (both yours as the principle and attending trade shows, providing proof sources etc)? Do they include kick-off or distributor meetings (both principles bringing the distributors together and the channel partners kick-off), or meetings where they invite the technical or business experts from the principle? Evaluating your reward system will reveal potential gaps in your partner motivation and alignment.

## IDEAL:

Ideally, you have an effective reward system that strongly aligns the incentives of your channel partners with your overall business strategy. This system should reward partners for achieving key objectives that contribute to your strategic goals, such as increased market share, customer acquisition, or specific product promotions. Having a mix of incentives for the distributor and their staff working on your ranges and participation in and actively seeking the principles involvement in their local activities.

## RELEVANCE:

Aligning partner incentives with your strategy is crucial for maximizing channel performance and achieving desired outcomes. A well-designed reward system can significantly motivate partners and drive better results. If your reward system is not effectively aligned with your strategy, this area is highly relevant. Reviewing and adjusting your reward system will improve partner motivation and drive better business outcomes.

# PRICING STRATEGIES FOR CHANNEL PARTNERS:

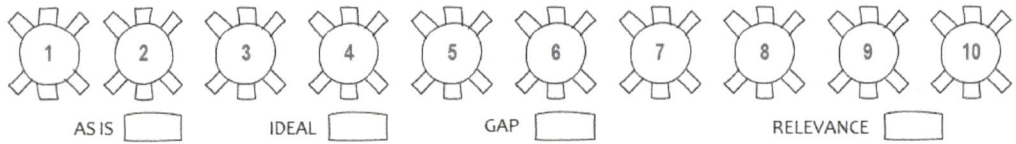

AS IS [ ]    IDEAL [ ]    GAP [ ]    RELEVANCE [ ]

## AS IS:

Consider how you set prices for your channel partners. Reflect on whether your pricing strategy is based on a deep understanding of your partners' roles, responsibilities, economics, and incentives to sell your products. Do market conditions have an input into pricing? How is this verified? Do you know what your competitor pricing is in the market? Are you utilizing a margin for the channel partner? Or are you using a cost-plus model? Does the expected price and margin align with other territories? Or is pricing determined more arbitrarily, potentially leading to partner dissatisfaction or reduced motivation? Evaluating your pricing strategy will reveal potential gaps in your partner relationship management.

## IDEAL:

Ideally, your pricing strategy for channel partners is based on a thorough understanding of their roles, responsibilities, economics, market dynamics and incentives to sell your products. This ensures that pricing is fair, competitive, and motivates partners to actively promote and sell your offerings.

## RELEVANCE:

A well-considered pricing strategy is crucial for maintaining healthy partner relationships and maximizing channel performance.
Appropriate pricing can significantly influence partner motivation and drive sales. If your pricing strategy does not adequately consider partner economics and incentives, this area is highly relevant. Reviewing and adjusting your pricing strategy will improve partner relationships and drive better business outcomes.

# DISCOUNT STRATEGIES FOR CHANNEL PARTNERS:

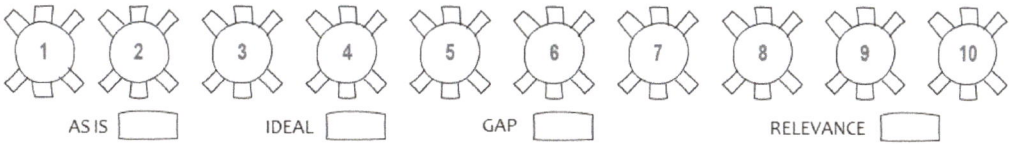

| 1 | 2 | 3 | 4 | 5 | 6 | 7 | 8 | 9 | 10 |

AS IS ☐    IDEAL ☐    GAP ☐    RELEVANCE ☐

## AS IS:

Consider your discount scheme for channel partners. Reflect on whether you have a differentiated approach that takes into account factors such as sales performance, volume, and exclusivity agreements. Does your discount scheme ensure partner competitiveness while also securing your desired margins? How does your scheme avoid "bull whip" effects (i.e. large orders to achieve a discount, then long periods without ordering)? How does your scheme avoid using stock to secure discounts? How does your scheme ensure a year-on-year achievement? Or does it allow "borrowing" from the future to achieve this periods results? Does the scheme discount for orders, or is it retrospective? Does the territory allow retrospective discounting? **(CHECK!)** What is the goal behind the discounts? Is it growth, margin capture, consistency of ordering? Or is the discount structure less nuanced, potentially leading to either reduced partner motivation or margin erosion? Evaluating your discount scheme will reveal potential gaps in your partner relationship management and pricing strategy.

## IDEAL:

Ideally, you have a well-defined and differentiated discount scheme that is based on factors such as sales performance, volume, exclusivity agreements, and other relevant criteria. The scheme will ensure that inventory is used for actual demand and not a method for gaining discounts. The scheme will be aligned with an actual year-on-year constant achievements. Where appropriate, the schemes may use one of the following methods. Order discounts, specials, year-end rebates, free stock or where possible retrospective discounts. This approach ensures that partners are motivated to perform well, while also protecting your margins and maintaining profitability.

## RELEVANCE:

An appropriate discount scheme is crucial for motivating channel partners for growth, compliance with corporate and optimizing profitability. A well-structured discount scheme can significantly influence partner behaviour and drive the channel partner's actions. If your discount scheme is not sufficiently aligned or sophisticated, this area is highly relevant. Reviewing and adjusting your discount structure will improve partner motivation and ensure healthy margins.

# CHANNEL MANAGER ROLES & RESPONSIBILITIES:

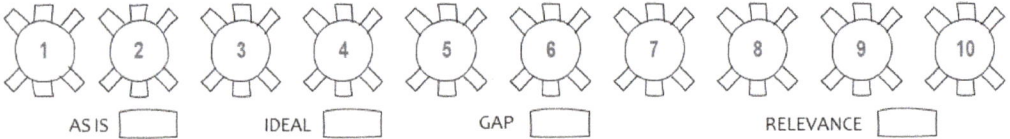

| 1 | 2 | 3 | 4 | 5 | 6 | 7 | 8 | 9 | 10 |

AS IS ☐   IDEAL ☐   GAP ☐   RELEVANCE ☐

## AS IS:

Consider the division of responsibilities between your channel partners and your internal sales and marketing teams. Reflect on how clearly these roles are defined and communicated, especially across different customer types, geographical segments, or product/service segments. Are there overlaps, gaps, or ambiguities in responsibilities that lead to confusion, duplicated efforts, or missed opportunities? How do you ensure coordination and prevent conflicts between partners and your internal teams? Evaluating the clarity of roles and responsibilities will reveal potential gaps in your channel management and internal collaboration.

## IDEAL:

Ideally, you have clearly defined and documented roles and responsibilities for both your channel partners and your internal sales and marketing teams. Managing or work with or through the channel partner. This includes establishing clear communication protocols, escalation paths, and processes for joint activities. A well-defined boundaries set and potential service level agreement or guide can clarify what is expected. A commercial operating model canvas created with the Channel Partner can be helpful as a starting point to focus these discussions with the distributor guiding a building out a RACI for each section.

Commercial Operating Model Canvas

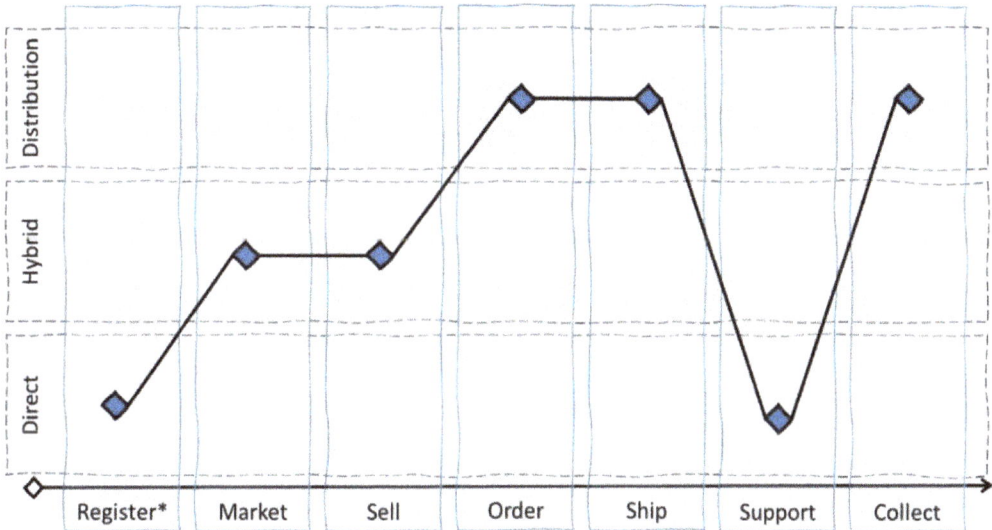

This eliminates confusion, maximizes efficiency, and fosters a coordinated approach to reaching target customers.

## RELEVANCE:

Clearly defined roles and responsibilities are crucial for effective channel management and internal collaboration. Well-defined responsibilities prevent conflicts, improve efficiency, and ensure that all necessary activities are covered. If roles and responsibilities are not clearly defined, this area is highly relevant. Investing in clarifying these roles and establishing clear communication protocols will improve coordination, reduce conflicts, and drive better channel performance.

# CHAPTER 28:

# Stock and Inventory Management

Score this chapter here

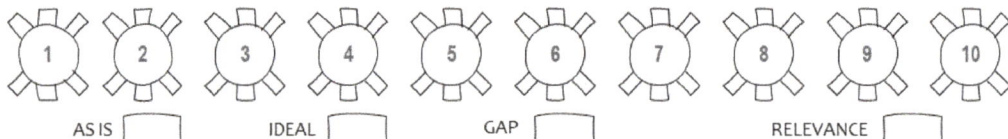

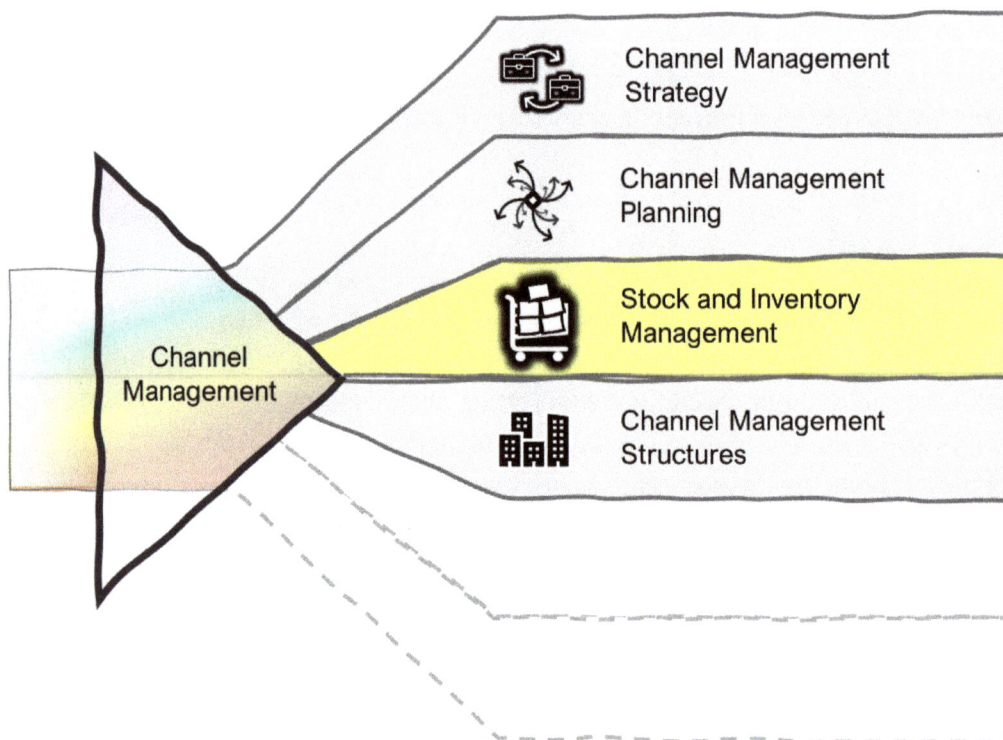

1 2 3 4 5 6 7 8 9 10

AS IS ☐    IDEAL ☐    GAP ☐    RELEVANCE ☐

Channel Management Strategy

Channel Management Planning

Stock and Inventory Management

Channel Management Structures

Channel Management

Stock and inventory has its own section here as it's the primary way a distributor (Channel Partner) can manipulate their margins and claim discounts, or achieve Minimum Purchase Requirements (MPR).

# PARTNER STOCK RIGHTSIZING:

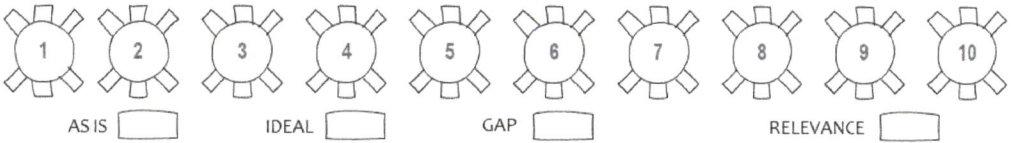

AS IS [ ]    IDEAL [ ]    GAP [ ]    RELEVANCE [ ]

## AS IS:

Consider how you support your channel partners in managing their inventory. Reflect on whether you actively assist them in "rightsizing" their stock, meaning ensuring they have a complete product offering to meet customer demand while also optimizing their working capital (i.e., minimizing excess inventory). Do you provide guidance on inventory levels, forecasting tools, or other support to help them balance these competing priorities? Or do you leave inventory management entirely to the partners, potentially leading to stockouts or overstocking? Do you understand their inventory position? What slow moving stock do they have? What are the average shipping quantities? Is there any slow-moving stock? Why is it slow? Is this stock slow moving in other territories of the business? Evaluating your level of support will reveal potential gaps in your channel partner support program.

## IDEAL:

Ideally, you provide proactive and effective support to your channel partners in rightsizing their stock. This includes offering guidance on optimal inventory levels based on market demand, product lifecycle, and other relevant factors. You may provide forecasting tools, inventory management systems, or other resources to help them make informed decisions. The goal is to ensure that partners have a complete offering to meet customer demand without tying up excessive working capital in unnecessary inventory. The system may look at over, under and slow-moving stock and compare against budgets, MPR, and forecasts. A system like EOQ utilizing safety and max / min stocking level would be helpful in ensuring rightsized channel partner stock, ensuring minimal stock loss because of expiry.

## RELEVANCE:

Supporting channel partners with stock rightsizing is crucial for maximizing their sales effectiveness and financial health. Helping partners optimize their inventory can significantly improve their profitability and strengthen your channel relationships. If you are not actively supporting partners in this area, this area is highly relevant. Does your channel partner attempt to or is entitled to claims for expired stock? Can they utilize stock to achieve their MPR? Or achieved discounts? Investing in providing inventory management support will improve partner performance and strengthen your channel.

## DATA-DRIVEN STOCK MANAGEMENT WITH CHANNEL PARTNERS:

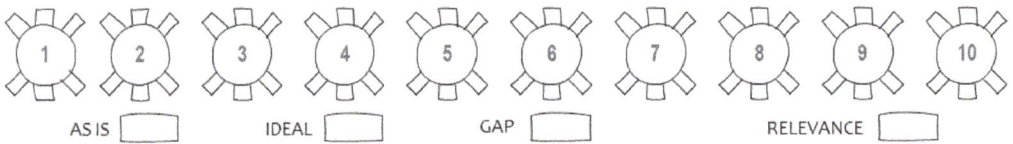

AS IS ⬚   IDEAL ⬚   GAP ⬚   RELEVANCE ⬚

## AS IS:

Consider how you utilize end-customer purchasing data in supporting your channel partners' stock management. Reflect on whether you actively collect and analyse this data to provide insights to partners on demand trends and optimal inventory levels. Do you utilize Vendor Managed Inventory (VMI) programs with partners where appropriate, taking on responsibility for managing their inventory based on real-time data? Or do you rely on less data-driven approaches, potentially leading to less accurate forecasting and less efficient inventory management? Evaluating your use of data and VMI will reveal potential gaps in your data utilization and channel collaboration.

## IDEAL:

Ideally, you actively use end-customer purchasing data to provide valuable insights to your channel partners on demand trends, optimal inventory levels, and potential stockouts or overstocking or slow-moving stock situations. Where appropriate, you implement (VMI) programs, taking responsibility for managing

The Commercial Excellence Playbook

partner inventory based on real-time data and agreed-upon service levels. Where there is a lack of VMI systems available, a system to correlate the stock levels with max and min levels usage versus sales volumes is in place. This enables a time based and expiry calculations and then appropriate max and min systems. Ideally, this can be linked to the appropriate incentive schemes to ensure there is no bull whip impact. This data-driven and collaborative approach ensures that partners have the right products in the right quantities at the right time, maximizing sales and minimizing inventory costs.

## RELEVANCE:

Utilizing end-customer purchasing data and implementing VMI programs can significantly improve channel efficiency and profitability, whilst avoiding bull whip situations. Data-driven inventory management can be a key differentiator, enabling more efficient usage of capital for the channel partner's market growth...whilst giving the principle more information and understanding of the market and a fuller picture of global trends, as well as better management of the channel partner. If you are not actively using data or utilizing VMI where appropriate, this area is highly relevant. Investing in data analytics capabilities and exploring VMI opportunities will improve channel efficiency and strengthen partner relationships.

# CHANNEL PARTNER SALES AND MARKETING SUPPORT SYSTEMS:

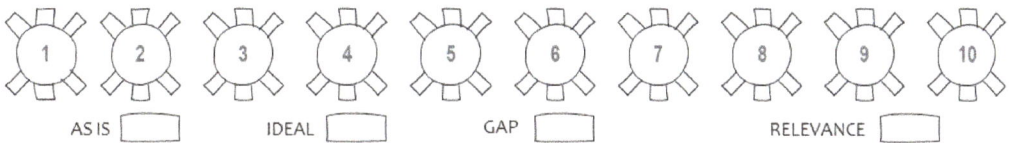

AS IS ☐          IDEAL ☐          GAP ☐          RELEVANCE ☐

## AS IS:

Consider the tools and resources available to your channel partners to support their sales and marketing efforts. Reflect on whether they have access to appropriate marketing materials, cost-benefit calculation models, and support for developing joint value creation programs with end customers. Or are they lacking the necessary tools to effectively promote and sell your products/services? Evaluating the availability of these tools will reveal potential gaps in your channel partner support program.

## IDEAL:

Ideally, you provide your channel partners with a comprehensive suite of tools and resources to support their sales and marketing efforts. This includes appropriate marketing materials (e.g., brochures, presentations, online content), cost-benefit calculation models that help them demonstrate the value of your offerings to customers, and support for developing joint value creation programs that address specific customer needs. These tools empower partners to effectively promote and sell your products/services and build strong customer relationships.

## RELEVANCE:

Providing the right tools and resources to channel partners is crucial for maximizing their sales effectiveness and driving channel performance. Equipping partners with the necessary tools is essential for achieving revenue targets and expanding market reach. If your partner's lack access to appropriate tools, this area is highly relevant. Investing in providing these resources will improve partner performance and strengthen your channel.

# CHAPTER 29:

# Channel Management Structures

Score this chapter here

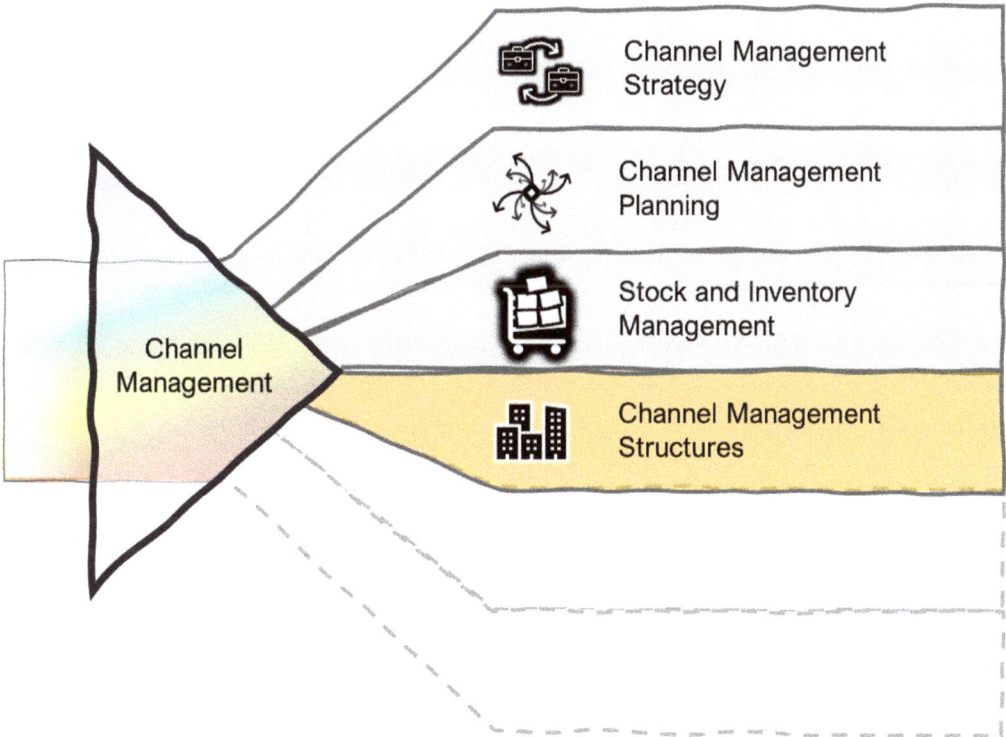

Channel Management

Channel Management Strategy

Channel Management Planning

Stock and Inventory Management

Channel Management Structures

# CHANNEL MANAGEMENT RESOURCING:

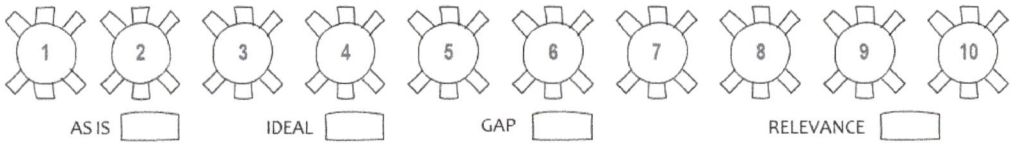

AS IS [ ]    IDEAL [ ]    GAP [ ]    RELEVANCE [ ]

## AS IS:

Consider the skills, experience, and competencies of your current channel management team. Reflect on whether they possess the necessary expertise to effectively manage your channel partners and meet the needs of your end customers. Do they have strong relationship-building skills, commercial acumen, market knowledge, and the ability to effectively collaborate with internal and external stakeholders? Are there any skill gaps that need to be addressed through training, development, or recruitment? Evaluating the capabilities of your channel management team will reveal potential gaps in your talent management strategy.

## IDEAL:

Ideally, you have a team of highly skilled and experienced channel managers who possess the optimal mix of competencies to effectively manage your channel partners and meet customer needs. This includes strong relationship management, negotiation skills, business acumen, market understanding, and the ability to develop and execute effective channel strategies. Ongoing training and development programs should be in place to ensure that the team stays current with industry best practices and evolving market dynamics.

## RELEVANCE:

Having the right channel management talent is crucial for maximizing channel performance and achieving business objectives. Investing in attracting, developing, and retaining top channel management talent is essential for driving growth and expanding market reach. If your channel management team lacks the necessary skills or experience, this area is highly relevant. Investing in talent development will significantly improve your channel management effectiveness.

The Commercial Excellence Playbook

# EMPOWERMENT OF CHANNEL MANAGERS:

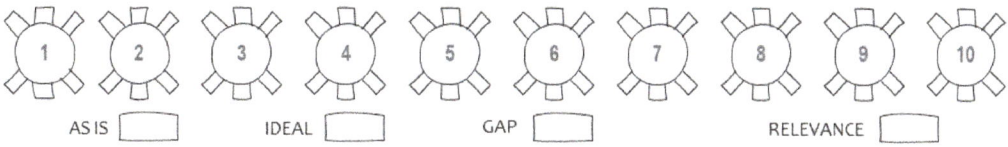

AS IS [ ]   IDEAL [ ]   GAP [ ]   RELEVANCE [ ]

## AS IS:

Consider the level of empowerment given to your dedicated Channel Managers. Reflect on whether they have the authority to make decisions related to their channel partners, or do they frequently need to seek approval from higher levels of management? Does this level of empowerment enable them to respond quickly and effectively to partner needs and market opportunities? Or does it create bottlenecks and delays in decision-making? Evaluating the level of empowerment will reveal potential gaps in your organisational structure and decision-making processes.

## IDEAL:

Ideally, your dedicated Channel Managers are fully empowered to make appropriate decisions related to their channel partners, within clearly defined guidelines and authority levels. This empowers them to act quickly, respond effectively to partner needs, and capitalize on market opportunities. It also fosters a sense of ownership and accountability within the channel management team.

## RELEVANCE:

Empowering Channel Managers is crucial for enabling them to effectively manage their partners and drive channel performance. Empowering channel managers to make timely decisions can significantly improve partner relationships and drive business growth. If your Channel Managers lack sufficient empowerment, this area is highly relevant. Investing in empowering them will improve their effectiveness and responsiveness.

# CHANNEL MANAGER INCENTIVE ALIGNMENT:

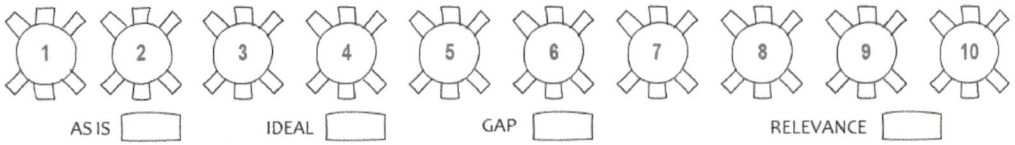

AS IS [      ]     IDEAL [      ]     GAP [      ]     RELEVANCE [      ]

## AS IS:

Consider the reward system in place for your Channel Managers. Reflect on how effectively this system aligns their incentives with both your overall business strategy and the strategies of your distributors. Does the reward structure motivate Channel Managers to work collaboratively with distributors to achieve shared goals? Or are there misalignments that could lead to conflicts of interest or suboptimal channel performance? Do your incentives drive revenue growth? Market share? Or profit growth? Do they reward using inventory to meet channel partner MPRs of budgets? For example, are your internal channel managers renumerated to cause stocking situations? Evaluating your reward system will reveal potential gaps in incentive alignment.

## IDEAL:

Ideally, you have an effective reward system for your Channel Managers that strongly aligns their incentives with both your overall business strategy and the strategies of your distributors. This system should reward Channel Managers for achieving key objectives that contribute to both your business goals and the success of your distributors. This fosters a collaborative environment and encourages Channel Managers to act as true partners with their distributors.

## RELEVANCE:

Aligning the incentives of Channel Managers with both your strategy and that of your distributors is crucial for maximizing channel performance and achieving mutual success. A well-designed reward system can significantly motivate Channel Managers to drive better results. If your reward system is not effectively aligned, this area is highly relevant. Reviewing and adjusting your reward structure will improve motivation and drive better business outcomes.

The Commercial Excellence Playbook

# ORGANISATIONAL INTEGRATION OF CHANNEL MANAGEMENT:

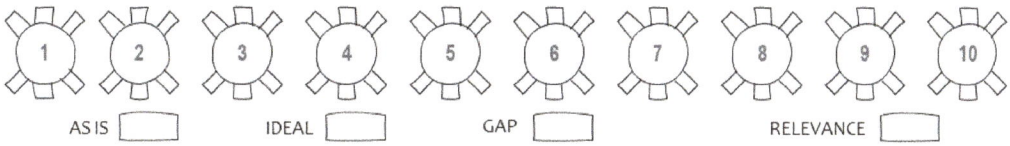

AS IS [ ]     IDEAL [ ]     GAP [ ]     RELEVANCE [ ]

## AS IS:

Consider how effectively your Channel Management organisation interacts with other commercial functions, particularly sales. Reflect on whether there are clearly defined internal processes, such as documented roles and responsibilities and clear pricing authority, that facilitate smooth communication and collaboration. Or are there ambiguities, overlaps, or conflicts that hinder effective teamwork and potentially create confusion for channel partners and stakeholders? Evaluating internal communication and collaboration will reveal potential gaps in your organisational effectiveness.

## IDEAL:

Ideally, your Channel Management organisation interacts seamlessly with other commercial functions, especially sales, through clearly defined internal processes. This includes documented roles and responsibilities, clear pricing authority, and established communication protocols. This ensures that everyone understands their respective roles and how they work together to support channel partners and achieve business objectives.

## RELEVANCE:

Effective interaction and collaboration between Channel Management and other commercial functions, especially sales, is crucial for maximizing channel performance and providing a consistent customer experience. Strong internal alignment is important for achieving business growth. If internal processes and communication are not well-defined, this area is highly relevant. Investing in clarifying roles, responsibilities, and communication protocols will improve collaboration and drive better channel outcomes.

# Section Conclusion

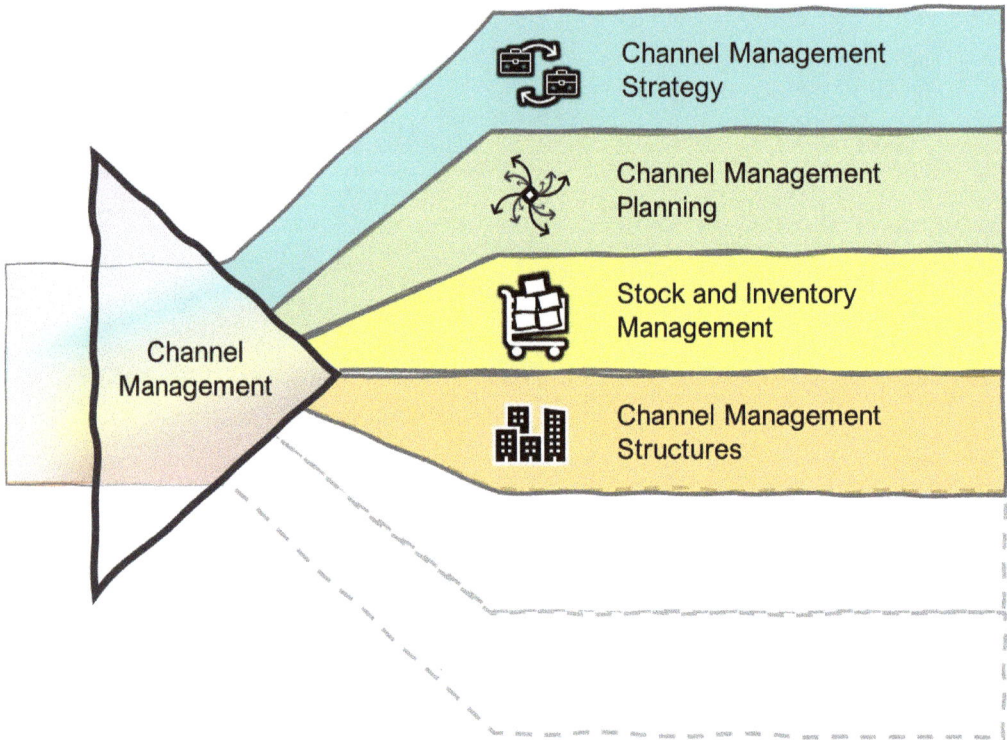

Channel Management

- Channel Management Strategy
- Channel Management Planning
- Stock and Inventory Management
- Channel Management Structures

**Transfer the ratings at the beginning of each chapter here:**

| Chapter | AS IS | Ideal | Gap | Relevance |
|---|---|---|---|---|
| Channel Management Strategy | | | | |
| Channel Management Planning | | | | |
| Stock and Inventory Management | | | | |
| Channel Management Structures | | | | |

Is there one area that is better or worse than the others?

Plot the chapters into the Channel Management box plot.

# CHANNEL MANAGEMENT PLOT:

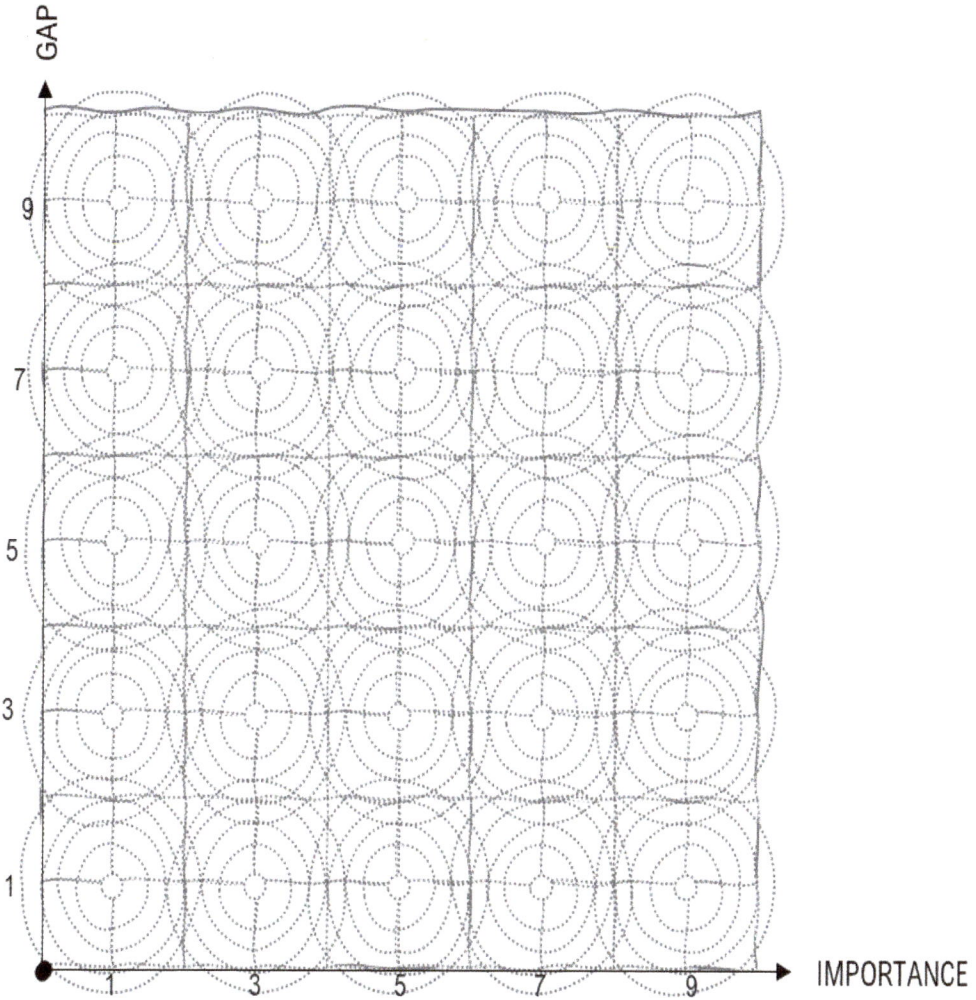

GAP

IMPORTANCE

Looking at the box plot what is your assessment of Channel Management?

# OVERALL EVALUATION:

| 1 | 2 | 3 | 4 | 5 | 6 | 7 | 8 | 9 | 10 |

AS IS [         ]     IDEAL [         ]     GAP [         ]          RELEVANCE [         ]

# SECTION 7:
# FINANCE & PRICING

---

## Value Capture Artisans

---

*Financial Areas, Analysing Pricing Models & Profitability*

**Strategy**

**Sales**

**Marketing**

**Key Accounts**

**Services**

**Channel Management**

**Finance & Pricing**

Are your financial strategies driving growth or merely keeping the lights on? In today's volatile economic landscape, effective financial management and pricing

The Commercial Excellence Playbook

strategies aren't just about balancing the books—they're about creating a sustainable competitive advantage. This chapter challenges you to critically examine your financial processes, pricing models, and value capture mechanisms. Are you truly leveraging financial insights to drive strategic decisions, or are you stuck in a reactive mode? Let's explore how to transform your finance and pricing functions from support roles into strategic powerhouses, ensuring that every financial decision and pricing strategy aligns with your overall business objectives and maximizes your market potential.

**Figure 28:** 4 Wavelengths of Finance & Pricing

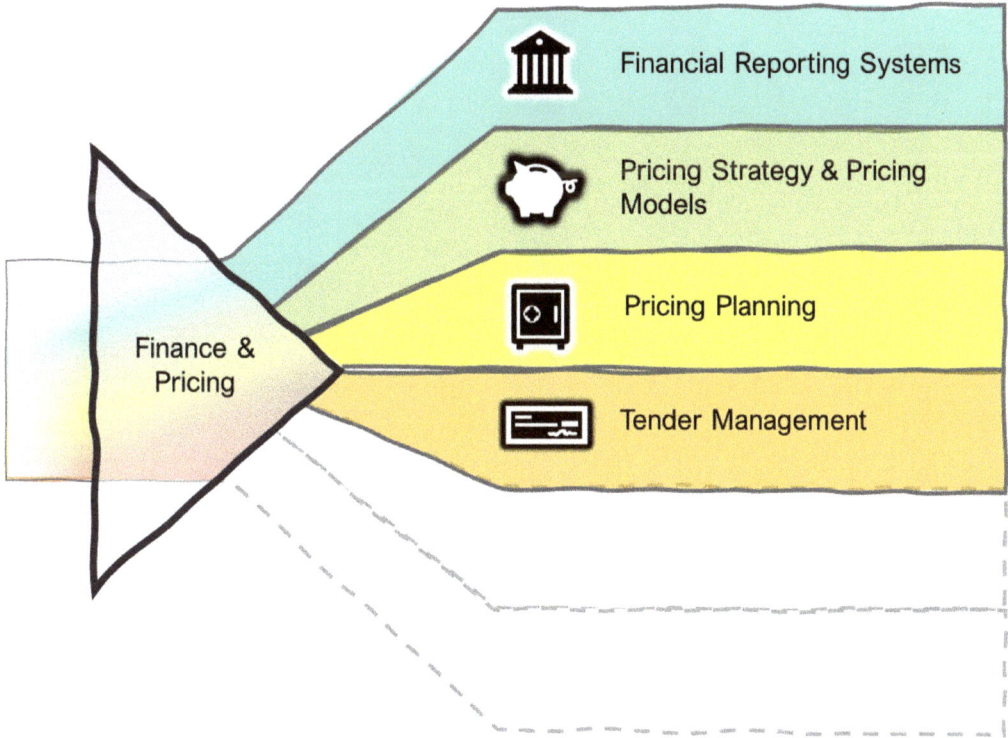

# CHAPTER 30:

# Financial Reporting Systems

Score this chapter here

| 1 | 2 | 3 | 4 | 5 | 6 | 7 | 8 | 9 | 10 |

AS IS [    ]     IDEAL [    ]     GAP [    ]     RELEVANCE [    ]

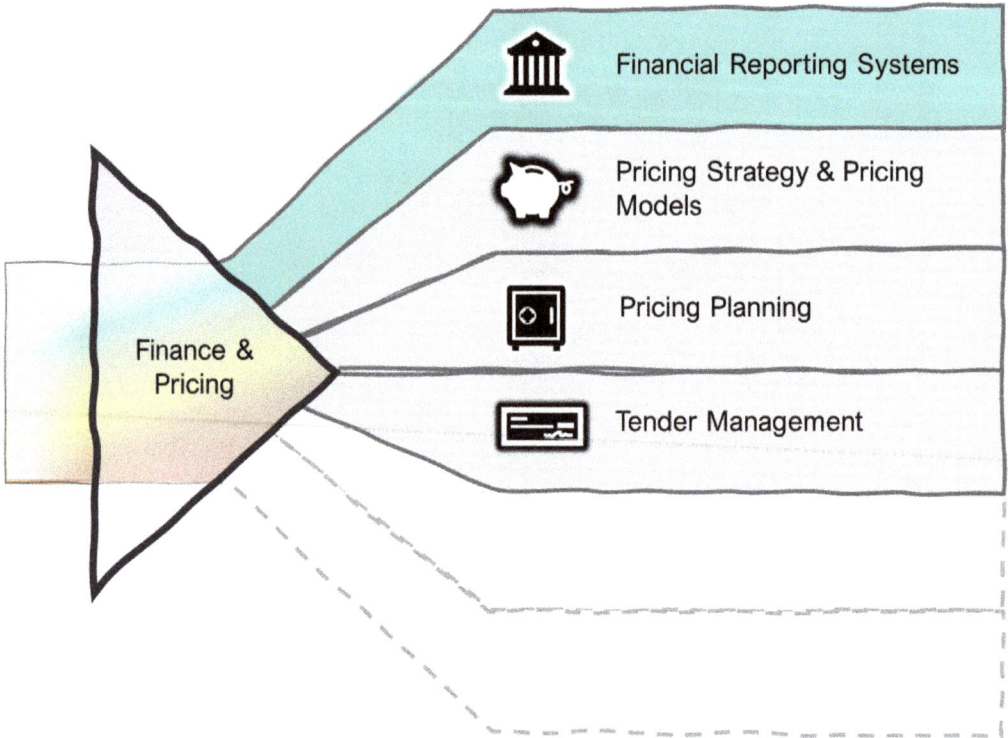

Finance & Pricing

- Financial Reporting Systems
- Pricing Strategy & Pricing Models
- Pricing Planning
- Tender Management

This chapter represents the foundation needed to carry out a commercial excellence program with any level of accuracy. Without the use of allocation keys using activity based costings, it's impossible to get to net profit reporting for customers and product ranges. As it all starts with allocation keys, let's begin there.

# ALLOCATION KEYS:

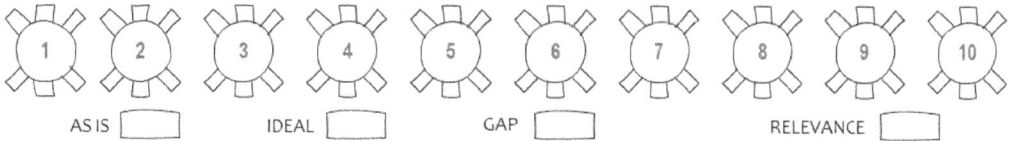

AS IS    IDEAL    GAP    RELEVANCE

## AS IS:

How sophisticated is your cost allocations systems? Do you have a system that can allocate both the direct and indirect costs? Does this system have allocation keys for each of the main direct and indirect sources? Does this system use multiple types of allocations? Does it include allocation keys such as time based, through-put or usage time based, or others? Or does your business rely on broad estimates or simply allocate overhead costs based on revenue or sales volume?

## IDEAL:

Ideally, the finance team would have a robust and refined cost allocation methodology, utilizing a sophisticated allocation key that accurately captures the true cost drivers for each product and customer. This might involve activity-based costing (ABC) methods, which allocate costs based on the specific activities that drive them. This level of cost granularity would enable the business to accurately determine the true profitability of each product and customer segment, make informed pricing decisions based on actual cost-to-serve.

## RELEVANCE:

Accurate cost allocation is critical for commercial excellence activities. Regardless of whether or not this allocation system is used for product costings, the ability to fully understand business decisions on product mix, customer or product targeting is critical to a successful commercial excellence program. Without this as a foundation, minimal accuracy can be achieved from any correction programs as an output of this book.

# P&L LEVEL REPORTING:

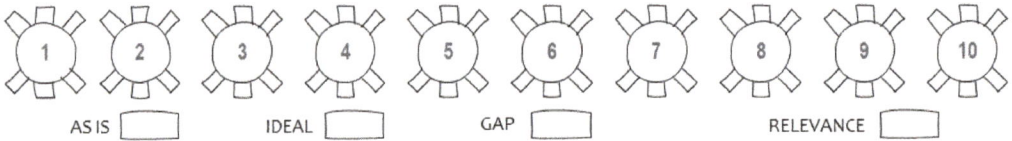

| 1 | 2 | 3 | 4 | 5 | 6 | 7 | 8 | 9 | 10 |

AS IS [        ]    IDEAL [        ]    GAP [        ]    RELEVANCE [        ]

## AS IS:

Is your business able to produce an income statement at the customer level? Are your allocation methods sophisticated enough to accurately allocate overheads? Can you determine the impact of an individual customer on the organisation's profitability? Can you determine if the product mix were to change within a customer what impact that would have on the customer's profitability? Do you share this information with the organisation? At what level is it shared?

## IDEAL:

Ideally, the finance team could produce a detailed Profit & Loss (P&L) statement for each customer, including a breakdown of all direct and indirect costs associated with serving that customer. This would involve a robust cost allocation system that accurately captures the true cost drivers for each customer interaction, such as order fulfilment, customer support, and sales and marketing efforts. This level of granularity would allow for a deep understanding of customer profitability, enabling the business to identify high-value customers, optimize pricing and service levels, and make data-driven decisions about customer acquisition and retention strategies. Combined with product costings at a similar net level would allow modelling of mix changes. Ideally such a system would have a profitability classification incorporated. (Examples will be discussed later in this chapter). Such a classification facilitates the business to perform more accurate "what if" and scenario analysis? This would be linked with the customer targeting systems (sometimes called Customer Value

Management) and the Sales Incentives Plans (SIP) to drive profitable top and bottom-line growth for the company.

## RELEVANCE:

The ability to generate customer-level P&L statements is critical for full commercial excellence integration. This level of financial analysis provides crucial insights for informed business decisions. By understanding the true profitability of each customer, businesses can utilise the customer profitability optimisation funnel (Figure 29)

**Figure 29:** Customer Profitability Optimisation Funnel

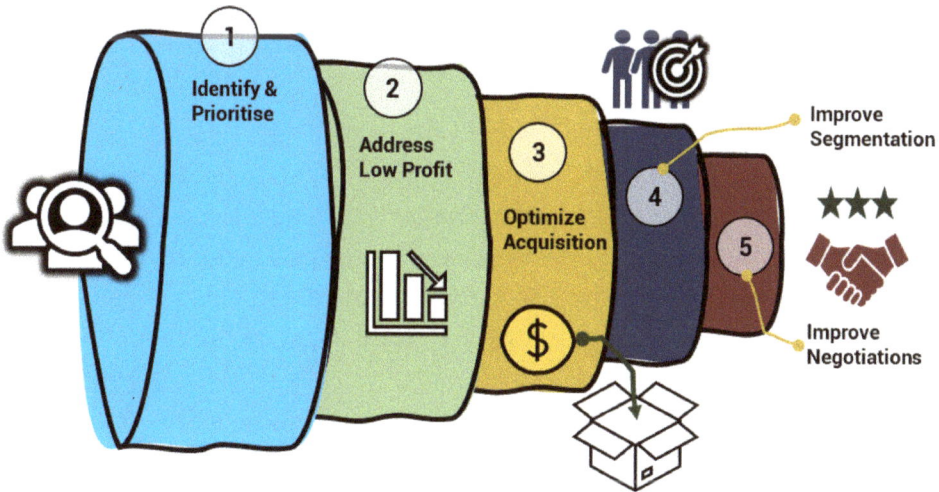

:

**1.** Identify and prioritize high-value customers and focus on retaining and growing this segment.

**2.** Identify and address unprofitable customer segments, potentially through price adjustments, service level adjustments, or customer attrition strategies.

**3.** Make data-driven decisions about customer acquisition costs and marketing spend.

**4.** Improve customer segmentation and develop more targeted marketing campaigns.

**5.** Negotiate more effectively with key customers based on a clear understanding of the true cost of serving them.

While the initial setup and ongoing maintenance of such a system may require some investment, the insights gained from customer-level P&L statements can significantly improve profitability and inform strategic business decisions.

# PRODUCT COSTING SYSTEMS:

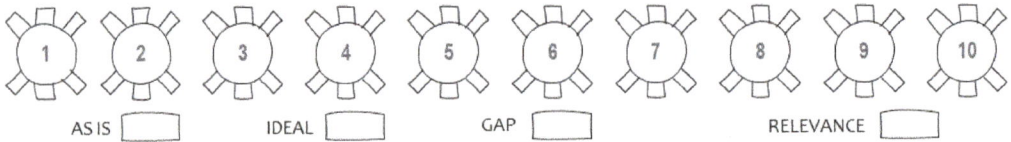

| 1 | 2 | 3 | 4 | 5 | 6 | 7 | 8 | 9 | 10 |

AS IS ☐      IDEAL ☐      GAP ☐      RELEVANCE ☐

## AS IS:

How sophisticated is your product costing system? Is it able to cost to a net profit level? Or is it more generic? What level of detail does your current system allow? Does it rely heavily on broad allocations of overhead costs? If you wanted to allocate further, what inaccuracies would there be? Do you have an Activity-Based Costing System?

## IDEAL:

Ideally, the product costing process would go beyond simply calculating the cost of goods sold. It should incorporate a robust Activity-Based Costing (ABC) methodology. ABC involves identifying and analysing the key activities that drive costs and allocating overhead costs based on the consumption of these activities by each product. This allows for a more accurate and granular understanding of the true cost of producing and selling each product, including all direct and indirect costs. By costing products at the net profit level, the business can identify and address under-priced or unprofitable products, understand product mix affects and understand customer purchasing behaviours better.

## RELEVANCE:

Accurate product costing is critical for a successful commercial excellence program. The more accurate the costings, the more accurate any model is for predicting the future or understanding the commercial business. If you lack the ability to make more informed pricing decisions, identify and address under-priced or unprofitable products, or understand the impact of discounting this area is critical.

**NOTE:** While implementing an ABC costing system may require an initial investment in time and resources, the long-term benefits in terms of improved pricing, profitability, and strategic decision-making can be significant.

# PROFITABILITY CLASSIFICATION SYSTEMS:

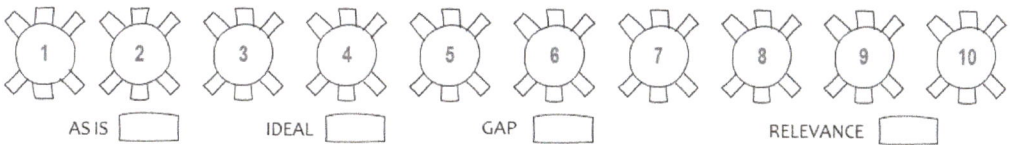

AS IS [          ]    IDEAL [          ]    GAP [          ]    RELEVANCE [          ]

## AS IS:

Do you have a basic understanding of product and customer profitability? Or is it more sophisticated? Do you know if the customer or product is contributing to or diluting your gross margin? Do you have a formalized process for classifying products and customers based on their profitability contribution to the overall business? How do you decide on customer X versus customer Y or Product A versus product B?

## IDEAL:

Ideally, the business would have a well-defined product profitability process that goes beyond a simply guess. This process would, classify products and customers as "margin contributively" or "margin dilutive" based on whether their individual gross margin exceeds or falls below the company's overall gross margin.

**Figure 30:** Financial Segmentation

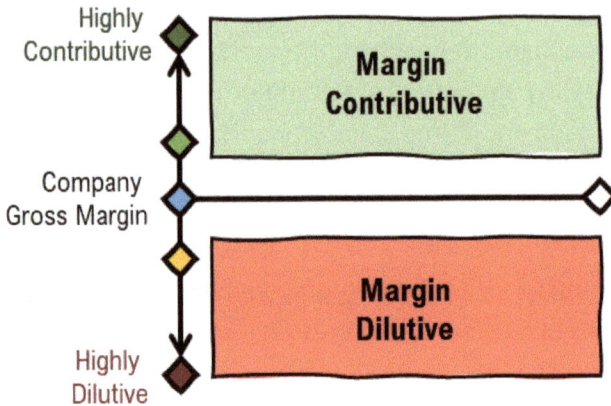

# RELEVANCE:

A robust product profitability process is highly relevant. By classifying products and customers as "margin contributive" or "margin dilutive," businesses can:

**1.** Focus their efforts on high-margin products and customers to drive overall profitability.

**2.** Identify and address underperforming products and customers, potentially through price adjustments, service level adjustments, or customer attrition strategies.

**3.** Make more informed decisions about product development, marketing, and sales efforts.

**4.** Optimize their product mix and customer portfolio to maximize overall profitability.

This process can provide valuable insights for strategic decision-making and help businesses achieve sustainable growth and profitability.

# PRODUCT PORTFOLIO OPTIMISATION:

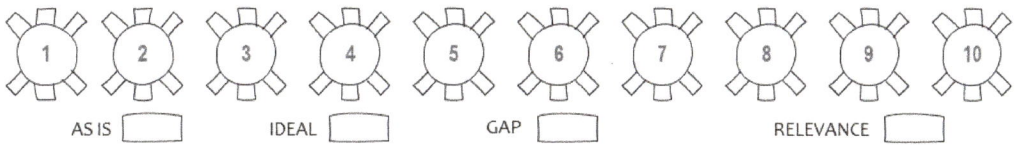

AS IS [ ]   IDEAL [ ]   GAP [ ]   RELEVANCE [ ]

## AS IS:

Do you have a process to cull your unprofitable product ranges? How do you measure product portfolio performance? Are there products that you know lose money or are in declining sales? How do you remove those from the marketplace with minimal customer complaints or issues? Or does the business rely on gut feeling or anecdotal evidence to make these decisions?

## IDEAL:

Ideally, the business would have a robust and systematic process for optimizing its product portfolio. This process would involve a regularly (potentially annual) review of product performance. Analysing key metrics such as sales volume, market share, profitability margins, customer demand, and competitive pressures. Then utilizing the profitability segmentation and customer targeting segmentation to pinpoint targets for removal, A review process to evaluate the financial impact and customer loyalty impact would be in place. The program would look into potential alternatives, product modifications: such as packaging changes, feature enhancements, pricing adjustments, product extensions: such as introducing new variants or complementary products and finally product discontinuation: For highly dilutive products a deadline date may be appropriate for end of life. Whilst in moderately dilutive products to high-value customer may warrant a phased approach to discontinuing underperforming products. Mapping the number and Value of the revenue from them onto a Product Portfolio Optimisation Canvas can provide actionable incites see Figure 31

**Figure 31:** Product Portfolio Optimisation Canvas.

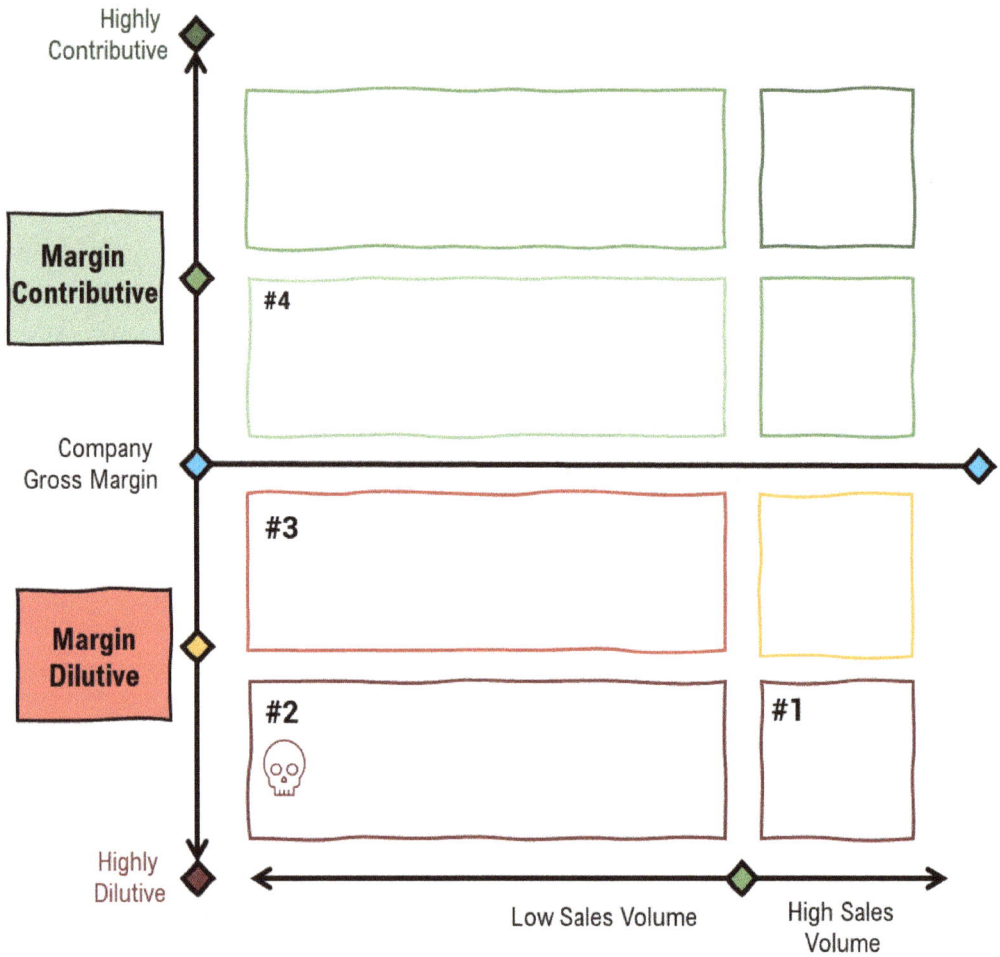

## RELEVANCE:

A robust product portfolio optimization process is highly relevant. By systematically reviewing and adjusting their product offerings, businesses can improve profitability, allowing the focusing on high-margin products and eliminating underperformers. It can free up resources that can be allocated to more promising products and initiatives, whilst enhancing customer satisfaction by offering a more focused and relevant product portfolio.

While the process of optimizing the product portfolio may require time, effort and discipline, the long-term benefits in terms of improved profitability and competitive advantage can be significant.

# CHAPTER 31:

# Pricing Strategy and Pricing Models

'Score this chapter here

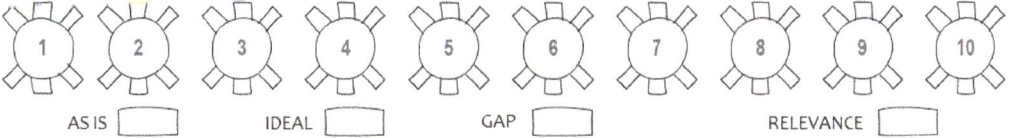

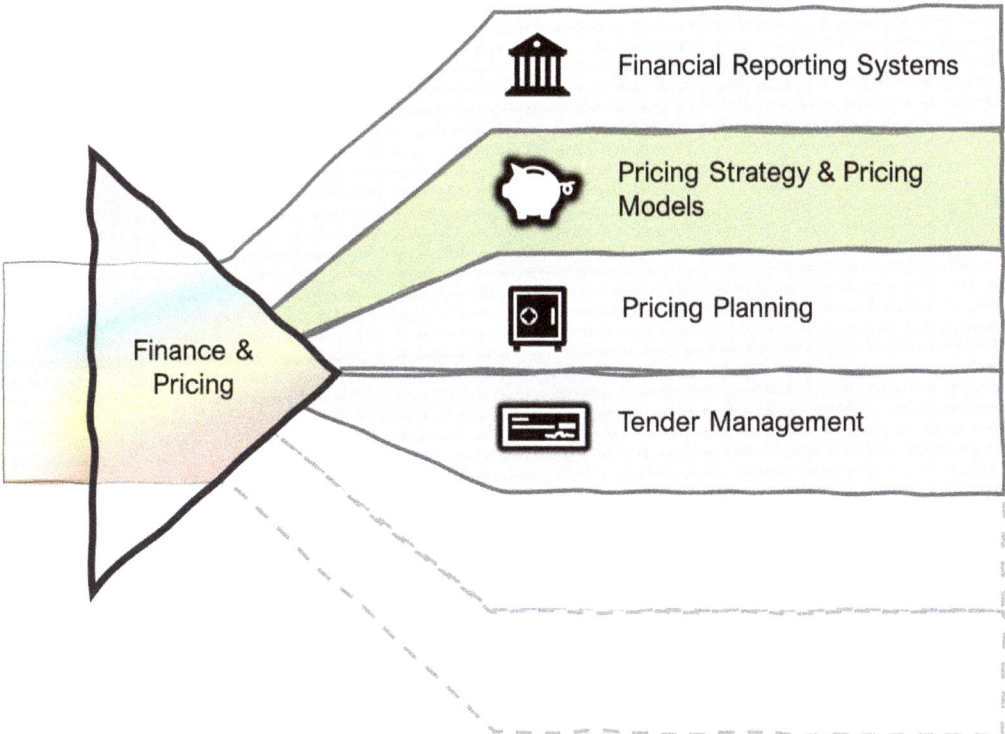

Financial Reporting Systems

Pricing Strategy & Pricing Models

Pricing Planning

Tender Management

Finance & Pricing

# PRICING MODEL:

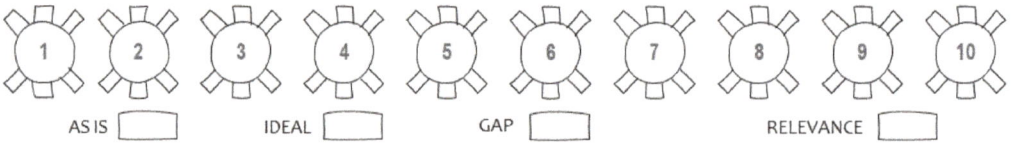

AS IS [ ]  IDEAL [ ]  GAP [ ]  RELEVANCE [ ]

## AS IS:

Consider how you currently calculate pricing for your products and services? Is it done on a method or is it basic and absent a model? What model is currently used? How far up the pricing method hierarchy is it?

**Figure 32:** Pricing Hierarchy: Based upon concepts from The Pricing Model

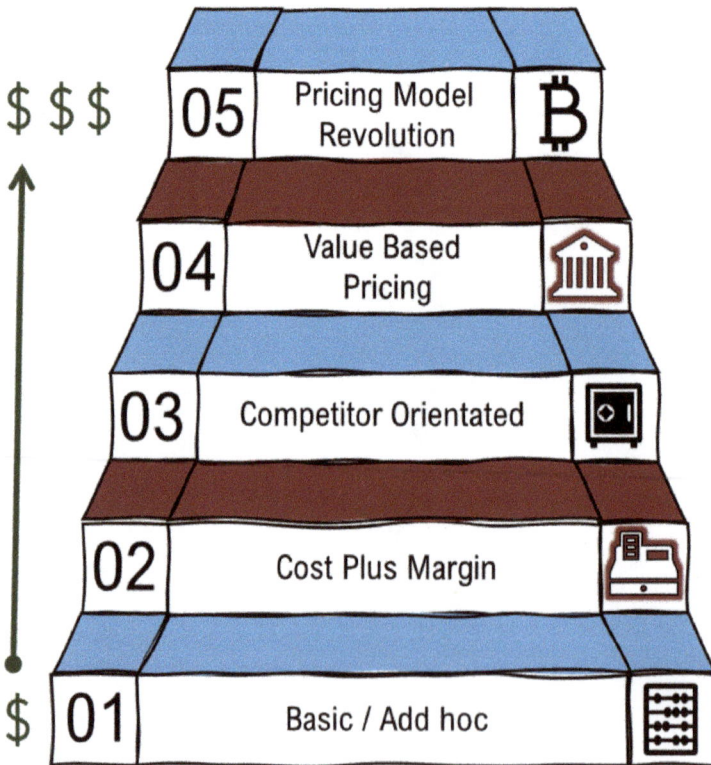

Revolution (Zatta, 2022).

## IDEAL:

Where on the hierarchy would you like to be? Ideally, your business would be as high up the hierarchy as they currently have access to. For businesses that know their competitors, pricing Stage 3 may be suitable. For businesses that understand the benefits that the customer gets from purchasing and what that is worth, then Stage 4 is optimal. For those businesses who have their own AI model that can take the statistical methods and improve the customer experience or multilevel nodes possible they, geo pricing, churn probability, discount predictors and price elasticity models can be generated.

## RELEVANCE:

Choosing the right pricing model is important to maximise review. As price is the fastest way to affect profit levels, this should be of importance to most businesses. If you have high churn, low levels of details about the competition or have limited understanding of the value your products / services bring, this area is of critical importance.

## WILLINGNESS-TO-PAY ANALYSIS:

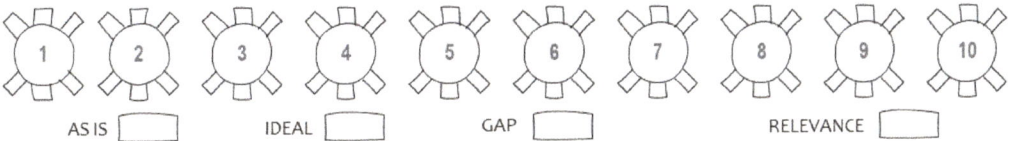

AS IS ☐     IDEAL ☐     GAP ☐     RELEVANCE ☐

## AS IS:

Consider how often and how thoroughly you analyse the willingness to pay for your products. Reflect on whether you actively compare this willingness to pay against available options and budget constraints within your different market segments. Do you conduct market research, customer surveys, or other analyses to understand these dynamics? Or do you rely on less formal methods? What do your competitors' strong accounts pay for their products? What volume are they taking? Does that fit into or align with your pricing corridor? How often do you beta test a price by raising it with 1 or 2 no regret customers until they no longer purchase? Similarly, if you run a promotion or discounting what additional volume do you achieve? Evaluating your approach to understanding willingness to pay will reveal potential gaps in your market research and pricing analysis.

## IDEAL:

Ideally, you conduct an analysis of the willingness to pay for your products, comparing them against available treatment options and budget constraints within each relevant market segment. Then with a no regret / no visit customer, raise the pricing time and time again until they stop purchasing. Repeating this one time every 12-18 months, allowing to set an upper limit of "list price" for all others to be benchmarked and discounted from. The results of these analyses and beta testing inform your pricing decisions and ensure that your pricing is aligned with market realities.

## RELEVANCE:

Understanding willingness to pay is important for setting effective prices that maximize revenue. Giving you an idea of the upper limits of your pricing corridor. If you are not frequently analysing willingness to pay, or if you don't routinely raise pricing, this area is relevant. Investing in market research, pricing analysis and beta testing will improve your pricing decisions and drive better business outcomes.

## COMPETITOR PRICING AND STRATEGY:

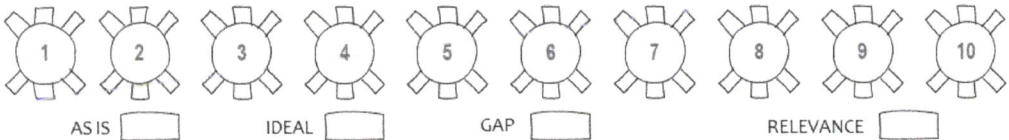

1   2   3   4   5   6   7   8   9   10

AS IS [    ]    IDEAL [    ]    GAP [    ]    RELEVANCE [    ]

## AS IS:

Consider how thoroughly you explore your competitors' pricing strategies. Reflect on whether you regularly analyse their pricing behaviour, including discounts, promotions, and contracting structures. Do you actively monitor their pricing changes and analyse the impact on your own business? Do you know their pricing model? Are they cost plus? Value-based? Are they using bundling or buy 1 get 1 offers to supplement a higher list / advertised price? Or is your competitive pricing intelligence less comprehensive? How do they find out your pricing strategy? Evaluating your competitive pricing analysis will reveal potential gaps in your market intelligence.

The Commercial Excellence Playbook

## IDEAL:

Ideally, you regularly conduct in-depth analyses of your competitors' pricing strategies, behaviour, and contracting structures. You will follow their marketing and promotional activities that can give you pricing insights. You'll take advantage of competitor accounts to gain pricing knowledge. This involves actively monitoring their pricing changes, analysing their promotional activities, and understanding their contracting terms. This information is used to inform your own pricing strategy and ensure that you remain competitive in the marketplace.

## RELEVANCE:

Understanding your competitors' pricing strategies is crucial for setting competitive prices and maintaining market share. Effective competitive pricing intelligence is essential for remaining competitive. If you are not regularly exploring your competitors' pricing, this area is highly relevant. Investing in competitive pricing analysis will improve your pricing decisions and strengthen your competitive position.

# PRICING STRATEGY AND COMMERCIAL OBJECTIVE ALIGNMENT:

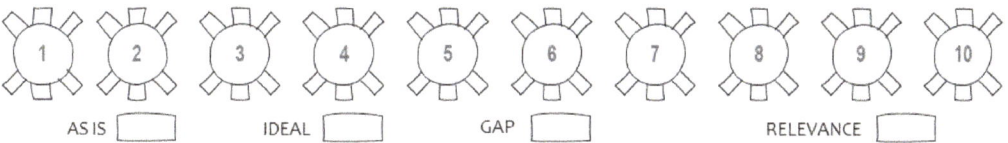

| 1 | 2 | 3 | 4 | 5 | 6 | 7 | 8 | 9 | 10 |

AS IS [    ]    IDEAL [    ]    GAP [    ]    RELEVANCE [    ]

## AS IS:

Consider the alignment of your pricing strategy with your overall commercial strategy and business objectives. Reflect on whether your pricing decisions are consistent with your product positioning (e.g., premium versus commodity), your target customer segments, your channel strategies, and your business objectives (e.g., volume and margin targets). Or are there inconsistencies or conflicts between these different elements, potentially leading to suboptimal business outcomes? Evaluating the alignment of your pricing strategy will reveal potential gaps in your overall strategic coherence.

## IDEAL:

Ideally, your pricing strategy is fully aligned with your overall commercial strategy and business objectives. This means that your pricing decisions are consistent with your product positioning, target customer segments, channel strategies, and desired volume and margin targets. This alignment ensures that your pricing supports your overall business goals.

## RELEVANCE:

Alignment between pricing strategy, commercial strategy, and business objectives is crucial for maximizing profitability and growing both the top and bottom lines simultaneously. Strategic alignment is essential for driving growth and achieving financial targets. If your pricing strategy is not aligned with your other strategic elements, this area is relevant. Investing in ensuring alignment will improve your business outcomes.

# MARKET DYNAMICS AND PRICING STRATEGY:

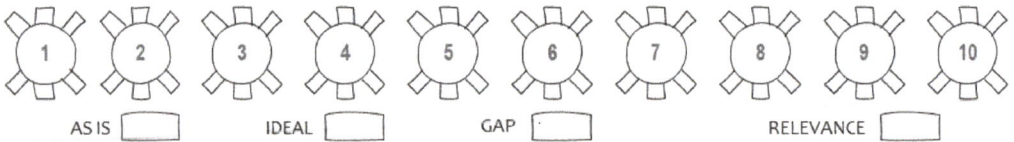

AS IS [ ]     IDEAL [ ]     GAP [ ]     RELEVANCE [ ]

## AS IS:

Consider how well your pricing strategy reflects current market dynamics. Reflect on whether your pricing decisions take into account factors such as market structure, your market position, competitive pricing, and customer purchasing behaviour. Or are your pricing decisions made in isolation? Do you have a pricing corridor that you understand? How does the market dynamics affect it? Is it the same as other territories? Evaluating the market-responsiveness of your pricing strategy will reveal potential gaps in your market understanding.

## IDEAL:

Ideally, your pricing strategy appropriately reflects all relevant market dynamics, including market structure, your market position, competitive pricing, and customer purchasing behaviour. In rapidly growing markets, pricing strategy can see a higher or lower pricing corridor depending upon the level of competition. This ensures that your pricing is competitive and aligned with market conditions.

## RELEVANCE:

A market-responsive pricing strategy is crucial for remaining competitive and maximizing market share. Adapting to market dynamics is essential for maintaining a competitive edge. If your pricing strategy does not adequately reflect market dynamics, this area is relevant.

## PARTNER ECONOMICS AND PRICING:

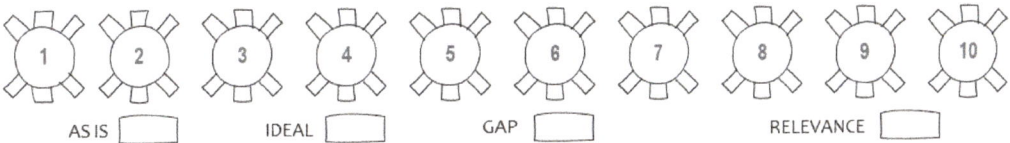

AS IS ▢    IDEAL ▢    GAP ▢    RELEVANCE ▢

## AS IS:

If you work with third-party partners, channel partners, distributors or agents, consider how well your pricing strategy reflects their economics and incentives. Reflect on whether you understand their cost structures, profit margins, and motivations for selling your products. Does your pricing structure adequately reward them to promote and sell your offerings? Or does it create disincentives or conflicts of interest? Evaluating your partner pricing strategy will reveal potential gaps in your channel management and partner relationships.

## IDEAL:

If you cooperate with third parties or distributors, your pricing strategy should reflect a deep understanding of their economics and incentives to sell your products. This ensures that your pricing structure is fair, competitive, and motivates partners to actively promote and sell your offerings.

## RELEVANCE:

A partner-focused pricing strategy is crucial for maintaining strong channel relationships and maximizing channel performance. Effective pricing is essential for motivating partners and driving sales. If your pricing strategy does not adequately consider partner economics and incentives, this area is highly relevant. Reviewing and adjusting your pricing strategy will improve partner relationships and drive better channel outcomes.

## PRICING STRATEGY OPTIMISATION:

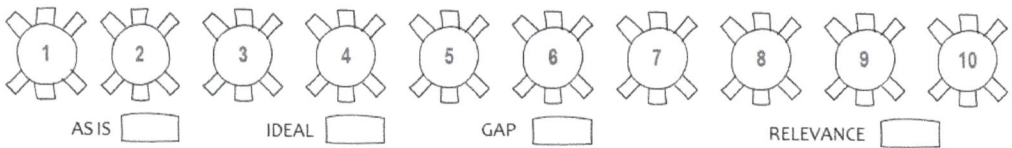

AS IS [        ]    IDEAL [        ]    GAP [        ]    RELEVANCE [        ]

### AS IS:

Consider how often you review and optimize your pricing strategy. Reflect on whether you have a regular process for reviewing your pricing decisions and making adjustments based on market changes, competitive dynamics, and business performance. Is this review conducted at least every two years, or is it less frequent? When is the last time that you challenged the assumption "I can't change price, they will leave"? Evaluating the regularity of your pricing strategy review will reveal potential gaps in your pricing management.

### IDEAL:

Ideally, you have a formal process for regularly reviewing and optimizing your pricing strategy at least every two years – or more frequently, if market conditions warrant. This review should involve analysing market data, competitive intelligence, customer feedback, and internal performance metrics. This ensures that your pricing strategy remains aligned with market realities and business objectives.

### RELEVANCE:

Regular optimization of your pricing strategy is important to keep pace with the market. Adapting your pricing to changing market conditions is essential for long-term success. If you are not regularly reviewing your pricing strategy, this

302                                                    The Commercial Excellence Playbook

area is relevant. Implementing a regular review process will improve your pricing decisions and drive better business outcomes.

# VALUE BASED PRICING LOGIC:

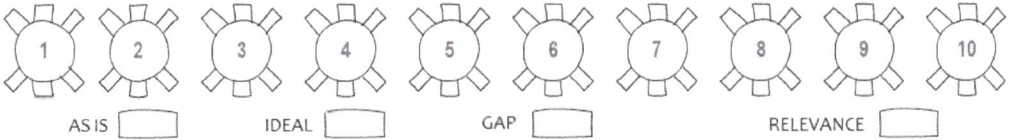

| | | | |
|---|---|---|---|
| 1 | 2 | 3 | 4 | 5 | 6 | 7 | 8 | 9 | 10 |

AS IS [____]    IDEAL [____]    GAP [____]    RELEVANCE [____]

## AS IS:

Consider the basis for your pricing decisions. Reflect on whether you use a clear value-based pricing logic that considers the value your products/services deliver to customers. Do you quantify the benefits and cost savings that customers realize by using your offerings? Or do you rely on cost-plus pricing, competitor-based pricing, or other less value-oriented approaches? Evaluating your pricing logic will reveal potential gaps in your pricing methodology.

## IDEAL:

Ideally, you determine your prices based on a clear and well-defined value-based pricing logic. This involves quantifying the value your products/services deliver to customers, including tangible benefits such as cost savings, increased efficiency, and improved outcomes. Once this is understood new and novel models can be utilised to change from a red to a blue ocean. Look at what this value is then used as the basis for setting prices that accurately reflect the worth of your offerings to customers.

## RELEVANCE:

Value-based pricing is crucial for maximizing profitability and justifying premium prices. Demonstrating value to customers is essential for achieving pricing power. If you are not using a value-based pricing logic, this area is highly relevant. Investing in developing a value-based pricing methodology will improve your pricing decisions and increase profitability.

# COMPREHENSIVE PRICING MANAGEMENT:

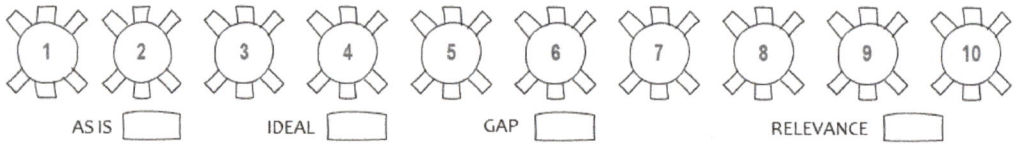

AS IS [ ]   IDEAL [ ]   GAP [ ]   RELEVANCE [ ]

## AS IS:

Consider the full range of pricing elements you manage. Reflect on whether you actively manage not only list prices and explicit discounts but also "hidden discounts" such as product services, free shipping, spare parts, rebates, warranties, and payment terms. Do you understand the total cost of these hidden discounts and their impact on profitability? Or are these elements managed less strategically, potentially leading to unintended price reductions and margin erosion? Evaluating the breadth of your pricing management will reveal potential gaps in your pricing control.

## IDEAL:

Ideally, you manage all aspects of pricing, including not only list prices and discounts but also "hidden discounts" such as product services, free shipping, spare parts, rebates, warranties, and payment terms. You have a clear understanding of the cost and impact of each of these elements and manage them strategically to optimize profitability.

## RELEVANCE:

Managing all pricing elements is crucial for maintaining profitability and maximizing revenue. Effective control of all pricing aspects is essential for achieving financial targets. If you are not actively managing "hidden discounts," this area is highly relevant. Implementing a more comprehensive approach to pricing management will improve profitability and prevent unintended price reductions.

# CROSS-COUNTRY PRICE CONSIDERATIONS:

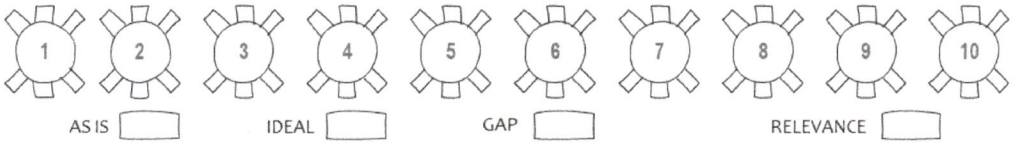

1  2  3  4  5  6  7  8  9  10

AS IS [        ]    IDEAL [        ]    GAP [        ]    RELEVANCE [        ]

## AS IS:

If you operate in multiple countries, consider how your pricing model addresses cross-country price differences. Reflect on whether your model adequately accounts for factors such as exchange rates, local market conditions, taxes, and regulatory requirements. Does it effectively control price differences between countries to prevent arbitrage or other unintended consequences? Or are cross-country pricing issues managed less effectively, potentially leading to pricing inconsistencies and lost revenue? Evaluating your cross-country pricing model will reveal potential gaps in your global pricing management.

## IDEAL:

If you operate in multiple countries, your pricing model should sufficiently account for and control cross-country price differences. This involves considering factors such as exchange rates, local market conditions, taxes, regulatory requirements, and competitive landscapes in each country. The model should also include mechanisms to prevent arbitrage and ensure consistent pricing across markets, where appropriate.

## RELEVANCE:

Managing cross-country price differences is crucial for maintaining profitability and preventing unintended consequences in global markets. For businesses operating internationally, effective cross-country pricing management is essential for maximizing global revenue. If your pricing model does not adequately address cross-country differences, this area is highly relevant. Investing in developing a robust cross-country pricing model will improve your global pricing management and prevent revenue leakage.

# COMPETITIVE ADVANTAGES FROM PRICING AND CONTRACT STRUCTURES:

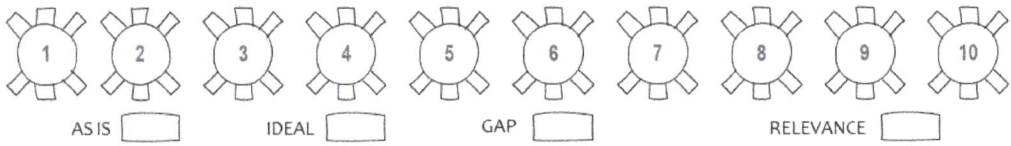

AS IS [ ]    IDEAL [ ]    GAP [ ]    RELEVANCE [ ]

## AS IS:

Consider the innovativeness of your price, contract, and discount structures. Reflect on whether you are using traditional pricing approaches or exploring innovative structures that can drive volume growth, improve price realization, and differentiate you from competitors. Do you offer value-based contracts, performance-based pricing, or other innovative pricing mechanisms? Or are your pricing structures relatively standard, potentially limiting your ability to stand out in the market? Evaluating the innovativeness of your pricing will reveal potential gaps in your competitive differentiation.

## IDEAL:

Ideally, you have innovative price, contract, and discount structures that differentiate you from competitors and drive positive business outcomes. This may include value-based contracts, performance-based pricing, bundled offerings, tiered pricing, or other creative pricing mechanisms that align with customer needs and create a competitive advantage.

## RELEVANCE:

Innovative pricing structures can be a powerful differentiator and drive business growth. Exploring new pricing models can create a competitive edge. If your pricing structures are not innovative, this area is highly relevant. Investing in developing innovative pricing approaches will improve your competitive position and drive better business outcomes.

# FINANCING TAILORING:

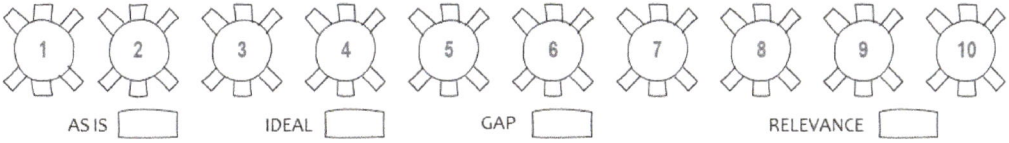

## AS IS:

Consider the financing options you offer your customers. Reflect on whether you provide a range of options, such as purchase versus leasing, that take into account their respective economic situations. Do you offer flexible payment terms or other financing arrangements that make it easier for customers to purchase your products/services? Or are your financing options limited, potentially restricting access for some customer segments? Evaluating your financing options will reveal potential gaps in your customer accessibility.

## IDEAL:

Ideally, you offer a range of financing options that cater to the diverse economic situations of your customers. This may include purchase options, leasing arrangements, flexible payment terms, financing partnerships, or other mechanisms that make your products/services more accessible and affordable.

## RELEVANCE:

Offering flexible financing options can significantly increase customer accessibility and drive sales. Providing financing options can be a key differentiator and attract a wider range of customers. If your financing options are limited, this area is highly relevant. Investing in developing more flexible financing arrangements will improve customer accessibility and drive sales growth.

# CHAPTER 32:

# Pricing Planning

Score this chapter here

| 1 | 2 | 3 | 4 | 5 | 6 | 7 | 8 | 9 | 10 |

AS IS ⬚    IDEAL ⬚    GAP ⬚    RELEVANCE ⬚

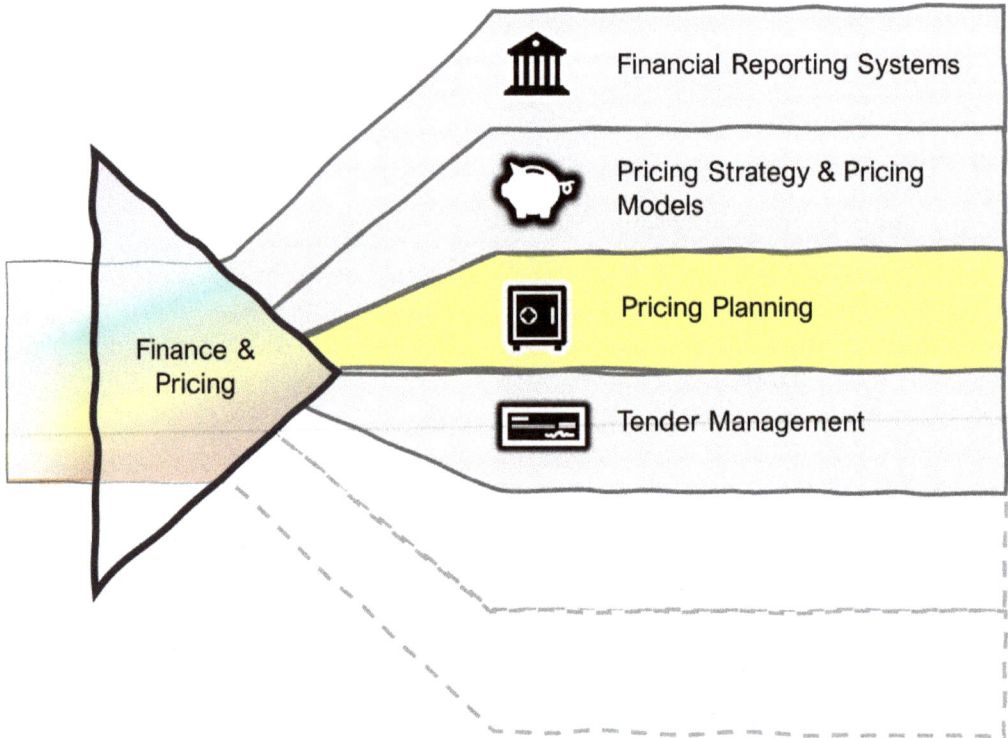

Financial Reporting Systems

Pricing Strategy & Pricing Models

Pricing Planning

Tender Management

Finance & Pricing

# STRATEGIC PRICING NEGOTIATION

# PREPARATION:

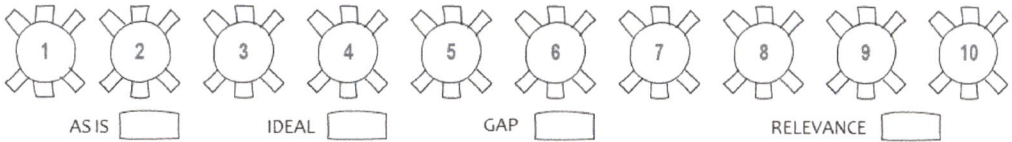

AS IS [        ]    IDEAL [        ]    GAP [        ]    RELEVANCE [        ]

## AS IS:

Consider your organisation's approach to pricing negotiations. Reflect on whether you systematically prepare for these negotiations, including gathering relevant data, defining objectives, and developing negotiation strategies. Do you capture lessons learned from previous negotiations and use them to inform future interactions? Or is your preparation less structured, potentially leading to suboptimal outcomes? Evaluating your negotiation preparation process will reveal potential gaps in your pricing execution.

## IDEAL:

Ideally, your organisation has a systematic and well-defined process for preparing for pricing negotiations. This includes gathering market intelligence, understanding customer needs and priorities, defining clear negotiation objectives, developing various negotiation scenarios and tactics, and documenting lessons learned from previous negotiations. This structured approach ensures that you are well-prepared to achieve favourable pricing outcomes.

## RELEVANCE:

Systematic preparation is crucial for successful pricing negotiations. Effective negotiation can significantly affect profitability. If your preparation process is not systematic, this area is highly relevant. Investing in developing a robust negotiation preparation process will improve your pricing execution and drive better business outcomes.

# PRICING DECISION MECHANISMS:

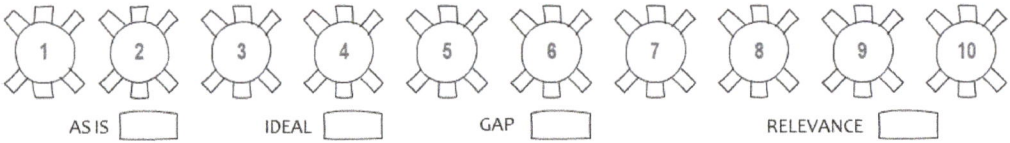

1  2  3  4  5  6  7  8  9  10

AS IS [        ]    IDEAL [        ]    GAP [        ]    RELEVANCE [        ]

## AS IS:

Consider the efficiency of your processes for reviewing contracts and bids and making decisions on discounts and terms. Reflect on whether these processes are rapid and efficient, enabling you to respond quickly to customer requests and market opportunities. Or are there bottlenecks or delays in the approval process, potentially leading to lost deals or missed opportunities? Evaluating your contract/bid review process will reveal potential gaps in your pricing ability.

## IDEAL:

Ideally, your organisation has rapid and efficient processes for reviewing contracts and bids and making decisions on discounts and terms. This involves clear decision-making authority, streamlined workflows, and effective communication channels. This enables you to respond quickly to customer needs and market opportunities, maximizing your chances of winning deals.

## RELEVANCE:

Rapid and efficient contract/bid review processes are crucial for maximizing sales effectiveness and responding to market opportunities. Agility in pricing decisions can be a significant competitive advantage. If your review processes are slow or inefficient, this area is highly relevant. Investing in streamlining these processes will improve your pricing agility and drive better business outcomes.

# PRICING VS VOLUME CONSIDERATIONS:

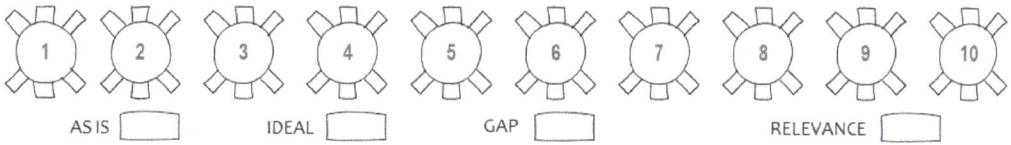

## AS IS:

Consider how your pricing strategy balances price and volume. Reflect on whether your strategy effectively sets prices that maximize profitability by finding the right trade-off between price and volume. Do you have data and analysis to support your pricing decisions? Or are these trade-offs made based on intuition or less formal methods, potentially leading to suboptimal results? Evaluating your price-volume trade-off strategy will reveal potential gaps in your pricing optimization.

The following is a table (Figure 33) to calculate the new volume needed to maintain the existing margin of a **1000-unit** sale.

**Figure 33:** Effect of Discounting on Volume to **Maintain** Margins

| New Volume to maintain existing Gross Margin | Gross Margin | | | | |
|---|---|---|---|---|---|
| | 60% | 50% | 40% | 30% | 20% |
| Proposed Discount — 5% | 1,091 | 1,111 | 1,143 | 1,200 | 1,333 |
| 10% | 1,200 | 1,250 | 1,333 | 1,500 | 2,000 |
| 15% | 1,333 | 1,429 | 1,600 | 2,000 | 4,000 |
| 20% | 1,500 | 1,667 | 2,000 | 3,000 | LOSS |

## IDEAL:

Ideally, your pricing strategy is based on a thorough understanding of the relationship between price and volume, and it effectively sets prices that maximize profitability. This involves analysing market data, customer demand, and cost structures to determine the optimal price-volume trade-off for each product/service and market segment.

# RELEVANCE:

Finding the right price-volume trade-off is crucial for maximizing profitability. Optimizing this trade-off is essential for achieving revenue and profit targets. If your pricing strategy does not effectively balance price and volume, this area is highly relevant. Investing in data analysis and pricing optimization will improve your pricing decisions and drive better financial results.

# DISCOUNTING GUARDRAILS:

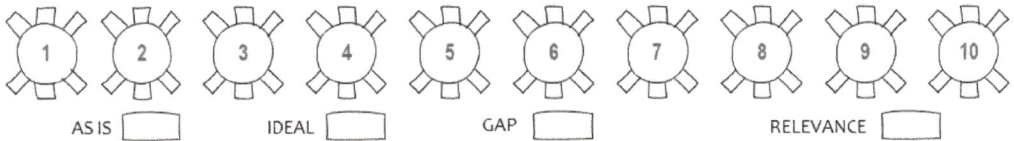

AS IS [     ]       IDEAL [     ]       GAP [     ]       RELEVANCE [     ]

# AS IS:

Consider the pricing guardrails you have in place. Reflect on whether you have established clear and objective criteria to prevent disruptively low prices that could negatively affect profitability or brand image. Are these guardrails documented, communicated, and consistently enforced? Or are pricing decisions made with less oversight, potentially leading to unintended price erosion? Evaluating your pricing control mechanisms will reveal potential gaps in your pricing governance.

# IDEAL:

Ideally, you have well-defined pricing guardrails based on objective and compliant criteria. These guardrails are documented, communicated, and consistently enforced to prevent disruptively low prices and maintain profitability. They should consider factors such as cost of goods sold, market conditions, competitive pricing, and strategic objectives. Volume and the cost of discounting:

## RELEVANCE:

Appropriate pricing guardrails are crucial for protecting profitability and maintaining brand value. Effective pricing control is essential for achieving financial targets. If you lack clear pricing guardrails, this area is highly relevant. Implementing robust pricing control mechanisms will prevent price erosion and protect profitability.

## DECISION MAKING AUTHORITY ON PRICE:

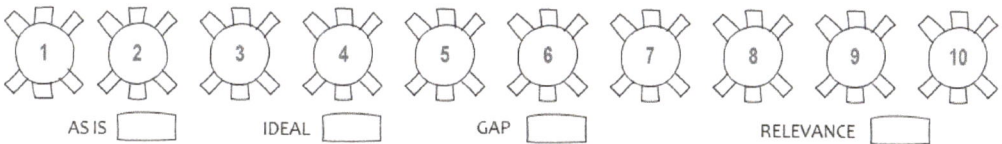

AS IS ☐    IDEAL ☐    GAP ☐        RELEVANCE ☐

## AS IS:

Consider the clarity of decision-making authority for different types of pricing decisions. Reflect on whether there is a clear and undisputed understanding within your organisation regarding who has the authority to set list prices, establish discount structures, and approve deal/tender bid prices. Or are there ambiguities or overlaps in authority, potentially leading to delays, inconsistencies, or internal conflicts? Evaluating the clarity of your pricing authority will reveal potential gaps in your pricing governance.

## IDEAL:

Ideally, your organisation has a clear and undisputed understanding of decision-making authority for each type of pricing decision, including list prices, discount structures, and deal/tender bid prices. This should be documented and communicated throughout the organisation to prevent confusion and ensure efficient decision-making.

## RELEVANCE:

Clear decision-making authority is crucial for efficient and effective pricing management. Well-defined authority levels can significantly improve pricing agility and prevent internal conflicts. If your pricing authority is unclear, this area is highly relevant. Investing in clarifying decision-making roles will improve pricing governance and streamline decision-making.

# DATA & TOOLS FOR PRICING DECISION AUTHORITY:

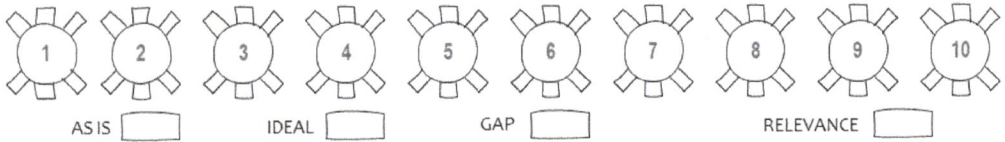

AS IS [          ]    IDEAL [          ]    GAP [          ]         RELEVANCE [          ]

## AS IS:

Consider the data, tools, and systems used to support your pricing and contracting processes and to monitor pricing performance. Reflect on whether you have the necessary resources to effectively analyse market data, track pricing performance, and manage contracts. Do you have clear visibility of price realization and variability across different segments, customers, regions, and territories? Or are there gaps in your data, tools, or systems that hinder effective pricing management? Evaluating your pricing infrastructure will reveal potential gaps in your pricing analytics and control.

## IDEAL:

Ideally, you have the necessary data, tools, and systems to fully support the pricing and contracting process and to effectively monitor pricing performance. This includes access to market data, pricing analytics tools, contract management systems, and reporting dashboards that provide transparency to price realization and variability across different segments, customers, regions, and territories.

## RELEVANCE:

Adequate data, tools, and systems are crucial for effective pricing management and performance monitoring. Investing in appropriate pricing infrastructure can significantly improve pricing decisions and drive better business outcomes. If

The Commercial Excellence Playbook

you lack the necessary resources, this area is highly relevant. Investing in improving your pricing infrastructure will enhance your pricing analytics and control.

# PRICING STRATEGY KPIS:

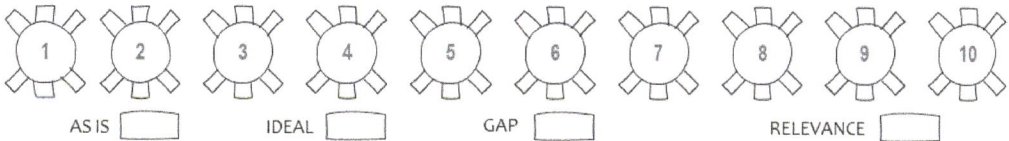

AS IS [ ]    IDEAL [ ]    GAP [ ]    RELEVANCE [ ]

## AS IS:

Consider the Key Performance Indicators (KPIs) you used to measure the effectiveness of your pricing strategy and model. Reflect on whether you have clearly defined KPIs that provide meaningful insights into pricing performance. Are these KPIs regularly tracked and analysed? Or is your performance measurement less systematic, potentially missing opportunities for improvement? Evaluating your pricing performance measurement will reveal potential gaps in your pricing analytics.

## IDEAL:

Ideally, you have a set of well-defined KPIs that provide comprehensive insights into the effectiveness of your pricing strategy and model. These KPIs should be aligned with your business objectives and include metrics such as price realization, gross margin, average selling price, price elasticity, and customer profitability. These KPIs are regularly tracked, analysed, and used to inform pricing decisions and strategy adjustments.

## RELEVANCE:

Defining and tracking relevant KPIs is crucial for evaluating the success of your pricing strategy and identifying areas for improvement. Data-driven performance monitoring is essential for optimizing pricing decisions and maximizing profitability. If you lack clearly defined pricing KPIs, this area is highly relevant.

Investing in developing and tracking appropriate KPIs will improve your pricing management and drive better business outcomes.

# PRICING PROCESS RESOURCING:

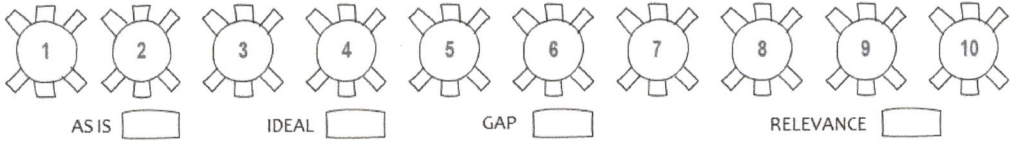

AS IS [____]    IDEAL [____]    GAP [____]    RELEVANCE [____]

## AS IS:

Consider the resources dedicated to pricing within your organisation. Reflect on whether you have sufficient personnel focused on pricing to effectively support both strategy development and execution. Are your pricing teams adequately staffed to handle the workload and complexity of pricing decisions? Or are resources stretched too thin, potentially leading to suboptimal pricing outcomes? Evaluating your pricing resource allocation will reveal potential gaps in your pricing capacity.

## IDEAL:

Ideally, you have sufficient personnel dedicated to pricing to effectively support both strategy development and execution. This ensures that pricing decisions are made with appropriate expertise and resources, maximizing their effectiveness. The size and structure of the pricing team should be aligned with the complexity of your pricing strategy and the size of your business.

## RELEVANCE:

Adequate resources are crucial for effective pricing management. Having dedicated pricing personnel can significantly improve pricing decisions and drive better business outcomes. If you lack sufficient resources dedicated to pricing, this area is highly relevant. Investing in appropriate staffing will improve your pricing management and drive better results.

# EXPERTISE IN EXECUTING PRICING STRATEGY:

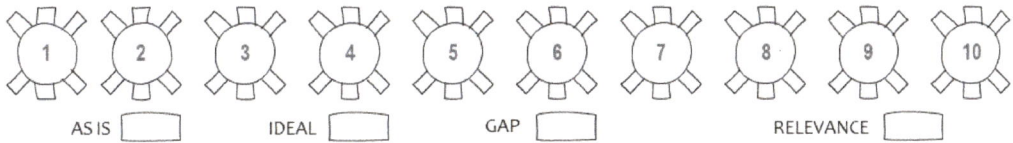

| 1 | 2 | 3 | 4 | 5 | 6 | 7 | 8 | 9 | 10 |

AS IS [       ]     IDEAL [       ]     GAP [       ]     RELEVANCE [       ]

## AS IS:

Consider the skills, experience, and functional understanding of your pricing team. Reflect on whether they possess the necessary competencies to fully and successfully execute your pricing strategy. Do they have strong analytical skills, market knowledge, financial acumen, and an understanding of pricing best practices? Or are there skill gaps that need to be addressed through training or recruitment? Evaluating the capabilities of your pricing team will reveal potential gaps in your pricing expertise.

## IDEAL:

Ideally, your pricing team possesses the optimal mix of skills, experience, and deep functional understanding required to fully and successfully execute your pricing strategy. This includes strong analytical skills, market knowledge, financial acumen, negotiation skills, and a thorough understanding of pricing best practices. Ongoing training and development programs should be in place to ensure that the team stays current with industry trends and evolving pricing methodologies.

## RELEVANCE:

Having a highly skilled and knowledgeable pricing team is essential for effective pricing management and achieving strategic objectives. Investing in talent development within the pricing function can be a significant differentiator. If your pricing team lacks the necessary skills or experience, this area is highly relevant. Investing in training and development will improve pricing decisions and enhance business performance.

# INCENTIVISING PRICING STRATEGIES:

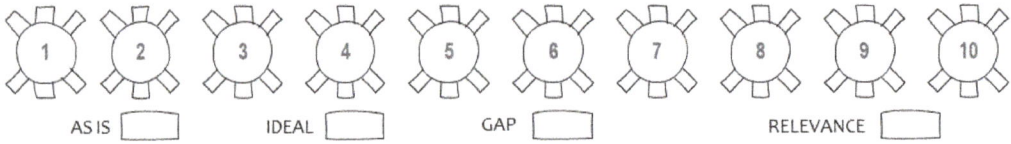

```
1    2    3    4    5    6    7    8    9    10
```

AS IS [    ]    IDEAL [    ]    GAP [    ]    RELEVANCE [    ]

## AS IS:

Consider the incentive and compensation structures in place for your sales, marketing, and management. Reflect on how effectively these structures support the execution of your pricing strategies. Do they motivate sales teams to achieve desired pricing outcomes, such as maintaining price integrity or promoting value-based selling? Or are there misalignments that could lead to discounting pressures or suboptimal pricing behaviour? Evaluating your incentive and compensation structures will reveal potential gaps in your pricing execution and sales motivation.

## IDEAL:

Ideally, you use effective incentive and compensation structures that strongly support the execution of your pricing strategies. These structures should reward sales teams for achieving desired pricing outcomes, such as maintaining price integrity, promoting value-based selling, and achieving profitability targets. The incentives should be aligned with your overall pricing strategy and business objectives.

## RELEVANCE:

Aligning incentives with pricing strategies is crucial for ensuring effective pricing execution, and maintaining or growing profitability. A well-designed incentive structure can significantly motivate sales teams to achieve desired pricing outcomes. If your incentive and compensation structures are not effectively aligned, this area is highly relevant. Reviewing and adjusting these structures will improve pricing execution and drive better business outcomes.

# CHAPTER 33:

# Tender Management

Score this chapter here

1  2  3  4  5  6  7  8  9  10

AS IS ☐     IDEAL ☐     GAP ☐     RELEVANCE ☐

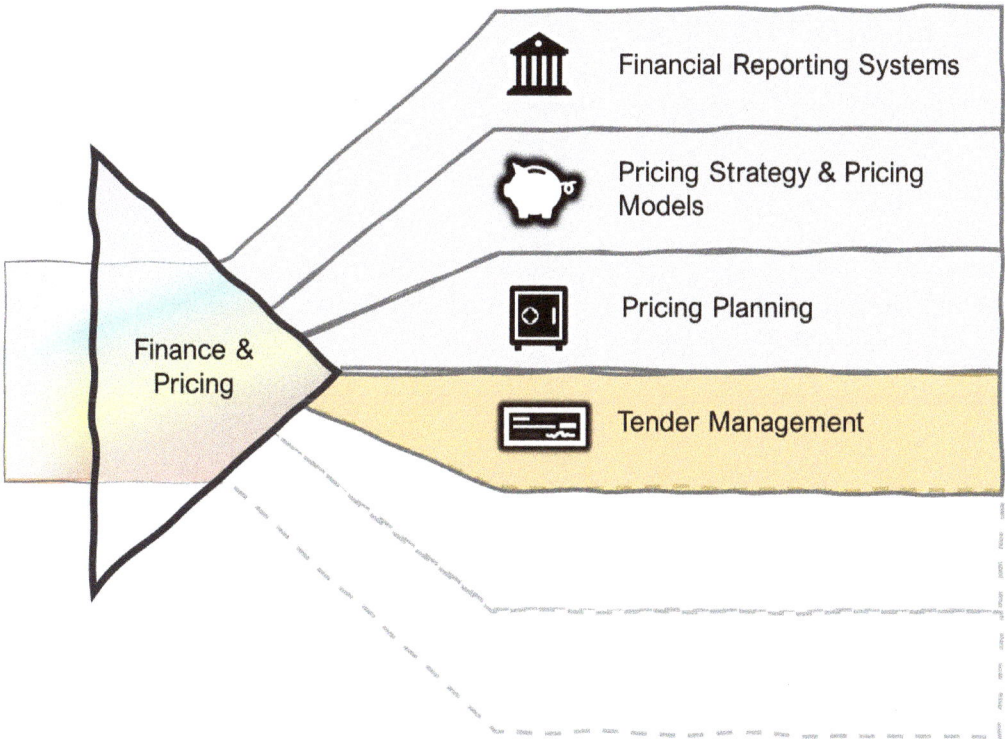

Financial Reporting Systems

Pricing Strategy & Pricing Models

Pricing Planning

Finance & Pricing

Tender Management

# COMPREHENSION OF TENDERING PROCESS:

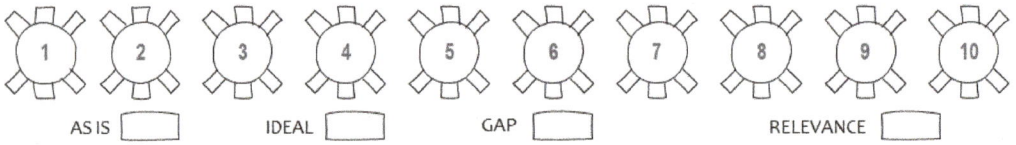

| | | | | | | | | | |
|---|---|---|---|---|---|---|---|---|---|
| 1 | 2 | 3 | 4 | 5 | 6 | 7 | 8 | 9 | 10 |

AS IS [ ]    IDEAL [ ]    GAP [ ]    RELEVANCE [ ]

## AS IS:

Consider your organisation's understanding of the tendering process in your target markets. Reflect on how thoroughly you understand the evaluation and assessment criteria used in tenders, any upcoming changes in relevant regulations (such as the shift towards value-based procurement), and the key decision-makers involved. Do you actively monitor regulatory changes and maintain relationships with key stakeholders? Or is your understanding less comprehensive, potentially putting you at a disadvantage in competitive tenders? Evaluating your knowledge of the tendering landscape will reveal potential gaps in your tender preparation.

## IDEAL:

Ideally, your organisation possesses a deep and comprehensive understanding of the tendering process in your target markets. This includes detailed knowledge of evaluation criteria, upcoming regulatory changes (such as value-based procurement), and the key decision-makers involved. You actively monitor regulatory developments and maintain strong relationships with key stakeholders to stay ahead of the curve.

## RELEVANCE:

A thorough understanding of the tendering process is crucial for developing winning tender strategies. For businesses in the $20-50 million range that participate in tenders, this knowledge is essential for maximizing win rates. If your understanding of the tendering landscape is lacking, this area is highly relevant. Investing in market research, regulatory monitoring, and stakeholder relationship management will improve your tender success rate.

# COMPETITION TENDERING STRATEGIES:

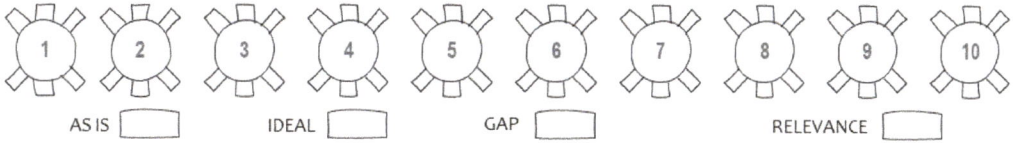

AS IS [      ]    IDEAL [      ]    GAP [      ]    RELEVANCE [      ]

## AS IS:

Consider how thoroughly you analyse your competitors' tendering strategies. Reflect on whether you regularly explore their bidding behaviour, pricing tactics, and contracting structures. Do you actively monitor their tender wins and losses and analyse their strategies? Or is your competitive intelligence in tendering less comprehensive, potentially leaving you vulnerable to their competitive bids? Evaluating your competitive tender analysis will reveal potential gaps in your market intelligence.

## IDEAL:

Ideally, you regularly conduct in-depth analyses of your competitors' tendering strategies and contracting structures. This includes monitoring their bidding patterns, pricing tactics, win/loss records, and any other relevant information. This intelligence is used to inform your own tender strategy and improve your competitiveness.

## RELEVANCE:

Understanding your competitors' tendering strategies is crucial for developing effective counter-strategies and maximizing your chances of winning tenders. Strong competitive intelligence in tendering is essential for maintaining a competitive edge. If you are not regularly exploring your competitors' tendering approaches, this area is highly relevant. Investing in competitive analysis will improve your tender win rate.

# TENDER SUCCESS TRACKING:

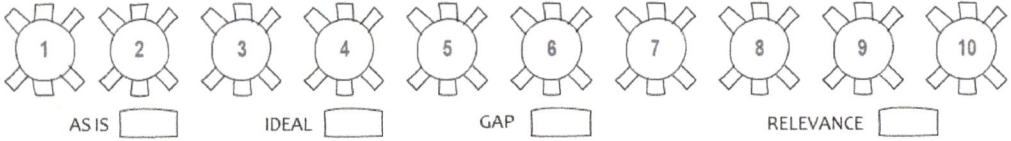

[Rating scale 1-10 with table settings graphics]

AS IS [  ]    IDEAL [  ]    GAP [  ]    RELEVANCE [  ]

## AS IS:

Consider how you track your performance in tenders. Reflect on whether you consistently track both your wins and losses, and whether you systematically analyse the reasons behind these outcomes. Do you use this information to learn from experiences and improve your future tender submissions? Or is your performance tracking less structured, potentially missing valuable opportunities for learning and improvement? Evaluating your tender performance tracking will reveal potential gaps in your continuous improvement efforts.

## IDEAL:

Ideally, you have a robust system for consistently tracking your wins and losses in tenders. This system includes a detailed analysis of the reasons for each outcome, including factors such as pricing, technical specifications, and relationship management. These insights are then used to inform future tender strategies and improve your win rate.

## RELEVANCE:

Consistent performance tracking and analysis are crucial for continuous improvement in tendering. Learning from experiences is essential for maximizing future success. If your performance tracking is weak, this area is highly relevant. Investing in a robust tracking and analysis system will improve your tender win rate over time.

# PROACTIVE TENDER MANAGEMENT:

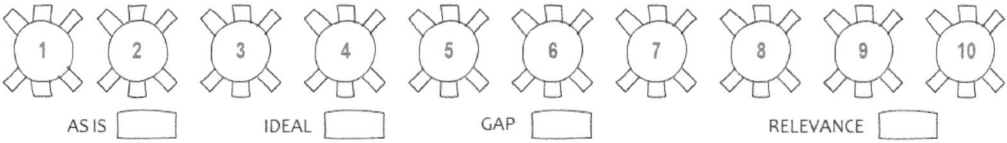

AS IS [___]    IDEAL [___]    GAP [___]    RELEVANCE [___]

## AS IS:

Consider the proactiveness of your tendering strategy. Reflect on whether your strategy includes active upfront shaping of the tender content, influencing the requirements and specifications before the tender is officially released. Do you also focus on building and maintaining strong relationships with key decision-makers within the tendering organisations? Or is your approach more reactive, simply responding to published tenders? Evaluating your proactive engagement will reveal potential gaps in your tender influence.

## IDEAL:

Ideally, your tendering strategy is proactive and includes active upfront shaping of the tender content. This involves engaging with potential clients early in the process to understand their needs and influence the tender requirements. You also prioritize building and maintaining strong relationships with key decision-makers to enhance your understanding of their priorities and increase your chances of success.

## RELEVANCE:

Proactive engagement and relationship building are crucial for influencing tender outcomes. Shaping the tender content and building strong relationships can significantly improve your win rate. If your approach is primarily reactive, this area is highly relevant. Investing in proactive engagement and relationship management will improve your tender success.

# PARTNERING FOR TENDER SUCCESS:

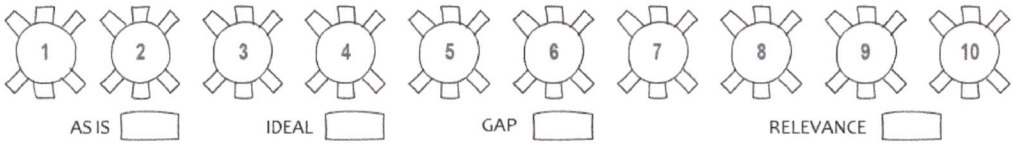

AS IS [ ]   IDEAL [ ]   GAP [ ]   RELEVANCE [ ]

## AS IS:

Consider your approach to partnerships and joint ventures in tendering. Reflect on whether you are willing to form temporary partnerships or joint ventures with other organisations if it is necessary to qualify for a tender or improve your chances of winning. Do you have a process for identifying and evaluating potential partners? Or is your approach more independent, potentially limiting your ability to compete for certain tenders? Evaluating your partnership strategy will reveal potential gaps in your tender competitiveness.

## IDEAL:

Ideally, you are open to forming temporary partnerships or joint ventures with other organisations if it is strategically advantageous for tendering. You have a well-defined process for identifying, evaluating, and establishing such partnerships, ensuring that they are aligned with your business objectives and enhance your competitiveness.

## RELEVANCE:

Strategic partnerships can significantly enhance your competitiveness in tenders, particularly for large or complex projects. Forming strategic alliances can open up new opportunities and improve win rates. If you are not actively considering partnerships, this area is highly relevant. Developing a partnership strategy will improve your tender competitiveness and open up new opportunities.

# VALUE OFFER TAILORING:

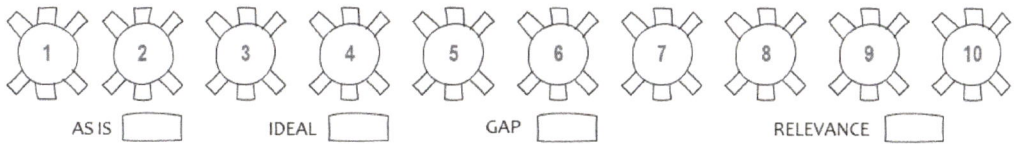

AS IS [　　]     IDEAL [　　]     GAP [　　]     RELEVANCE [　　]

## AS IS:

Consider how you develop tender offers. Reflect on whether you create tailored value propositions for each tender, including specific product benefit calculations and customized pricing models that are adapted to the individual account situation, tender criteria, and relevant regulations (such as value-based procurement). Or do you use more standardized offers, potentially missing opportunities to maximize your competitiveness? Evaluating your offer customization will reveal potential gaps in your tender strategy.

## IDEAL:

Ideally, you create highly tailored value offers for each tender, including detailed product benefit calculations and customized pricing models. These offers are specifically adapted to the individual account situation, the specific tender criteria, and all relevant regulations, including any movements towards value-based procurement. This personalized approach maximizes your chances of winning the tender by demonstrating a clear understanding of the client's needs and offering the most interesting solution.

## RELEVANCE:

Tailoring value offers is crucial for maximizing competitiveness in tenders. A customized approach can significantly improve win rates. If your offers are not sufficiently tailored, this area is highly relevant. Investing in developing customized offers will improve your tender success.

# BALANCING MARGIN, VOLUME & PRICE PRESSURES:

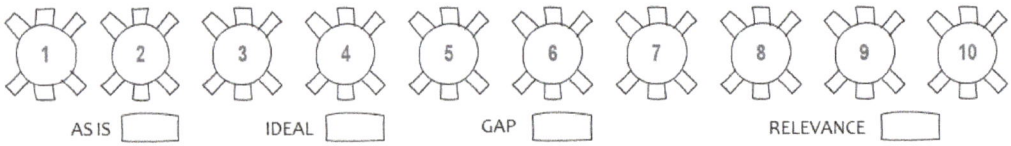

AS IS ☐     IDEAL ☐     GAP ☐     RELEVANCE ☐

## AS IS:

Consider the controls you have in place to manage the balance between margin and volume in tender business. Reflect on whether you have established appropriate guardrails to ensure that you are not sacrificing profitability in pursuit of higher volumes. Are these guardrails clearly defined, communicated, and consistently enforced? Or are pricing decisions made with less oversight, potentially leading to margin erosion? Evaluating your pricing control mechanisms will reveal potential gaps in your tender pricing strategy.

## IDEAL:

Ideally, you have well-defined and consistently enforced guardrails in place to ensure the right trade-off between securing margin and volume in tender business. These guardrails should be based on objective criteria, such as cost of goods sold, market conditions, and profitability targets, and should be regularly reviewed and updated.

## RELEVANCE:

Balancing margin and volume is crucial for achieving sustainable profitability in tender business. Effective pricing control is essential for long-term financial health. If you lack clear pricing guardrails, this area is highly relevant. Implementing robust pricing control mechanisms will protect your margins and ensure sustainable profitability.

# TENDER ROLES & RESPONSIBILITIES:

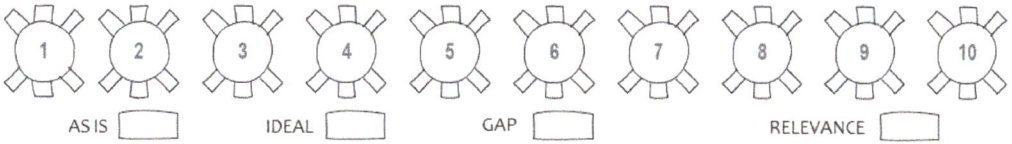

AS IS [ ]  IDEAL [ ]  GAP [ ]  RELEVANCE [ ]

## AS IS:

Consider the clarity of responsibilities and process coordination related to tendering within your organisation. Reflect on whether there is a clear understanding of roles, responsibilities, and workflows for all involved parties. Does this structure enable you to respond to tenders in a timely manner and make well-informed decisions? Or are there ambiguities, overlaps, or communication breakdowns that hinder efficiency and potentially lead to missed deadlines or suboptimal decisions? Evaluating your tender management structure will reveal potential gaps in your organisational effectiveness.

## IDEAL:

Ideally, your organisation has a clear and well-defined structure for managing tenders, with clearly assigned responsibilities, established workflows, and effective communication channels. This enables you to respond to tenders promptly and efficiently, while also ensuring that all decisions are made systematically and based on sound information.

## RELEVANCE:

Clear responsibilities and efficient processes are crucial for effective tender management. A well-defined structure can significantly improve responsiveness and decision-making. If your tender management structure is unclear or inefficient, this area is highly relevant. Investing in clarifying roles and streamlining processes will improve your tender response and overall efficiency.

# TENDERING RESOURCING:

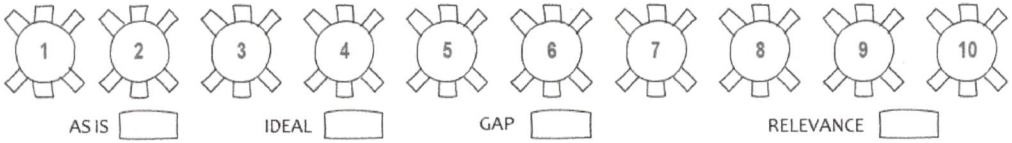

| 1 | 2 | 3 | 4 | 5 | 6 | 7 | 8 | 9 | 10 |

AS IS [       ]    IDEAL [       ]    GAP [       ]    RELEVANCE [       ]

## AS IS:

Consider the resources dedicated to tender management within your organisation. Reflect on whether you have a sufficient field force and back-office support team with the necessary skills and expertise to achieve optimal tender outcomes. Are your teams adequately staffed and trained to handle the workload and complexity of tender submissions? Or are there resource constraints or skill gaps that could hinder your tender success? Evaluating your resource allocation will reveal potential gaps in your tender capabilities.

## IDEAL:

Ideally, you have a sufficient field force and back-office support team with the right skills and experience to effectively manage all aspects of the tender process. This includes expertise in areas such as market research, competitive analysis, proposal writing, pricing strategy, and contract negotiation. Adequate staffing levels and ongoing training programs ensure that your teams are well-equipped to achieve optimal tender outcomes.

## RELEVANCE:

Adequate resources and skilled personnel are crucial for maximizing tender success. Investing in appropriate resources is essential for competing effectively in tenders. If you lack sufficient resources or skilled personnel, this area is highly relevant. Investing in strengthening your tender teams will improve your win rate.

# MARGIN DEFENCE:

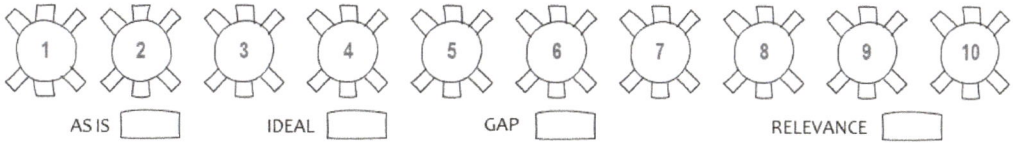

AS IS [    ]   IDEAL [    ]   GAP [    ]   RELEVANCE [    ]

## AS IS:

Consider your ability to maintain healthy margins in tender business. Reflect on whether you can secure profitable contracts while remaining competitive in tenders. Are you able to effectively manage costs and avoid excessive discounting that erodes margins? Or are you frequently forced to lower prices to win tenders, potentially affecting profitability? Evaluating your margin management will reveal potential gaps in your tender pricing strategy.

## IDEAL:

Ideally, you can defend your margins effectively in tender business, securing profitable contracts while remaining competitive. This involves careful cost management, strategic pricing, and effective negotiation. You avoid excessive discounting and focus on demonstrating the value of your offerings to justify your prices.

## RELEVANCE:

Maintaining healthy margins in tender business is crucial for sustainable profitability. Effective margin management is essential for long-term financial health. If you are struggling to defend your margins in tenders, this area is highly relevant. Investing in improving your cost management and pricing strategy will improve your profitability in tender business.

# Section Conclusion

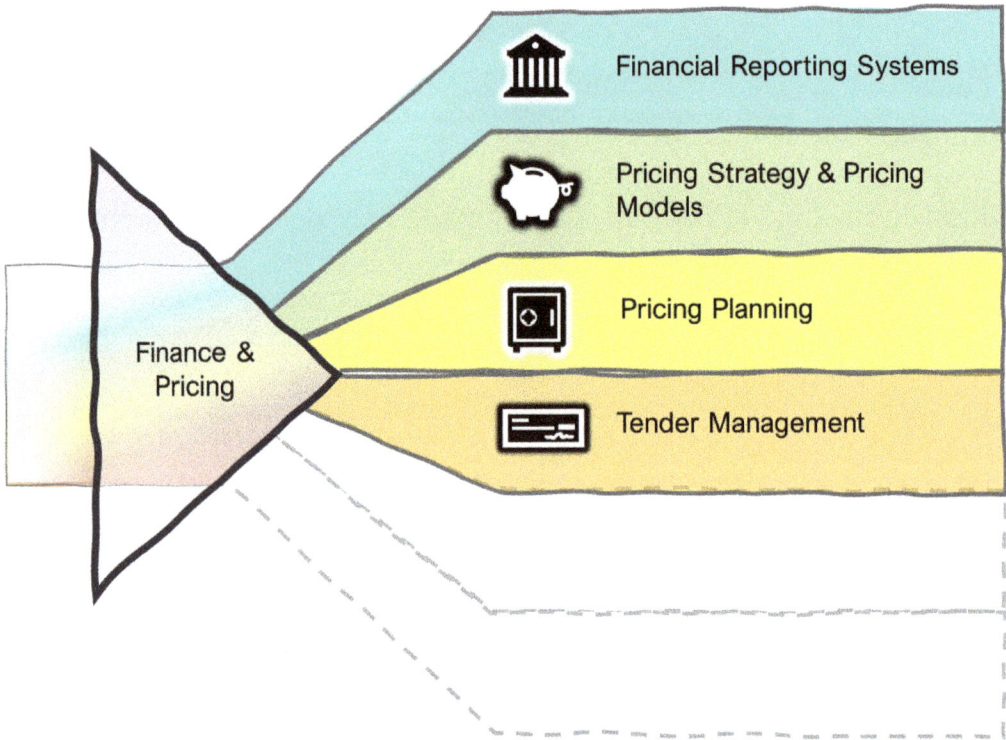

Finance & Pricing

- Financial Reporting Systems
- Pricing Strategy & Pricing Models
- Pricing Planning
- Tender Management

**Transfer the ratings at the beginning of each chapter here:**

| Chapter | AS IS | Ideal | Gap | Relevance |
|---|---|---|---|---|
| Financial Reporting Systems | | | | |
| Pricing Strategy | | | | |
| Pricing Planning & Execution | | | | |
| Tender Management | | | | |

Is there one area that is better or worse than the others?

Transfer the results onto the box plot.

# PRICING BOX PLOT:

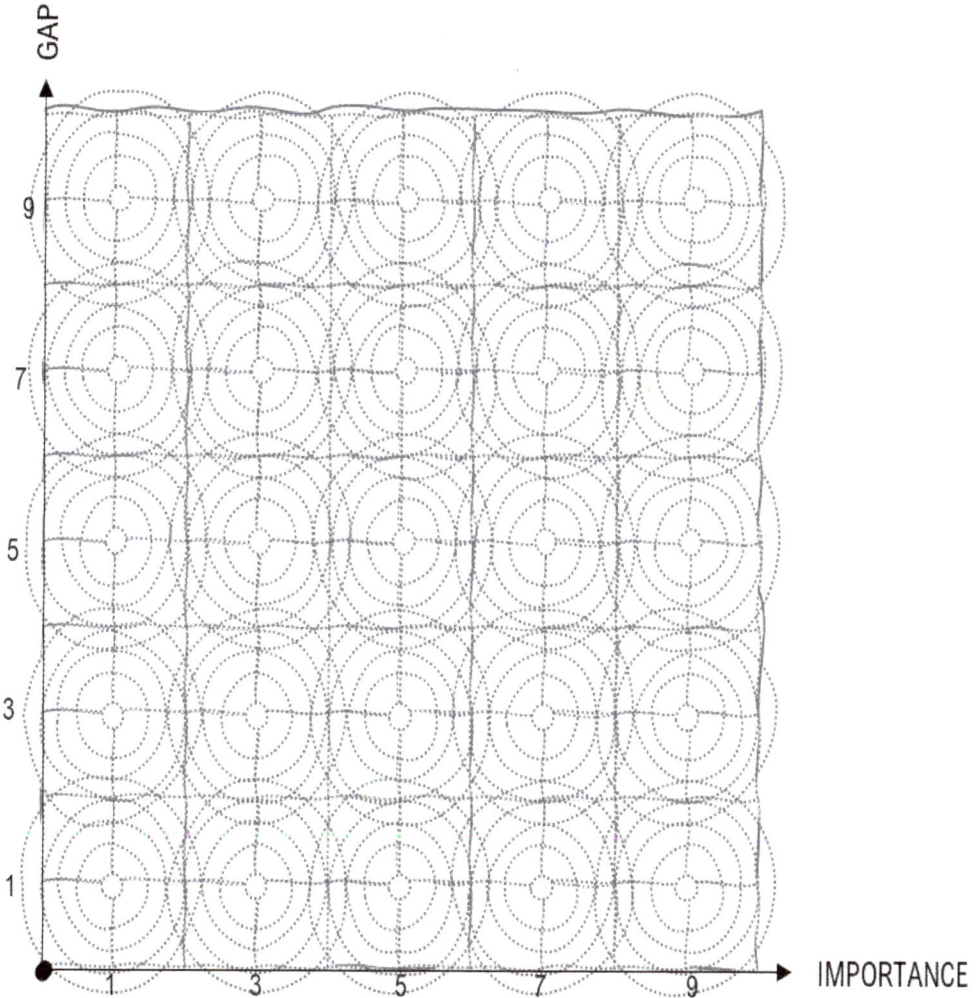

GAP

IMPORTANCE

# OVERALL EVALUATION:

AS IS [       ]    IDEAL [       ]    GAP [       ]    RELEVANCE [       ]

# Commercial Excellence Diagnostic Road Map

Putting it all together.

For each section you should now have a plot showing each chapter's relevance to your organisation and an overall AS IS, Ideal, Gap and Importance score. Transfer those below and complete the final plot for you to plot the sections. This will allow you to have a helicopter view of the organisation and deep dive into each of the sections.

I hope this was a valuable exercise and you got the most out of this book.

## COMMERCIAL EXCELLENCE ANALYSIS:

Transfer your overall evaluation scores from each section below. This is here to give you an overall picture and allow us to easily transfer them onto one final plot.

**Transfer the overall ratings listed at the end of each of the sections here:**

| Chapter | AS IS | Ideal | Gap | Relevance |
|---|---|---|---|---|
| Strategy | | | | |
| Sales | | | | |
| Marketing | | | | |
| Key Accounts | | | | |
| Services | | | | |
| Channel Management | | | | |
| Finance and Pricing | | | | |

For one final time transfer these onto the following box plot.

# COMMERCIAL EXCELLENCE PLOT:

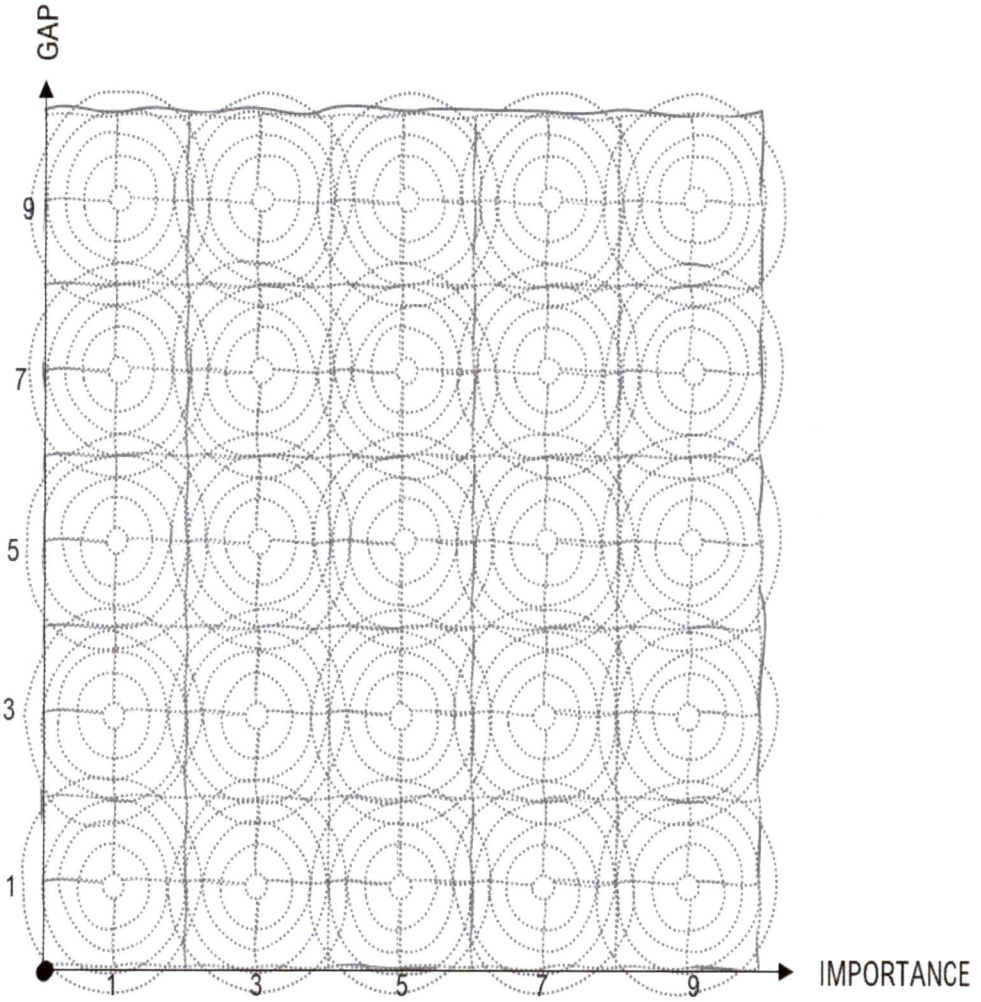

# Conclusion:

This concludes *The Commercial Excellence Playbook*.

From the Final Commercial Excellence Plot you should be able to determine exactly where you want to tackle improvements first.

## NOW – USE THE BOOK BACKWARDS:

Find the section you want to tackle first, then go to that section and have a look at the chapter's plot. This will tell you where within the section to focus your attention. Then go to the individual questions, that will show you in the make-up of that chapter what the biggest gap is.

This book does repeat certain aspects, but this is only in the quest for commercial excellence. I hope you could see past this repetition to gain the benefit of having a clear road map for the commercial side of your business.

# References

Adamson, M. D. (2011). *The Challenger Sale. Taking control of customer conversations.* Pengiun Random House.

Aguilar, F. (1967). *Scanning the business environment.*

Ansoff, H. I. (1957). *Strategies for Diversification.* Harvard Business Review.

Collins, J. &. (2004). *Built to Last: Successful Habits of Visionary Companies.* Harper Business.

Dapena-Baron, C. N. (2015). *Marketing Management: the big Picture.* Wiley.

Doerr, M. S. (2011). *Rainmaking Conversations: Influence, Persuade and sell in any situation.* Wiely.

Geir, D. D. (1989). *Personality Analysis .* Aristos Pub House.

Harnish, V. (2014). *Scaling Up: How a few companies make it... and why the rest dont.* Gazelles.com.

Mauborgne, c. K. (2005). *Blue Ocean Strategy.* Harvard Business School Publishing Corporation.

Mercuri-International. (circa 2012). *DAPA (Discover, Accept, Present, Accept).*

Miller Heiman, T. T. (1991). *The New Successful Large Account Management.* Miller Heiman.

Porter, M. (1979). *How Competitive Forces Shape Strategy.* Harvard Business Review.

Rackham, N. (1988). *Spin Selling: Situation, Problem Implication Need - Payoff.* McGraw-Hill Education.

Reichheld, F. (2006). *The Ultimate Question: Driving Good PRofits and True Growth.* Harvard Business Press .

SINEK, S. (2009). *Start with Why: How great leaders Inspire everyone to take action.* Penguin.

Whitmore, S. J. (2011). *Coaching for Performance .* John Murray Business.

Zatta, D. (2022). *The Pricing Model Revolution.*

# ACRONYMS AND TERMS USED IN THIS

# BOOK.

| Term | Definition |
|------|-----------|
| Allocation Keys | A key that describes how costs are allocated to products or customers. Particularly for Indirect costs examples could be via: Floor space used, Number of orders, to allocate Sales Admin time, Number of service orders for services teams, Number of Visits doe Sales Activities to a customer, Number of, Amount of time for marketing per segment to allocate marketing spend. |
| B2B | Business to Business |
| B2C | Business to Consumer |
| BHAG ® | Big Hairy Audacious Goal |
| Big Rocks | Big rocks are goals. To completely fill a jar you need to put the big rocks in first. |
| Bull Whip Effect | The Effect upon stock from a situation where everyone buys at the same time then does not purchase, leading to feast and famine situations |
| COM | Commercial Operating Model |
| CRM | Customer Relationship Management |
| CVM | Customer Value Management. A program used for Customer Targeting. A system where the customer who provides the company the most value is prioritised. |
| DAPA | A proprietary sales method of Mercuri International standing for Discover Accept Present Accept. |
| Decision Maker | The person with the power to say yes to a opportunity |
| DISC | Dominant (RED) Influence (Yellow) Steadiness (Green) Conscientious (Blue) |
| DMU | Decision Making Unit. |
| EBIT | Earnings Before Interest and Tax |
| EOQ | Economic Ordering Quantity. The Ideal ordering quantity to meet demand and minimise Inventory costs. |
| G2M | Go To Market model |
| Gate Keeper | The person who has the power to say No to a deal but does not have the power to say yes. |

| Term | Definition |
| --- | --- |
| GROW | Goal, Reality, Options, What will you do next time |
| GTM | Go To Market model |
| IDP's | Individual Development Plans |
| KA | Key Account. |
| KOL | Key Opinion Leader The terms for Influencers in the Medical field. |
| Margin Contributive | A product or service or customer where the Gross Margin is higher than the overall gross margin of the company. i.e. every $ they buy contributes to growing the Gross Margin of the company. |
| Margin Dilutive | A product or service or customer where the Gross margin is lower than the overall gross margin of the company. i.e. The more they spend with us the more it dilutes or brings down the overall Gross Margin of the company. |
| Market Penetration | Similar to Market Share but calculated on the number of total people using your solution in a market. Usually calculated in number of Customers Vs total market customers. |
| Market Share | The amount of share your company has of the total market. Usually calculated by Revenue. |
| MPR | Minimum Purchase Requirement. The minimum amount that a channel partner is obligated to purchase. |
| NPS | Net Promotor Score |
| NPV | Net Present Value |
| Payback | The time it takes to earn enough to pay back the investment. |
| PESTEL | Political, Economic, Social, Technological, Legal, Environmental |
| RACI | A system where each tasks or areas are assigned to different groups being R = Responsible A = Accountable = C = Consulted I = Informed. |
| RAIN | A sales process from the book Rainmaking conversations. Standing for Rapport Accentuate Implications New reality |
| Retrospective Discounting | A system where a discount is applied retrospectively to a product after that product sales reaches a threshold volume. i.e. we'll discount 10% on all units once we achieve 100,000 units of sales. NOTE: in certain countries this practice is illegal please check. |
| ROI | Return On Investment |
| SIP | Sales Incentive Plans |

| Term | Definition |
|------|-----------|
| **SMART** | Specific Measurable Achievable Relevant and Time bound goals. |
| **SOW** | Share of Wallet the amount spend you get from the total spend that the customer has available |
| **SPIN** | A sales from the book SPIN Selling. Standing for Situation, Problem, Implication and Need Payoff. |
| **SWOT** | Strengths Weaknesses Opportunities & Threats |
| **TOWS** | SWOT backwards. Used to assess where 1 aspect of your SWOT can complement or build on another aspect of the SWOT. |
| **TTT** | Train the Trainer |
| **USP** | Unique Selling Point This is the unique feature / benefit or other points that you use to sell your product. |
| **UVP** | Unique Value Proposition |
| **VMI** | Vendor Managed Inventory, A system where the principle manages the inventory levels of the channel partner. Many modern inventory management systems have this built into them. |

# SPARE GRADING SHEETS

AS IS [ ]    IDEAL [ ]    GAP [ ]    RELEVANCE [ ]

AS IS [ ]    IDEAL [ ]    GAP [ ]    RELEVANCE [ ]

AS IS [ ]    IDEAL [ ]    GAP [ ]    RELEVANCE [ ]

AS IS [ ]    IDEAL [ ]    GAP [ ]    RELEVANCE [ ]

AS IS [ ]    IDEAL [ ]    GAP [ ]    RELEVANCE [ ]

AS IS [ ]    IDEAL [ ]    GAP [ ]    RELEVANCE [ ]

# SPARE PLOTS

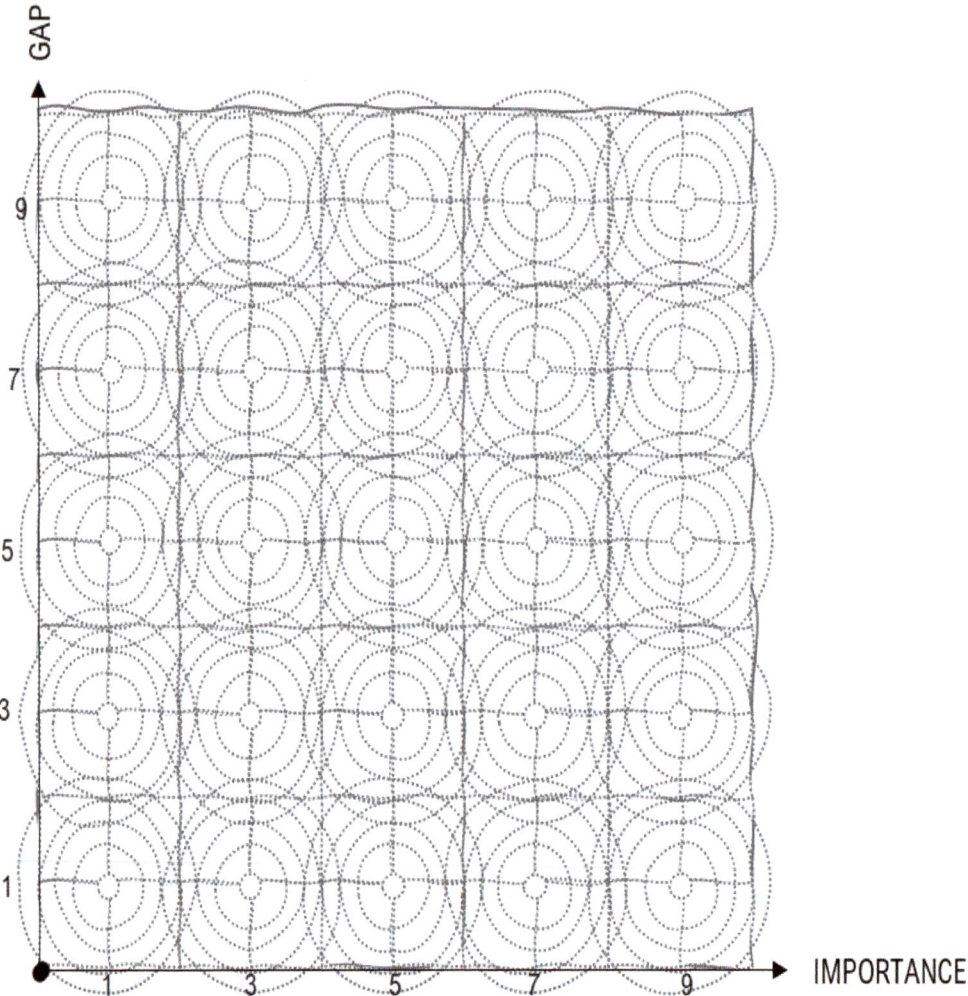

# About the Author:

Philip is a 51-year-old father of 3 and avid boatie. His passions include being on the water and Commercial Excellence. With over 30 years industry experience in medical diagnostics, medical devices, and the pharma and cosmetics industry, in both country leadership and Asia Pacific regional leadership. Philip has over 10 years CEO experience and 8 years executing Commercial Excellence across Asia Pacific. for Tier 1 Multinationals.

**"**
*In almost a decade of implementing commercial excellence programs across Asia pacific, I noticed that all the top consulting firms (such as Bain & Co, LEK, BCG, EY etc.) have commercial excellence programs that are in the millions of dollars to run.*

*This is* <u>*way*</u> *out of reach for the average business. The good news is that this is something that every business could do themselves with minimal costs, the right structure, and some thinking time of the C-suite. Sure, they may not get the same level of benchmarking, but they may get 80% of the value just by properly considering the topics covered within this book.*

*My hope is that this book helps you to understand and build a stronger business.*
*I'm at your disposal.*
**Cheers and best regards**
**Phil.**

P.S. Meanwhile I'd love to hear your feedback, see your plots, and share your success stories from using this book. If that's of interest, please connect with me on LinkedIn: **www.linkedin.com/in/Philip-d-bowler**

I have two follow-up books planned at this stage:

**1.** *Commercial Excellence: Customer Targeting Systems – How Customer Value Management Can Unite Departments.*

**2.** *Commercial Excellence: Channel Management: Systems for Managing*

*Distributors.* **"**

www.ingramcontent.com/pod-product-compliance
Lightning Source LLC
Chambersburg PA
CBHW051924190326
41458CB00026B/6403